PHILLIPS BROOKS:

SELECTED SERMONS

Phillips Brooks was born in Boston, Mass., December 13, 1835. In 1859 he was ordained deacon in the Protestant Episcopal Church and became rector of the Church of the Advent, Philadelphia. In 1860 he was ordained priest and in 1862 he became rector of the Church of the Holy Trinity, Philadelphia. In 1869 he was made rector of Trinity Church, Boston, where for over twenty years he "dominated—'nay glorified'—the city of Boston." In 1891 he was consecrated bishop of Massachusetts. He died on January 23, 1893. In addition to his sermons, which have continued to be read and studied, he is also remembered as the author of the Christmas hymn, *O Little Town of Bethlehem.*

Phillips Brooks

PHILLIPS BROOKS:
SELECTED SERMONS

EDITED AND WITH AN INTRODUCTION

BY

THE RT. REV. WILLIAM SCARLETT, D.D.

BISHOP OF MISSOURI

NEW YORK

E. P. DUTTON & COMPANY, INC.

1949

CONTENTS

INTRODUCTION

FORTUNATE indeed are they who still remember the occasion when they heard Phillips Brooks preach. For as they read these sermons they will see again in the pulpit of Trinity Church, Boston, the tall, majestic figure, standing six feet four inches in height, "symmetrically massive" in build, the magnificently modeled head, the strong, exceedingly handsome face—"he was the most beautiful man I have ever seen," said Justice Harlan of the United States Supreme Court— the large, dark glowing eyes. They will hear again the low voice increasing in strength, fullness and clarity as he proceeded, the impetuous utterance gathering momentum until he averaged over two hundred words per minute and giving the effect of "an express train" rushing through a station. They will remember the vast, hushed congregation caught up in intense emotion while the Preacher, in his earlier years, poured out his mind and soul while himself apparently unmoved.

Never in the history of the Protestant Episcopal Church has there been sustained preaching such as this. From his early days in Philadelphia until his death it was maintained on the same high level. Indeed a great church historian has said that there had hardly been anything like it in the history of the Christian Church. Certainly the comments of his contemporaries indicate that in a day of great preachers he was pre-eminent. Dr. Tulloch, Principal of St. Mary's College in the University of Aberdeen, whose profession required of him a study of the history of preaching, himself distinguished as a preacher and exceedingly able as a critic, wrote in a letter to his wife:

I have just heard the most remarkable sermon I ever heard in my life (I use the word in no American sense) from Mr. Phillips Brooks, an Episcopal clergyman here: equal to the best of Frederick Robertson's sermons, with a vigor and force of thought which he has not always. I never heard preaching like it, and you know how slow I am to praise preachers. So much thought and so much life combined;

7

such a reach of mind, and such a depth and insight of soul. I was electrified. I could have got up and shouted.*

And James Bryce, comparing Phillips Brooks to other great preachers—Bishop Wilberforce, Mr. Spurgeon, Dr. Liddon and Henry Ward Beecher—said:

All these famous men were, in a sense, more brilliant, that is to say, more rhetorically effective, than Dr. Brooks, yet none of them seem to speak so directly to the soul. With all of them it was impossible to forget the speaker in the words spoken, because the speaker did not seem to have quite forgotten himself. . . . With him it was otherwise . . . there was no sign of art . . . no touch of self-consciousness. He spoke to his audience as a man might speak to his friend, pouring forth with swift, yet quiet and seldom impassioned earnestness the thoughts and feelings of a singularly pure and lofty spirit. The listeners never thought of style or manner, but only of the substance of the thoughts. They were entranced and carried out of themselves by the strength and sweetness and beauty of the aspects of religious truth and its helpfulness to weak human nature which he presented. Dr. Brooks was the best because the most edifying of preachers. . . . In this blending of perfect simplicity of treatment with singular fertility and elevation of thought, no other among the famous preachers of the generation that is now vanishing approached him.†

For over twenty years Phillips Brooks dominated—"nay, glorified"—the City of Boston. He gave himself without stint wherever he was needed. He seemed to have the leverage for moving the world, someone said. When he died, at the early age of fifty-seven, the whole community became a house of mourning. A prominent Bostonian was caught in a traffic jam on Harvard Bridge, when "a teamster leaned over from his seat and said in an awed voice, 'Do you know what has happened? Phillips Brooks is dead.' They buried him like a king. Harvard students carried his body on their shoulders. All barriers of denomination were down. Roman Catholics and Unitarians felt that a great man had fallen in Israel." ‡

Dr. S. Weir Mitchell said he had known a number of men whom

---

* *Life and Letters of Phillips Brooks,* by Alexander V. G. Allen (New York: E. P. Dutton & Co., Inc.), Vol. II, p. 247.

† *Life and Letters of Phillips Brooks,* by Alexander V. G. Allen, Vol. III, p. 393.

‡ Mrs. Edward S. Drown, in *The Witness,* March 21, 1940.

we call great but Phillips Brooks was the only one he ever knew
who seemed to him entirely great.

It is sometimes said that in Phillips Brooks's sermons there is little
of the "social gospel." On this point several things may be said. First,
I imagine that they who selected the sermons in the previous volumes, since they also were seeking the most enduring of his sermons,
passed over those which dealt with particular but transient issues of
the day. For example, none of the passionate antislavery sermons are
to be found in these volumes, not even the most famous one, "Our
Mercies of Reoccupation."

But also the phrase itself is a misnomer. For there is no Social Gospel. There is only the Gospel. And it is indivisible. But it has profound and sweeping social principles and implications. And those
who do not see these implications and try rigorously to apply them
to the world in which they live really do not have the Gospel. But
if anyone thinks that Phillips Brooks was not profoundly aware of
all this nor gave it full expression, let him read in Dr. Allen's great
biography the chapters covering the period of the Civil War. For in
his Philadelphia days his biographer tells us he appeared almost as a
reformer and agitator, with a work to do outside the pulpit which
rivaled in importance and popular interest his work as a preacher.
After Abraham Lincoln's Emancipation Proclamation had set Phillips Brooks's mind entirely free, he threw himself into the cause of
the abolition of slavery with all his soul and mind and strength,
bringing to bear on it with rare intensity all his gifts of intellect and
eloquence. He attacked slavery in words that still burn and sting.
"It is useless to talk around and around it when we know and are
sure that slavery, its existence in the South and its approval in the
North, is the great crushing, cursing sin of our national life and the
cause of our evils." In his sermon on Lincoln's death he said, "By all
the goodness that there was in him, by all the love we had for him—
and who shall tell how great it was?—by all the sorrow that has burdened down this desolate and dreadful week, I charge this murder
where it belongs—on Slavery. I bid you remember where the charge
belongs, to write it on the door-posts of your mourning-houses, to
teach it to your wondering children, to give it to the history of these
times, that all times may come to hate and dread the sin that killed
our noblest President." *

* *Phillips Brooks*, by M. A. De Wolfe Howe, p. 31.

In the sermon* which made the greatest impression on the Philadelphia of that day where sentiment was greatly divided,† after thanking God that the institution of slavery was one year nearer its inevitable end, he continues, "What has done it? Not the proclamation of last New Year's Day, though we ought to thank God, as not the least mercy of these times, that we have had a man to lead us, so honest and so true, so teachable at the lips of the Almighty, as to write those immortal words that made a race forever free. Not any public document, not any public act has done the work: nothing but the hand of God, leading back his chosen people into the land of universal freedom into which He led the fathers and out of which the children went so woefully astray. Which God is greater —He who let the fathers in or He who leads the children back? At any rate, the Lord grant us to be truer to the new charter of emancipation than (we own it with shamefacedness and contrition) we have been to the declaration of freedom and human equality which the fathers wrote." Because of the vigorous stand which Phillips Brooks had taken on the slavery issue, Judge Woodward, the defeated candidate for Governor of Pennsylvania, himself a close friend of Phillips Brooks, resigned from the Vestry of Holy Trinity Church. No "social gospel" in all this? These years in Philadelphia when he stood forth as the great leader of his people in a great cause are in some respects his most fruitful period.

In Boston he was preoccupied in his early years by a great parochial task. He still dealt frequently and firmly with issues as they arose. But more and more he gave himself to one central theme. Often he said, "I have only one sermon." And this theme—"the sacredness, the beauty, the glory of life, because all men were the children of God, and Christ the eternal Son"—he saw through a hundred facets, and expressed in as many ways. But the essence of the whole Gospel is in these sermons. And no one can read the sermons in this volume and not find in them profound social principles of the Gospel of Christ, to which Phillips Brooks gave expression. But he lived the greater part of his ministry in another day than ours. The first volume of his sermons was published over seventy years ago.

* "Our Mercies of Reoccupation," *The Life and Letters of Phillips Brooks,* by Alexander V. G. Allen, Vol. I, p. 466 ff.

† *The Life and Letters of Phillips Brooks,* by Alexander V. G. Allen, Vol. I, p. 448 ff.

He died fifty-six years ago. His age was a different one, in which men looked forward to the future with a rosy, and now we see quite unwarranted, optimism, a day in which many of the ominous issues of our age were not yet acute. This needs to be remembered.

But Phillips Brooks himself was not caught by any shallow optimism. He once defined optimism as "a great belief in a great purpose, underlying the world for good, absolutely certain to fulfil itself somewhere, somehow." * But he knew what was in man. And while he believed profoundly in God and greatly in man and tried passionately to evoke the best that was in men, his sermons are full of awareness of the truth of Saint Paul's tragic words, "The good that I would I do not: but the evil which I would not, that I do . . . O wretched man that I am! who shall deliver me from the body of this death."

If there was any secret to the life of Phillips Brooks beyond the fact that he was a man uniquely endowed by God in mind, soul and body, it was an open secret and a simple one. "Keep close to Christ, Philly" had been his mother's constant refrain. And how faithfully and well he followed this charge is shown in a letter he wrote to a young clergyman who had asked him what the secret of his life might be:

"I am sure you will not think that I dream that I have any secret to tell. I have only the testimony to bear which any friend may fully bear to his friend when he is cordially asked for it, as you have asked me.

"Indeed the more I have thought it over, the less in some sense I have seemed to have to say. And yet the more sure it has seemed to me that these last years have had a peace and fullness which there did not use to be. I say it in deep reverence and humility. I do not think it is the mere quietness of advancing age. I am sure it is not indifference to anything which I used to care for. I am sure that it is a deeper knowledge and truer love of Christ. . . .

"I cannot tell you how personal this grows to me. He is here. He knows me and I know Him. It is no figure of speech. It is the reallest thing in the world. And every day makes it realler. And one wonders with delight what it will grow to as the years go on. . . ."

* *The Life and Letters of Phillips Brooks*, by Alexander V. G. Allen, Vol. III, p. 509.

It would be a vast pity if this great tradition, this exceedingly rich heritage, should grow dim. Phillips Brooks's influence on the young men of his day, to whom he seemed to speak in almost every sermon, was enormous. How many have counted him the decisive influence in their lives we shall never know. And many who never heard him or saw him, but who have met him intimately in Dr. Allen's magnificent biography, likewise have come under his influence and have been persuaded by him, "like light caught from leaping flame." The "nature" of anything, Plato argued, is shown by the best it can grow into. And here was the Christian ministry at its highest and most revealing level. Here was a calling evoking all which the ablest of men had to give. Here in Phillips Brooks himself was a most powerful argument for the Christian ministry. Many indeed have been the men who would acknowledge that Phillips Brooks was a major factor in their decision to enter the ministry. He still has the capacity to inspire and infuse men with the same purpose, the same vision, which animated his life, however differently we might express it. One wishes earnestly that Dr. Allen's moving biography were still widely read. Certainly it should be a "must" in every theological seminary.

*   *   *   *   *   *

The task which the publisher has assigned me, to select from the more than two hundred published sermons of Phillips Brooks the twenty or thirty which seem the most timeless, has been a happy but exceedingly difficult one. A few of Phillips Brooks's sermons stand out beyond their fellows. But just behind, close behind, come a host of others, each with its own peculiar claim. Another editor would have chosen differently. And some who still remember Phillips Brooks will be disappointed because a favorite sermon has been omitted. But the attempt is made here to select the sermons which best survive the test of time and yet most fully express the essential message which Phillips Brooks was sent to give. We must remember that he lived in a different age from ours and that between him and us there seems to be a great gulf fixed. Thought has changed. Theology has shifted its ground and its emphases. Yet though many would state it in different theological language, the timeless message of Phillips Brooks stands—the message of the sacredness and beauty of life, which is the gift to men because they are God's children; the

Word of God in its appeal to the human soul, rebuking, moving to repentance, evoking the best, setting man about his Father's business of building God's new world.

* * * * * *

I turned to a few friends for assistance, though none is responsible for the final selection of these sermons. And to them I must express my gratitude: to Bishop Edward L. Parsons, Bishop Robert E. L. Strider, Dr. W. Russell Bowie, Dean H. E. W. Fosbroke, especially to Dr. Harry Emerson Fosdick. And above all to Mrs. Edward S. Drown of Cambridge, brought up as a child under the wing of Phillips Brooks, in whose home he was a constant visitor and who still remembers hearing many of the sermons in this volume.

WILLIAM SCARLETT

Saint Louis, January, 1949.

PHILLIPS BROOKS:
SELECTED SERMONS

THE SACREDNESS OF LIFE

"He asked life of thee and thou gavest it him, even length of days for ever and ever."—PSALMS xxi. 4.

THE poetry of the twenty-first Psalm is very picturesque. King David is the writer, but the whole people of Israel are represented as the speakers. First they address themselves to God and praise Him for the blessings which he has given to their monarch. Then they turn to the king himself and rejoice with him upon the victory over his enemies and the escape from his troubles which is before him. And then in the last verse they turn back again to God and ascribe the glory and power entirely to Him. "Be thou exalted, Lord, in thine own strength, so will we sing and praise thy power."

The Psalm is therefore, in most spirited and poetic form, the expression of David's own gratitude and hope and devotion.

The verse which I have quoted for our text fixes our attention on the first part of the Psalm, the gratitude of David. The people are singing of God's mercy to their beloved king. They remember how, perhaps in some special emergency when his life seemed in danger, perhaps in that long aspiration of youth which is one long prayer for life, David had begged God to let him live. "He asked life of thee," and then they record how God was better to David than his prayer. "Thou gavest it him, even length of days for ever and ever," or, as our Prayer-Book version has it, "He asked life of thee and thou gavest him a long life, even for ever and ever." It is this verse which I wish to study with you. What does it mean? Surely David does not dream that God in answer to his prayer for life had really made his life immortal. Already as he wrote he must have felt in eye and hand some of those symptoms of advancing age which even in the full strength of maturity prophesy decay. It must have been that David caught sight of that other kind of earthly immortality which has always fascinated noble minds. He saw the perpetuation of his influence. He saw that the spiritual dynasty which was represented in him was to continue in long power over unborn generations of

17

mankind. The Christ who was to come in the fulfilment of that which he prefigured was to reign forever. This was the immortality which he heard God promising him. He asked life. Asked to be saved from death by sickness, or by the paw of the lion or the paw of the bear, or by the soldiers of Saul. And God gave him life. And at first, it may be, he thought that God had given him no more than he had asked for, only the immediate escape from dying. But by and by he found that the life which God had given him was a long and deep and mysterious thing. It was vastly richer in character and destiny than he had dreamed of. Slowly it opened to him and he saw that it was something with vast connections, something whose power touched spiritual forces and never should decay, something belonging to the unending life of God. It was eternal life which God had given him. "He had asked life and God had given him a long life even for ever and ever."

It is thus that these words of David have suggested to me the subject of which I wished to speak to you to-day. I have wondered whether I could make you see how that same deepening sight of life which came to David may come to us, does come to many men who get below the first appearance, the mere surface of life and see its deeper meaning. We too ask God for life. Every struggle for self-support; every shudder at the thought of dying, every delight in existence is a cry for life. We may not mean it for a prayer. We may not turn it Godward. With us, as we utter it, it may be a mere vague cry into the darkness, but God hears it as a cry to Him, just exactly as if you walked upon the beach at night and heard a drowning man shouting in terror, his shout would be in your ears a prayer to you, although he did not know that you were there, and only shouted in the vagueness of his terror. So every struggle that we make to live is a prayer to God for life. And the continuance of our existence is God's answer to our prayer. But when we first take the life which He gives us we do not know what it is. Its depth, its richness only opens to us gradually. Only gradually do we learn that God has given to us not merely the power of present being and present enjoyment, but that wrapt up and hidden in that He has given us the power of thinking, feeling, loving, living in such deep and lofty ways that we may be in connection with the great continuous unbroken thoughts and feelings and movements of the universe. The life which He has given us is in its capacities not merely a thing of this moment. It is a part of the life of the universe. It is eternal life.

We can understand it best perhaps if we look back to the very beginning of life and follow the human spirit in its development. It is possible for our imaginations even to picture the soul praying for life before it has begun to live. We all remember those verses from Pope's Messiah which are made into one of the hymns of our hymnal. The poet is singing of the kingdom of God that is to come, the new Jerusalem and its inhabitants:

> "See a long race thy spacious courts adorn,
> See future sons and daughters yet unborn,
> In crowding ranks on every side arise
> Demanding life, impatient for the skies."

The cry of the unborn for life! That is the sound which fills the poet's vision. By and by comes God's answer to that prayer. The unborn come to the birth and life is given. We all know how that life seems to be merely life, life in its first and simplest form at the beginning, and so it goes on through all the earliest years. The unconscious infant lives in a mere animal existence, and later when the strong and healthy boy begins to grow conscious of the delight of life, it is pure life, life simply as a fact, life not with reference to the deeper powers it contains or the far-off issues with which it has to do that gives him such hourly delight in living. There comes back to many of us, I am sure, the ringing verse in which Browning has made this very David, when he was a boy, sing in the presence of King Saul of this pure consciousness of joy in the mere fact of being alive.

> "Oh, the wild joys of living! the leaping from rock up to rock
> The strong rending of boughs from the fir-tree; the cool silver shock
> Of the plunge in a pool's living water,—the hunt of the bear,
> And the sultriness showing the lion is couched in his lair.
> And the meal—the rich dates yellowed over with gold dust divine
> And the locust's flesh steeped in the pitcher! the full draught of wine,
> And the sleep in the dried river-channel where bulrushes tell
> That the water was wont to go warbling so softly and well.
> How good is man's life, the mere living! how fit to employ
> All the heart and the soul and the senses forever in joy."

"Truly the light is sweet, and a pleasant thing it is for the eyes to behold the sun." So Ecclesiastes, the Preacher, sings the same truth, the truth of man's, the healthy man's, pure delight in life, long before he has looked down into the depth of life to ask what treasures are hidden there, or looked out along the distant vista of life to ask what he shall do with it. In his placing of a bright, unquestioning boyhood at the beginning of every man's career, does it not seem as if God had meant to indicate that this sense of life as a blessing in itself must be the basis out of which all the sense of the special blessedness of special events in life must grow, as if He meant to have us take life as a whole and thank Him for our creation before we looked deeper and saw what were the true purposes of life. But by and by the time for that deeper look must come. Not always can David be content with the leaping from rock to rock, the plunge in the pool and the sleep in the dry bed of the summer brook. The thoughts and anxieties and duties of a man come crowding up into the life of the light-hearted boy. Care for things to which he once was all indifferent, hopes of things about which he once never dreamed, ambitions and desires of influence and power, the delight in half-discovered faculties, and as the crown of all, conscious religion or the realized relationship with God, the love of and the obedience to Christ, all of these become his one after another. One after another life comes to mean these things. And now what shall we say? How have these things come to the man. See him at forty rich in all these, the earnest, thoughtful, religious man, full of associations with the world and with his fellow-man and God. This is the same being with the boy who played in simple health and thoughtlessness thirty years ago. How have all these things come to him? Have angels come down one by one, each bringing one of these new gifts and put them one by one into his life. Have they not rather opened one by one out of that life itself, called out by God, urged out by the half-blind desire to be all that it had within itself the capacity of being, but certainly coming forth out of the very substance of the life itself, and therefore having been in the life from the beginning. There never was a moment when the hand of God touched Shakespeare's lips and bade him be the poet. Never a time when as a new endowment a breath from Heaven gave to St. John the capacity to be a saint. Never a day when the nature of Raphael was filled with genius. These things were in these men from the beginning of their lives.

When as in Pope's imaginative picture their spirits prayed for life, and when God gave them life, this was what God gave them. This poetry, this genius, the sublimeness was all wrapped up in that first gift of life when God said "Let this man be." All that has to do with His own unending life was there. The eternal life of these men, this God gave to them. All that was to open out of their being forever, all that they were to be on to the endless end, all this God gave them when He answered the prayer of their unborn spirits. They asked life of Him, and He gave them a long life, even forever and ever.

We talk of Raphael, and Shakespeare, and St. John. But we might talk of any men. We talk of them only because their illustrious excellence makes glorious and clear what is true of all mankind. In all men the life which God gives has in it the capacity of all which the man forever hereafter is to be. In all men, the first life that appears, that which we commonly call life, the mere vitality, is the foundation of the entire life, the basis upon which must rest all the structure of the growing character. How interesting this makes the beginning of a life appear. Some day I walk along one of our streets and men are laying the foundations of a new house which is going to be built. It is interesting in itself,—the driving of the piles, the laying of the massive stones, the exercise of power and of skill. But the true interest of what they are doing lies in the consciousness that this is a foundation. The lines on which these great stones are laid mark the dimensions and partitions of the coming house. I look up and the air already seems to be quivering with the yet unbuilt walls. He who is laying these stones has the walls in his brain and is already building them. That makes it interesting. But let it stop, and then you feel instantly how destitute of value the foundation is in itself. A foundation that has never been built upon is the saddest sight upon a city street. A crumbling foundation on which a building which is now burnt down once stood is sad. Still it has the memory of having once done its true work. But a foundation that has been well laid and then stopped short and had no house built on it is the most sad of all. At once it suggests its human parallel. "This man began to build but was not able to finish," we say. "So is he who layeth up treasure for himself but is not rich toward God." The first life that has stopped short and never gone on to complete itself in the higher lives, mere vitality which has advanced and opened into no great character and usefulness, these are the human parallels of the foundation stones upon which the bankrupt or discouraged or fickle-minded builder never has gone on to build his house.

You have only to add one element to our simple metaphor and it becomes complete. You have only to conceive of the foundation stones becoming conscious of themselves and knowing what is happening to them, and then they represent completely that earliest, rudimentary life upon the basis of which all the other lives rest and which finds its value in its power to carry and develop them. Let the foundation feel the unbuilt building, and what joy must fill it as it finds itself growing more compact and solid. Every blow of the hammer which makes it more fit for what it is to carry rings like a bell from the steeple that is some day to pierce the sky. Surely there is something which corresponds to that in the human life. Surely the mere vitality, the mere animal living, if we choose to call it so, may be a different thing in the young human animal from what it is or can be in the young animal of any other kind, because of the premonitions, however dim and vague, of the life of intellect and of love and of religion which are to rest upon it. And when the years pass and no house is built, when only the foundation stands, must not that, too, if we imagine into it a consciousness, be disappointed and full of the sense of failure in a way which will find its parallel in the life of every man whose life lingers as the years go by in the first rudimentary conditions and never advances to any of the higher uses for which it was made. O the unused foundations of character which stand along our human streets and make the city of our human life so tragical. O the men here who are nothing but grown-up boys, who have never built upon their boyhood any real manly life. O the bodily vigor that has never been put to any strong work for God or fellow-man; the quick senses that have never been put to any higher employment than the shooting of a bird; the observation of our brethren that once was healthy sympathy but has developed into no true interest in our brethren's best good and so remains to-day only in the wretched shape of the old man's or the old woman's taste for gossip and scandal. O the fresh spontaneity which never having found its true task wanders still in dilettante dissipation among a thousand fancies. O the first crude imaginations about God, which never having been refined and elevated by careful and loving thought about Him have settled down into the bigotries and idolatries of middle life. These are the specimens of what I mean by the primary, rudimentary life becoming sad and miserable because it does not go boldly and freely on to fulfil itself in the higher lives. The temporal life which is not allowed to open into the eternal life becomes corrupt and feeble in its temporalness. The man who does not carry forward his care for himself and complete it with a loving care for God and for God's children, loses the best power of self-care. He who having asked God for life does not take the deeper and longer life which comes in answer to his prayer loses the best joy of the life which he does try to take.

I have prolonged these definitions and illustrations because I was very anxious to make clear even by much reiteration how there are these two lives in every full grown man, the life for which man asks and the deeper life which God gives; and how these two stand always related to one another, as the house to the foundation on which it is built, or, perhaps better, as the pattern to the stuff into whose substance it is woven. And I have done all this because I wanted to get at this further question which seems to me to be very pressingly important. What effect upon our treatment of the lower life will such a vision of the higher life which ought to be built on it produce? At first it might seem as if the mere physical life and all that belongs to it would seem contemptible and only worthy of neglect to one who had caught sight of the diviner purposes of living. But very soon we see that that is not so. It gives us new ideas about the mere fact of life when we thus discern the loftier purposes of life, but it does not make life contemptible or insignificant. Let us see what one or two of such ideas are.

The first of them is obedience. Any man who knows that his bodily life and all that immediately belongs to it has its real value as the scene of experience and the material of operations which belong to the mind and the soul, must of necessity seek for some power to whom the mind and body belong and ask of Him to make the body ready for the high and mysterious functions of which it can itself be most imperfectly aware, for which it can but most imperfectly prepare itself. To give ourselves into the will of God that He may do in us that which He made us for, which we ourselves but dimly understand, that is the only true completion of our life. O how we talk of submission to God as if it were the hard concession to necessity or else as if it were the last refuge of despair instead of being what it is, the fulfilment and consummation of our life. As if you took the chisel which had been trying to carve by itself and put it into the hand of Michael Angelo, so only infinitely higher is it when you teach your soul to say "O Lord, not my will but thy will be done." It is no cry of a defeated man. It is the soul seizing on the privilege and the right of having itself completed after God's pattern. The parable of the prodigal son has the whole story in it. The man submitting is the man completed. O if our brave, self-confident young men only knew this. Full of pure joy in life as life, full of the delight of "mere living," they look forward and the dream comes to them that sometime or other life may break and then they will go to God for repair, sometime or other (so they shuddering feel) they may fall into terrible sin and then they will go to God for forgiveness. But to go to God now for completeness, to go and lay life into the obedience of God as a diamond lays itself into the sunshine that the mere surface brilliancy may deepen and region behind region of splendor be revealed below, that does not seem to come into their thought. The cry "submit, submit," "obey, obey," seems to them to mean "come down! come down!" But it really means "come up!" Let God who has given you so abundantly the earthly life, the life of time, give you into and through it, the life of Heaven, the eternal life.

2. Again our doctrine enforces most impressively, I think, the need of purity in the life of the body for the soul's sake. Here are you, let us say, just where King David was when as a boy he lived in that bright, sunny, superficial life which Mr. Browning describes in the verses which I quoted some time ago, the life of the mountain and the fountain and the river bed, the life of physical spirits and the joy of mere existence. Not yet have opened the deeper depths to you. Not yet have you begun to hunger after truth, to puzzle over the problems of the world, to seek for spiritual holiness. But you know the time for all those deeper lives must come to you. You would not bear to think of yourself as possibly going on forever living thus only on the outside. You mean to be religious some day. Of course the true, the only true way is to be religious now. Now is the real time to open these deeper lives which you do mean some day to live. But till you open them, while you are lingering and hesitating and living still in the fresh delights of the external life, it is good that you should feel already the influence of that deeper life which is

to be some day, begging you to keep the life in which you are living even now pure for its sake. O if I could let you see the men who, when they come to the great effort to be Christians, find a terrible remonstrance in the dulness and heaviness of their whole being brought on them by years of dissipation or of idleness. Here is the young man who is not a Christian yet. He might be. Let him not think for a moment that it is only for old men to give themselves to the gracious service of the Son of man. Thank God, there are some boys among you who have learned better than that the chances and privileges of our human life. But this young man is not a Christian yet. Can he do anything even now? Surely he can! If ever he gives himself to God's service it must be with these hands that he will do the will of the Lord whom he will then love with all his heart. Therefore let him keep these hands pure and make them alert and strong. If ever he seeks for the signs of his then acknowledged God in all creation, it must be through these eyes and through all these senses that the rich, overwhelming witness must pour in. Therefore let him guard those senses from the least taint of impurity, from the sluggishness and obstruction which falls like a curse upon the body in which a man has lived a dissipated life. If this young man ever, made a Christian, is to enter into the deep and helpful associations with his fellow-men which are the delight and duty of the Christian life, it will be by the profounder opening and the broader extension of these social relations in which he is living now that that new social life will come, therefore let him keep these social relations scrupulously clean and true. This is the way in which you may be faithful already to whatever unguessed deeper life God has in His intentions for you. No man is living worthily who is not faithful already to the future life which he does not yet understand, but which he knows must come. "Your bodies are the temples of the Holy Ghost," says Paul. Before the God has occupied the temple, the temple must feel the influence of his promised coming and keep its empty courts clean for Him. Are there not some men here, not yet devoted to the highest life which is Christ's service, who are yet conscious enough of some mysterious richness of experience of life before them, to make them ready to listen when one begs them to keep their whole present life, their whole bodily life pure and true and active, so that whatever may claim them in the days to come shall find them with natures so fresh and sound that they can answer to its claim.

I know indeed that it is out of the very substance of our sins that God's unbounded and ingenious mercy can make the new life. I know that into the shattered structure of a misused and degraded body He can pour His spiritual strength. I know that on the tattered canvas of a profligate life he can weave the glorious patterns of His grace. But truths like these, confirmed by multitudes of notable histories, must never make us think so base a heresy as that a man must go through wickedness to get to goodness, or that a pure youth does not display a fairer theatre for the work of grace than a young life all torn and stained with sin. Every man's youth, be it as pure as it may, will offer enough for God to forgive, enough from which the soul, come to its conversion, can gather the fruits of humble penitence. But it will always be the hills which lift themselves the highest in the dark and look most frankly toward the quarter from which the promising must come when it does come; it will always be these hills that will first and most easily and most richly catch the glory of the rising sun. Therefore keep your life pure that some day God may make it holy! Be faithful already to the faith which shall be yours some day.

3. Let me say one single but most earnest word about the necessary sacredness and inviolability which this truth of ours when it is thoroughly accepted gives to our physical life. Nothing, I believe, can give a man a sure, reliable conviction that under no circumstance of pain or disappointment has he a right to cast away his life, nothing can give and keep to a man a true and manly certainty that he is bound, no matter how he hates it, to stand at the post where God has put him till the God who put him there calls him away, except the clear perception that this physical life is but the material and condition of deeper spiritual life which is the only finally valuable thing. The man whose whole nature is steeped in and pervaded by that truth will stand in spite of everything, while God in any way, through the pain of the body, if need be, calls up the soul and bids it live its life, and makes the man by suffering which he will not run away from, a spiritual man.

Every now and then a strange phenomenon appears which shows how the sacredness of life depends upon the preservation of clear ideas of the deepest purposes of life. Every now and then some physician or some other man whose eye is fastened principally on man's physical structure stands up with the plea that if a man is sick with an incurable disease and doomed to hopeless suffering it is the right and even the duty of science to relieve him of his sufferings by gently taking away his life. It is an atrocious insult to the essential and inalienable sacredness of life. "There is nothing but suffering for this poor creature," cries such an arrogant doctor, "therefore let him die!" Nothing but suffering! As if God were not every day using the body's suffering to cultivate the soul's eternal life. As if just as soon as there was a hard lesson to be learned you ought to kill the scholar. One trembles as he thinks what pictures of human patience, what visions of ripened character which have been revelations and inspirations to generations of mankind, what spectacles of the spiritual possibilities of humanity, nay, what sights of refined and exalted happiness in the triumph of the spirit over the flesh, must have been lost to the world if doctors such as these had had their way from the beginning. No! The life of the human body is a sacred thing, because in it and through it comes the deeper life. Man must stand by his post, and no other man must drive him from it, because so only can God give man His best revelations and use him for His most effective work.

And so we come back to King David and our text. The old, old prayer for life. How the whole world has rung with it! In what various tones it has gone up to God. Not merely from sick beds where life seemed to be just slipping away out of the grasp of desperate men. Not merely at the foot of thrones where wretches begged their tyrants not to cut short their wretched days. But all the stir of living is a cry for life. All the struggle of business is an appeal of man to live. All industry, all enterprise, all thought, echoes with the dread of death, the prayer for life! And God hears it and gives the world, and gives to you and me, day by day, the life we ask. But oh, that as He gives it to us day by day we may know the full richness of what He gives. Every morning He puts into our hands anew the mystery of our existence. The chance to think true thoughts, to do brave and kind deeds, to love him, and to help our brethren—these, the great chances of the soul, these, the eternal life, the "long life even forever and ever" He gives us day by day when we ask for life. O may He give us something more, the gift of His own sight that we may know as He knows all the depth of this life which He gives to us, and live it obediently and purely and patiently, and so come in it and by it always nearer to Him who gives it to us.

THE CANDLE OF THE LORD

"The spirit of man is the candle of the Lord."—Prov. xx. 27.

THE essential connection between the life of God and the life of man is the great truth of the world; and that is the truth which Solomon sets forth in the striking words which I have chosen for my text this morning. The picture which the words suggest is very simple. An unlighted candle is standing in the darkness and some one comes to light it. A blazing bit of paper holds the fire at first, but it is vague and fitful. It flares and wavers and at any moment may go out. But the vague, uncertain, flaring blaze touches the candle, and the candle catches fire and at once you have a steady flame. It burns straight and clear and constant. The candle gives the fire a manifestation-point for all the room which is illuminated by it. The candle is glorified by the fire and the fire is manifested by the candle. The two bear witness that they were made for one another by the way in which they fulfil each other's life. That fulfilment comes by the way in which the inferior substance renders obedience to its superior. The candle obeys the fire. The docile wax acknowledges that the subtle flame is its master and it yields to his power; and so, like every faithful servant of a noble master, it at once gives its master's nobility the chance to utter itself, and its own substance is clothed with a glory which is not its own. The disobedient granite, if you try to burn it, neither gives the fire a chance to show its brightness nor gathers any splendor to itself. It only glows with sullen resistance, and, as the heat increases, splits and breaks but will not yield. But the candle obeys, and so in it the scattered fire finds a point of permanent and clear expression.

Can we not see, with such a picture clear before us, what must be meant when it is said that one being is the candle of another being? There is in a community a man of large, rich character, whose influence runs everywhere. You cannot talk with any man in all the city but you get, shown in that man's own way, the thought, the feeling of that central man who teaches all the community to think, to feel. The very boys catch something of his power, and have something about them that would not be there if he were not living in the town. What better description could you give of all that, than to say that that man's life was fire and that all these men's lives were candles which he lighted, which gave to the rich, warm, live, fertile nature that was in him multiplied points of steady exhibition, so that he lighted the town through them? Or, not to look so widely, I pity you if in the circle of your home there is not some warm and living nature which is your fire. Your cold, dark candle-nature, touched by that fire, burns bright and clear. Wherever you are carried, perhaps into regions where that nature cannot go, you carry its fire and set it up in some new place. Nay, the fire itself may have disappeared, the nature may have vanished from the earth and gone to heaven; and yet still your candle-life, which was lighted at it, keeps that fire still in the world, as the fire of the lightning lives in the tree that it has struck, long after the quick lightning itself has finished its short, hot life and died. So the man in the counting-room is the candle of the woman who stays at home, making her soft influence felt in the rough places of trade where her feet never go; and so a man who lives like an inspiration in the city for honesty and purity and charity may be only the candle in whose obedient life burns still the fire of another strong, true man who was his father, and who passed out of men's sight a score of years ago. Men call the father dead, but he is no more dead than the torch has gone out which lighted the beacon that is blazing on the hill.

And now, regarding all this lighting of life from life, two things are evident, the same two which appeared in the story of the candle and its flame: First, there must be a correspondency of nature between the two; and second, there must be a cordial obedience of the less to the greater. The nature which cannot feel the other nature's warmth, even if it is held close to it; and the nature which refuses to be held where the other nature's flame can reach it,—both of these must go unlighted, no matter how hotly the fire of the higher life may burn.

I think that we are ready now to turn to Solomon and read his words again and understand them. "The spirit of man is the candle of the Lord," he says. God is the fire of this world, its vital principle, a warm pervading presence everywhere. What thing of outward nature can so picture to us the mysterious, the subtle, the quick, live, productive and destructive thought, which has always lifted men's hearts and solemnized their faces when they have said the word GOD, as this strange thing,—so heavenly, so unearthly, so terrible, and yet so gracious; so full of creativeness, and yet so quick and fierce to sweep whatever opposes it out of its path,—this marvel, this beauty and glory and mystery of fire? Men have always felt the fitness of the figure; and the fire has always crowded, closest of all earthly elements, about the throne on which their conception of Deity was seated. And now of this fire the spirit of man is the candle. What does that mean? If, because man is of a nature which corresponds to the nature of God, and just so far as man is obedient to God the life of God, which is spread throughout the universe, gathers itself into utterance; and men, aye, and all other beings, if such beings there are, capable of watching our humanity, see what God is, in gazing at the man whom He has kindled,—then is not the figure plain? It is a wondrous thought, but it is clear enough. Here is the universe, full of the diffused fire of divinity. Men feel it in the air, as they feel an intense heat which has not broken into a blaze. That is the meaning of a great deal of the unexplained, mysterious awfulness of life, of which they who are very much in its power are often only half aware. It is the sense of God, felt but unseen, like an atmosphere burdened with heat that does not burst out into fire. Now in the midst of this solemn, burdened world there stands up a man, pure, God-like, and perfectly obedient to God. In an instant it is as if the heated room had found some sensitive, inflammable point where it could kindle to a blaze. The vague oppressiveness of God's felt presence becomes clear and definite. The fitfulness of the impression of divinity is steadied into permanence. The mystery changes its character, and is a mystery of light and not of darkness. The fire of the Lord has found the candle of the Lord, and burns clear and steady, guiding and cheering instead of bewildering and frightening us, just so soon as a man who is obedient to God has begun to catch and manifest His nature.

I hope that we shall find that this truth comes very close to our personal, separate lives; but, before we come to that, let me remind you first with what a central dignity it clothes the life of man in the great world. Certain philosophies, which belong to our time, would depreciate the importance of man in the world, and rob him of his centralness. Man's instinct and man's pride rebel against them, but he is puzzled by their speciousness. Is it indeed true, as it seems, that the world is made for man, and that from man, standing in the centre, all things besides which the world contains get their true value and receive the verdict of their destiny? That was the old story that the Bible told. The book of Genesis with its Garden of Eden, and its obedient beasts waiting until the man should tell them what they should be called, struck firmly, at the beginning of the anthem of the world's history, the great note of the centralness of man. And the Garden of Eden, in this its first idea, repeats itself in every cabin of the western forests or the southern jungles, where a new Adam and a new Eve, a solitary settler and his wife, begin as it were the human history anew. There once again the note of Genesis is struck, and man asserts his centralness. The forest waits to catch the color of his life. The beasts hesitate in fear or anger till he shall tame them to his service or bid them depart. The earth under his feet holds its fertility at his command, and answers the summons of his grain or flower-seeds. The very sky over his head regards him, and what he does upon the earth is echoed in the changes of the climate and the haste or slowness of the storms. This is the great impression which all the simplest life of man is ever creating, and with which the philosophies, which would make little of the separateness and centralness of the life of man, must always have to fight. And this is the impression which is taken up and strengthened and made clear, and turned from a petty pride to a lofty dignity and a solemn responsibility, when there comes such a message as this of Solomon's. He says that the true separateness and superiority and centralness of man is in that likeness of nature to God, and that capacity of spiritual obedience to Him, in virtue of which man may be the declaration and manifestation of God to all the world. So long as that truth stands, the centralness of man is sure. "The spirit of man is the candle of the Lord."

This is the truth of which I wish to speak to you to-day, the perpetual revelation of God by human life. You must ask yourself first, what God is. You must see how at the very bottom of His existence, as you conceive of it, lie these two thoughts—purpose and righteousness; how absolutely impossible it is to give God any personality except as the fulfilment of these two qualities—the intelligence that plans in love, and the righteousness that lives in duty. Then ask yourself how any knowledge of these qualities—of what they are, of

what kind of being they will make in their perfect combination—
could exist upon the earth if there were not a human nature here in
which they could be uttered, from which they could shine. Only a
person can truly utter a person. Only from a character can a character be echoed. You might write it all over the skies that God was
just, but it would not burn there. It would be, at best, only a bit of
knowledge; never a Gospel; never something which it would glad-
den the hearts of men to know. That comes only when a human
life, capable of a justice like God's, made just by God, glows with
His justice in the eyes of men, a candle of the Lord.

I have just intimated one thing which we need to observe. Man's
utterance of God is purely an utterance of quality. It can tell me
nothing of the quantities which make up His perfect life. That God
is just, and what it is to be just—those things I can learn from the just
lives of the just men about me; but how just God is, to what uncon-
ceived perfection, to what unexpected developments of itself, that
majestic quality of justice may extend in Him,—of that I can form no
judgment, that is worth anything, from the justice that I see in fellow-man. This seems to me to widen at once the range of the truth
which I am stating. If it be the quality of God which man is capable
of uttering, then it must be the quality of manhood that is necessary
for the utterance; the quality of manhood, but not any specific quantity, not any assignable degree of human greatness. Whoever has in
him the human quality, whoever really has the spirit of man, may be
a candle of the Lord. A larger measure of that spirit may make a
brighter light; but there must be a light wherever any human being, in virtue of his humanness, by obedience becomes luminous
with God. There are the men of lofty spiritual genius, the leaders
of our race. How they stand out through history! How all men
feel as they pass into their presence that they are passing into the
light of God! They are puzzled when they try to explain it. There
is nothing more instructive and suggestive than the bewilderment
which men feel when they try to tell what inspiration is,—how men
become inspired. The lines which they draw through the continual
communication between God and man are always becoming unsteady and confused. But in general, he who comes into the presence of any powerful nature, whose power is at all of a spiritual
sort, feels sure that in some way he is coming into the presence of
God. But it would be melancholy if only the great men could give

us this conviction. The world would be darker than it is if every human spirit, so soon as it became obedient, did not become the Lord's candle. A poor, meagre, starved, bruised life, if only it keeps the true human quality and does not become inhuman, and if it is obedient to God in its blind, dull, half-conscious way, becomes a light. Lives yet more dark than it is, become dimly aware of God through it. A mere child, in his pure humanity, and with his easy and instinctive turning of his life toward the God from whom he came,—it is one of the commonplaces of your homes how often he may burn with some suggestion of divinity, and cast illumination upon problems and mysteries whose difficulty he himself has never felt. There are great lamps and little lamps burning everywhere. The world is bright with them. You shut your book in which you have been holding communion with one of the great souls of all time; and while you are standing in the light which he has shed about him, your child beside you says some simple, childlike thing, and a new thread of shining wisdom runs through the sweet and subtle thoughts that the great thinker gave you, as the light of a little taper sends its special needle of brightness through the pervasive splendor of a sun-lit world. It is not strange. The fire is the same, whatever be the human lamp that gives it its expression. There is no life so humble that, if it be true and genuinely human and obedient to God, it may not hope to shed some of His light. There is no life so meagre that the greatest and wisest of us can afford to despise it. We cannot know at all at what sudden moment it may flash forth with the life of God.

And in this truth of ours we have certainly the key to another mystery which sometimes puzzles us. What shall we make of some man rich in attainments and in generous desires, well educated, well behaved, who has trained himself to be a light and help to other men, and who, now that his training is complete, stands in the midst of his fellow-men completely dark and helpless? There are plenty of such men. We have all known them who have seen how men grow up. Their brethren stand around them expecting light from them, but no light comes. They themselves are full of amazement at themselves. They built themselves for influence, but no one feels them. They kindled themselves to give light, but no one shines a grateful answer back to them. Perhaps they blame their fellow-men, who are too dull to see their radiance. Perhaps they only wonder what is the matter, and wait, with a hope that never quite dies out into despair, for the long-delayed recognition and gratitude. At last they die, and the men who stand about their graves feel that the saddest thing about their death is that the world is not perceptibly the darker for their dying. What does it mean? If we let the truth of Solomon's figure play upon it, is not the meaning of the familiar failure simply this: These men are unlighted candles; they are the spirit of man, elaborated, cultivated, finished to its very finest, but lacking the last touch of God. As dark as a row of silver lamps, all chased and wrought with wondrous skill, all filled with rarest oil, but all untouched with fire,—so dark in this world is a long row of cultivated men, set up along the corridors of some age of history, around the halls of some wise university, or in the pulpits of some stately church, to whom there has come no fire of devotion, who stand in awe and reverence before no wisdom greater than their own who are proud and selfish, who do not know what it is to obey. There is the explanation of your wonder when you cling close to some man whom the world calls bright, and find that you get no brightness from him. There is the explanation of yourself, O puzzled man, who never can make out why the world does not turn to you for help. The poor blind world cannot tell its need, nor analyze its instinct, nor say why it seeks one man and leaves another; but through its blind eyes it knows when the fire of God has fallen on a human life. This is the meaning of the strange helpfulness which comes into a man when he truly is converted. It is not new truth that he knows, not new wonders that he can do, but it is that the unlighted nature, in the utter obedience and self-surrender of that great hour, has been lifted up and lighted at the life of God, and now burns with Him.

But it is not the worst thing in life for a man to be powerless or uninfluential. There are men enough for whom we would thank God if they did no harm, even if they did no good. I will not stop now to question whether there be such a thing possible as a life totally without influence of any kind, whether perhaps the men of whom I have been speaking do not also belong to the class of whom I want next to speak. However that may be, I am sure you will recognize the fact that there is a multitude of men whose lamps are certainly not dark, and yet who certainly are not the candles of the Lord. A nature furnished richly to the very brim, a man of knowledge, of wit, of skill, of thought, with the very graces of the body perfect, and yet profane, impure, worldly, and scattering scepticism of all good and truth about him wherever he may go. His is no un-lighted candle. He burns so bright and lurid that often the purer lights grow dim in the glare. But if it be possible for the human candle, when it is all made, when the subtle components of a human nature are all mingled most carefully,—if it be possible that then, in-stead of being lifted up to heaven and kindled at the pure being of Him who is eternally and absolutely good, it should be plunged down into hell and lighted at the yellow flames that burn out of the dreadful brimstone of the pit, then we can understand the sight of a man who is rich in every brilliant human quality, cursing the world with the continual exhibition of the devilish instead of the godlike in his life. When the power of pure love appears as a capacity of brutal lust; when the holy ingenuity with which man may search the character of a fellow-man, that he may help him to be his best, is turned into the unholy skill with which the bad man studies his victim, that he may know how to make his damnation most com-plete; when the almost divine magnetism, which is given to a man in order that he may instil his faith and hope into some soul that trusts him, is used to breathe doubt and despair through all the substance of a friend's reliant soul; when wit, which ought to make truth beautiful, is deliberately prostituted to the service of a lie; when earnestness is degraded to be the slave of blasphemy, and the slave's reputation is made the cloak for the master's shame,—in all these cases, and how frequent they are no man among us fails to know, have simply the spirit of man kindled from below, not from above, the candle of the Lord burning with the fire of the devil. Still it will burn; still the native inflammableness of humanity will show it-self. There will be light; there will be power; and men who want nothing but light and power will come to it. It is wonderful how mere power, or mere brightness, apart altogether from the work that the power is doing and the story that the brightness has to tell, will win the confidence and admiration of men from whom we might have expected better things. A bright book or a bright play will draw the crowd, although its meaning be detestable. A clever man will make a host of boys and men stand like charmed birds while he draws their principles quietly out of them and leaves them moral idiots. A whole great majority of a community will rush like foolish sheep to the polls and vote for a man who they know is false and brutal, because they have learned to say that he is strong. All this is true enough; and yet while men do these wild and foolish things, they know the difference between the illumination of a human life that is kindled from above and that which is kindled from below. They know the pure flames of one and the lurid glare of the other; and however they may praise and follow wit and power, as if to be witty or powerful were an end sufficient in itself, they will always keep their sacredest respect and confidence for that power or wit which is inspired by God, and works for righteousness.

There is still another way, more subtle and sometimes more dangerous than these, in which the spirit of man may fail of its completest function as the candle of the Lord. The lamp may be lighted, and the fire at which it is lighted may be indeed the fire of God, and yet it may not to God alone who shines forth upon the world. I can picture to myself a candle which should in some way mingle a peculiarity of its own substance with the light it shed, giving to that light a hue which did not belong essentially to the fire at which it was lighted. Men who saw it would see not only the brightness of the fire. They would see also the tone and color of the lamp. And so it is, I think, with the way in which some good men manifest God. They have really kindled their lives at Him. It is His fire that burns in them. They are obedient, and so He can make them His points of exhibition; but they cannot get rid of themselves. They are mixed with the God they show. They show themselves as well as Him. It is as when a mirror mingles its own shape with the reflections of the things that are reflected from it, and gives them a curious convexity because it is itself convex. This is the secret of all pious bigotry, of all holy prejudice. It is the candle, putting its own color into the flame which it has borrowed from the fire of God. The violent man makes God seem violent. The feeble man makes God seem feeble. The speculative man makes God look like a beautiful dream. The legal man makes God look like a hard and steel-like law. Here is where all the harsh and narrow part of sectarianism comes from. The narrow Presbyterian or Methodist, or Episcopalian or Quaker, full of devoutness, really afire with God,—what is he but a candle which is always giving the flame its color, and which, by a disposition which many men have to value the little parts of their life more than the greater, makes less of the essential brightness of

the flame than of the special color which it lends to it? It seems, perhaps, as if, in saying this, I threw some slight or doubt upon that
individual and separate element in every man's religion, on which,
upon the contrary, I place the very highest value. Every man who is
a Christian must live a Christian life that is peculiarly his own. Every
candle of the Lord must utter its peculiar light; only the true individuality of faith is marked by these characteristics which rescue
it from bigotry: first, that it does not add something to the universal
light, but only brings out most strongly some aspect of it which is
specially its own; second, that it always cares more about the essential light than about the peculiar way in which it utters it; and third,
that it easily blends with other special utterances of the universal
light, in cordial sympathy and recognition of the value which it finds
in them. Let these characteristics be in every man's religion, and
then the individuality of faith is an inestimable gain. Then the different candles of the Lord burn in long rows down His great palace-
halls of the world; and all together, each complementing all the rest,
they light the whole vast space with Him.

I have tried to depict some of the difficulties which beset the full
exhibition in the world of this great truth of Solomon, that "the spirit
of man is the candle of the Lord." Man is selfish and disobedient, and
will not let his life burn at all. Man is wilful and passionate, and kindles his life with ungodly fire. Man is narrow and bigoted, and makes
the light of God shine with his own special color. But all these are accidents. All these are distortions of the true idea of man. How can
we know that? Here is the perfect man, Christ Jesus! What a man He
is! How nobly, beautifully, perfectly human! What hands, what feet,
what an eye, what a heart! How genuinely, unmistakably a man! I
bring the men of my experience or of my imagination into His presence, and behold, just when the worst or best of them falls short of
Him, my human consciousness assures me that they fall short also of
the best idea of what it is to be a man. Here is the spirit of man in
its perfection. And what then? Is it not also the candle of the Lord?
"I am come a light into the world," said Jesus. "He that hath seen
Me hath seen the Father. "In Him was life and the life was the light
of men." So wrote the man of all men who knew Him best. And in
Him where are the difficulties that we saw? where for one moment is
the dimness of selfishness? O, it seems to me a wonderful thing that
the supremely rich human nature of Jesus never for an instant turned

with self-indulgence in on its own richness, or was beguiled by that besetting danger of all opulent souls, the wish, in the deepest sense, just to enjoy himself. How fascinating that desire is. How it keeps many and many of the most abundant natures in the world from usefulness. Just to handle over and over their hidden treasures, and with a spiritual miserliness to think their thought for the pure joy of thinking, and turn emotion into the soft atmosphere of a life of gardened selfishness. Not one instant of that in Jesus. All the vast richness of His human nature only meant for Him more power to utter God to man.

And yet how pure His rich life was. How it abhorred to burn with any fire that was not divine. Such abundant life, and yet such utter incapacity of any living but the holiest; such power of burning, and yet such utter incapacity of being kindled by any torch but God's; such fulness with such purity was never seen besides upon the earth; and yet we know as we behold it that it is no monster, but only the type of what all men must be, although all men but Him as yet have failed to be it.

And yet again there was intense personality in Him without a moment's bigotry. A special life, a life that stands distinct and self-defined among all the lives of men, and yet a life making the universal God all the more universally manifest by its distinctness, appealing to all lives just in proportion to the intensity of the individuality that filled His own. O, I think I need only bid you look at Him, and you must see what it is to which our feeble lights are struggling. There is the true spiritual man who is the candle of the Lord, the light that lighteth every man.

It is distinctly a new idea of life, new to the standards of all our ordinary living, which this truth reveals. All our ordinary appeals to men to be up and doing, and make themselves shining lights, fade away and become insignificant before this higher message which comes in the words of Solomon and in the life of Jesus. What does the higher message say? "You are a part of God! You have no place or meaning in this world but in relationship to Him. The full realtionship can only be realized by obedience. Be obedient to Him, and you shall shine by His light, not your own. Then you cannot be dark, for He shall kindle you. Then you shall be as incapable of burning with false passion as you shall be quick to answer with the true. Then the devil may hold his torch to you, as he held it to the heart of Jesus in the desert, and your heart shall be as uninflammable as His. But as soon as God touches you, you shall burn with a light so truly your own that you shall reverence your own mysterious life, and yet so truly His that pride shall be impossible." What a philosophy of human life is that. "O, to be nothing, nothing!" cries the mystic singer in his revival hymn, desiring to lose himself in God. "Nay not that; O to be something, something," remonstrates the unmystical man, longing for work, ardent for personal life and character. Where is the meeting of the two? How shall self-surrender meet that high self-value without which no man can justify his living and honor himself in his humanity? Where can they meet but in this truth? Man must be something that he may be nothing. The something which he must be must consist in simple fitness to utter the divine life which is the only original power in the universe. And then man must be nothing that he may be something. He must submit himself in obedience to God, that so God may use him, in some way in which his special nature only could be used, to illuminate and help the world. Tell me, do not the two cries meet in that one aspiration of the Christian man to find his life by losing it in God, to be himself by being not his own but Christ's?

In certain lands, for certain holy ceremonies, they prepare the candles with most anxious care. The very bees which distil the wax are sacred. They range in gardens planted with sweet flowers for their use alone. The wax is gathered by consecrated hands; and then the shaping of the candles is a holy task, performed in holy places, to the sound of hymns, and in the atmosphere of prayers. All this is done because the candles are to burn in the most lofty ceremonies on most sacred days. With what care must the man be made whose spirit is to be the candle of the Lord! It is his spirit which God is to kindle with Himself. Therefore the spirit must be the precious part of him. The body must be valued only for the protection and the education which the soul may gain by it. And the power by which his spirit shall become a candle is obedience. Therefore obedience must be the struggle and desire of his life; obedience, not hard and forced, but ready, loving, and spontaneous; the obedience of the child to the father, of the candle to the flame; the doing of duty not merely that the duty may be done, but that the soul in doing it may become capable of receiving and uttering God; the bearing of pain not merely because the pain must be borne, but that the bearing of it may make the soul able to burn with the divine fire which found it in the furnace; the repentance of sin and acceptance of forgiveness, not merely that the soul may be saved from the fire of hell, but that it may be touched with the fire of heaven, and shine with the love of God, as the stars, forever.

Above all the pictures of life,—of what it means, of what may be made out of it,—there stands out this picture of a human spirit burning with the light of the God whom it obeys, and showing Him to other men. O, my young friends, the old men will tell you that the lower pictures of life and its purposes turn out to be cheats and mistakes. But this picture can never cheat the soul that tries to realize it. The man whose life is a struggle after such obedience, when at last his earthly task is over, may look forward from the borders of this life into the other, and humbly say, as his history of the life that is ended, and his prayer for the life that is to come, the words that Jesus said—"I have glorified Thee on the earth; now, O Father, glorify Me with Thyself forever."

[When this sermon was preached in Westminster Abbey, on the evening of Sunday, the Fourth of July, 1880, the following sentences were added:—]

MY FRIENDS,—May I ask you to linger while I say to you a few words more, which shall not be unsuited to what I have been saying, and which shall, for just a moment, recall to you the sacredness which this day—the Fourth of July, the anniversary of American Independence—has in the hearts of us Americans. If I dare—generously permitted as I am to stand this evening in the venerable Abbey, so full of our history as well as yours—to claim that our festival shall have some sacredness for you as well as us, my claim rests on the simple truth that to all true men the birthday of a nation must always be a sacred thing. For in our modern thought the nation is the making-place of men. Not by the traditions of its history, nor by the splendor of its corporate achievements, nor by the abstract excellencies of its constitution, but by its fitness to make men, to beget and educate human character, to contribute to the complete humanity, the "perfect man" that is to be,—by this alone each nation must be judged to-day. The nations are the golden candlesticks which hold aloft the candles of the Lord. No candlestick can be so rich or venerable that men shall honor it if it holds no candle. "Show us your man," land cries to land.

In such days any nation, out of the midst of which God has led another nation as He led ours out of the midst of yours, must surely watch with anxiety and prayer the peculiar development of our common humanity of which that new nation is made the home, the special burning of the human candle in that new candlestick; and if she sees a hope and promise that God means to build in that new land some strong and free and characteristic manhood which shall help the world to its completeness, the mother-land will surely lose the thought and memory of whatever anguish accompanied the birth, for gratitude over the gain which humanity has made, "for joy that a man is born into the world."

It is not for me to glorify to-night the country which I love with all my heart and soul. I may not ask your praise for anything admirable which the United States has been or done. But on my country's birthday I may do something far more solemn and more worthy of the hour. I may ask you for your prayer in her behalf. That on the manifold and wondrous chance which God is giving her,—on her freedom (for she is free, since the old stain of slavery was washed out in blood); on her unconstrained religious life; on her passion for education, and her eager search for truth; on her jealous care for the poor man's rights and opportunities; on her countless quiet homes where the future generations of her men are growing; on her manufactures and her commerce; on her wide gates open to the east and to the west; on her strange meetings of the races out of which a new race is slowly being born; on her vast enterprise and her illimitable hopefulness,—on all these materials and machineries of manhood, on all that the life of my country must mean for humanity, I may ask you to pray that the blessing of God the Father of man, and Christ the Son of man, may rest forever.

Because you are Englishmen and I am an American; also because here, under this high and hospitable roof of God, we are all more than Englishmen and more than Americans; because we are all men, children of God, waiting for the full coming of our Father's kingdom, I ask you for that prayer.

THE DIGNITY AND GREATNESS
OF FAITH

"No man can say that Jesus is the Lord but by the Holy Ghost."—I COR.
xii. 3.

THESE words must mean their deepest, or else they cannot mean anything for us. They were written long ago when Christianity was new. To say, then, that Jesus Christ was the divine Lord of the world was something different in the demand it made upon a man's powers and character from what it is to-day. In some respects it must have been much harder then than now: in some respects much easier. We cannot tell wholly, I suppose, what Paul's verse meant in the ears of the Corinthians who heard it first. But when we bring his words over to our own time and try to realize them now, it is evident that they mean nothing unless they mean their deepest. "No man can say that Jesus is the Lord but by the Holy Ghost." Evidently it is not true that a divine help is needed simply to declare as an article of one's creed, a conviction of one's mind, that Jesus Christ is Master of the world. Thousands of people are doing that all the time, and doing it evidently by themselves, not "by the Holy Ghost" at all, often saying the great words wilfully, obstinately, controversially, with a spirit and an impulse so essentially earthly that we know they did not come from heaven; with a vehemence so unholy and unspiritual that we know it is not the work of the Holy Spirit. Evidently it cannot be the mere saying of the words or the mere acceptance of the fact that proves a divine influence. It must be the saying of the words, "Jesus is the Lord," filled with the most earnest faith and the richest experience; the saying of them by a man to whom they represent the deepest fact and the most powerful impulse of his life. It must mean this, and, if it does, then it involves one of the greatest and most urgent subjects of which we can think or speak. That subject is the dignity and greatness of a faith in Christ. It is only, so says St. Paul, it is only by an action which outgoes his own powers and shares

42

the strength of God that a man is able to own Christ as the master of his life.

The Dignity and Greatness of faith! There are two classes of people, very different from one another, both of whom deny the proposition which I have announced and of which I wish to speak. The first denier is the ordinary flippant church-member or partisan controversialist, who treats faith as if it were one of the easiest and most casual functions of a human life, and a confession of faith as if it were an indifferent sort of action to be slipped in almost anywhere, between two other acts of wholly other kinds. Such a man dishonors faith by the trivialness with which he treats it. His denial of its dignity and greatness is a practical one, and while he makes it he may be all the time talking the grandest talk about the faith which all his life discredits. The other denier is more serious, and his denial deals with the whole idea and theory of faith. Many and many men there are to-day who most deliberately hold and teach that the idea of man's depending upon a loftier power than himself is a delusion of human immaturity, that it belongs to the infancy of the human mind, that for the world or for any man to give it up and count the human life sufficient for itself is a distinct advance, that faith is fetich-worship gradually passing out into the light, slowly becoming that full enlightenment of man in which, when it becomes complete, there shall be no longer any such thing possible as faith. In protest against both denials, the practical denial of the frivolous communicant in our churches, and the dogmatic denial of the positivist philosopher, we want to assert the dignity and greatness of faith. I would like to think that as I speak I see two faces before me— one the easy, careless face of the commonplace professor of religion. Looking into his trifling eyes I would like to say: "Poor soul, this earthly, uninspired thing of yours is not real faith. No man can have real faith but by the Holy Spirit." The other face shall be the earnest, puzzled, eager face of the young man who is trying, as he has been taught, to despise and pity the victims of the supernatural. To him one wants to say: "Do not dare to despise what is the noblest act that man has ever tried to do. You degrade yourself when you do that. It is only by a divine, Holy Spirit that any man can have faith."

Begin with this, then: that the greatness of any act is to be estimated by the faculties of man which it employs. It is a greater act for a man to write a book than for him to build a fence, because the writing of the book demands the use of deeper powers. The man must think,—at least a little,—and arrange his thought, and give it utterance in language. To govern a State requires still nobler faculties, faculties rarer, finer, more profound, faculties that must be summoned for their work out of yet deeper chambers of our human nature. When I know what faculties any man's work requires, at once I know where that work stands in comparative dignity among the works of men. When a new act of man is offered to me which I have not been called upon to estimate before, I ask myself what powers the man will have to use who does that act, and when I know that, then I am sure that I can judge it rightly.

This is the test that we must apply here: What faculties are needed in an act of faith? What powers must a man use who says with all his heart of an unseen Jesus, "He is my Lord and Master"? Let us see—and first of all there is the power of dealing with the unseen at all. Back from the visible to the invisible which lies behind it, the mind of man is always pressing; and as it presses back, there are new powers coming out into consciousness and use. The first man in his immaturity deals with things. Man as he grows maturer deals also with ideas. The things are visible and tangible. The ideas no eye has seen, no hand has ever touched. Subtle, elusive, and yet growing to be more real to the mind of the man who truly deals with them than are the bricks of which his house is built, or the iron tool with which he does his work, the great ideas of justice, of beauty, of sublimity, become at once the witnesses and the educators of man's deeper powers which must come out to do their work. The birth of the power of recognizing and dealing with ideas, the birth of ideality, is an epoch in the history of the world or of a man. Or, again, you know your friend by the seeing of the eye; all the distinct intercourses of the senses introduce your life to his; and then your friend goes away from you, out of your sight, to China or Peru; and as your power of friendship reaches out to follow him, as the thought of him takes the place of the sight of him, as association, and memory, and hope, and imagination come out at your need to bind your life with his, —is not your friendship growing greater with the new faculties it requires, has not your love for your unseen friend become a nobler exercise than any delight in his visible presence possibly could be? These are instances and illustrations of the glories of the faculty in man by which he has to do with things which he cannot see. And when the unseen one is Christ, a being whom the man never has seen, whom yet he is compelled to realize, not as an idea, but as a living person capable of being loved, and trusted, and obeyed, there surely is a noble demand there for one of the loftiest of human faculties; and the loftiness of the faculty which must be used in doing it bears testimony to the loftiness of the act which the man does who says of the unseen Jesus Christ, "He is my Lord."

Another of the faculties which is involved in faith, and whose necessity is a sign that a true act of faith is one of the completest acts which man can do, is the faculty of personal admiration and trust. In its fullest exercise faith is personal. We speak indeed of faith in principles, and that is a noble and ennobling thing; but the fullest trust comes with the perception of trustworthy character, and the entire reliance of one nature on another. Is it a great power or a great weakness in a man's life that makes him capable of doing that? I am tempted, in answer to that question, to point you simply to that which I am sure that you have all seen and felt, the strange and sometimes terrible deterioration which so often comes in men's characters as they grow up from boyhood into manhood, leaving the years of docility behind them, pass into the years of self-reliance and independence. The poetry and beauty and richness of a boy's life lie in his power of admiration for, and trust in, something greater than himself. If you fathers make your homes what they ought to be, the boys will find the object of that admiration and trust in you. If you will not let them find it there, they will find it somewhere else. Somewhere they will surely find it. And in their admiration and their trust, the outreaching and uplifting of their life will come. What does it mean when men as they grow older become narrow, sordid, and machine-like, when a vulgar self-content comes over them, and all the limitations of a finished life that hopes for and expects no more than what it is makes the sad picture which we see in hosts of men's middle life? Is it not certainly that those men have ceased to admire and ceased to trust? The objects of their childhood's trust and admiration they have outgrown, and like young scholars who imagine that the story-books of infancy are the only books in the world, and so, when those books cease to interest the maturing mind, lay by their power of reading as if there were no further use for it, so these men, when they can no longer admire and trust their fellow-men completely, as they used to do when they were boys, think that the faculty of perfect trust and admiration has no further use. The blight that falls upon their admiring and trusting natures is the token of what a lofty and life-giving faculty it is which they have put out of use. It was this faculty which made them at every moment greater than themselves, which kept them in communion with the riches of a higher life, which preserved all the enthusiasm of active energy, and yet preserved humility which held all the other faculties to their best work. This is the faculty whose disuse makes the mature life of so many men barren and dreary, and whose regeneration, when the man is lifted up into the new admiration and the new trust, the admiration for and trust in God, makes a large part of the glory of the full-grown life of faith.

One other quality I mention which must be in the man who sends his faith out into the unseen and fastens it in trust and admiration on a divine person. I know not what to call it except a hopeful sense of need,—not only a sense of need, for that, if it be not hopeful, may merely grovel and despair,—but a sense of personal deficiency, filled and lighted up all through and through with the conviction that somewhere in the world, in some place not desperately beyond its reach, there lies, waiting for its finding, the strength and the supply that it requires. This is the faculty in which has lain the coiled mainspring of all human progress. Barbarism, filled with the hopeful sense of need, has pressed onward and onward into civilization. Ignorance, hopefully knowing its need, has scaled the heavens and fathomed the seas and cleft the rocks for knowledge. Man, in all ages, has struggled and achieved, has wrestled with his present condition and laid his daring hand on higher things, under the power of this faculty in which were met the power of his clear perception of his deficiencies and his deep conviction that his deficiencies might be supplied. Is this a noble faculty or not? I would be willing to appeal again to your own consciousness. There are times when this faculty is very sluggish and dull within you, and there are other times when it seems full of life. Some days there are when the story of your need falls on your ears like an unmeaning tale; when either you are self-contented and feel no lack in heart or brain or character, or, feeling it, have no hope but that you must go on forever the poor, half-developed, crippled thing you are. Then there are other days when you look through and through yourself, and any thought of keeping on constantly just as you see yourself now is terrible. You know your sin and sordidness. But at the same time voices are calling you to come and get the things that you require. The whole great voice of all the world seems to be promising you escape and supply. As deep and strong as the sense of need is the hope. Of those two days, which is the greater? On which of them are you the stronger man? Is this faculty, which on the second of these days is awake in you, a degradation or an exaltation of your life? There can be but one answer, only one. You know you never are so great, never so thoroughly a man, as when with manly honesty you see yourself through and through, and, filled with shame, are yet inspired and held up by hope. But all that must come to pass, this faculty of hopeful neediness must wake and live, before a man can with true faith call Jesus Christ, the Saviour of the world, his Lord.

And now once more I say, it is the faculties which any act demands which indicate the degree of dignity and greatness in that act. Behold, then, what we have reached. In the act of faith, by which you or I trust ourselves to the keeping and make ourselves the servants of Christ, there must meet these faculties, or else the act cannot be done: the power of dealing with the unseen, the power of personal loyalty and trust, the power of a hopeful sense of need. Those three great powers in their aggregate meet in the man who is Christ's servant. Now what I claim is this, that the belief and personal devotion for whose attainment that aggregate of qualities must meet is a most great and glorious action. I do not say now that it is an action possible or impossible, or whether the man who thinks with all his soul that he is doing it is congratulating himself upon the great fact of his life, or hugging to his heart the most shadowy of all delusions. I only say that the description of the act involves a picture of the most complete and lofty and thoroughly human action which a man can be conceived of as doing; and that if man, having thought himself capable of such an action, should be completely proved to be incapable of it, his whole life would have suffered an incalculable loss. The world of human existence would have been robbed of its sunlight and its sky. On this I am sure that we ought to insist. There are bold, trenchant writers and talkers to-day who are congratulating the world that the days of faith are over, that the glorious liberty of unbelief has come. That certainly will never do. You must not pluck the jewel off of the forehead of the man who has counted himself a king and then ask him to thank you as if you had broken fetters from his wrists. You must not pull down the sun out of the sky and then bid men rejoice that they have escaped from the slavery of sunlight. If there is no God whom I can come to and obey and thrust, I want to know the dreadful fact, and not to go on thinking that there is; for it is better for every man to know the fact, however dreary and dreadful it may be, than to believe a lie, however sweet and gracious. But that is something utterly different from saying that it would not be better for us all if faith were possible, and that to be robbed of the possibility of faith is the desolation and ruin of human life.

One wants to say the same thing to men who do believe with all their hearts, men who believe with all the strength of an experience which no man can disturb, in the possibility and the reality of faith. I seem to hear a certain sort of apologetic tone among men of faith, which is not good. They sometimes seem to plead that their faith may be left to them, much as a baby pleads that he may keep his toys, or a lame man that he may keep his crutches. It is the appeal of weakness. The man who trusts God sometimes seems almost to say to his unbelieving brother, "Forgive me. I am not as strong as you are. I cannot do without this help. You are more strong and do not need it. But let me keep it still." No open foe of faith can do faith so much harm as that kind of believer. Shall the disciple be ashamed of that which is the glory of his manhood, its highest reach, requiring the combination of its noblest powers? The only thing to be said about such feeble-hearted faith as that is that it is not faithful enough to know the essential dignity of faith. It is a sick man apologizing to death because he is not quite ready yet to die. It is the meagreness of health in him that prompts his poor apology. Let him grow healthier and he begins to look not down to death with apologies, but up to life with hopes and aspirations. So let the weak disciple grow more strong in faith, and he will have no longer feeble words of shame and self-excuse to say about his trust in Christ; only his whole life will grow one earnest prayer for an increase of faith, as the child's life is one continued hope and prayer for manhood.

O young disciples, whatever other kind of falseness to your faith you may fall into, may you be saved at least from ever being ashamed of it. It is the noblest, the divinest, thing on earth. You may have only got hold of the very borders of it, but if in any true sense you can say, "Jesus is the Lord," you have set foot into the region wherein man lives his completest life. Go on, without one thought or dream of turning back, and with no shamefaced hiding of the new mastery under which you are trying to live. If your Christian service is too small in its degree for you to boast of, it is too precious in its kind for you to be ashamed of. Go on forever craving and forever winning more faith and obedience, and so learning more and more forever that faith and obedience are the glory and crown of human life.

But now let us return to our text. We have been talking about the dignity and greatness of faith. But St. Paul says something else about it. It is the gift and inspiration of God. "No man can say that Jesus is the Lord but by the Holy Ghost." Not merely, it is a great and noble thing to feel through all life the grasp and influence of Jesus, but this great and noble thing no man can do unless God the Holy Ghost inspires and helps him to do it. This statement of St. Paul seems to me to have at its heart the profoundest and most beautiful conception of the relation between God and man. Suppose that it were not true. Suppose that faith in Christ being, as I have tried to show it, the crowning act of man, it were yet an act which man could do without any inspiration or help of God; suppose that in this, or any other of the greatest actions of his life, man could first conceive the wish to do it all by and of himself, and then could quietly gather up his powers and go and do it all by and of himself,—have you not in such a supposition broken the absoluteness, the essentialness, the permanency, of the whole relation between our life and God's? The true idea of that relationship involves the presence of God in every highest activity of man. It often seems to me as if men had got such a low and inadequate conception of all this! Men talk, very religious men, as if God were a sort of reserve force to be called in when He was needed—a sort of last resort when man's strength failed. And so I sometimes think that the whole Christian thought of man's being dependent upon God continually seems to a good many people like something cowardly, unmanly, a miserable calling up of the reserve when we ought to be fighting out the battle for ourselves. The thought of God which Christ came to reveal, the thought of God of which all Christ's own life was full, is something totally different from that. To Christ's thought God and man are part of one system —one structure, one working-force. To separate them is not simply to deny man a power that he needs: it is to break a unity, and to set a part of the power to the attempt to do what the whole power ought to do as one. The strength, the force, which is appointed to lift your burden, to run your race, to find your truth, to hold the canopy of faithfulness over your life, is not you. It is you and God. For you to try to do it alone is unnatural. It is almost as if the engine tried to run without its steam, or as if the chisel tried to carve without the artist. It is engine and steam that are to make the running-power. It is artist and chisel that are to carve the statue. It is God and you that live your life. For you to try to live it alone is to try to do all the work with one part of the power. God is not a crutch coming in to help your lameness, unnecessary to you if you had all your strength. He is the breath in your lungs. The stronger you are, the more thoroughly you are yourself, the more you need of it, the more you need of Him.

How clear this became in the life of Jesus Himself! There was humanity at its best. Could it do without those supplies of God which the lower humanity required? Did it throw away its crutch and walk in its own self-sufficient strength? Oh, no! It breathed deeper than any other human life has ever breathed of the breath of God. It filled itself with His Spirit. It did nothing by itself, but everything with, in, by Him. Oh, my dear friends, there is the everlasting testimony that utter dependence on God is no accident of man's sin or misfortune, but is the intrinsic and eternal necessity and glory of man's nature.

And so when man comes to that which I have claimed to be his completing act, when he says that Jesus is the Lord, it is not strange that he cannot do that alone, not by himself, a poor half-life, crippled and broken. It needs the whole of him—and he is not the whole of himself unless God is in him. He cannot do it "but by the Holy Ghost." The man with a duty says, "Jesus is the Lord," and he is brave. The man with a temptation says, "Jesus is the Lord," and he is firm. The man with a suffering says, "Jesus is the Lord," and he is patient. The man with a bewilderment says, "Jesus is the Lord," and he sees light. Is it not a true and precious part of the value of those great experiences, that in each of them there is both the struggle of the human soul up to God, and also the uprising of the divine soul carrying the man deeper into itself—that neither of those men says "Jesus is the Lord" but by the Holy Ghost?

There is one other point of which I wish to speak before I close. I have been magnifying faith. I have been painting it as what I know it is, the consummate action of the human soul, requiring the soul's best faculties working at their best. I can imagine while I speak thus that some hearts here may be asking themselves, "What then? If faith be such a supreme act, must it not be the privilege of a few, must it not be within the power only of the supreme souls? Can I, one of the weakest and worldliest of men, can I do such an act, an act that needs such powers?" And so perhaps I may seem to have lifted the very thing which all men ought to do out of the possibility of many men. I would not leave any such doubt in any soul. God forbid that in trying to make faith seem glorious I should make it seem impossible! But it is true of God's gifts always that the most complete of them are also the most possibly universal. Is it not so? Think of this illustration: wealth is a lower gift than health, and wealth is evidently limited in its possibility; all men are not intended to be rich —but health is for all men. It is unnatural for any man to be sick. And so of admiration and of love. To be loved is better than to be admired—and admiration is the privilege of a few brilliant natures, while love is within the reach of any pure and loving heart. And so of the subtler beauties of art and the simpler beauties of nature. Art is the privilege of the few, but nature opens her treasures wide. "There is no price set on the lavish summer, and June may be had by the poorest comer." But nature is as much more beautiful as she is more free than art. It is a splendid law of all God's world, a law that makes the whole world shine with the splendor of His love, that everywhere the finest is the freest. The lower blessings are often the exceptions, but the higher blessings are meant to be not the exception, but the rule. If this be so, then how must it be with that blessing which outgoes all others, the blessing of faith, the blessing of living under the perpetually recognized lordship of Christ? The finest of all gifts of God—may we not look for it to be the freest too? Free as the air, which is the most precious thing the world contains, and yet struggles as nothing else in all the world struggles to give itself away —crowds itself in wherever it can go, and moves whatever will let itself be moved by its elastic pressure.

And this grows clearer and surer still when we remember that the part of us to which the pressure of God, the power of his Holy Ghost asking to be admitted to govern our lives, applies for its admission is the part which is most universally open and active in all the degrees of mankind; namely, the moral part. Think how often you are ready to listen to a poor ignorant creature's judgment of right and wrong, and pay the deepest reverence to it, when you would not care in the least for that same creature's judgment of any question of the intellect. Think how a little child can look you in the eye with his pure, clear glance, as you are telling your well-disguised falsehood, and say, "That is not true," and make you quail. Think how you can touch a child's conscience long before you can waken his brain. All these are illustrations and signs of the universalness of moral life. It is in all men and in all times of each man's life. And so a blessing which must enter by that door can find in every nature a door to enter by. A Holy Spirit, having its power in its holiness, need not be shut out of any heart that is capable of knowing holiness and being holy. Therefore no soul of dunce or boor or little child is too low to be brought by the Holy Spirit to the place where, answering back by the divine within it to the divine above it, it may say that "Jesus is the Lord." I have claimed already that no soul is too high to find in that announcement of its faith the consummation of its life. Here, then, is where the highest and the lowest meet. Here is where they have met through all the ages. Glorious thinkers, great strong workers, sufferers whose lives were miracles of patience, all of these singing as they went their ways, "Jesus is Lord, Jesus is Lord." And all around them, and in among them, dull, plodding souls, and minds whose thought was all confused and bewildered with emotion, and little children, with their crude clear pictures in their simple brains, all these too singing, in their several tones and with their several clearness, "Jesus is Lord, Jesus is Lord."

Would you be able to say that, to join that great human chorus, to claim Christ for your Lord with some especial claim of your own which shall make the great human chorus which claims Him for the world a little more complete? You can do it. But you can do it only "by the Holy Ghost." Only by letting God enter into you can you go up to God, and own with joy and thankfulness the mastery of his Son. And oh, my friends, remember that the owning of Christ's mastery here is but the beginning of the participation in Christ's glory in heaven.

Into that may we all come at last by His great love!

WHOLE VIEWS OF LIFE

"And Balak said unto him, Come, I pray thee, with me unto another place, from whence thou mayest see them. Thou shalt see but the utmost part of them, and shalt not see them all: and curse me them from thence."—NUMBERS xxiii: 13.

MANY of you will recall the story from which these words are taken, and the striking picture which it draws. The Israelites are travelling through the desert. They are approaching the domain of Balak, King of Moab. Balak is frightened, and sends for the Mesopotamian wizard, Balaam, and bids him curse the dangerous intruders. But Balaam, filled with a higher spirit than he understands, blesses instead of cursing. Again the effort is made and the disappointment follows in another place. And then it is that there occurs to the monarch the idea which is recorded in the text. Perhaps if the prophet did not see the whole host in its multitude the curse would come more readily. "Let us stand where we can only see a part of them," he says. "Peradventure thou canst curse me them from thence."

It was a vain expedient. The blessing came still pouring forth more richly than before. Why should it not? It was not the quantity but the quality of Israel which drew the blessing. It was not because there were so many of them, but because they were set on lofty purposes and carried in their bosom mighty spiritual issues, that God took care of them and made them strong. It was a hopeless hope of Balak. And it was like a child. It was the transparent self-cheat of infancy. So children play with themselves and one another, saying, "Let us see only a part and make believe that that is all."

It is this childlikeness, this primitive simplicity about the incident, which makes it capable of being expanded and of applying to all life. The wisdoms and policies of childhood find their illustrations everywhere. They are so simple that they fit on every life. A child says a wise word, and the sage catches surprised sight in it of complications in his life of which the little head has never dreamed. A child does some act of transparent folly, and by it you easily understand the

53

elaborate superstition or the intricate villainy of the full-grown con-
spirator or bigot. The children go about with the keys of our conditions in their hands. They hold them up before us, and we take them
and unlock our problems and give them back again, and the children
know nothing of what they have done.

So is it with this childish act of the barbarian Balak—so fresh and
simple is it that I feel sure I shall not fail to find the repetitions of it
everywhere. And I do! It is about its repetitions that I want to talk
this morning. I would speak about the modern Balaks, who think
they can indulge their passions and scatter their curses as they please,
by shutting their eyes to all but some small portion of that with
which they have to deal. They are the men who wilfully take partial
views, who will see nothing which will interfere with that which
they have already made up their minds to think or do—especially
the men who have made up their minds to curse, and who refuse to
look at that part of a subject or a life which will make cursing impossible, and compel a blessing upon that which they choose to hate.

Of such a disposition—and I am sure that you recognize the disposition which I mean—the first thing that impresses one is its lack
of absoluteness. There is an absolute truth about everything, something which is certainly the fact about that thing, entirely independent of what you or I or any man may think about it. No man on earth
may know that fact correctly—but the fact exists. It lies behind all
blunders and all partial knowledges, a calm, sure, unfound certainty,
like the great sea beneath its waves, like the great sky behind its
clouds. God knows it. It and the possession of it makes the eternal
difference between God's knowledge and man's.

It is a beautiful and noble faith when a man thus believes in the
absolute truth, unfound, unfindable perhaps by man, and yet surely
existent behind and at the heart of everything. It is a terrible thing
when a man ceases to believe in it, and ceases to seek for it. He sinks
out of the highest delight and purity. For him the great glory of life
is gone. Petty and selfish economies sweep in and overwhelm him.
Not what is true, but what will tell for the advantage of something
which he thinks valuable, becomes the object of his search. He questions everything, as the lawyer questions a witness, in the interest of
a cause. Then comes the Balak folly. Then the man shuts his eyes
to everything which will not tell upon his side. Then he refuses to
look upon the whole of things, and sees only the portion which will

minister to his passion or his spite. Oh, keep your faith in, your love for, the absolute, my friends! Be sure that it exists. To find it, to come a little nearer to finding it,—that, and not the gaining of a new argument or the sustaining of an old prejudice, is what you must be craving when you seek for truth.

In the loss of this faith lies the secret of all partisanship. The partisan always is a Balak. What is a partisan? Is he not simply a man who will see only a part of truth, lest he should be compelled to abandon a position which he loves, or to adopt a position which he chooses to dislike? How many men are there to-day—Republicans or Democrats or anything beside—who are genuinely and really as ready to give its full value to a fact when, if it is true, it tells upon the other party's side as if it told on theirs? "Behold," you say, "look at the total case. Take in the entire situation, and then condemn this party and its leaders and its policies as all foolish or all false." Your friend looks, and, Balaam-like, to your dismay he breaks out into telling of the good which he sees even in this party you despise. What impulse is more natural than yours to say, "Come I pray thee, unto another place. Thou shalt not see them all. Thou shalt see only that which I choose to let thee see of them, and thou shalt curse me them from thence." This is not—he would completely misunderstand what I am saying who thought it was—a mere assertion that there is good and bad in everything, and the preaching of a feeble vacillation that could never come to any decisive action. There is just the difference between partisanship and reasonable choice. The reasonable man who has surveyed the whole condition, by and by strikes his balance and announces his result. He finds that which is genuinely and hopelessly bad, the base, the false, and the impure, and he denounces that unsparingly. Then, among honest and honorable differences, he judges what he thinks comes nearest to the absolute truth, and sustains that with all his strength. But he has no curse for the man upon the other side. He will not impute miserable motives. He is brave as well as bold. He must be just and generous as well as strong. And so the policy which he contends for is in the end not weaker, but stronger, for his breadth of view.

Away with cursing! Away with vehement denunciation which prevents right judgment with the intensity of personal passion and dislike! One man denounces civilization. He sees the wretchedness and misery of which its streets are full. He hears the cry of out-

raged natures and of ruined souls. He says it is an organized selfishness, and he curses it with all his heart. Another man denounces education. He says it is superficial and misplaced. He says that instead
of fitting children, it unfits them, for the work of life. He says it
makes cultivated villains and useless burdens on society; and so he
curses edcation very loudly. Another man denounces society. He
tells us how selfish and narrow and corrupting is the intercourse
of man with man. He shows us the social world all honeycombed
with insincerity. He says, "Is that the way for the children of God
to live with one another?" And so he curses society and turns ascetic.
Another man curses the scientific spirit. "Behold, how hard it is," he
says, "how unbelieving! How arrogant in its self-conceit! How it
would reduce life to a desert and the world to a machine! How it
despises the spontaneous affections! How it worships its idols!" And
his curses fall upon it furious and fast.

Now notice that all these accusations have their truth. Each of
these mighty and benignant interests is guilty of the sin with which
it is charged. But it is only as one shuts out all except a little portion
of it from his view that any man is able to see each of these interests
absolutely given up to its sin, so that he can curse it. In each case if a
man takes into view the whole of civilization or education or society
or science, he sees its graciousness and beauty, and cannot curse, but
bless. And so it is with life in general. There are parts of it and aspects of it which, if they were all, would make existence an accursed
thing. "Come," says the pessimist, "you shall not see the whole. I
will set you where you shall only see a part, and curse me it from
thence." There is where pessimism is made. The man who sees the
whole of life must be an optimist. I know dark points of view, grim
grim gloomy crags of moral vision, hideous observatories on which
if a man stands he can see nothing but the dreadful side of life, its
wretchedness, its disappointment, its distress, its reckless, wanton,
defiant sin. I can see gathered on those horrible observation points
the despisers, the revilers, the cursers of our human life. I know that
if I went up there and stood by their side, my tongue would curse
like theirs. But there I will not go. If there be any point whence I
can see it all, however dimly, through whatever clouds, there I will
go. So will I keep my faith that life is good, and work with what
strength I can against its evils, knowing that I work in hope.

Upon those dark places of partial vision I know that I should never find the great Seer of human life, who is Christ. Christ saw all life in God. That means that He saw life in its completeness. No being ever saw the evil and misery as He beheld it. He saw sin with all the intensity of holiness. But nobody ever has dared call Jesus Christ a pessimist. He saw the end from the beginning. He saw the depth from the surface. He saw the light from the darkness. He saw the whole from the parts. Therefore He could not despair. There was no curse of life upon His lips. Infinite pity! A pity that has folded itself around the world's torn and bleeding heart like a benediction ever since—but no curse! And who are we, with our little feeble rage and petulance, flinging our testy curses where the Lord's blessing descended like the love of God? Oh, if you ever find yourself cursing life, get your New Testament and read what Jesus said looking down on Jerusalem from the height of the Mount of Olives, looking down on man from the measureless height of the cross!

Do I talk too generally? Let me then illustrate and enforce all this with instances. A man's career—every man's career, we may truly say—is made up of struggles and victories or defeats. More defeats than victories there are in most men's lives, we think. But, however that may be, at least the defeats, the weak and wretched failures, the troublesome, exasperating, disappointing incompetency for the work of life, force themselves most upon the eyes of those who watch their fellow-men. And to a very great many people there is a continual temptation to ignore the fact of struggle and remember only the fact of defeat. It is so satisfactory to take a simple sweeping view about your neighbor's life, to give him one broad judgment that has no qualifications, to trample on him in the gutter and never ask how he got there. Then you can freely curse. Then you cannot merely condemn the deed, but utterly denounce the doer.

But men do struggle, even those who fall at last most utterly. It would seem as if anybody needed only to remember his own history and to study his own consciousness to be assured of that. You think of the days when you have sinned most dreadfully. Are you willing to accept any man's judgment of those days who simply sees the sin. You know, though you dare not tell any one besides, of how you fought with your temptation. You know the nights of darkness and the days of hope. You remember the misery of the last yielding, and you say, "He could not curse me if he knew it all."

This is the meaning of the soul's appeal to God. "Let my judgment come forth from Thy presence," David cries. Is it that God does not hate sin as man does? Certainly not that. It is that God knows all. The struggle and the fall and the repentance all make one unit of experience to Him. Therefore He may condemn and He may punish, but He cannot curse.

And when we thus look at ourselves and into our own consciousness, must we not look abroad on other men and say, "No prejudice shall force or tempt me to a place where I shall see only the blank fact that this man has sinned? No desire of my own soul to simplify and emphasize his life shall shut out of my sight the wrestling before the fall, the good which pleaded against his resistance, and which, though outraged and insulted, is in him still, and will not leave him at peace in his wickedness?"

There is indeed the other vice. Sometimes a man insists that you shall stand where you can see nothing except the good in him with whom you are to deal. He insists on having you make such allowance for the temptation that you shall disregard the sin, or having you give such value to the struggle that the defeat shall seem a small affair. That is not what we want. The easy apology or even the profused admiration which may come down from that point of observation is not the true and serious man's greeting and judgment of the life of his brother-man. It is as foolish and false as the curse, however more generous and kindly it may be.

Neither of these is just and true, because neither of them is complete. Both of them are partial. It is a "blessing" that man wants to give to man, and the quality of a true blessing is that it is complete. Whenever man blesses his brother-man, if he is doing the act in all its fulness, it is the completeness of one nature taking in all the completeness of the other. Whatever it is,—the mother giving her blessing to her boy as he goes out from the home-gate into the dangerous world, the friend who finds no words of sympathy for his friend in his great sorrow except "God bless you," the priest consecrating the hero as he rushes to his duty in the field, the king who looks across the millions of his people and pours upon them all the blessing of his kingly heart, the people who set their king or president into his place of burdensome honor with shouts of benediction, the neighbor who greets his neighbor with sacred words which have not lost their meaning, or the children who gather round their father's grave and drop their blessings on his dear memory along with their tears,—

wherever there is real blessing there is the sight of the whole nature, there is the comprehension of the total life. Weaknesses are not forgotten. It is the remembrance of their presence which makes the voice tremble as it blesses. Struggle is not ignored. It keeps the blessing hopeful when it is trembling on the margin of despair. The whole pathetic mixture of the human life is gathered up together. Its evil and its good are both in sight. The danger and the possibility, the fear and the hope, the darkness and the light, are blended in one great profound conception of what this wonderful human life is; and when, standing where it is all clear before him, one human being says to another, "I bless you," it is the largest act which man can do to man. Rebuke, and pity, and exhortation, and encouragement, and warning, and exaltation, and prayer—all are in it. It is soul meeting soul in the highest region and with the closest grasp.

Jesus "led His disciples out as far as Bethany, and He lifted up His hands and blessed them." There was no curse on His lips as He left the poor, frightened, wilful, ignorant, and stumbling men. "He lifted up His hands and blessed them." So may the total result of the pressure of our lives upon our brethren's lives be blessing! May we see them so largely that a curse shall be impossible!

I must say a few words upon two other applications of our truth that it is the limited and partial sight of the things which makes the curse.

The first of them refers to the way in which men form their judgments about religion. We listen to the platform orator, we read the novel of the day, and what impresses us is this: the way in which a hundred misconceptions have their origin in the perpetual tendency to see a part and not the whole, and utter vehement and sometimes furious judgments on that which finds its reasonableness and meaning only when it is set into the system of which it rightly makes a portion. Religion is the whole larger life of man, seen in the presence and the light of God. The Christian religion is the life of man, seen in the broad illumination of the supreme and wondrous Christ. In Him it finds its wholeness, and its parts grow into reconciliation and significance.

Take for a single instance what is called the fact of miracle; not this or that miraculous event, but the whole element of miracle as it appears pervading everywhere and coloring the Christian story. I wish that I could tell in simple words how the whole matter seems to me to stand concerning miracles. "The trouble with miracles is that they don't happen," is the cry. And men look up and say, "Yes, that is true. They do not happen. All moves on unmiraculously. We see no wonders." Is that all? Have those eyes, looking up, beheld the whole of Christianity? Have they seen a Being, strange, unique, unprecedented, moving majestically among men with whom He certainly is one, and yet from whom, both by the words He says about Himself and by the self-witness which His figure bears, is greater than the men He walks among, greater than any man who ever walked upon the earth? Have they seen Him, living His most exceptional and lofty life, and then looked, ready for whatever they might witness, to see whether obedient Nature had no response to make to Him greater and richer than she makes to the long, crowded generations of ordinary human life? If not, is it not right to say that they have shut out a part, and then judged of the part which still was left as if it were the whole?

Here is the true philosophy of miracle. All the history of the earth is full of the record of what Nature has to say to man, of what she does and says in answer to his invitations, to his very presence in her courts. That is her natural history as it relates to man. But what man? Who is he that speaks to her and whom she answers? Is it man in his common capacity and character, the ordinary man, man as he has been for ages? For him miracles do not happen. To him Nature replies in the same old sweet and solemn voices in which for ages she has spoken. But when a new man comes, a new manhood, a divine man, his newness and divinity being attested for us not by his miracles, but by his character, then miracles do happen; nay, more than that, it is altogether probable that miracles must happen, being the natural outflow of his life—being, we almost may say, no miracles for him—being as natural in the world of power where he lives as it is in our world that the echo should fly back from the mountain, or the seed we planted should come piercing through the soil.

You must see Christ and the tomb, both of them, before it can seem possible that Lazarus will rise. Let any one take you where you will see the tomb only and not see Christ, and you will of course reject the thought of resurrection and declare it a superstition or a fraud. You have got the task without the power, the load without the lifting-strength. Power and task make one great whole. They greet and answer to each other. Stand where you see Him, and miracle is not merely explained—it is demanded. He is miraculous, and miracle surrounds Him as the sunshine issues from the sun.

The same is true of many of the questions of religion. Stand where you cannot see man's greatness, and the incarnation seems a wild, inexplicable dream. Stand where no music reaches you from the deep harmonies of man's present spiritual life, and it is out of your power to believe in heaven. Lose sight of sin, and the darker possibilities of eternity are hideous impossibilities. The religious truth which you see by itself, out of its position in the great whole which ought to hold it, fails to bear witness of its truth. Strive then for wholes, and let the parts reveal themselves within them. Strive for God, who is the whole. Not immediately for particular religious doctrines, but for that vast religious and divine conception of existence which shall make special religious doctrines credible. By obedience, by communion, climb to the height where you shall be with God, and then the truths about God shall open their reasonableness, their richness, and their harmony. So, I think, Jesus was religious. So may we be.

I must do little more than allude to the one other application of our truth which is in my mind; but I must not let you go without alluding to it. It is the saddest and most terrible of all. I am thinking of the desperation and bitterness which come with the sight of pain without the sight of the higher consequences and results of pain. It is the old tragedy of the Book of Job, and of the books of thousands of tortured lives. "Curse God and die," seems sometimes to be the only outcome of it all. Perhaps, nay almost certainly, there are some to whom it seems so here this morning. It is the only outcome of it all, if the pain you feel or see is all. But if the whole of a man's life from its beginning to its endless end, from its surface in to its inmost heart, is capable of being taken into account, then that desperate outcome is not the only one. There is a blessing and a thankfulness which may overcome and drown the curse. Suppose that, looking at pain, and with the curse just growing into shape upon your lips, a great hand takes you up and lifts you. And as you rise your vision widens. And slowly education grows into your view, surrounding pain, and drawing out its sense of cruelty, and crowding in upon it its own sense of love and purpose. Then, in the larger vision, must not the curse perish? And if the lips are not strong enough to open into thankfulness, at least the eyes, still full of pity, may wait in peace.

This is the fear we have to-day. The sense of human pain grows stronger all the time. And it sometimes seems as if the sense of purpose and education grew weaker in a multitude of souls. It is the heart of man taken, Balaam-like, to a place whence it can see the part and not the whole; and who that listens does not hear the muttering of the curse? Where is the help, first for your soul, then for the whole great world? Not in saying that pain is not pain, not in shutting the eyes to the part which is so awfully manifest, but in seeing, in insisting upon seeing, the whole.

> "To feel, although no tongue can prove,
> That every cloud that spreads above,
> And veileth love, itself is love."

That is the only help. He who lets his heart bear witness, he who lets the experience of countless sufferers bear witness, he who lets Christ bear witness, that no suffering ever yet came to any human creature by which it was not possible that that human creature should be made better and purer and greater,—he has caught sight of the whole; and though he walks in silence and perplexity and suspense, he does not curse.

And so we come to this,—the sacredness and graciousness of the whole. He who sees the part, grows bitter. He who sees the whole, is full of hope. We curse the part, but not the whole. The reason must be that he who grasps the whole, touches God, and the human soul cannot really curse Him. The whole is sacred. It is more than the sum of its parts. It has its own quality and character. It is great and mysterious. In it is peace. He who sees it all finds rest unto his soul. He who catches glimpses of how he shall see it all some day has something of the power of that rest already.

Remember I have not preached to you blind satisfaction and complacency. I have tried to press on you the old noble and ennobling exhortation, "Lift up your eyes," see all you can. What you cannot see with your eyes, see with your faith. Then go through life not feebly scattering curses by the way, but bravely hopeful, strong in God whose being and love surround it all, blessing and being blessed, at every step and at the end.

THE PILLAR IN GOD'S TEMPLE

"Him that overcometh will I make a pillar in the temple of my God, and he shall go no more out; and I will write upon him the name of my God, and the name of the city of my God, . . . and my new name."—Rev. iii. 12.

It is very many years since these great words were sent abroad into a world of struggle. We can hardly read them without remembering on what countless souls they have fallen in a shower of strength. Men and women everywhere, wrestling with life, have heard the promise to "him that overcometh;" and, though much of the imagery in which the promise was conveyed was blind to them, though they very vaguely identified their conflict with the battle which these far-off people in the Book of the Revelation were engaged in fighting, still, the very sound of the words has brought them inspiration. Let us study the promise a little more carefully this morning. Perhaps it will always be worth more to us if we do. A text which we have once studied is like a star upon which we have once looked through the telescope. We always see it afterwards, full of the brightness and color which that look showed us. Even if it grows dim behind a cloud, or other nearer stars seem to outshine it, we never think it dull or small after we have once looked deep into its depths.

"To him that overcometh," reads the promise; and the first thing that we want to understand is what the struggle is in which the victory is to be won. It is the Saviour Christ who speaks. His voice comes out of the mystery and glory of heaven to the church in Philadelphia, and this book, in which His words are written, stands last in the New Testament. The gospel story is all told. The work of incarnation and redemption is all done. Jesus has gone back to His father, and now is speaking down to men and women on the earth, who are engaged there in the special struggle for which He has prepared the conditions, and to which it has been the purpose of His life and death to summon them. Let us remember that. It is a special struggle. It is not the mere human fight with pain and difficulty which every living mortal meets. It is not the wrestling for place, for knowledge,

63

for esteem, for any of the prizes which men covet. Nay, it is not absolutely the struggle after righteousness; it is not the pure desire and determination to escape from sin, considered simply as the aspiration of a man's own nature and the determination of a man's own will. It is not to these that Christ looks down and sends His promise. He had called out a special struggle on the earth. He had bidden men struggle after goodness, out of love and gratitude and loyalty to Him.

If the motive, everywhere and always, is the greatest and most important part of every action, then there must always be a difference between men who are striving to do right and not to do wrong, according to the love which sets them striving. If it is love of themselves, their struggle will be one thing. If it is love of the abstract righteousness, it will be another. If it is love of Christ, it will be still another. Jesus is talking to the men and women there among the Asian mountains, and to the hosts of men and women who were to come after them upon the earth, who should be fighters against sin, against their own sin, who should struggle to be pure and brave and true and spiritual and unselfish, because they loved Christ, because He had lived and died for them, because they belonged to Him, because He would be honored and pleased by their goodness, grieved and dishonored by their wickedness; because by goodness they would come into completer sympathy with Him, and gain a fuller measure of His love. It is to men and women in this struggle that Christ speaks, and promises them the appropriate reward which belongs to perseverance and success in just that obedience of loyalty and love.

For one of the discoveries that we make, as soon as we grow thoughtful about life at all, is that the world is not merely full of struggle, but full of many kinds of struggle, which vary very much in value. We begin by very broad and superficial classifications. Men are happy or unhappy; men are wise or foolish; men are generous or stingy. But by and by such broad divisions will not satisfy us. The great regions into which we have classified our fellow-men begin to break up and divide. There are all kinds of happiness, all kinds of wisdom, all kinds of generosity. It means little to us, when we have once found this out, to be told that a man is happy, wise, or generous, until we have learned also the special quality of this quality as it appears in him, how he came to possess it, and how he works it out in life. And so in all the world-full of struggling men, as we observe them we find by and by that there are differences. A great, broad mass of eager, dissatisfied, expectant faces it appears at first; a wild and restless tossing hither and thither, as if a great ship had broken asunder in mid-ocean, and her frightened people, with one common fear and dread of being drowned, were struggling indiscriminately in the waves. But at last all that changes, and we wonder how it ever could have looked so to us. Struggle comes to seem as various as life. The objects for which men struggle, and the strength by which men struggle, grow endlessly various. And then, among the mass that seemed one general and monotonous turmoil, there stand out these—there shine out these—whose struggle is against sin, for holiness, and by the love of Christ. Other men struggle against poverty, against neglect; for ease, for power, for fame; and by the love of self, the noble abstract love of righteousness; but, scattered through the whole mass thickly enough to give it character and add a new, controlling strain to the eternal music of aspiring discontent which rises from the swarm of human living, there are these strugglers against sin, by the love of Christ. They are by your side. They are in your houses. They meet you in the street. Your children are catching sight of that struggle, and its fascination and its power, in the times when they are silent and thoughtful, and seem to be passing out of your familiar understanding. Your friend, whose carelessness concerning the things about which you are eager seems so strange to you, is careless about them only because he is fighting a deeper fight. He is fighting against sin, by the love of Christ. Therefore, he does not dread the poverty and the unpopularity against which your selfishness makes you so eager to fear and fight.

This then is the peculiar struggle to the victory in which Christ, out of heaven, gives His promise. And now the promise can be understood if we understand the struggle. The two belong together. "Him that overcometh will I make a pillar in the temple of my God, and he shall go no more out." The ideas of the pillar in a building, in a temple, are these two: incorporation and permanence. The pillar is part of the structure; and when it is once set in its place it is to be there as long as the temple stands. How clear the picture stands before us. There is a great, bright, solemn temple, where men come to worship. Its doors are ever open; its windows tempt the sky. There are many and many things which have to do with such a temple. The winds come wandering through its high arches. Perhaps the birds stray in and build their nests, and stray away again when the short summer is done. The children roam across its threshold, and play for a few moments on its shining floor. Banners and draperies are hung upon its walls awhile, and then carried away. Poor men and women, with their burdens and distress, come in and say a moment's prayer, and hurry out. Stately processions pass from door to door, making a brief disturbance in its quiet air. Generation after generation comes and goes and is forgotten, each giving its place up to another; while still the temple stands, receiving and dismissing them in turn, and outliving them all. All these are transitory. All these come into the temple and then go out again. But a day comes when the great temple needs enlargement. The plan which it embodies must be made more perfect. It is to grow to a completer self. And then they bring up to the doors a column of cut stone, hewn in the quarry for this very place, fitted and fit for this place and no other; and, bringing it in with toil, they set it solidly down as part of the growing structure, part of the expanding plan. It blends with all the other stones. It loses while it keeps its individuality. It is useless, except there where it is; and yet there, where it is, it has a use which is peculiarly its own, and different from every other stone's. The walls are built around it. It shares the building's changes. The reverence that men do to the sacred place falls upon it. The lights of sacred festivals shine on its face. It glows in the morning sunlight, and grows dim and solemn as the dusk gathers through the great expanse. Generations pass before it in their worship. They come and go, and the new generations follow them, and still the pillar stands. The day when it was hewn and set there is forgotten; as children never think when an old patriarch, whom they see standing among them, was born. It is part of the temple where the men so long dead set it so long ago. From the day that they set it there, it "goes no more out."

Can we not see perfectly the meaning of the figure? There are men and women everywhere who have something to do with God. They cannot help touching and being touched by Him, and His vast purposes, and the treatment which He is giving to the world. They cross and recross the pavement of His providence. They come to Him for what they want, and He gives it to them, and they carry it away. They ask Him for bread, and then carry it off into the chambers of their own selfishness and eat it. They ask Him for power, and then go off to the battlefields or workshops of their own selfishness and use it. They are forever going in and out of the presence of God. They sweep through His temple like the wandering wind; or they come in like the chance worshipper, and bend a moment's knee before the altar. And then there are the other men who are struggling to escape from sin, by the love of Christ. How different they are. The end of everything for them is to get to Christ, and put themselves in Him, and stay there. They do not so much want to get to Christ that they may get away from sin, as they want to get away from sin that they may get to Christ. God is to them not merely a great helper of their plans; He is the sum of all their plans, the end of all their wishes, the Being to whom their souls say, not "Lord, help me do what I will;" but, "Lord, show me Thy will that I may make it mine, and serve myself in serving Thee." When such a soul as that comes to Christ, it is like the day when the marble column from the quarry was dragged up and set into the temple aisle. Such a soul becomes part of the great purpose of God. It can go no more out. It has no purpose or meaning outside of God. Its life is hid there in the sacred aisles of God's life. If God's life grows dark, the dusk gathers around this pillar which is set in it. If God's life brightens, the pillar burns and glows. Men who behold this soul, think instantly of God. They cannot picture the pillar outside of the temple; they cannot picture the soul outside of the fear, the love, the communion, the obedience of God.

The New Testament abounds with this idea and the discrimination which we have been trying to make. When the Prodigal Son comes back to his Father, he cries out, "I am not worthy to be called Thy son; make me as one of Thy hired servants;" but the Father answers, "This, My son, was dead, and is alive again;" and the pillar is set up in the temple. When Jesus looks into His disciples' faces at the last supper, He says: "Henceforth I call you not servants, for the servant knoweth not what his Lord doeth; but I have called you friends, for all things which I have heard of my Father I have made known unto you." The servant is the drapery hung upon the nails; the friend is the pillar built into the wall. Paul writes to the Romans: "Who shall separate us from the love of Christ? Shall tribulation, or distress, or persecution, of famine, or nakedness, or peril, or sword? I am persuaded that neither death, not life, nor angels, nor principalities, nor powers, nor things present, nor things to come, nor height, nor depth, nor any other creature, shall be able to separate us from the love of God." It is the calm assurance of the pillar which feels the pressure of the wall around it, and defies any temptation to entice it, or any force to tear it away.

Nor is there anything unphilosophical, or unintelligible, or merely mystical in all this. The same thing essentially occurs everywhere. Two men both come to know another man, richer and larger than either of them. Something called friendship grows up between each of them and him. But the first of the two men who seek this greater man, comes and goes into and out of his great neighbor's life. He keeps the purposes of his own life distinct. He comes to his rich friend for knowledge, for strength, for inspiration, and then he carries them off and uses them for his own ends. The other friend gives up all ends in life which he has valued, and makes this new man's, this greater man's purposes, his. He wants what this great man wants, because this great man wants it. Naturally and easily we say that he "lives in" this other man. By and by you cannot conceive of him as separate from this greater life. The reward of his loving devotion is that he is made a pillar in the temple of his friend, and goes no more out.

Two men both love their country. One loves her because of the advantage that he gets from her, the help that she gives to his peculiar interests. The other loves her for herself, for her embodiment of the ideas which he believes are truest and divinest and most human. One uses the country. The other asks the country to use him. One goes into the country's service and gathers up money or knowledge or strength, and then, as it were, goes out and carries them with him to help the tasks which he has to do in his own private life. The other takes all his private interests, and sacrifices them to the country's good. And what is the reward of this supreme devotion, which there will always be some little group of supremely patriotic men ready to make in every healthy state? Will they not belong to the state, and will it not belong continually to them? They will never be lost out of its history. They will become its pillars and share its glory, as they helped to support its life.

The same is true about the church. There are the multitudes who go in and out, who count the church as theirs, who gather from her thought, knowledge, the comfort of good company, the sense of safety; and then there are others who think they truly, as the light phrase so deeply means, "belong to the church." They are given to it, and no compulsion could separate them from it. They are part of its structure. They are its pillars. Here and hereafter they can never go out of it. Life would mean nothing to them outside the church of Christ.

And, to give just one more example, so it is with truth. The men who seek truth for what she has to give them, who want to be scholars for the emoluments, the honors, the associations, which scholarship will bring, these are the men who will turn away from truth so soon as she has given them her gifts, and leave herself dishonored, —who will turn away from any truth which has no gifts to give. But, always, there are a few seekers who want truth's self, and not her gifts. Once scholars, they are scholars always. They really put their lives into the structure of the world's advancing knowledge. There those lives always remain, like solid stones for the scholarship of the years to come to build upon. There is no world conceivable to which their souls can go, where they will not turn to seek what it is possible there for souls like theirs to know.

Thus everywhere, in every interest of human life, there is a deeper entrance and a more permanent abiding which is reserved for those who have come into the profoundest sympathy with its principles, and the most thorough unselfish consecration to its work. Come back, then, from these illustrations, to the Christian life, and see there the larger exhibition of the same law which they illustrate. God is the Governor of all the world. The purpose of His government, the one design on which it all proceeds, is that the whole world, through obedience to Him, should be wrought into His likeness, and made the utterance of His character. Let that thought dwell before your mind, and feel, as you must feel, what a sublime and glorious picture it involves. Then remember that God does not treat the world in one great, vague generality. He sees the world all made up of free souls, of men and women. The world can become like Him by obedience, only as the souls of men and women become like Him by obedience. Each soul, your soul and mine, must enter into that consummation, must realize the idea of that picture by itself, by its own free submission; helped, no doubt, by the movement of souls all about it, and by the great promise of the world's salvation, but yet acting for itself, by its own personal resolve. To each soul, then, to yours and mine, God brings all the material of this terrestrial struggle,—all the temptations, all the disappointments, all the successes, all the doubts and perplexities, all the jarring of interests, all the chances of hindrance and chances of help which come flocking about every new-born life. The struggle begins, begins with every living creature, is beginning to-day with these boys and girls about you, just as you can remember that years and years ago it began with you. What is it to succeed in that struggle? What success shall you set before them to excite their hope and energy? On what success shall you congratulate yourself? Is it success in the struggle of life simply to get through with decency and die without disgrace or shame? Is it success in the struggle of life just to have so laid hold on God's mercy, to have so made our peace with Him, that we know we shall not be punished for our sins? Is it success in the struggle of life even to have so lived in His presence that every day has been bright with the sense that He was taking care of us? These things are very good; but if the purpose of God's government of the world and of us is what I said, then the real victory in the struggle can be nothing less than the accomplishment in us of that which it is the object of all His government to accomplish in the world. When, truly obedient, we have been made like Him whom we obey, then, only then, we have overcome in the struggle of life. And then we must be pillars in His temple. With wills harmonized with His will; with souls that love and hate in truest unison of sympathy with His; with no purposes left in us but His purposes,—then we have come to what He wants the world to come to. We have taken our places in the slowly rising temple of His will. To whatever worlds He carries our souls when they shall pass out of these imprisoning bodies, in those worlds these souls of ours shall find themselves part of the same great temple; for it belongs not to this earth alone. There can be no end of the universe where God is, to which that growing temple does not reach, the temple of a creation to be wrought at last into a perfect utterance of God by a perfect obedience to God.

O my dear friends, that is the victory that is awaiting you. Slowly, through all the universe, that temple of God is being built. Wherever, in any world, a soul, by free-willed obedience, catches the fire of God's likeness, it is set into the growing walls, a living stone. When, in your hard fight, in your tiresome drudgery, or in your terrible temptation, you catch the purpose of your being, and give yourself to God, and so give Him the chance to give Himself to you, your life, a living stone, is taken up and set into that growing wall. And the other living, burning stones claim and welcome and embrace it. They bind it in with themselves. They make it sure with their assurance, and they gather sureness out of it. The great wall of divine likeness through human obedience grows and grows, as one tried and purified and ripened life after another is laid into it; and down at the base, the corner-stone of all, there lies the life of Him who, though He was a son, yet learned obedience by the things which He suffered, and, being made perfect, became the author of eternal salvation unto all them that obey Him.

In what strange quarries and stone-yards the stones for that celestial wall are being hewn! Out of the hillsides of humiliated pride; deep in the darkness of crushed despair; in the fretting and dusty atmosphere of little cares; in the hard, cruel contacts that man has with man; wherever souls are being tried and ripened, in whatever commonplace and homely ways;—there God is hewing out the pillars for His temple. O, if the stone can only have some vision of the temple of which it is to lie a part forever, what patience must fill it as it feels the blows of the hammer, and knows that success for it is simply to let itself be wrought into what shape the Master wills.

Upon the pillar thus wrought into the temple of God's loving kingdom there are three inscriptions. I can only in one word ask you to remember what they are: "I will write upon him the name of my God, and the name of the city of my God, and my new name." The soul that in obedience to God is growing into His likeness, is dedicated to the divine love, to the hope of the perfect society, and to the ever new knowledge of redemption and the great Redeemer. Those are its hopes; and, reaching out forever and ever, all through eternity, those hopes it never can exhaust. Those writings on the pillar shall burn with purer and brighter fire the longer that the pillar stands in the temple of Him whom Jesus calls "My God."

May all this great promise ennoble and illumine the struggle of our life; keep us from ever thinking that it is mean and little; lift us above its details while it keeps us forever faithful to them; and give us victory at last through Him who has already overcome.

THE GLORY OF SIMPLICITY

"But let your communication be 'Yea, yea'; 'Nay, nay': for whatsoever is more than these cometh of evil."—MATTHEW v. 37.

THIS is the Quaker's verse. It is associated always with the spirit and the habits of that interesting company of men and women who have devoted themselves to the cultivation of simplicity, and have enthroned quietude and peace as the gentle and mighty monarchs of their life. And yet it must not be their verse alone. No grace and no condition can be given up to any one group of men as if it belonged to them exclusively. No doubt, as Christendom divides itself at present, it is true that each of the groups or sects into which it is divided is notable for the pre-eminence of some one quality, or ambition, or form of Christian thought, but evidently it holds that special treasure by no exclusive charter. It holds it in trust and charge for all the rest. It is almost as if each of these groups were a peculiar garden into which each new plant that was to be acclimated and appropriated into the great kingdom of the Christian life were brought for special cultivation. There it is made much of, and surrounded by the best conditions, and guarded from the dangers which most easily beset it. The walls are built to keep away the winds which this plant dreads. The streams bring it the water which it most loves. The gardeners of that special garden studies its peculiar character and habits. In every way that garden devotes itself to that one plant, but it is not because the plant belongs to that one garden and to it alone. It is the property of all the kingdom; and by and by, when the nursery has done its work and the plant is thoroughly naturalized and acclimated, it is sent abroad and blooms on every hillside and in every valley through the land. So it is when a particular quality or a particular truth is committed to a certain church or to a certain age to cultivate. It belongs to universal life—to all the churches and to all the ages. It is but trusted to this special group for special cultivation. All the time that it is being specially cultivated there it is flourishing also as it may in all the larger world; and by and by the special cultivation sends it out into the larger world to be the property and portion of the whole. Therefore it is not for itself alone, but for all Christendom and all mankind, that Quakerism has made its assertion and cultivation of simplicity.

I want to speak this morning about the glory of simplicity. All life continually tends to complication. It is so with the individual life as it grows up from youth to manhood. It is so with the corporate life of men as it grows more and more highly civilized. Where is the man who does not look back to his youth and think how few were the things which he had then to do, how uncomplicated were the arrangements which he had then to make, compared with the intricate confusion which fills his life to-day? And where is the community which does not look back with longing to the primitive standards and natural habits in which history tells it that its fathers lived only a few short centuries ago? When Jesus came into Jerusalem He found this complication flourishing abundantly about Him. Elaborateness was everywhere. Great, tedious ceremonials occupied the temple service. Long lists of rules and arbitrary laws had overspread the simplicity of the ten commandments. Society was a most intricate system of castes and classes. Thought, as the Rabbis guided it, turned and twisted and retwisted on itself in endless subtleties. Every hair had to be split and split again. Every definition had to be defined and re-defined a thousand times. Now there are various indications in the Gospels that the Jews wanted Jesus to accept this system of things, and to come in among them and join in their hairsplitting, and be a Rabbi like themselves. But the glory of His conduct, the testimony of His divinity, was that He refused. He struck this whole mass of complication and elaboration aside, and set a few big, broad simple truths and laws in the place which they had occupied, and bade them reflect the broad sunshine of God; and so He saved the world.

What He did all the great teachers and saviours of the world have done. They have all been simplifiers. The second order of the world's helpers has been largely made of those who brought in some new bit of helpfulness, and so added to the complication of which the world is full. But the first order of helpful men, to which but few of the greatest of mankind belong, has been made up of those who so asserted and illuminated and glorified and made powerful the eternal, elementary truths and forces that they stood out sufficient and alone, and burnt up, as it were, all the half-lights and pale reflections of themselves of which the sky had become full.

How passionate sometimes in the midst of the most beautiful and interesting of complicated life becomes this craving for simplicity! What strange forms of exhibition it assumes! The youth leaves impatiently the gilded and cushioned luxury where he was born and bred, and is found by and by in the depths of the prairies herding his cattle like a true son of Adam. The man of many learnings casts his many books away and goes to some manual toil which seems to bring him back to the hard primitive things by whose touch he reclaims the earth and identifies himself as man. The king disappears from the throne, and his voice is heard chanting in the cloister. The woman turns from the complicated whirl of society and becomes the sister of charity. The connoisseur sweeps all the accumulated bric-à-brac of a lifetime away and sits down to ponder on one single statue or to fathom the secret of a single picture, or takes refuge in the loveliness of nature which lies behind all the pictures. Everywhere this craving for simplicity is at the bottom of all complication. The barbarian is at the heart of every son of civilization. The fresh morning is within the hot bosom of every noon, filling it with dim aspirations and regrets and hopes.

But all is not said when we say this. Still, sing the praises of simplicity as loudly as we will, the question comes most urgently "What kind of simplicity is possible for a man or for a race which has once left the primary simplicity behind and developed into the elaborate conditions of ripened life?" It cannot be the old simplicity back again just as it used to be. The full-blown rose can never fold itself into a bud again. The world is never going to tear down its cities, and dress itself once more in bearskins, and take to the wigwams and the woods again. And if a man or two leaves the study for the workshop or the palace for the monastery, we are almost sure that they find they have carried within them the complication away from which they ran; and that while their hands are busy at the primary toils of man, their hearts are tossed and crossed with the old problems and contradictions which they brought with them out of the heart of their puzzled books or of the tumultuous world. No, it is not by any mere reversion to a long-past childhood that the man's life or the world's life is to be simplified again. That is all past and over. It never can return. And by the same token it cannot be by mere excision and exclusion till, interest after interest being lopped away, only one or two interests are left. That will not do. You do not truly make life simple by making it meagre. It is as if you tried to simplify a tree by cutting off its branches. You either kill the tree and it is a tree no longer, or else, if it still lives, it instantly puts forth new branches and the old complication is there again before you know. Not so! Not so! It is not by excision and rejection that the simplicity of life is gained. The unity which comes by meagreness is far too dearly bought and is not really unity.

And how, then, can it come? Is not its method felt in those deep words of Jesus, "Seek ye first the kingdom of God and His righteousness, and all these things shall be added unto you?" Seek ye the centre and ye shall possess the sphere.

There is a great principle, a great truth, large enough, elementary, absolute, universal enough to enclose and enfold all the fragmentariness of living and make life one. "The kingdom of God and His righteousness," so Jesus calls it. It is the fact of the power and the goodness of God, the fact that the good God is king, which is able thus to embrace all life and make it one. Take a king out of a kingdom and it falls to pieces. He is at once its centre and its envelope. By his force within it and his pressure round it he holds it into unity; and all its parts within it freely play without disturbing its simplicity.

What is the meaning of this religiously to us? If we believe in God, if God is a reality to us, our life is not distracted whatever be the multiplicity of its details. You are a score of things, and life seems to be pulled a score of ways by the conflicting claims of the score of things you are. Your family pulls you one way and your business another, and your ambition another, and by and by one fragment of you is working here and another there; and your self, that core and heart of you which cannot be torn apart by any distraction, is flying and rushing here and there, and trying to regulate and rule these tumultuous kingdoms, and failing always. What then? Can you believe in God? Do you know that He loves you? Do you know that you are His? If you do, the moment that you do, it is as if a great hand was put underneath and around all this complexity and distraction, and—without any true part of your life being crowded out, all being kept complete—the whole was gently, strongly pressed into a whole, a unit. One motive fills all these parts of life, and they become harmonious. One love pervades them and they love each other. The simplicity of a system asserts itself—a simplicity like the God's from whom it comes—so that as we declare of Him, in the same way the harmonized parts of us declare of us, "In Him we live and move and have our being." Each man is a true universe, a cosmos, an order all the more simple for its complexity of parts.

Do you know what this means? Indeed you must know, or else you have got to do one or other of two things. Either you have got to strip piece after piece, interest after interest, of your life away until you attain the meagre simplicity of the unorganized atom; or else you have got to give up the hope and thought of all simplicity, and just lie loose and dejected—a score of pieces of a man, each running independently and spasmodically, but not one man at all. You cannot do either of these things, and so you must come to the simplicity of the child of God.

Thus I have tried to describe the only method of simplicity which lies open to the life of the busy and thoughtful man, the man who cannot starve his life into meagreness, and at the same time cannot be satisfied with mere multitudinousness of life which has no principle of unity.

And now let us see how such a simplicity as that, when it has entered into a man's life, satisfies and fills and rules it. Here is a growing and expanding nature. It is always reaching forward, always desiring to be more and to do more to-morrow than to-day. Now the question of that nature's activity will practically be this: whether it shall expand itself by leaving the old and going abroad to find new things for its possession, or by more and more complete possession of the things it has. The first is the method of ever-increasing complication. The second is the method of perpetual simplicity. The first is full of restlessness, the second is all calm.

Do we not know the difference? How many of our lives are feverish with the perpetual search after new things when the things which we have now have not begun to be exhausted. We are like children with our houses strewn with half-read books and half-played games and half-eaten fruit; who stand at the doorway crying out into the open world for more instead of giving ourselves to the richer uses of what we have already.

The reason of such a state of things must be either that what we already have is not large enough and rich enough, or that its largeness and richness have not been enough apprehended by us. We have not found our simplicity in God. If we had we should never dream of exhaustion.

The clear illustration of this I find in the New Testament. Christ comes and preaches, the new teacher, the great revealer of the truth of God to man. I think that all men have been surprised sometimes at what seemed the simplicity, almost the meagreness, of the teachings of Jesus. There are such multitudes of questions for which every philosopher has had his answer, but which Christ never touches. There are such wide regions of curious speculation where all our feet insist on wandering, but which He never enters. Think of what we should have expected. "He is coming to us direct from God. Now we shall know everything. He will tell us everything." But, on the contrary, how was it? How calmly the old truths fell from His lips! What richness and novelty opened in them as He spoke them! Ho, to those who heard with ears worthy of the lips with which He spoke, the old truths—the truths of God and the soul and immortality—became enough, so deep they grew as He proclaimed them! What need was there for Him to go afield for far-fetched truths, when right here at His feet the old world was so rich? It is His simple "Yea, yea," spoken of the eternal verities which the world has always seemed to know, that has flooded the world with new light and salvation.

Wonderful is he who takes us by the hand and leads us into regions of whose very existence we had not known before. This wonderfulness there is certainly in Jesus. More wonderful still is he who on the old ground where we stand bids the mine open and the diamond shine, bids the fountain burst and the waters flow; and it is this wonderfulness that makes Jesus truly and entirely the Saviour of the world.

Again, think how men use their Bibles. There are so many of the Bible students who are forever finding obscure, difficult, out-of-the-way passages, and treating them as if they had the marrow and substance of the Gospel in them. Some mystic verse in St. John's revelation, some occult computation from the prophecy of Daniel, has often so taken possession of a man or of a sect that all the great remainder of the Bible seemed to fade back into insignificance. It was as if these readers had exhausted all that the great, simple, healthy Gospels had to say, and had nothing left to listen to except this enigmatical and dubious voice speaking out of the darkness in a language which no man could understand. Very often it has seemed as if "knowledge of the Bible" consisted in the possession of theories regarding such comet-like texts which shoot across the sky of Revelation, rather than devout intimacy with the majestic simplicity of the revelation of God and the revelation of man, which are the tranquil stars that burn always and lighten all the heavens.

Indeed, one of the strange things in the whole history of Christianity has been the way in which many souls have seemed not merely to miss but to prefer to miss its great simplicity. What an amount of reverent and devoted study has been given to strange doctrines, such as the doctrine of the historic fall of man, or the doctrine of the second advent of the Saviour, or the doctrine of the correspondence of the types of the Old Testament with the events of the New, or the doctrine of the imputed righteousness of Christ. Men's minds have hovered around them with a strange, unhealthy fascination. Theories have risen from them like mists out of dim fields, often very beautiful, as beautiful as they were thin and unsubstantial; while all the time the great solid truths, of man's divine lineage and God's much-manifested love and Christ's redemption of the soul by sacrifice have lain, not denied, but unopened, unsounded for the depths of unfound richness that is in them. I am sure that much of the character of a Christian's faith may be tested by its simplicity, by whether he finds abundant richness in the great, primary fundamental truths or whether his mind wanders among fantastic doctrines, and values ideas not for their naturalness but for their strangeness; not for the way in which they satisfy and feed, but for the way in which they startle and surprise the human soul.

There is no region in which all this is more true than in men's speculation about the life which lies beyond the grave. Nowhere does the difference between the healthiness of simplicity and the unhealthiness of complicated and elaborate curiosity so visibly appear. People who hardly believe that there is such a thing as a future life at all will speculate on its details, will sit holding their breath while mediums who have no touch of common sympathy try to bring souls together in carnal manifestation, whose intimacy is too sacred for any but themselves to share. It is not this that brings comfort and peace. It is not this that lifts the souls on earth to live already the divine life which their kindred souls are living in the celestial world. No morbid dream of knowledge which is not for me, no fancied sight into the detailed occupations of the spiritual life—only the great, broad, simple certainty that the friend I love is in the perfect company and care, is held fast in the tender and majestic love of God—only this I want to satisfy my soul. The Bible tells us one thing—only one—about the dead who have passed out of our sight. They are with God. How simple that is! How sufficient it becomes! How cheap and tawdry, as we dwell in it, it makes the guesses and conceits with which men try to make real to themselves what the dead are doing! They are with God. Their occupations are ineffable. No tongue can tell their new, untasted joy. The scenery in the midst of which they live speaks to the spirit with voices which no words born of the senses can describe. But the companionship and care,—those are the precious, those are the intelligible things. The dead are with God. O you who miss even to-day the sound of the familiar voices, the sight of the dear, familiar faces, believe and be more than satisfied with that.

There is no sign of ripening life which is more gracious and more beautiful than the capacity and disposition to find richness in the simplest and healthiest associations. Have you never had an experience like this? Have you never had a friend whom you have long known, in whom you found much to enjoy and to be grateful for, but whom at last you seemed to have exhausted and outgrown? You went abroad to natures which fascinated you more. You felt the power of some man in whom there was some sort of one-sided and fantastic power, in whom there was more violence of light and shade, in whom the very manifestness of defect made certain promontories of possession peculiarly picturesque and attractive. You revelled in his strange unhealthy power. Something, it may be, almost weird came out in yourself to answer his romantic inspiration. But by and by he too failed you and did not satisfy. Some morning that which had been so dramatic looked only theatrical to you. His high lights and great gulfs of darkness wearied you. And then have you never turned back to the simplicity of your first friendship, and found to your amazement how unexhausted, how inexhaustible it was? There stood the deep, quiet nature on whose surface you had scratched and fumbled, but where profoundness lay yet all untouched. His healthiness refreshed you as if you came out of a torch-lighted cavern into the sunlight and the breeze. His calm "Yea, yea; nay, nay," truthful and strong, swept all the frantic extravagances and over-strained exaggerations out of your soul, and you rejoiced in a great cleanness and freshness. Giving yourself to him again you found him opening to you treasures which you never found before, —as men come back with the tools of civilization in their hands, and work great wealth of gold out of the mines which their barbarian ancestors thought they had exhausted ages ago.

Sometimes the truth about God and His relation to our human life seems to shape itself exactly into this, that He stands waiting, in infinite patience, till His children out of their restlessness and wanderings come back to find the satisfaction of their souls in Him. We just touch Him in our childhood; our first implicit faith gets just the surface blessings of His love, as the childish savages gather the grains of gold which lie shining on the surface of the ground. Then we go off, fascinated by some eccentric, tumultuous utterance of power, and we give ourselves up to some passion for the distorted or unreal. We make long journeys in search of bags of gold which spirits tell us that the genii have hidden in the holes of rocks across the seas; and all the while there lies the mine with its good, hidden gold. All the while there waits God with His great satisfaction for the soul of man; and some day we come to ourself and say "I will arise and go to my Father." Some day the false lights fade, the partial shows its partialness. Out of the depth of the earth where the gold is hidden the call sounds, "Come unto me." Out of the healthiness of the divine life our hearts recognize the summons as we come back to the God we thought we had exhausted, forsooth, when we left Him in our nursery, and find in humiliation and in joy that He is the strength of our life and "our portion forever," that which eternity itself cannot exhaust.

God is so healthy. That is indeed the meaning of His holiness. In Him no part or quality grows tyrannical over the rest. In His timeless existence the present cannot be sacrificed to the future, nor the future to the present. The eternal necessities are in Him, so that He does not submit His will to them; they are His will. His Yea and Nay are the creations and distinctions of the world. When He says to your disturbed, distracted, restless soul, or mine, "Come unto me," He is saying, come out of the strife and doubt and struggle of what is at the moment where you stand, into that which was and is and is to be,—the eternal, the essential, the absolute. Let go the fascination of the unhealthy and the exceptional, come to the everlasting health, the great natural and normal life which lies under the fretfulness of living as the great sea underlies the fretful waves,—"Come unto me."

Even in regions which we do not call religious, we recognize this power of the absolute and simple to call souls to itself; and we see how the truest souls are they who answer to the call, and how the souls which answer to the call become the truest. The healthiness and simplicity of the highest genius is remarkable. Genius of the second rank may be fantastical, complicated, living in regions of its own, lighted by fitful stars of morbid fascinating brilliance; but genius of the first order, the few very highest souls—Shakespeare, Plato, and Homer—live in the universal light and air. They speak intelligently to their fellow-men. They shine with a true, colorless light. They move upon the world like the true air of heaven. Their "yea" and "nay" are inexhaustible because they are the essential affirmations and denials of the universe; they are the positives and negatives of the eternal truth. Therefore it is that we come back to them for peace and highest inspiration out of the turmoil of excited literature which eddies and foams about us, and tosses us to distraction. Therefore it is that men of their quality, however small they may be, have always life-giving and peace-giving power; and men turn back to the man who is simple, broad, healthy, and true, as the sailor who has rejoiced in the contortions and distractions of the sea, turns, when the twilight comes, to the peace of the deep-rooted shore and the rest of the meadows where the flowers grow out of the unmeasured depth of fruitful earth.

Thus we talk of the simplicity of God, thus we talk of the simplicity of the profoundest and truest men. It is the exhibition of both of these simplicities which we behold in Jesus, and which makes His healthiness, His holiness. One of the noblest signs of how true our human nature is at the bottom is the way in which, notwithstanding all the fascination which the unhealthy forms of power have had for men, the strongest hold that ever has been laid upon the human heart has been laid there by the simple, healthy Christ. It is not His miracles, it is His nature which holds the world and will not let it go. Men are shouting and screaming all about Him with their partial truths, their temporary standards, their intoxicated joys, their frantic and galvanic shows of power. You are wondering to which fanaticism you shall give up your life, which form of unhealthy thought or action you shall make your own, since it seems as if only in unhealthiness was power or joy to be attained; and just then, when you are all ready to throw yourself into the fire of some frenzy, Jesus steps before you and says, "Give yourself to Me"; and then, looking into His face, you see that there is your true master. For look, what it will be to serve Him. He never will ask you to distort a truth even for the very highest purpose. He never will ask you to do wrong to-day that you or other men may do right to-morrow. He not merely will not tempt you, He will not allow you to bring the high standards of living down to what seem the powers of your life. He will bid you trust your fellow-men and not suspect them; assuring you that it is better to be cheated a hundred times and to be imposed upon continually than to fail to help one soul which you might help, or to shut the door of the better life in the face of any child of God who is trying to come in. Above all, He will open to you the great simple sources of truth and power, and make them the exhaustless feeders of your soul. These things He has done wherever souls have got genuinely and thoroughly at Him. Sometimes His church has not done these things for men. Sometimes she has done just the opposite of these things. But wherever His church has really brought Him and men together, and wherever He and men have ever really met, this has been always the result. He has done for them all these things, and the great outcome of it all has been that their lives have grown healthy and grown natural. The fantastic has been cast out. They have felt and known themselves in as true relations to the earth they lived on as its mountains or its trees. And so peace has come to them, and with peace, power.

My friends, the world we live in, the time and town we live in, are full of unhealthiness. There are exaggerations, affectations, complications, thin frenzies, theatrical excitement, fashions of passions, conventionalities of unconventionalities, till our souls grow sick and tired of it all. Where is the escape from it? Only in what St. Paul calls "The simplicity which is in Christ." Go up into the mountain of His love and service, and you shall leave all these mists and fogs below. Drink of the water that He shall give you, and "it shall be in you a fountain of living water, springing up to everlasting life." That is the true health of the soul. May we all come to it by Him!

THE WINGS OF THE SERAPHIM

Above it stood the seraphim. Each one had six wings; with twain he covered his face, and with twain he covered his feet, and with twain he did fly.—ISAIAH vi. 2.

IN THE majestic vision of Isaiah the Lord Jehovah sits upon His throne, and around Him as He sits there stand mighty figures such as do not appear in just the same guise anywhere else in Scripture. Isaiah calls them "the seraphim." They are not angels; they are rather the expressions of the forces of the universe waiting there beside the throne of God. They are titanic beings, in whom is embodied everything of strength and obedience which anywhere, in any of the worlds of God, is doing His will. Since man is the noblest type of obedient power, these majestic seraphim seem to be human in their shape; but, as if farther to express their meaning, there are added to each of them three pairs of wings, whose use and disposition are with particularity described.

It is from what is said about these wings of the seraphim that I want to take my subject for this morning. You can see what right we have to treat the seraphim themselves as types and specimens of strength offering itself obediently to God. And if the highest attitude of any man's life is to stand waiting for what use God will choose to make of him, then we have a right to seek for something in the fullest life of consecrated manhood—of manhood standing by the throne of God—correspondent to each indication of temper and feeling which Isaiah shows us in the seraphim.

How shall man stand, then, in a world where God sits in the centre on His throne? This is the question for which I seem to find some answer in the picture of the mighty creatures, each with his six wings,—with two of which he covered his face, and with two he covered his feet, and with two he did fly. We gather so many of our impressions of humanity from poor stunted human creatures—poor wingless things who strut or grovel in their insignificance—that it will surely be good if we can turn for once and see the noblest image of consecrated power, and say to ourselves, "This is what man is meant to be. This it is in me to be if I can use all my powers and let God's presence bring out in me all that it really means to be a man."

Each of the three pairs of wings has its own suggestion. Let us look at them each in turn and see how they represent the three qualities which are the conditions of a complete, effective human life.

With the first pair of wings, then, it is said that the living creature, standing before God, "covered his face." There was a glory which it was not his to see. There was a splendor and exuberance of life, a richness of radiance coming from the very central source of all existence which, although to keep close to it and to bathe his being in its abundance was his necessity and joy, he could not search and examine and understand. There was the incomprehensibleness of God!

We talk about God's incomprehensibleness as if it were a sad necessity; as if, if we could understand God through and through, it would be happier and better for us. The intimation of Isaiah's vision is something different from that. It is the glory of his seraphim that they stand in the presence of a God so great that they can never comprehend Him. His brightness overwhelms them; they cover their faces with their wings, and their hearts are filled with reverence, which is the first of the conditions of complete human life which they represent.

We have only to think of it a moment to become aware how universal a necessity of human life we are naming when we speak of reverence,—meaning by it that homage which we feel for what goes beyond both our imitation and our knowledge, and shrouds itself in mystery. No man does anything well who does not feel the unknown surrounding and pressing upon the known, and who is not therefore aware all the time that what he does has deeper sources and more distant issues than he can comprehend. It is not only a pleasing sentiment, it is a necessary element of power,—this reverence which veils its eyes before something which it may not know. What would you give for the physician who believed that he had mastered all the truth concerning our human bodies and never stood in awe before the mystery of life, the mystery of death? What would you give for the statesman who had no reverence, who made the State a mere machine, and felt the presence in it of no deep principles too profound for him to understand? What is more dreadful than irreverent art which paints all that it sees because it sees almost nothing, and yet does not dream that there is more to see; which suggests nothing because it suspects nothing profounder than the flimsy tale it tells, and would fain make us all believe that there is no sacredness in woman, nor nobleness in man, nor secret in Nature, nor dignity in life. Irreverence everywhere is blindness and not sight. It is the stare which is bold because it believes in its heart that there is nothing which its insolent intelligence may not fathom, and so which finds only what it looks for, and makes the world as shallow as it ignorantly dreams the world to be.

When I say this, I know, of course, how easily corruptible the faculty of reverence has always proved itself to be. The noblest and finest things are always most capable of corruption. I see the ghosts of all the superstitions rise before me. I see men standing with deliberately blinded eyes, hiding from their inspection things which they ought to examine, living in wilfully chosen delusions which they prefer to the truth. I see all this in history; I see a vast amount of this to-day and yet all the more because of this, I am sure that we ought to assert the necessity of reverence and of the sense of mystery, and of the certainty of the unknown to every life. To make the sentiment of reverence universal would be the truest way to keep it healthy and pure. It must not seem to be the strange prerogative of saints or cranks; it must not seem to be the sign of exceptional weakness or exceptional strength; it must be the element in which all lives go on, and which has its own ministry for each. The child must have it, feeling his little actions touch the Infinite as his feet upon the beach delight in the waves out of the boundless sea that strike them. The mechanic must have it, feeling how his commonest tools are ministers of elemental forces, and raise currents in the air that run out instantly beyond his ken. The scientist needs it as he deals with the palpable and material which hangs in the impalpable and spiritual, and cannot be known without the knowledge of the mystery in which it floats. Every true scientist has it; Newton or Tyndal pauses a moment in his description of the intelligible, and some hymn of the unintelligible, some psalm of delight in the unknown, comes bursting from his scientific lips. Every man holds his best knowledge of himself bosomed on an ignorance about himself,—a perception of the mystery of his own life which gives it all its value. You can know nothing which you do not reverence! You can see nothing before which you do not veil your eyes!

But now take one step farther. All of the mystery which surrounds life and pervades life is really one mystery. It is God. Called by His name, taken up into His being, it is filled with graciousness. It is no longer cold and hard; it is all warm and soft and palpitating. It is love. And of this personal mystery of love—of God—it is supremely true that only by reverence, only by the hiding of the eyes, can He be seen. He who thinks to look God full in the face and question Him about His existence, blinds himself thereby, and cannot see God. He sees something, but what he sees is not God but himself. In Christ Himself there is the perpetual intimation of His ignorance. There is the continual awe of a nature from the perfect knowledge of which the conditions of His human life excluded him. And if He could not know the Father perfectly, while He lived here in the flesh, shall we complain that we cannot? Shall we not rather rejoice in it? Shall it not be a joy to us to feel, around and through the familiar things which we seem perfectly to understand, the wealth and depth of Divinity, out-going all our comprehension?

Sometimes life grows so lonely. The strongest men crave a relationship to things more deep than ordinary intercourses involve. They want something profounder to rest upon,—something which they can reverence as well as love; and then comes God.

> "Call ye life lonely? Oh, the myriad sounds
> Which haunt it, proving how its outer bounds
> Join with eternity, where God abounds!"

Then the sense of something which they cannot know, of some one greater, infinitely greater than themselves surrounds their life, and there is strength and peace, as when the ocean takes the ship in its embrace, as when the rich warm atmosphere enfolds the earth.

But I do not think that we have reached the fulness of Isaiah's description of reverence as one of the great elements of life until we have looked more carefully at the image which he sets before us. He says of the seraphim not merely that their eyes were covered, but that they were covered with their wings. Now the wings represent the active powers. It is with them that movement is accomplished and change achieved and obedience rendered; so that it seems to me that what the whole image means is this,—that it is with the powers of action and obedience that the powers of insight and knowledge are veiled. The being who rightly approaches God, approaches Him with the powers of obedience held forward; and only through them does the sight of God come to the intelligence which lies behind. The mystery and awfulness of God is a conviction reached through serving Him. The more He is served the more the vastness of His nature is felt. The more obedience, the more reverence. That, I take it, is the meaning of Isaiah's seraphim with their two wings covering their faces.

Behold, what a lofty idea of reverence is here! It is no palsied idleness. The figure which we see is not flung down upon the ground, despairing and dismayed. It stands upon its feet; it is alert and watchful; it is waiting for commandments; it is eager for work; but all the time its work makes it more beautifully, completely, devoutly reverent of Him for whom the work is done. The more work the more reverence. So man grows more mysterious and great to you, oh, servant of mankind, the longer that you work for him. Is it not so? So Nature grows more mysterious to you, oh, naturalist, the longer that you serve her. Is it not so? So God grows more sublime and awful as we labor for Him in the tasks which He has set us. Would you grow rich in reverence? Go work, work, work with all your strength; so let life deepen around you and display its greatness.

Poor is the age which has not reverence. Men say it sometimes of this age of ours. But just because it is an age of active over-running work, I cannot, I do not believe that it is really so. At least, I feel sure that it cannot be so in the end. Its work may make it at first arrogant and merely trustful of itself. A little work like a little knowledge is a dangerous thing. It may not easily and all at once submit to be obedient; but as it goes deeper and touches more mighty tasks it must come into the presence of the power which is behind all powers, and feel God. Until it does that it may trifle, it may grow profane; but all the time it is on the way to reverence, the highest reverence,—the reverence which comes not by idle contemplation, but by obedient work.

Poor is the soul which has not reverence! You may have many powers and gifts, but if you have not reverence there is a blight upon them all. Only be sure you seek for reverence aright. Not by shutting your eyes to God or any of His truth, but by spreading your wings before your eyes, by putting your active powers in the forefront of your life, by doing your work as deeply, in as true a sense of obedience to God, as possible, so shall you touch the Infinite, and live in a serene and cheerful awe. The veiling of intelligence with obedience shall give it light and not darkness. The reverence which comes in service shall be not paralysis, but strength.

Let us pass on to the second element in Isaiah's image of a strong and consecrated life. With twain of his wings, he says, each of the seraphim "covered his feet." The covering of the feet represents the covering of the whole body. As the covering of the face means not seeing, the covering of the feet means not being seen. It signifies the hiding of oneself, the self-effacement which belongs to every effective act and every victorious life.

Here is a man entirely carried away by a great enthusiasm. He believes in it with all his soul. His heart and hands are full of it. What is the result? Is it not true that he entirely forgets himself? Whether he is doing himself credit or discredit, whether men are praising him or blaming him, whether the completion of the work will leave him far up the hill of fame or down in the dark valley of obscurity, he literally never thinks of that. He is obliterated. It is as if he did not exist, but the work did itself, and he was only a spirit to rejoice in its success. Some morning the work is done. It is successful; and he is famous and amazed. Another man's work is all filled with self-consciousness. He never loses himself out of it for a moment. It may be a noble self-consciousness. He may be anxious all the time that the work he is doing should make him a better man; but the work is weak just in proportion as he thinks about himself. It is strong just in proportion to his self-forgetfulness.

Is it not so? Consider your own lives. Have you not all had great moments in which you have forgotten yourselves, and do you not recognize in those moments a clearness and simplicity and strength which separates them from all the other moments of your life? There was a moment when you saw that a great truth was true and accepted it without asking what the consequences of its acceptance to your life might be. There was a moment when you saw a great wrong being done, and resisted it with an impulse which seemed to be born directly out of the heart of the eternal justice and had nothing to do with your personal dispositions,—hardly anything, even, with your personal will. There was a moment when you were in battle; and whether you lived or died was unimportant, but that the citadel should be taken was a necessity. Those are the great moments of your life.

The man who forgets himself in his work has but one thing to think of,—namely, his work. The man who cannot forget himself has two things to think of,—his work and himself. There is the meaning of it all. There is the distraction and the waste. The energy cannot be concentrated and poured in directly on its one result. Who wants to see a governor, whose whole thought might be given to the welfare of the State, forever pulled aside to think how what he proposes to do will affect his popularity, his credit, his chance of being governor again? My friend comes and sits down beside me, and begins to give me his advice. I listen, and his words are wise. I am just catching glimpses of his meaning and seeing how there may be truth in what he tells, when suddenly there breaks out through his talk a lurid flash which spoils it all. The man is thinking of himself. He is trying to be wise. He is remembering how wise he is. He is trying to impress me with his wisdom; and so his power is gone. A student sits and seeks for truth, but mingled with his search for truth there is a seeking after fame or some position; and truth hides her deepest secrets from a man like him. So everywhere the noblest streams grow muddy with self-consciousness. Only here and there a stream refuses to be muddied; and then, whether it be great or small, a mighty torrent or a silver thread of quiet water, in its forgetfulness of self it flows on to its work, and makes men's hearts joyous and strong. Efface yourselves, efface yourselves; and the only way to do it is to stand in the presence of God, and be so possessed with Him that there shall be no space or time left for the poor intrusion of your own little personality.

Here also, as before, it is possible to follow out the image of Isaiah. Here, as before, it may mean something to us that the feet are not merely covered, but covered with the wings. The wings, we saw, meant the active powers; and so the meaning is that the thought of oneself is to be hidden and lost behind the energy and faithfulness and joy of active work. I may determine that I will not be self-conscious, and my very determination is self-consciousness; but I become obedient to God, and try enthusiastically to do His will, and I forget myself entirely before I know it. It is not because men make so much of their work that their work makes them vain and fills itself with secondary thoughts of their own advantage; it is because they make so little of their work, because they do not lift themselves up to the thought of obedience to God. The effacement of self is not to come by sinking into sleep, but by being roused into intensest action at the call of God,—by a passionate desire that His will should be done, whether by us or by another. When that is in our soul, we shall do the part of His will which is ours to do, and in our eagerness for the doing of the work forget the worker. Here is the true death of personal ambition, into the higher life of desire for the attainment of results. "Père Jandel is myself without the inconvenience of myself," said Lacordaire when his brother-monk was elevated above himself to the master-generalship of their order. Behind the wings the feet are growing always strong and beautiful. Within the obedience the obedient nature is growing vigorous and fair; but its own growth is not its purpose, and by and by when the obedience is complete, the soul itself most of all is surprised at the unguessed, unhoped-for life which has come to it in its voluntary death.

This is the history of all self-sacrifice, of all the martyrdoms, of all the crosses. This is what is going on in the sick-rooms where souls are learning patience, and on battle-fields where brave young soldiers are fighting for the truth. This is what true life does for true men as the years go on. Work for God somewhere, in some form, takes gradual possession of a man until at last the thought of self, even in its highest interests, has passed away. It seems to be dead, and only wakens into conscious life again when the great salutation greets it at the end, "Well done, good and faithful servant. Thou hast been faithful. Enter into My joy." Then the wings part, and the uncovered feet walk by the river of the water of life.

One pair of wings remains. After the twain which hid the face of the seraph, and the twain which hid his feet, Isaiah says still, "And with twain did he fly." We have spoken of obedience as the method of reverence, and of obedience as the method of self-effacement; but here there comes the simpler and perhaps the healthier thought of obedience purely and solely for itself,—the absolute joy and privilege of the creature in doing the Creator's will.

> "His state
> Is kingly. Thousands at his bidding speed
> And post o'er land and ocean without rest."

So sang the poet of divinity. And though he goes on to turn his great truth into consolation of his own affliction, yet in the lines themselves we cannot help feeling a true and simple joy in the great glory of a universe all thrilled and beaten with the wings of hurrying obedience.

To live in such a universe of obedient activity, to feel its movement, to be sensible of its gloriousness, and yet to make no active part of it would be dreadful. Milton felt this, and in his last great line was compelled to pierce down to the deepest truth about the matter, and assert that he too, even in his blindness, had share in the obedience of the untiring worlds.

"They also serve who only stand and wait."

Here is the deepest reason, here is the reasonable glory of that which is perpetually exalted and belauded in cheap and superficial ways,—the excellence of work, the glory of activity. Many of our familiar human instincts live and act by deeper powers than they know. That which is really the noble, the divine element in the perpetual activity of man is the sympathy of the obedient universe. The circling stars, the flowing rivers, the growing trees, the whirling atoms, the rushing winds,—all things are in obedient action, doing the will of God. It is the healthy impulse of any true man who finds himself in this active world to share in its activity. It is the healthy shame of any true man to find himself left out, having no part in that obedience which keeps all life alive.

This is the power of the flying wings,—the simple glory of active obedience to God. Somewhere, in some sphere, to do some part of the Eternal Will, to bear some message, to fulfil some task,—no human being can be complete, no human being can be satisfied without that. You may have the face-covering wings and hide your eyes behind them,—that is, you may be full of reverence; you may feel most overwhelmingly the majesty of God; you may stand all day in the most sacred place, crying, "Holy, holy, holy," through the clouds of incense all day long. You may have the feet-covering wings; you may efface yourself; you may tear out the last roots of vanity from your life; you may mortify your pride; you may even deny facts in your eager depreciation of yourself; but reverence and self-effacement come to nothing unless the spirit of active obedience fills the life.

I think this appears to be ever more and more critically true. If a man wants to do God's will, there can be no misbelief in him so dangerous as to be his ruin, there can be no prison of false sentiment or feeling in him that is not already being cast out. It is not that belief is unimportant. God forbid! Belief is of the very substance of the life. "As he thinketh in his heart, so is he." It is not that false feelings, pride, and self-consciousness are insignificant. They are the soul's corruption and paralysis. But it is that through active service, through the will to do God's will, belief is ever struggling to become true, and feeling is ever struggling to grow healthy. No man is fool enough to think that an active arm and a big muscle can be a substitute for a slow beating heart or a torpid brain. It is to set the dull brain thinking and the slow blood running that you take your exercise. Not as a substitute for doctrine or for love, but as a means of both, the Christian says, "O Lord, what shall I do?" And so his act of service has in it all the richness of faith not yet believed, and love not yet kindled into consciousness.

There are two extremes of error. In the one, action is disparaged. The man says, "Not what I do but what I am is of significance. It is not action. It is character." The result is that character itself fades away out of the inactive life. In the other extreme, action is made everything. The glory of mere work is sung in every sort of tune. Just to be busy seems the sufficient accomplishment of life. The result is that work loses its dignity, and the industrious man becomes a clattering machine. Is it not just here that the vision of the wings comes in? Activity in obedience to God. Work done for Him and His eternal purposes. Duty conscious of Him and forgetful of the doer's self, and so enthusiastic, spontaneous,—there is the field where character is grown, there is at once the cultivation of the worker's soul and the building of some corner of the Kingdom of God.

Oh, my young friends, listen to the great modern Gospel of Work which comes to you on every breeze, but do not let it be to you the shallow, superficial story that it is to many modern ears. Work is everything or work is nothing according to the lord we work for. Work for God. Let yourself do no work which you cannot hold up in His sight and say, "Lord, this is Thine!" and then your work indeed is noble. Then you are standing with your flying wings which will assuredly bear you into fuller light as they carry some work of God toward its fulfilment.

These then are the three,—reverence and self-forgetfulness and active obedience,—"With twain he covered his face, and with twain he covered his feet, and with twain he did fly." It is because of irreverence and self-conceit and idleness that our lives are weak. Go stand in the sight of God and these wings of salvation shall come and clothe your life. They perfectly clothed the life of Jesus. Reverence and self-sacrifice and obedience were perfect in Him. In the most overwhelmed moments of His life,—crushed in the garden, agonized upon the cross,—he was really standing, like the strong seraphim, at the right hand of God.

You want to be strong. Oh, be strong in the Lord and in the power of His might,—strong as He was by reverence and self-surrender and obedience. The opportunity for that strength is open to every man who bears a soul within him, and over whom is God, and around whom is the world all full of duty and need!

THE SERIOUSNESS OF LIFE

Let not God speak to us, lest we die.—Ex. xx. 19.

THE Hebrews had come up out of Egypt, and were standing in front of Sinai. The mountain was full of fire and smoke. Thunderings and voices were bursting from its mysterious awfulness. Great trumpet-blasts came pealing through the frightened air. Everything bore witness to the presence of God. The Hebrews were appalled and frightened. We can see them cowering and trembling. They turn to Moses and beg him to stand between them and God. "Speak thou with us, and we will hear; but let not God speak to us, lest we die."

At first it seems as if their feeling were a strange one. This is their God who is speaking to them, their God who brought them "out of the Land of Egypt, out of the House of Bondage." Would it not seem as if they would be glad to have Him come to them directly, to have Him almost look on them with eyes that they could see, and make unnecessary the interposition of His servant Moses, bringing them messages from Him? Will they not feel their whole history of rescue coming to its consummation when at last they find themselves actually in the presence of the God who has delivered them, and hear His voice?

That is the first question, but very speedily we feel how natural that is which actually did take place. The Hebrews had delighted in God's mercy. They had come singing up out of the Red Sea. They had followed the pillar of fire and the pillar of cloud. They had accepted God's provision for their hunger. They had received Moses, whom God had made their leader. But now they were called on to face God Himself. In behind all the superficial aspects of their life they were called on to get at its centre and its heart. In behind the happy results, they were summoned to deal with the mysterious and mighty cause. There they recoiled. "Nay," they said, "let us go on as we are. Let life not become so terrible and solemn. We are willing to know that God is there. We are willing, we are glad, that Moses

94

should go into His presence and bring us His messages. But we will not come in sight of Him ourselves. Life would be awful. Life would be unbearable. Let not God speak with us, lest we die!"

I want to bid you think this morning how natural and how common such a temper is. There are a few people among us who are always full of fear that life will become too trivial and petty. There are always a great many people who live in perpetual anxiety lest life shall become too awful and serious and deep and solemn. There is something in all of us which feels that fear. We are always hiding behind effects to keep out of sight of their causes, behind events to keep out of sight of their meanings, behind facts to keep out of sight of principles, behind men to keep out of the sight of God. Because that is such poor economy; because the only real safety and happiness of life comes from looking down bravely into its depths when they are opened to us, and fairly taking into account the profoundest meanings of existence; because not death but life, the fullest and completest life, comes from letting God speak to us and earnestly listening while He speaks,—for these reasons I think this verse will have something to say to us which it will be good for us to hear.

We have all known men from whom it seemed as if it would be good to lift away some of the burden of life, to make the world seem easier and less serious. Some such people perhaps we know to-day; but as we look abroad generally do we not feel sure that such people are the exceptions? The great mass of people are stunted and starved with superficialness. They never get beneath the crust and skin of the things with which they deal. They never touch the real reasons and meanings of living. They turn and hide their faces, or else run away when those profoundest things present themselves. They will not let God speak with them. So all their lives lack tone; nothing brave, enterprising, or aspiring is in them. Do you not know it well? Do you not feel it everywhere?

For we may lay it down as a first principle that he who uses superficially any power or any person which he is capable of using profoundly gets harm out of that unaccepted opportunity which he lets slip. You talk with some slight acquaintance, some man of small capacity and little depth, about ordinary things in very ordinary fashion; and you do not suffer for it. You get all that he has to give. But you hold constant intercourse with some deep nature, some man of great thoughts and true spiritual standards, and you insist on dealing merely with the surface of him, touching him only at the most trivial points of living, and you do get harm. The unused capacity of the man—all which he might be to you, but which you are refusing to let him be—is always there, demoralizing you. If you knew that a boy would absolutely and utterly shut his nature up against the high influences of the best men, would you not think it good for him to live not with them but with men of inferior degree, in whom he should not be always rejecting possibilities which he ought to take? A dog might live with a wise man, and remaining still a dog, be all the better for the wise man's wisdom, which he never rejected because he could not accept it. But a brutish man who lived with the sage and insisted that he would be still a brute, would become all the more brutish by reason of the despised and neglected wisdom.

Now we have only to apply this principle to life and we have the philosophy and meaning of what I want to preach to you this morning. It is possible to conceive of a world which should offer the material and opportunity of nothing but superficialness,—nothing but the making of money and the eating of bread and the playing of games; and in that world a man might live superficially and get no harm. On the other hand it is possible to conceive of a man who had no capacity for anything but superficialness and frivolity and dealing with second causes; and that man might live superficially even in this deep, rich world in which we live, and get no harm. But—there is the point—for this man with his capacities to live in this world with its opportunities and yet to live on its surface and to refuse its depths, to turn away from its problems, to reject the voice of God that speaks out of it, is a demoralizing and degrading thing. It mortifies the unused powers, and keeps the man always a traitor to his privileges and his duties.

Take one part of life and you can see it very plainly. Take the part with which we are familiar here in church. Take the religious life of man. True religion is, at its soul, spiritual sympathy with, spiritual obedience to God. But religion has its superficial aspects,—first of truth to be proved and accepted, and then, still more superficial, of forms to be practised and obeyed. Now suppose that a man setting out to be religious confines himself to these superficial regions and refuses to go further down. He learns his creed and says it. He rehearses his ceremony and practises it. The deeper voice of his re-

ligion cries to him from its unsounded depths, "Come, understand
your soul! Come, through repentance enter into holiness! Come,
hear the voice of God." But he draws back; he piles between himself and that importunate invitation the cushions of his dogma and
his ceremony. "Let God's voice come to me deadened and softened
through these," he says. "Let not God speak to me, lest I die. Speak
thou to me and I will hear." So he cries to his priest, to his sacrament,
which is his Moses. Is he not harmed by that? Is it only that he loses
the deeper spiritual power which he might have had? Is it not also
that the fact of its being there and of his refusing to take it makes his
life unreal, fills it with a suspicion of cowardice, and puts it on its
guard lest at any time this ocean of spiritual life which has been shut
out should burst through the barriers which exclude it and come
pouring in? Suppose the opposite. Suppose the soul so summoned
accepts the fulness of its life. It opens its ears and cries, "Speak,
Lord, for thy servant heareth." It invites the infinite and eternal
aspects of life to show themselves. Thankful to Moses for his faithful
leadership, it is always pressing through him to the God for whom
he speaks. Thankful to priest and church and dogma, it will always
live in the truth of its direct, immediate relationship to God, and
make them minister to that. What a consciousness of thoroughness
and safety; what a certain, strong sense of resting on the foundation
of all things is there then! There are no closed, ignored rooms of the
universe out of which unexpected winds may blow, full of dismay.
The sky is clear above us, though we have not soared to its farthest
height. The ocean is broad before us, though we have not sailed
through all its breadth.

Oh, my dear friends, do not let your religion satisfy itself with
anything less than God. Insist on having your soul get at Him and
hear His voice. Never, because of the mystery, the awe, perhaps the
perplexity and doubt which come with the great experiences, let
yourself take refuge in the superficial things of faith. It is better to be
lost on the ocean than to be tied to the shore. It is better to be overwhelmed with the greatness of hearing the awful voice of God
than to become satisfied with the piping of mechanical ceremonies or
the lullabies of traditional creeds. Therefore seek great experiences
of the soul, and never turn your back on them when God sends
them, as He surely will!

The whole world of thought is full of the same necessity and the same danger. A man sets himself to think of this world we live in. He discovers facts. He arranges facts into what he calls laws. Behind his laws he feels and owns the powers to which he gives the name of force. There he sets his feet. He will go no further. He dimly hears the depth below, of final causes, of personal purposes, roaring as the great ocean roars under the steamship which, with its clamorous machineries and its precious freight of life, goes sailing on the ocean's bosom. You say to him, "Take this into your account. Your laws are beautiful, your force is gracious and sublime. But neither is ultimate. You have not reached the end and source of things in these. Go further. Let God speak to you." Can you not hear the answer? "Nay, that perplexes all things. That throws confusion into what we have made plain and orderly and clear. Let not God speak to us, lest we die!" You think what the study of Nature might become, if, keeping every accurate and careful method of investigation of the way in which the universe is governed and arranged, it yet was always hearing, always rejoicing to hear, behind all methods and governments and machineries, the sacred movement of the personal will and nature which is the soul of all. Whether we call such hearing science or poetry, it matters not. If we call it poetry, we are only asserting the poetic issue of all science. If we call it science, we are only declaring that poetry is not fiction but the completest truth. The two unite in religion, which when it has its full chance to do all its work shall bring poetry and science together in the presence of a recognized God, whom the student then shall not shrink from, but delight to know, and find in Him the illumination and the harmony of all his knowledge.

The same is true about all motive. How men shrink from the profoundest motives! How they will pretend that they are doing things for slight and superficial reasons when really the sources of their actions are in the most eternal principles of things, in the very being of God Himself. I stop you and ask you why you give that poor man a dollar, and you give me some account of how his poverty offends your taste, of how unpleasant it is to behold him starve. I ask you why you toil at your business day in and day out, year after year. I beg you to tell me why you devote yourself to study, and you reply with certain statements about the attractiveness of study and the way in which every extension or increase of knowledge makes the world more rich. All that is true, but it is slight. It keeps the world thin. This refusal to trace any act back more than an inch into that world of motive out of which all acts spring, this refusal especially to let acts root themselves in Him who is the one only really worthy cause why anything should be done at all,—this is what makes life grow so thin to the feeling of men who live it; this is what makes men wonder sometimes that their brethren can find it worth while to keep on working and living, even while they themselves keep on at their life and work in the same way. This is the reason why men very often fear that the impulse of life may give out before the time comes to die, and shudder as they think how awful it will be to go on living with the object and the zest of life all dead. Such a fear never could come for a moment to the man who felt the fountain of God's infinite being behind all that the least of God's children did for love of Him.

I know very well how all this which I have undertaken to preach this morning may easily be distorted and misunderstood. It may seem to be the setting forth of a sensational and unnatural idea of life, the struggle after which will only result in a histrionic self-conscious-ness, a restless, discontented passion for making life seem intense and awful, when it is really commonplace and tame. "Let us be quiet and natural," men say, "and all will be well." But the truth is that to be natural is to feel the seriousness and depth of life, and that no man does come to any worthy quietness who does not find God and rest on Him and talk with Him continually. The contortions of the sen-sationalist must not blind us to the real truth of that which he gro-tesquely parodies. His blunder is not in thinking that life is earnest, but in trying to realize its earnestness by stirring up its surface into foam instead of piercing down into its depths, where all is calm. Yet even he, grotesque and dreadful as he is, seems almost better than the imperturbably complacent soul who refuses to believe that life is serious at all.

The whole trouble comes from a wilful or a blind underestimate of man. "Let not God speak to me, lest I die," the man exclaims. Is it not almost as if the fish cried, "Cast me not into the water, lest I drown," or as if the eagle said, "Let not the sun shine on me, lest I be blind." It is man fearing his native element. He was made to talk with God. It is not death, but his true life, to come into the divine so-ciety and to take his thoughts, his standards, and his motives directly out of the hand of the eternal prefectness. Man does not know his own vitality, and so he nurses a little quiver of flame and keeps the draught away from it, when if he would only trust it and throw it bravely out into the wind, where it belongs, it would blaze into the true fire it was made to be. We find a revelation of this in all the deepest and highest moments of our lives. Have you not often been surprised by seeing how men who seemed to have no capacity for such experiences passed into a sense of divine companionship when anything disturbed their lives with supreme joy or sorrow? Once or twice, at least, in his own life, almost every one of us has found himself face to face with God, and felt how natural it was to be there. Then all interpreters and agencies of Him have passed away. He has looked in on us directly; we have looked immediately upon Him; and we have not died,—we have supremely lived. We have known that we never had so lived as then. We have been aware how natural was that direct sympathy and union and communication with God. And often the question has come, "What possible reason is there why this should not be the habit and fixed condition of our life? Why should we ever go back from it?" And then, as we felt ourselves going back from it, we have been aware that we were growing unnatural again; we were leaving the heights, where our souls breathed their truest air, and going down into the valleys, where only long habit and an educated distrust of our own high capacity had made us feel ourselves more thoroughly at home.

And as this is the revelation of the highest moments of every life, so it is the revelation of the highest lives; especially it is the revelation of the highest of all lives, the life of Christ. Men had been saying, "Let not God speak to us, lest we die"; and here came Christ, the man,—Jesus, the man; and God spoke with Him constantly, and yet He lived with the most complete vitality. He was the livest of all living men. God spoke with Him continually. He never did a deed, He never thought a thought, that He did not carry it back with His soul before it took its final shape and get His Father's judgment on it. He lifted His eyes at any instant and talked through the open sky, and on the winds came back to Him the answer. He talked with Pilate and with Peter, with Herod and with John; and yet his talk with them was silence; it did not begin to make His life, to be His life, compared with that perpetual communion with His Father which made the fundamental consciousness as it made the unbroken habit of His life. All this is true of Jesus. You who know the rich story of the Gospels know how absolutely it is true of Him. And the strange thing about it is that the life of which all this is true is felt at once to be the most natural, the most living life which the world has ever seen. Imagine Jesus saying those words which the Hebrews said: "Let not God speak to me, lest I die." You cannot put those words upon His lips. They will not stay there. "O God, speak to me, that I may live,"—that is the prayer with which He comes out of the stifling air of the synagogue or the temple, out of the half-death of the mercenary streets, out of the foolish rivalries and quarrellings of His disciples.

And every now and then a great man or woman comes who is like Christ in this. There comes a man who naturally drinks of the fountain and eats of the essential bread of life. Where you deal with the mere borders of things he gets at their hearts; where you ask counsel of expediencies, he talks with first principles; where you say, "This will be profitable," he says, "This is right." Remember I am talking about him now only with reference to this one thing,—that when men see him they recognize at once that is is from abundance and not from defect of vitality that this man lives among the things which are divine. Is there one such man—it may be one such boy—in the store where all the rest of you are working for rivalry or avarice? Is there one who works from principle, one who works for God; and will you tell me whether you do not all count him the most genuinely living of you all?

The student of history knows very well that there are certain ages and certain races which more than other ages seem to have got down to the fundamental facts, and to be living by the elemental and eternal forces,—ages and races which are always speaking with God. So we all feel about the Hebrews. The divine voice was always in their ears. Often they misunderstood it. Often they thought they heard it when it was only the echo of their own thoughts and wishes that they heard; but the desire to hear it, the sense that life consisted in hearing it,—that never left them. And so, too, we feel, or ought to feel, about the great Hebrew period of our own race, the Puritan century, in which everything was probed to the bottom, all delegated authorities were questioned, and earnestness everywhere insisted upon having to do immediately with God. Plenty of crude, gross, almost blasphemous developments of this insistence set themselves forth; but the fact of the insistence was and still is most impressive. It never frightened the Puritan when you bade him stand still and listen to the speech of God. His closet and his church were full of the reverberations of the awful, gracious, beautiful voice for which he listened. He made little, too little, of sacraments and priests, because God was so intensely real to him. What should he do with lenses who stood thus full in the torrent of the sunshine? And so the thing which makes the history of the Puritans so impressive is the sense that in them we come close to the great first things. We are back behind the temporary, special forms of living, on the bosom of the primitive eternal life itself.

When we turn suddenly from their time to our own time what a difference there is! At least what a difference there is between all their time and a part of ours. For our time is not capable of being characterized as generally and absolutely as theirs. It has many elements. Certainly it has much of Puritanism. The age which has had Carlyle for its prophet, and which has fought out our war against slavery has not lost its Puritanism. But the other side of our life, how far it is from the first facts of life, from God, who is behind and below everything! When I listen to our morals finding their sufficient warrant and only recognized authority in expediency; when I behold our politics abandoning all ideal conceptions of the nation's life and talking as if it were only a great mercantile establishment, of which the best which we can ask is that it should be honestly run; when I see society conceiving no higher purpose for its activities than amusement; when I catch the tone of literature, of poetry, and of romance, abandoning large themes, studiously and deliberately giving up principles and all heroic life, and making itself the servant and record of what is most sordid and familiar, sometimes even of what is most uncomely and unclean; when I think of art grown seemingly incapable of any high endeavor; when I consider how many of our brightest men have written the word Agnostic on their banner, as if not to know anything, or to consider anything incapable of being known, were a condition to shout over and not to mourn over,— when I see all these things, and catch the spirit of the time of which these things are but the exhibitions and the symptoms, I cannot help feeling as if out of this side, at least, of our time there came something very like the echoes of the old Hebrew cry, "Let not God speak to us, lest we die." We are afraid of getting to the roots of

things, where God abides. What bulwarks have you, rich, luxurious
men, built up between yourselves and the poverty in which hosts
of your brethren are living? What do you know, what do you want
to know, of the real life of Jesus, who was so poor, so radical, so full
of the sense of everything just as it is in God? You tremble at the
changes which are evidently coming. You ask yourself, How many
of these first things, these fundamental things, are going to be disturbed? Are property and rank and social precedence and the relation of class to class going to be overturned? Oh, you have got to
learn that these are not the first things, these are not the fundamental
things! Behind these things stand justice and mercy. Behind everything stands God. He must speak to you. He will speak to you. Oh,
do not try to shut out His voice. Listen to Him that you may live.
Be ready for any overturnings, even of the things which have seemed
to you most eternal, if by them He can come to be more the King
of His own earth.

And in religion, may I not beg you to be vastly more radical and
thorough? Do not avoid, but seek, the great, deep, simple things of
faith. Religious people read thin, superficial books of religious sentiment, but do not meet face to face the strong, exacting, masculine
pages of their Bibles. They live in the surface questions about how
the Church is constituted, how it ought to be governed, what the
forms of worship ought to be. They shrink from the profound and
awful problems of the soul's salvation by the Son of God and preparation for eternity. Do we not hear—strangest of all!—in religion,
which means the soul's relationship to God, do we not hear there—
strangest of all—the soul's frightened cry, "Let not God speak with
me, lest I die"? In all your personal life, my friends, it is more thoroughness and depth that you need in order to get the peace which if
you spoke the truth you would own that you so woefully lack. You
are in God's world; you are God's child. Those things you cannot
change; the only peace and rest and happiness for you is to accept
them and rejoice in them. When God speaks to you you must not
make believe to yourself that it is the wind blowing or the torrent
falling from the hill. You must know that it is God. You must gather
up the whole power of meeting Him. You must be thankful that
life is great and not little. You must listen as if listening were your
life. And then, then only, can come peace. All other sounds will be

caught up into the prevailing richness of that voice of God. The lost proportions will be perfectly restored. Discord will cease; harmony will be complete.

I beg you who are young to think of what I have said to you to-day. Set the thought of life high at the beginning. Expect God to speak to you. Do not dream of turning your back on the richness and solemnity of living. Then there will come to you the happiness which came to Jesus. You, like Him, shall live, not by bread alone, but by every word that proceedeth out of the mouth of God!

THE EGYPTIANS DEAD
UPON THE SEASHORE

"And Israel saw the Egyptians dead upon the seashore."—Exodus xiv. 30.

IT WAS the Red sea which the children of Israel had crossed dry-shod, "which the Egyptians essaying to do were drowned." The parted waves had swept back upon the host of the pursuers. The tumult and terror, which had rent the air, had sunk into silence, and all that the escaped people saw was here and there a poor drowned body beaten up upon the bank, where they stood with the great flood between them and the land of their long captivity and oppression. It meant everything to the Israelites. It was not only a wonderful deliverance for them, but a terrible calamity for their enemies. It was the end of a frightful period in their history. These were the men under whose arrogant lordship they had chafed and wrestled. These hands had beaten them. These eyes they had seen burning with scorn and hate. A thousand desperate rebellions, which had not set them free, must have come up in their minds. Sometimes they had been successful for a moment; sometimes they had disabled or disarmed their tyrants; but always the old tyranny had closed back upon them more pitilessly than before. But now all that was over; whatever else they might have to meet, the Egyptian captivity was at an end. Each dead Egyptian face on which they looked was token and witness to them that the power of their masters over them had perished. They stood and gazed at the hard features, set and stern, but powerless in death, and then turned their faces to the desert, and to whatever new unknown experiences God might have in store for them.

It is a picture, I think, of the way in which experiences in this world become finished, and men pass on to other experiences which lie beyond. In some moods it seems to us as if nothing finally got done. When we are in the thick of an experience we find it hard to believe or to imagine that the time will ever come, when that experience shall be wholly a thing of the past and we shall have gone out beyond it into other fields. When we open our eyes morning after morning and find the old struggle on which we closed our eyes last night awaiting us; when we open our door each day only to find our old enemy upon the doorstep; when all our habits and thoughts and associations have become entwined and colored with some tyrannical necessity, which, however it may change the form of its tyranny, will never let us go,—it grows so hard as almost to appear impossible for us to anticipate that that dominion ever is to disappear, that we shall ever shake free our wings and leave behind the earth to which we have been chained so long. On the long sea-voyage the green earth becomes inconceivable. To the traveller in the mountains or the desert it becomes very difficult to believe that he shall some day reach the beach and sail upon the sea. But the day comes, nevertheless. Some morning we go out to meet the old struggle, and it is not there. Some day we listen for the old voice of our old tyrant, and the air is still. At last the day does come when our Egyptian, our old master, who has held our life in his hard hands, lies dead upon the seashore, and looking into his cold face we know that our life with him is over, and turn our eyes and our feet eastward to a journey in which he shall have no part. Things do get done, and when they do, when anything is really finished, then come serious and thoughtful moments in which we ask ourselves whether we have let that which we shall know no longer do for us all that it had the power to do, whether we are carrying out of the finished experience that which it has all along been trying to give to our characters and souls.

For while we leave everything behind in time, it is no less true that nothing is wholly left behind. All that we ever have been or done is with us in some power and consequence of it until the end. Is it not most significant that these children of Israel, whom we behold to-day looking the dead Egyptians in the face and then turning their backs on Egypt, are known and appealed to ever afterwards as the people whom the Lord their God had brought "out of the land of Egypt, out of the house of bondage"? In every most critical and sacred moment of their history they are bidden to recall their old captivity. When God most wants them to know Him, it is as the God of their deliverance that He declares Himself. The unity of life is never lost. There must not be any waste. How great and gracious is the economy of life which it involves! Neither to dwell in any experience always, nor to count any experience as if it had not been, but to leave the forms of our experiences behind, and to go forth from them clothed in their spiritual power, which is infinitely free and capable of new activities,—this is what God is always teaching us is possible, and tempting us to do. To him who does it come the two great blessings of a growing life,—faithfulness and liberty: faithfulness in each moment's task, and liberty to enter through the gates beyond which lies the larger future. "Well done, good servant: thou hast been faithful over a few things. Enter thou into the joy of thy Lord."

All this is true, but it is very general. What I want to do this morning is to ask you to think about the special experience to which our text refers, and consider how one truth is true of that, and of what corresponds to it in all men's lives. It was the end of a struggle which had seemed interminable. The hostility of Hebrew and Egyptian had gone on for generations. However their enmity may be disguised or hidden, the tyrant and the slave are always foes. If hope had ever lived, it had died long ago. Patient endurance, grim submission, with desperate revolt whenever the tyranny grew most tyrannical, —these had seemed to be the only virtues left to the poor serfs. Not to be demoralized and ruined by their servitude, to keep their self-respect, to be sure still that they were Abraham's children and that Abraham's God still cared for them, patience and fortitude,—these must have been the exhortations which they addressed to their poor souls as they toiled on in the brickyard or by the river.

It does not prove anything, if you please, about our present life, but it certainly sets us to asking new questions about it, perhaps to believing greater things concerning it, when in our typical story we behold all this changed. Behold, the day came when the chains were broken and the slaves went free. Are, then, our slaveries as hopeless as they seem? Are we condemned only to struggle with our enemies in desperate fight, and shall we not hope to see them some day dead like the Egyptians on the seashore?

Surely it is good for us to ask that question, for nothing is more remarkable than the way in which, both in public and personal life, men accept the permanence of conditions which are certainly some day to disappear. The whole of history which teaches us that mankind does conquer its enemies and see its tyrants by and by lying dead on the seashore, often appears to have no influence with the minds of men, all absorbed as they are in what seems a hopeless struggle. But look around! Where are the Egyptians which used to hold the human body and the human soul in slavery? Have you ever counted? The divine right of rulers, the dominion of the priesthood over the intellect and conscience, the ownership of man by man, the accepted inequality of human lots, the complacent acquiescence in false social states, the use of torture to extort the needed lie, the praise of ignorance as the safeguard of order, the irresponsible possession of power without corresponding duty, the pure content in selfishness—do you realize, in the midst of the cynical and despairing talk by which we are surrounded, can you realize, how these bad tyrants of the human race have lost their power over large regions of human life? They are dead Egyptians. Abominable social theories which fifty years ago, in the old days of slavery, in the old days of accepted pauperism, men stated as melancholy, but hopeless, truisms are now the discarded rubbish of antiquity, kept as they keep the racks and thumb-screws in old castle-dungeons for a tourists' show.

Is there anything more wonderful than the way in which men today are daring to think of the abolition and disappearance of those things which they used to think were as truly a part of human life as the human body, or the ground on which it walks? Ah! my friends, you only show how you are living in the past, not in the present, when you see nothing but material for sport in the beliefs of ardent men and brave societies which set before themselves and human kind the abolition of poverty, the abolition of war, the abolition of ignorance, the abolition of disease, the sweeping away of mere money competition as the motive power of life, the dethronement of fear from the high place which it has held among, aye, almost above, all the ruling and shaping powers of the destiny of man. I recognize in many a frantic cry the great growing conviction of mankind that nothing which ought not to be need be. I hear in many hoarse, ungracious tones man's utterance of his conviction that much which his fathers thought was meant to cultivate their patience by submission, is meant also to cultivate their courage by resistance till it dies. "The Egyptian must die." That is the assurance which is possessing the heart of man.

When any evil does finally perish, then there is something infinitely pathetic in the remembrance of the way in which mankind for generations accepted it as inevitable and drew out of its submission to it such blessing and education as pure submission to the inevitable

is able to bestow. The poor man, who thinks his poverty, and the ignorance and servitude which his poverty entails, all right, comforts
himself by saying that God made him poor in order that he might be
patient and learn to possess his soul in self-respect. By and by when
the iniquity of the system under which he has lived gives way and he
finds himself admitted to the full rights and duties of a man—what
then? Infinitely pathetic, as it seems to me, is the recognition that
he wins of the great love and wisdom with which God would not
let even that darkness be entirely fruitless of light; but while He
was making ready for the fuller life of which the poor man never
dreamed, at the same time fed him in the wilderness with manna
which the wilderness alone could give, so that no delight of freedom
to which he afterwards should come need make him wholly curse or
utterly despise the regions of darkness and restraint through which
he came to reach it.

Is it not thus that we may always explain at least a part, the best
part, of that strange longing with which the world, when it has entered into any higher life, still finds itself looking back to the lower
life out of which it has passed? It is not properly regret. It is not a
desire to turn back into the darkness. The age of real faith does not
covet again the chains of superstition. The world at peace does not
ask to be shaken once more by the earthquakes of war. But faith does
feel the beauty of complete surrender which superstition kept for
its sole spiritual virtue; and peace, with its diffused responsibility,
is kindled at the thought of heroic and unquestioning obedience
which the education of war produced. Still let superstition and war
lie dead. We will not call them back to life; but we will borrow their
jewels of silver and jewels of gold as we go forth into the wilderness
to worship our God with larger worship. Do you not feel this in all
the best progress? Do you not see it in the eyes of mankind, in the
depths of the eyes of mankind always, as it turns away from the dead
forms of its old masters and goes forth into the years to be; the
hoarded power of the past glowing beneath the satisfaction of the
present and the fiery hope of the unknown future?

Ah, well, there is always something fascinating in thus dwelling on
the fortunes of the world at large, peering, like fortune-telling gyp-
sies, into the open palm which she holds out to all of us. It is fascinating, and is not without its profit. But just as, I suppose, the shrewd-
est gypsy may often be the most recklessly foolish in the government

of her own life, so it is good for us always to turn speedily and ask how the principles which we have been wisely applying to the world, apply to that bit of the world which we are set to live.

Do we believe—you and I—in the death of our Egyptians? What is your Egyptian? Some passion of the flesh or of the mind?—for the mind has its tyrannical passions as well as the flesh. Years, years ago, you became its captive. Perhaps you cannot at all remember when. Perhaps, like these children of Israel, you were born into its captivity. It was your father, or your father's fathers, that first became its slaves. When you first came to know yourself, its chains were on your limbs. As you grew older you knew that it was slavery, but it was such a part of all you were and all you did that you accepted it. That has not made you cease to struggle with it, but it has made you accept struggle hopelessly, as something never to be outgrown and left behind. You have looked forward into the stretch of years, and in prophetic imagination you have seen yourself an old man, still wrestling with the tyranny of your covetousness, or your licentiousness, or your prejudice, getting it down, planting your foot upon its neck, even compelling it to render you, out of the unceasing struggle, new supplies of character; absolutely fixed and determined never to give up the fight until you die—to die fighting. All this is perfectly familiar. Countless noble and patient souls live in such self-knowledge and consecration. But there comes something vastly beyond all these, when the soul dares to believe that its enemy may die, that the lust, or the prejudice, or the covetousness may absolutely pass out of existence, and the nature be absolutely free—sure no doubt to meet other enemies and to struggle till the end, but done with that enemy forever, with that Egyptian finally dead upon the seashore.

When that conviction takes possession of a man, his fight is a new thing. The courage not of desperation, but of certain hope, fills every limb and gives its force to every blow. The victory which the soul believes is coming is here already as a power for its own attainment.

Has a man a right to any such hope as that, or is it the mere dream of an optimistic sermon? I dare appeal to you and ask you whether, in your own experience, God has not sometimes given you the right to such a hope? Are there no foes of your youth which you have conquered and left dead, passing on to greater battles? I am not speaking of the vices which you have miserably left behind, merely because the taste is exhausted and the strength has failed—vices which you would take up again if you were once more twenty years old. Those are poor victories. Those are no victories at all. But I mean this: Whether you are a better or a worse man now than you were twenty years ago. Are there not at least some temptations to which you yielded then to which you know that you can never yield again? Are there not some meannesses which you once thought glorious which now you know are mean? Are there no places where you once stumbled where now you know you can walk firm? I pity you if there are not. Other enemies which you then never dreamed of you have since encountered, but those enemies are done with. The Moabites and Midianites are before you and around you, but the Egyptians are dead. And in their death your right and duty are to read the prophecy of the death of every power which stands up between you and the Promised Land!

The appeal is not only to experience. It is to the first Christian truth concerning man. I have preached it to you a thousand times. I will preach it again and again until the end. The great truth of Christianity, the great truth of Christ, is that sin is unnatural and has no business in a human life. The birth of Christ proclaimed that in one tone: His cross proclaimed it in another! And that which is unnatural is not by any necessity permanent. The struggle of all nature is against the unnatural—to dislodge it and cast it out. That beautiful struggle pervades the world. It is going on in every clod of earth, in every tree, in every star, and in the soul of man. First to declare and then to strengthen that struggle in the soul of man was the work of Christ. That work still lingers and fails of full completion, but its power is present in the world. When He takes possession of a nature He quickens that struggle into life. No longer can that nature think itself doomed to evil. Intensely sensitive to feel the presence of evil as he never felt it before, the Christian man instantly and intensely knows that evil is a stranger and an intruder in his life. The wonder is not that it should some day be cast out: the wonder is not that it should ever have come in. The victory promised in the sinless Son of man is already potentially attained in the intense conception of its naturalness. This is Christianity.

Is not this the change which you can see coming in the faces of the sinners who meet Jesus and feel His power in the wonderful stories which fill the pages of the Gospels? The first thing which comes to them, the great thing which comes to them all, is a change in their whole conception of life. What used to seem natural comes to seem most unnatural. That which they called unnatural becomes so natural that they cannot see why it should not immediately come to pass. The rich young man's money begins to fade in his hand, and he feels its tyranny passing away. The Magdalen's face grows luminous with a new vision of purity as the only true human life. Bigotry looks to Nicodemus what it really is. The simple naturalness in the hope that the children of God should live the life of God comes and folds itself around each of them. And in that atmosphere of their new life the old life with its old bondages dies.

You see how positive all this is. And that, too, seems to me to be depicted in the old Hebrew story, which we are using for our parable. It was on the farther seashore of the Red sea that the Egyptian pursuers of the Israelites lay dead. It was when the people of God had genuinely undertaken the journey to the land which God had given them, that the grasp of their enemy gave way and the dead hands let them go. You may fight with your enemy on his own ground, only trying to get the immediate better of him, and win what he claims for yourself, and your fight will go on, more or less a failure, more or less a victory, forever. You must go forth into a new land, into the new ambition of a higher life, and then, when he tries to follow you there, he perishes.

O selfish man! not merely by trying not to be selfish, but by entering into the new joy of unselfish consecration, so only shall you kill your selfishness. When you are vigorously trying to serve your fellow-men, the last chance that you will be unjust or cruel to them will disappear. When you are full of enthusiasm for truth, the cold hands of falsehood will let you go. Get the Egyptian off his own ground, seek not the same low things by higher means; seek higher things, and the low means will know that they cannot hold you their slave. They will lie down and die. And then the pillar of fire and the pillar of cloud will have you for their own and lead you on in your free journey.

With regard, then, to a man's permanent escape from evil, may we not say these two things,—that it must come about as the natural privilege of his life, and it must be positive? To the soul which has finally escaped from sin into the full freedom of the perfect life, the soul which has entered into the celestial liberty, must not these two things be clear,—first, that his old dream of life was a delusion, that he was never meant to be the thing which he so long allowed himself to be; and, second, that the great interests of the celestial life, the service of God which has there claimed the child of God, makes sure forever that there shall be no return to the old servitude? And what we dare to believe shall there in heaven come perfectly, and with reference to all wickedness, why may we not believe that here and now it may come in its degree with reference to some special sin? Know that it is not natural that you should steal, that you should lie; get rid of the first awful assumption that it is bound up with your constitution, cease to be a weak fatalist about it. That is the first thing. And then launch bravely forth into brave works of positive honesty and truth. Insist that your life shall not merely deny some falsehood, but that it shall assert some truth. Then, not till then, shall the lie let you go, and your soul count it impossible ever again to do—wonderful, almost incredible, that it ever should have done—what once it used to do from day to day.

I think that there are few things about our human nature which are more constantly marvellous than its power of acclimating itself in moral and spiritual regions where it once seemed impossible that it should live at all. The tree upon the hillside says: "Here and here alone can I live. Here my fathers lived in all their generations. Into this hard soil they struck their roots, and drank their sustenance out of its rocky depths. Take me down to the plain and I shall die." The gardener knows better. He takes the doubting and despairing plant and carries it, even against its will, to the broad valley, and sets it where the cold winds shall not smite it, and where the rich ground feeds it with luxuriance. And almost as they touch each other the ground and the root claim one another, and rich revelations of its own possibility flood the poor plant and fill it full of marvel with itself.

Of less and less consequence and meaning seem to me those easy things which men are always saying about their own natures and character. "I have no spiritual capacity," says one. "It is not in me to be a saint," another cries. "I have a covetous soul. I cannot live except in winning money." "I can make many sacrifices, but I cannot give up my drink." "I can do many things, but I cannot be reverent."

So the man talks about himself. Poor creature, does he think that he knows, down to its centre, this wonderful humanity of his? It all sounds so plausible and is so untrue! "Surely the man must know himself and his own limitations." Why must he? How can he know what lurking power lies packed away within the near-opened folds of this inactive life? Has he ever dared to call himself the child of God, and for one moment felt what that involves? Has he ever attacked the task which demands those powers whose existence he denies, or tried to press on into the region where those evil things cannot breathe which he complacently declares are an inseparable portion of his life? There is nothing on earth more seemingly significant and more absolutely insignificant than men's judgment of their own moral and spiritual limitations.

When the fallacy has been exposed, when the man has become something which he used to go about declaring that it was absolutely impossible that he should ever be, or has cast finally away that which he has counted a very part and portion of his life, it is often very interesting to see how he thinks of his cast-off sin. He, if he is a true man, counts his escape complete, but he never forgets his old bondage. He is always one whom God has led "out of the land of Egypt." Egypt is still there, although he has escaped from it. Egypt did not cease to be when the Egyptians with whom he had to do fell dead. Men are still doing the sin which has now become impossible for him. He understands those men by his past, while he cannot imagine himself sharing their life today. He is full of sympathy with the sinner, which is one with, of the same substance as, his security against the sin. Pity and hopefulness and humility and strength all blend into the peaceful and settled composure of his life.

It is a noble attitude towards a dead sin. You look into its dead face and are almost grateful to it. Not with a gratitude which makes you any way more tolerant of its character. You hate it with your heart—but look! Has it not given you self-knowledge, and made you cry out to God and set your face towards the new life?

My friends, get something done! Get something done! Do not go on forever in idle skirmishing with the same foe. Realize, as you sit here, who your chief enemy is, what vice of mind or body, what false or foul habit. Cry out to God for strength. Set your face resolutely to a new life in which that vice shall have no part. Go out and leave it dead. Plenty of new battles and new foes, but no longer that battle and that foe! Get something done! May He who overcame, not merely for Himself but for us all, give you courage and make you sharers in His victory and in the liberty which He attained.

THE GIANT WITH THE
WOUNDED HEEL

*"And I will put enmity between thee and the woman, and between thy seed and her seed. It shall bruise thy head, and thou shalt bruise his heel."—*GENESIS iii. 15.

THE scene in the story of which these words are written is fixéd deep in the imagination of mankind. We read it in our childhood, and it is never afterwards forgotten. As we go on, seeing more and more of life, life and this story of the Book of Genesis become mutually commentaries on each other. Life throws light on the story and the story throws light on life.

Let us take one passage from the story now, and try to hold it in the light of life and see its meaning brighten and deepen. God is represented as talking to the serpent who has been the tempter of mankind. The serpent, the spirit of Evil, has forced his way into the human drama. He has compelled the man and woman to admit him to their company. He cannot now be cast out by one summary act. He has come, and he remains. All that takes place in human history takes place in his presence. Upon everything he tries to exercise his influence. He is everywhere and always, and always and everywhere the same.

To this serpent, this spirit of evil in the world, God is speaking. What is it that he says? He might tell the monster that the world belonged to him. "Since man has let you in, he must abide the issue. He is yours. There is no help for it, and you must do with him as you will." On the other hand he might with one sweep of his omnipotence bid the hateful reptile depart. "Begone; for man belongs to me; and even if he has given himself to you, you can have no power over him at all, for he is mine." The words which are written in our text are different from both of these. What does God say? There shall be a long, terrible fight between man and the power of evil. The power of evil shall haunt and persecute man, cripple him and vex him, hinder him and make him suffer. It shall bruise his heel.

But man shall ultimately be stronger than the power of evil, and shall overcome it and go forth victorious, though bruised and hurt, and needing recovery and rest. He shall bruise its head.

Is there not in these words which the awful voice of God is heard speaking at the beginning of human history, a most clear and intelligible prophecy of human life? It separates itself at once from the crude theories which men have made on either side. It is not reckless pessimism nor reckless optimism. It is God's broad, wise, long-sighted prophecy of man, harassed, distressed and wounded on the way, but yet in spite of wounds and hindrances finally getting the better of his enemy and coming to success. With that promise of God—promise and warning together—sounding in his ears, man started on the long journey of existence, and has come thus far upon his way.

We want to ask ourselves how far that prophecy has been fulfilled, how far it has justified itself in history. We grow all out of patience with men's crude and sweeping and unqualified epitomes of life. One man says "It is all good," and will see none of the evil and sin and misery which are everywhere. Another man says "It is all bad," and for him all the brightness and graciousness and perpetual progress go for nothing. One man calls humanity a hopeless brute. Another man calls humanity a triumphant angel. God in these words of Genesis says, "Neither! but a wounded, bruised, strong creature, not running and leaping and shouting, often crawling and creeping in its pain, but yet brave, with an inextinguishable certainty of ultimate success, fighting a battle which is full of pain but is not desperate, sure ultimately to set his heel upon his adversary's head." Certainly there is a picture of man there which, in its most general statement, corresponds largely with the picture which history draws, and with that which our own experience presents. Let us look a little while first at the truthfulness of the picture; then at the way in which it comes to be true, and then at the sort of life which it will make in men who recognize its truth. The fact, the reason, and the consequence. Those are the natural divisions of any subject. Let them be the divisions of ours.

I look first at the institutions which mankind has formed for doing his work in the world. Institutions are nothing but colossal men. They are the great aggregations of humanity for doing those universal works which it is the interest not merely of this man, or of that man, but of all men to have done. Church institutions, state institutions, present the workings of human nature on a large scale, and so give excellent opportunity to study the fundamental facts of human life. And when we look at the great institutions of the world, what do we see? Everywhere, whether it be in Church or state, essentially the same thing. Noble principles, vast, beneficent agencies, gradually conquering barbarism and misery, making men better, making men happier, but always miserably hampered by wretched little sins of administration; stung in the heel by the serpents of selfishness, and sordidness, and insincerity and narrowness. Civilization, which is simply the sum of all the institutions which are shaped out of the best aspirations of mankind—it is simply amazing when we tell over to ourselves what the powers are which keep civilization to-day from putting its heel square and fair upon the head of barbarism, and finishing it forever. Popular government perverted by demagogues; Commerce degraded by the intrusion of fraud; the Church always weakened by hypocrisy; Charity perplexed by the fear of imposture and the dread of pauperism. Why, is not the image of institutionalism, embodying great principles, full of the consciousness of great ideas, and yet hindered and halting everywhere through the blunders and weaknesses of its administration—is it not just the picture of the giant with the bruised heel, the great strong creature, limping dubiously along the road over which he ought to be moving majestically to assured results?

Look again at society—that great mother and mistress of the thoughts and lives of so many of our old and younger people. It has its devotees and its denouncers. How few of us have ever seriously set ourselves to ask what is the real value and meaning of that social life which occupies so large a portion of the activity of civilized humanity? In its idea it is beautiful. Eagerness to take pleasure in the company of fellow-men—eagerness to give pleasure, by whatever contribution we can make—a wish to share with others all their gifts and ours—these are most true and healthy impulses. The society which is instinct with these impulses is the enemy of solitude; it puts its foot on selfishness; it makes men brothers; it kills out morbidness and self-conceit. Society is doing this—"What! our society?" you say, "this false, and foolish, and corrupt, and selfish, and frivolous uproar which takes possession of our city every winter, and runs its round of excitement, and jealousy, and dissipation, until Lent sets in?" Yes, even that! Sorely bruised in the heel it is, wounded and crippled in a melancholy fashion; a poor enough image of that divine communion of the children of God, which is the real society of men and women —but yet a thing to be cured and cleansed, not to be cast away, not a thing for any man to turn his back upon and be a misanthrope, but for all men and women to do what they can to rescue and to fill with the spirit of a nobler life.

Then, think again of learning. We have a perfect right to indulge our enthusiasm over man as a studying and learning creature. Man seeking after knowledge is felt at once to be man using very noble powers. It is man doing the work for which a very noble part of him was made. We think of the ready and cheerful self-sacrifice of the scholars, great and little, not merely of those who have been rewarded for the surrenders which they made by the applause of a delighted world, but of the scholars whose self-sacrifice has lain in obscurity, who have eaten their crusts in silence, and not even recompensed themselves with groans. We think of all that man's untiring pursuit of knowledge has attained; of the great conquests which have been rescued out of the kingdom of ignorance. We let our imagination run forward and picture in delighted bewilderment the future triumphs of the same divine audacity, man's brave determination to know all that is knowable. And then, while we are glowing with this large enthusiasm, what is this which comes to interrupt and chill it? What are these petty jealousies and hates of learned men? What is this pedantry? What is this narrowness which neglects and despises, and even tries to hinder other learning than its own? Close on the large ambition comes the miserable discontent, the carping criticism, the discouragement, the love of darkness. The worm is in the wood of the brave ship that sails so proudly out to sea. The rust is on the arrow which is sent flying through the air. What is the Poet's complaint, that "knowledge comes but wisdom lingers," except a declaration that here too the full completeness of a great process is prevented, the serpent is stinging at the heel which ultimately must be set upon the serpent's head and crush it.

And what shall we say about religion? The future of mankind is a religious future. It is man as religious, that is to rule the world. What changes of form religious thought may undergo, who can pretend to say? But that religion shall perish, none of us believes. And if religion continues, she must reign. We cannot imagine for her a merely subordinate or passive life. She must reign, reign till she has put all enemies under her feet. Indeed I do not know how any man can really believe in religion today, who does not believe in the destiny of religion to be the mistress of the world. I cannot believe in God without believing that he is the rightful Lord of everything; for that is what "God" means. A God who is not rightful Lord and Master, is not God. We say this with entire certainty, and then, we look up to see religion conquering the world. We do see what we look for. But we see something else besides. How the great conqueror is harassed and tormented. What petty annoyances and trouble she is beset with. Look at the crudeness, and the mercenariness, and mechanicalness with which men, even her own friends, misconceive her most spiritual truths. Look how her theories break down in human action. Behold the hypocrisy, the selfishness, the bigotry, the fanaticism, the untruthfulness, the formality, the cowardice, the meanness of religious people! Wounded in the house of her friends, is this great majestic Being who is some day to rule and save the world. And outside of her friends, among her enemies, men insult her and oppose her as if she were their worst foe, and not, what she really is, their only hope. The work which she is bound to do will none the less be done, but it will be done under perpetual opposition and persecution, done with torn and bleeding hands and feet.

Thus hurriedly I think over the great powers which are helping the world, and everywhere the case concerning all of them seems to be the same. All of them are doing good work. All of them are destined to ultimate success. Of none of them do we despair. But every one of them is working against hindrance and enmity and opposition. Not one of them goes freely and fearlessly to its victory. It is the combination of these two facts that gives the color and the tone to human history. From every century comes forth the same report. Great powers, sure to succeed, yet ever hindered at their work; never abandoning hope, yet moving timidly because they know, that sure as their final victory may be, their immediate lot is wounds and insult. Is it not exactly the old prophecy. The serpent whose head is ultimately to be crushed, now ever wounding the heel which is finally to be its destruction. Could any image picture human history so well?

Turn now away from this large look across the fields of history, and think how true the picture of the Book of Genesis is to our personal life. I might open the closed and sacred pages of any man's experience. Here is a man who for his thirty, forty, fifty years has been seeking after goodness, trying to conquer his passions and vices, and be a really good man. What will he say of his struggle as he looks back upon it? Let him stand upon this Sunday hillock, a little nearer to the sky perhaps than on the week-days; let him stand here and say how life looks to him as his eye runs back. You know the hindrances you have met. Paul's story has been your story. When you would do good evil was present with you. You never sprang most bravely from the low ordinary level of your living, that a hand did not seem to catch you and draw you back. You never felt a new power start up within you that a new weakness did not start up by its side. Terrible has been this quickness of the evil power, giving you the awful sense of being watched and dogged. Awful has grown this certainty that no good impulse ever could go straight and uninterrupted to its victorious result, and yet, is it not wonderful how you have kept the assurance that good and not evil is the true master-power of your life! The resolution has been broken. It has been wounded. It has limped and halted. It has stood for months, perhaps for years, in the same place and made no progress, but it has never died. There is no man here who has not failed; but is there any man here in all this multitude who has given up? Not one! Every man here, when he looks forward, means some day to enter into the gates of salvation, to leave his sins behind him and live the life of God. In such a hope, in the light of such a resolution only, is life tolerable. Everything that hinders and delays that resolution is an accident and an intruder. The resolution itself is the utterance of God's purpose for the life.

I think the same is true about our faith. To believe is the true glory of existence. To disbelieve is to give ourselves into the power of death, and, just so far, to cease from living. And you are living and not dead. You do believe. You are quite sure of spiritual verities. God is a truth to you. Your soul is your true self. Christ, the spiritual perfectness of manhood, the true Son of God, is really King of the world. This spiritual faith you would not part with for your life. It is your only hope. You look forward to the day when it shall have conquered and cast out every doubt in you, and reign supreme. But now, how doubt besets you! Now, how a denial comes like a shadow on the heels of every faith! Who is this man whom in your loftier and more hopeful moments you discern, far off, on some bright distant day, entering into the open portals of a perfect faith, and leaving doubt dead outside the door forever? Is he the victor of an easy fight? Does he come springing up the shining steps with muscles only just tried enough to feel themselves elastic from the long struggle? Indeed, not so! The man—yourself—whom you see finally victorious, comes crawling to the temple of entire faith, dragging after him the wounded heel which Doubt, for long years before at last he died, stung, and stung, and stung again. Wonderful is that faith in faith, a thing to be thankful for to all eternity; wonderful is that faith in faith by which the soul dares to be sure, even in the very thick of doubt, that in belief, and not in unbelief, is its eternal rest and home.

I have spoken of the prophecy of Genesis as if it referred to that total seed of the woman which is all humanity. I have no doubt that it does so refer. But it has also always been considered to have reference to that special representative humanity which was in Jesus Christ. To him it certainly applies. What is the story of that wondrous life which, centuries afterward, Christ lived in Palestine? It is the story of a life wounded again and again by an antagonist whom at the last it overthrew. Christ's victory was perfect on the cross. There, finally, he conquered the world, he conquered sin. There he went up upon his throne, and Sin and Death were under his feet. But how did he come to that throne? Behold him staggering, wounded, bruised, beaten, all the way from Pilate's brutal judgment hall to Calvary. Remember what the years before had been. All the time he had been conquering the world and sin, and yet all the time sin and the world had been apparently conquering him. At the tomb door of Bethany, he stands and groans and weeps. Death has cut deep into his affections. His friend is dead. We may well believe that he hesitates and almost doubts. Then he lifts up his head and cries, "Lazarus, come forth!" and as the dead man comes to life, is it not true in that moment that the bruised heel of the woman is set upon the head of the serpent which has bruised it? Is not the old prophecy of Genesis, in that moment, perfectly fulfilled?

May I not then rest here my statement and assertion of the fact? Is it not true that everywhere the good is hampered and beset and wounded by the evil which it is ultimately to slay; true also that the good will ultimately slay the evil by which it was wounded and beset? These two facts, in their combination, make a philosophy of life which, when one has accepted it, colors each thought he thinks, each act he does. The two facts subtly blend their influence in every experience. They make impossible either crude pessimism or crude optimism. No man can curse that world in which the best of men, and the best of manhood, is steadily moving onward to the victory over the serpent. No man can unqualifiedly praise the world where that onward movement of the best is always being wounded and retarded by the serpent, over which it is to triumph at the last. But surely it gives certainty to our own observation of the history of man; surely it gives dignity to what has seemed to be the mere accident of confusion in our own lives, when we find them both prophesied on the first page of the world's Book. Yes, that which puzzles you or me, that which so often seems to make life meaningless and cruel, at least it is no chance and thoughtlessness by which it comes, for it is written in the very prospectus and prophecy of human life.

It would be possible, I think, also to show that it is written, or at least the possibility of it is written in the very necessity of things. On that I must not linger. I have dwelt so long upon the fact, that I must say but a few words of the cause and the consequence.

Of the cause I may say only this, that there is one conceivable state of things which in its operation must produce just that phenomenon which we have been studying at such length this morning. That state of things is a vast general purpose for the best good of mankind, submitted for its execution to the wills of men. Granted a God who means all good for his creatures, and who, as a part of his benevolent designs for them, calls their free agency to help in bringing about his purposes, and what shall we behold? Indubitable evidences that the good is stronger than the evil; a great, slow, steady progress of the good, forever gaining on the evil; and all the time reactions and detractions, rebellions of the evil against its conquest by the good. A stream with grand majestic onward flow, whose broad strong bosom is not smooth, but flecked all over with eddies, little twists and turns, in which the water for a time is running the wrong way. A stately figure of humanity, slowly pressing down its heel upon the serpent's head, yet with its face full of disturbance and of pain, because the serpent on whose head the heel is set is always stinging with the very venom of despair the heel that crushes it.

Tell me, my friends, if this is what would come if there were a great divine purpose in the world necessarily submitted for its execution to the will of man: then, since this has come, since this is the very picture which our eyes behold, shall we not let ourselves believe that the cause which I have described does indeed lie behind this wonderfully interesting, pathetic, fearful, hopeful life we live? A great divine purpose, dependent for its detailed execution on the will of men! Let me believe that, and then I know what means this ineradicable hope and this perpetual discouragement. Let me know that, and then I understand both why the good does not conquer now, and why the good must conquer at the last.

Our last question still remains. What sort of human life will this world tend to make in the mean time, or what will be the truest and most fitting life to live in a world such as this which we have seen our world to be. For man is capable of many lives, and is able to answer to the world in which he lives with its appropriate response.

Two qualities, I think, must certainly appear in the man who has thoroughly caught the spirit and is susceptible to the best influences of this world. One quality I call watchful hope, and the other I call anxious charity. We need our adjectives as well as our nouns when we describe the true temper in which a man must live. The nouns describe the fundamental confidence which must arise from the conviction of a divine purpose for the life of man. The adjectives depict the sense of danger which comes from the knowledge that this divine purpose is committed for its execution to the unstable wills of men. Hope and charity, these must both spring up from the soul of faith. If God has truly a purpose for our lives, who dare be hopeless? If God has really a purpose for our brother's life, who dare despair of him? Ah, we do only half believe it. Therefore our hope is such a colorless and feeble thing; therefore our charity so doubts and hesitates. But they are in us still. They must be in us just in proportion to our faith in God.

And yet the hope must be a watchful hope, the charity must be an anxious charity. Neither can fling itself out broadcast and without reserve. Hope is aware of danger; charity is full of fear; in this world where God has done all God can, and yet leaves the last decision of his own destiny in the hands of man.

A watchful hope! An anxious charity! Are not these very clear and recognizable qualities? Do they not make a very clear and recognizable character? They make a character which has stamped the life of humanity wherever it has really known and felt the conditions of its life.

One sometimes thinks how it would be if to each star which floats in space the life which its inhabitants are living should impart a color, which other stars might see as they pass by it in the never resting chorus of the planets. Can we not picture to ourselves with what a special hue the long spiritual experience of the men who live upon it must have clothed this earth of ours? A sober glory, a radiance of indescribable depth and richness; and yet a certain tremulousness as of a perpetual fear; no outburst of unquestioning, unhesitating splendor, but a restrained effulgence, hoping for more than it dare yet to claim, pathetic with a constant, age-long discontent.

Whether our sister stars discover it or not, we know it well; we who live here and see the highest typical life of man upon the earth. Do we not know how all the best and holiest men live in a hope so great that its own greatness clothes it in a mystery which is almost doubt, as the sun clothes itself in sunlight which is almost a hiding of the splendor it displays. We cannot describe it to ourselves or one another, but how well we know it; that watchful hope and anxious charity; that sober, earnest, cheerful, and careful richness which have filled the lives and shone out of the faces of the best men the world has seen, and given its profoundest meaning to the name of Man!

When we look up to Christ and catch the color of His wondrous life, is there not there the confirmation and supreme exemplification of all this? In him are watchful hope and anxious charity complete. This story of his life is no wild shout, flung forth out of the cloudless sky, but a rich, solemn, deep, beautiful music, wherein the sense of danger always trembles and sways beneath the constancy of an unalterable certainty of God.

If we are saved by Christ, it will be into the life of Christ that we are saved, into the inextinguishable hope and into the watchful fear together. Not intoxicated by the hope and not discouraged by the fear, we shall go on our way expecting both parts of the old prophecy to be fulfilled in us, as they were both fulfilled in Him. Expecting to be stung and bruised by the serpent, but sure ultimately, if we let God give us all His strength, to set the bruised and stung heel on the serpent's head. That life may we all have the grace to live.

THE CURSE OF MEROZ

"Curse ye Meroz, saith the angel of the Lord, Curse ye bitterly the inhabitants thereof; because they came not to the help of the Lord, to the help of the Lord against the mighty."—JUDGES v. 23.

DEBORAH and Barak had gained a great victory in the plain of Esdraelon and along the skirts of the mountain of Little Hermon. Their enemy Sisera had fled away completely routed, and the wild, fierce, strong woman who "judged Israel in those days," and the captain of the Israelitish army, sang a splendid proud song of triumph. In it they recount the tribes who had come up to their duty, who had shared the labor and the glory of the fight. And then, in the midst of the torrent of song there comes this other strain of fiery indignation. One town or village, Meroz, had hung back. Hidden away in some safe valley, it had heard the call which summoned every patriot, but it knew it was in no danger. It had felt the shock of battle on the other side of the hills, and nestled and hid itself only the more snugly. "Curse ye Meroz, saith the angel of the Lord; curse ye bitterly the inhabitants thereof, because they came not to the help of the Lord, to the help of the Lord against the mighty." It is a fierce vindictive strain. It bursts from the lips of an exalted furious woman. But it declares one of the most natural indignations of the human heart.

Meroz is gone. No record of it except this verse remains. The most ingenious and indefatigable explorer cannot even guess where it once stood. But the curse remains; the violent outburst of the contempt and anger which men feel who have fought and suffered and agonized, and then see other men who have the same interest in the result which they have, coming out cool and unwounded from their safe hiding places to take a part of the victory which they have done nothing to secure. Meroz stands for that. It sometimes happens that a man or a town passes completely away from the face of the earth and from the memory of men, and only leaves a name which stands as a sort of symbol or synonym of some quality, some virtue or

126

some vice, forever. So Meroz stands for the shirker; for him who is willing to see other people fight the battles of life, while he simply comes in to take the spoils. No wonder Deborah and Barak were indignant. Their wounds were still aching; their people were dead and dying all around them; and here was Meroz, idle and comfortable, and yet, because she was part of the same country, sure to get the benefit of the great victory as much as any.

It was not only personal anger. This cowardly and idle town had not come "to the help of the Lord." Deborah knew that the cause of Jehovah had been in terrible danger. It seemed as if it had only barely been saved. She was filled with horror when she thought what would have been the consequences if it had been lost. And here sat this village, whose weight perhaps might have furnished just what was needed to turn the doubtful scale; here it had sat through all the critical and dreadful day, looking on and doing nothing. It was all her passionate sense of the preciousness of God's government and the danger in which it had stood which burst from her lips when she cursed Meroz.

There are many people always who are in the community and in the world what Meroz was in Palestine. For there is an everlasting struggle going on against wickedness and wretchedness. It never ceases. It changes but it never ceases. It shifts from one place to another. It dies out in one form only to burst out in some other shape. It seems to flag sometimes as if the enemy were giving way, but it never really stops; the endless struggle of all that is good in the world against the enemies of God, against sin and error and want and woe. And the strange and sad thought which comes upon our minds sometimes is of how few people after all are really heartily engaged in that struggle, how few have cast themselves into it with all their hearts, how many there are who stand apart and wish it well but never expose themselves for it nor do anything to help it.

Look at the manifest forms in which men show their will to work for God and goodness. Those of you who have had any occasion to observe it know full well by what a very small number of persons the charitable and missionary works of the church and all operations which require public spirit in a community are carried on. If there is a reform to be urged; if there is an abuse to be corrected in the administration of affairs; if there is some oppressed and degraded class whose rights, which they cannot assert themselves, must be asserted for them; if there is a palpable wrong done every day upon our streets,—most of you know how very few are the people in this city, who, apart from any private interest in the matter, are looked to as likely to take any concern for the public good. The subscription papers which one sees passing about for public objects might almost as well be stereotyped as written, so constantly do they repeat the same limited list of well known names.

These are superficial signs. But ask yourself again, How many of the people among us who are in the positions of influence in various occupations, feel any kind of responsibility for the elevation of their occupation, feel any desire of making it a stronghold against the power of evil? How many merchants feel that it belongs to them to elevate the standards of trade? How many teachers value their relation to the young because they have the chance to strengthen character against temptation? How many men and women in social life care to develop the higher uses of society, making it the bulwark and the educator of men's purer, finer, deeper life? Every occupation is capable of this profounder treatment, besides its mere treatment as a means of livelihood or of personal advancement. In every occupation there are some men who conceive of it so. How few they are! How the mass of men who trade and teach and live their social life, never get beyond the merely selfish thought about it all! The lack of a sense of responsibility, the selfishness of life, is the great impression that is forced upon us constantly.

It is so even in religion. To how many Christians does the religious life present itself in the enthusiastic and inspiring aspect of working and fighting for God? How almost all Christians never get beyond the first thought of saving their own souls! I think I am as ready as any man to understand the vast variety of forms under which self-devotion may be shown, and not to impute selfishness to that which simply is not unselfish in certain special forms. But, making all broad allowances, I think there is nothing which so comes to impress a man as the way in which the vast majority of men hold back and, with no ill-will but all good wishes, let the interests of their fellow-men and of goodness and of God take care of themselves. I should like to speak to-day of the curse of Meroz, the curse of uselessness, the curse of shirking; and I should rejoice indeed if I could make any young man see how wretched it is and inspire him with some noble desire to do some of the work, to fight some of the enemies of God.

Notice then first of all that the sin for which Meroz is cursed is pure inaction. There is no sign that its people gave any aid or comfort to the enemy. They merely did nothing. We hear so much about the danger of wrong thinking and the danger of wrong doing. There is the other danger, of not doing right and not thinking right, of not doing and not thinking at all. It is hard for many people to feel that there is danger and harm in that, the worst of harm and danger. And the trouble comes, I think, from the low condition of spiritual vitality, from the lack of emphasis and vigor in the whole conception of a man's own life. A man who is but half alive, a poor helpless invalid shut up in his room, hears the roar of human life going on past his windows, and it causes him no self-reproach that he is not in it, that he has no part or share in all this work. He does not expect it of himself. He recognizes still the positive sins. He knows that he has no right to commit murder, or to forge, or to lie as he sits there. His helplessness has not released him from any of those obligations. But he does feel released from enterprise and activity. He is not called upon to do a well man's work. His task is only to keep himself alive. Now the spiritual and moral vitality of many men is low. What can revive it? What can put strength and vigor into it? There is a verse of St. John which, among many other things which it tells, tells this, I think. "He that hath the Son hath life," John says, "and he that hath not the Son of God hath not life." That is a great declaration. It says that if a man takes Christ, that is to say if a man loves and serves Christ because Christ has redeemed him into the family of God, he really lives, vigor comes into him, responsibility lays hold upon him. The work of the world becomes his work. God's tasks become his tasks. The enemies of God become his enemies. This is the meaning of countless passages which people make to mean so much shallower, so much smaller things. "God sent His only begotten Son into the world that we might live through Him," John says again. When Christ has redeemed a man, and the man knows his redemption and wants to serve Christ in gratitude, then the invalidism of the soul is gone. The man lives all through and through, and wherever Christ needs him he is ready; which merely means that wherever there is any good work to be done, he does it.

Now there are in all our cities, and this city has its full share of them, a great multitude of useless men, and of men perfectly contented in their uselessness. Many a man looks back upon his life, and save for the kindly offices which he has rendered to his immediate associates, he cannot remember one useful thing he ever did. He never stood up for a good cause. He never remonstrated against an evil. He never helped a bad man to be better. A merely useless man! His life might drop out of the host to-morrow and none would miss a soldier from the ranks. No onset or defence would be the weaker for his going. I know not how he reconciles it to himself. It may be that the palsy of a fashionable education has been on him from his birth. Perhaps he grew up, as you perhaps are bringing up your children now, to think that because his life was plentifully provided against necessity, therefore it was free from duty. There is nothing so pitiable as to see a boy in some self-indulgent household, who evidently came into the world with faculties to make him be, and make him enjoy being, a strong and helpful worker for God and man, having all chance and taste for using these faculties quietly, steadily crushed out of him by the constant pressure of a fashionable home. It is the child of God being slowly made into the man of the world. But however it came about, let us take the only too familiar phenomenon of the useless man who excuses his uselessness, and let us see what are some of the various forms which his uselessness assumes. I shall speak of three; cowardice, and false humility, and indolence. Let us see how dead they make a man; and how the Son of God is the true life of all of them.

1. The first source then of the uselessness of good men, or, if you please, of men who are not bad, is moral cowardice. Cowardice we call the most contemptible of vices. It is the one whose imputation we most indignantly resent. To be called a coward would make the blood boil in the veins of any of us. But the vice is wonderfully common. Nay, we often find ourselves wondering whether it is not universal, whether we are not all cowards somewhere in our nature. Physical cowardice all of us do not have. Indeed physical cowardice is rarer than we think. A war or a shipwreck always brings out our surprise when we see how many men there are that can march up to a battery, or stand and watch the water creep up the side of their ship to drown them, and never quail. But moral courage is another thing. To dare to do just what we know we ought to do, without

being in the least hindered or distorted by the presence of men who we know will either hate or despise or ridicule us for what we are doing, that is rare indeed. Men think they have it till their test comes. Why, there is in this community; nay, there is in this congregation to-day, an amount of right conviction which, if it were set free into right action by complete release from moral cowardice, would be felt through the land. A man is deeply assured of Christianity. He is trying to serve Christ. He is always trying to be spiritual. If he can creep up at night and drive a spike into some cannon of infidelity or sin when no one sees him, there is something in his heart that makes him do it. He will give his anonymous dollar or thousand dollars to religious work. But he never stands out boldly on the Lord's side, never declares himself a Christian and says that the work of his Master shall be the work of his life. Is it cowardice? He says there is no man he is afraid of; and there is none. The fear is concentrated on no individual. But is there not a sense of hostile or contemptuous surroundings that lies like a chilling hand upon what ought to be the most exuberant and spontaneous utterance of life? Have not the long years of living in such an atmosphere enfeebled the power of the native will? One sees it in old men continually, the fear which keeps the best and most enthusiastic hopes and wishes chained. One has but little expectation of the breaking of that chain in them. But it is sad to see those same chains fastening themselves on younger men. The mere boy feels them growing. He wants to be generous, pure, devoted, Christian. Everything urges him to put his life from the first upon the side of righteousness and Christ. And what hinders him? He early learns to cloak it under various names, but the power itself is fear. Cowardice wrings the foul or profane word from the lips that hate it while they utter it. Cowardice stifles the manly and indignant rebuke at the piece of conventional and approved meanness of the college or the shop. Cowardice keeps the low standards of honor traditional and unbroken through generations of boys. Cowardice holds the young Christian back from a frank acknowledgment of his Lord.

It is easy to make an argument with such a moral cowardice. It is easy for the boy or man who finds that he is losing his best life out of fear of his fellows to reason with himself. "Come," he says to himself; "I am failing of my duty, I am dishonoring my best convictions, I am living a lie; and all because I am afraid of whom? Of a boy or a man, or of a company of boys or men whom I cannot respect. I know that he whom I fear is mean and low in his judgments. He is wicked, and in his heart there is no doubt the misgiving of wickedness. He probably distrusts and only half believes in his own abuse or his own sneer. And yet I am afraid of him. And what am I afraid that he will do? Why, either that he will detest me or ridicule me. Suppose he does. What is the value of these missiles? Do I really care for his praise so much that to lose it would really give me pain? And then am I not wrong in thinking that he cares enough about me to waste upon me either his hate or his contempt? Do I not overestimate the space which I fill in his thoughts? Am I not doing myself wrong in order that a man or a world may think well of me, which in reality never thinks of me at all?" This is the argument which the conscious coward holds with himself. It is unanswerable. It ought to break the chains instantly and set the coward free. A man ought to cast his fears to the winds when he comes to realize that he is fearing contemptible people, and fearing that they will do to him contemptible things which in all probability they will never care enough about him to do at all. That is what many a man does realize about his cowardice; and does it set him free? Almost never, I believe. Almost never is a man made independent and brave by having it proved to him that it is a foolish thing to be afraid. No, men do not escape from their cowardice so. Nothing except the inflow of a larger consecration which oversweeps and drowns their cowardice can really put it out of the way forever. Nothing but the knowledge of God's love, taking such possession of a man that his one wish and thought in life is to glorify and serve God, can liberate him from, because it makes him totally forget, his fear of man. "I will walk at liberty because I keep Thy commandments." O those great words of David! What an everlasting story they tell of the liberty that comes by lofty service. They tell of what you young people need to save you, at the very outset of your life, from cowardice. Not by despising men will you cease to fear them. People's worst slavery very often is to things and people that they despise. Only by loving God and fearing Him with that fear whose heart and soul is love; only by letting Christ show God to you so that you must see Him; only so shall you tread your cowardice under your feet and be free for your best life.

2. We must go on to the second of the causes of the uselessness

of men who might be useful, which I called false humility. Humility is good when it stimulates, it is bad when it paralyzes, the active powers of a man. It may do either. We have noble examples of humility as a stimulus; the sense of weakness making a man all the more ardent to use all the strength he has. But if conscious weakness causes a man to believe that it makes no difference whether he works or not, then his humility is his curse. Perhaps this was part of the trouble of Meroz. The little village in the hills, poor, insignificant perhaps, lay listening to the gathering of the tribes. She saw the signal fires and heard the summons of the trumpet run through all the land. She knew the summons was for her as well as all the rest. But who was she? What could she do? What strength could she add to the host? What terror could she inspire in the foe? What would Barak care for her support, or Sisera for her hostility? So she lay still and let the battle fight itself through without her. Do you not recognize the picture? Whenever men hide behind their conscious feebleness; whenever, because they can do so little, they content themselves with doing nothing; whenever the one-talented men stand with their napkins in their hands along the roadside of life,—there is Meroz over again. Once more the argument is clear enough; as clear with humility as it is with cowardice. Listen, how clear it is! You who say that you can do so little for any good cause that there is no use of your doing anything; you can give so little that it is not worth while for you to give anything; your word has so little weight that it need not be spoken for the Lord,—consider these things. First, what do you know about the uses of the Lord, of this great work which the Lord has to do; what do you know of it that gives you the right to say that your power is little? God may have some most critical use to put you to as soon as you declare yourself His servant. Men judge by the size of things; God judges by their fitness. Two pieces of iron lie together on a shelf. One is a great clumsy ploughshare; and the other is a delicate screw that is made to hold the finest joint of some subtle machinery in place. An ignorant boor comes up and takes the great piece and treasures it. The little piece he sees is little, and throws it away. Fitness is more than size. You can see something of your size; but you can see almost nothing of your fitness until you understand all the wonderful manifold work that God has to do. It is a most wanton presumption and pride for any man to dare to be sure that there is not some very important and critical place which just he and no one else is made to fill. It is almost as presumptuous to think you can do nothing as to think you can do everything. The latter folly supposes that God exhausted Himself when He made you; but the former supposes that God made a hopeless blunder when He made you, which it is quite as impious for you to think.

And remember, in the second place, what would happen if all the little people in the world held up their littleness like a shield before them as you hold up yours. Grant that you are as small as you think you are, you are the average size of moral and intellectual humanity. Let all the Merozes in the land be humble like you, and where shall be the army? Only when men like you wake up and shake the paralysis of their humility away, shall we begin to see the dawn of that glorious millennium for which we sigh; which will consist not in the transformation of men into angels, nor in the coming forth of a few colossal men to be the patterns and the champions of life, but simply in each man, through the length and breadth of the great world, doing his best.

Remember, too, that such a humility as yours, the humility that enfeebles and disarms you, comes, if you get at its root, from an over-thought about yourself, an over-sense of your own personality, and so is close akin to pride. It has run all around the circle in its desire to escape from pride, and has almost got back to pride again. Now pride is the thickest and most blinding medium through which the human eye can look at anything. If your humility is not transparent but muddy, so that you see things not more clearly but less clearly because of it, you may be sure there is pride in it. O my friends, there is a humility which some men are too humble to feel, a distrust of self which some men are too forgetful of self ever to experience.

The argument, then, against allowing any sense of weakness to keep us from doing all that we can do, is perfectly conclusive. But, once again, does this argument dispel the paralysis and set men free to work? Almost never, I believe, again. Not by studying himself, but by forgetting himself in the desire to serve his Lord, does a man exchange the false humility which crushes for the true humility which inspires. What has become of the self-distrust and shyness of that gentle scholar who has turned into a Boanerges of the truth; or of that timid shrinking woman who goes unmoved through the hooting of a rabble to the stake? Both have lost themselves in their

Lord. Both have learned the love of Christ till that became the one fact of their existence; and then the call of Him who loved them has drawn the soul out of all self-consciousness. They have forgotten themselves, forgotten even their humility, and are wholly His. And there is the door through which all morbid self-distrust, all the despair of conscious weakness, must find escape.

3. I shall not need to say much upon the third of the causes for men's shirking the duties and responsibilities of life. Not that it is not important, but that it is so simple. It is mere indolence mere laziness. Perhaps Meroz was not afraid. Perhaps she was not shy and self-distrustful. Perhaps she simply believed that the work of God would somehow get itself done without her, and so waited and waited and came not to the help of the Lord against the mighty. Ah, we are always giving elaborate and complicated accounts both of the virtues and the vices of our fellow-men which are really as simple and explicable as possible, as clear as daylight. A man does a good thing and we are not content to say that he does it because he is a good man, but we must find strange obscure motives for it, some far-off policies and plans, some base root for this bright flower. Another man lets his duty, his clear duty, go undone, and again we set our ingenuity to work to guess why he does not do it. He misconceives his duty, he is too modest, he is waiting for something; when the real trouble is in a simple gross laziness, a mere self-indulgent indolence, which makes him indifferent to duty altogether. Let me go back to the picture which I tried to draw at the beginning of this sermon; a man who was born in luxury has lived in luxury, and now is coming on to middle life with the habits of his youth about him. He belongs to that strange, undefined, and yet distinct condition of life which is called society or fashion or respectability. That is a strange condition. It is not characterized by remarkable intelligence, not by peculiar education, not always by the most perfect breeding; but the main thing about it is that over it there hovers a vague air of privilege. The men and women who live in it are not looked to by other people, and do not look to themselves, for the active energetic contributions to the labor of life. It does not furnish the workers to the state or to the church. With this condition many of you are perfectly familiar. To it many of you belong, and feel its influence. Nothing is expected of you, and you do nothing. A well-bred, good-natured selfishness fills up the life of such a man.

Duty? It seems as if he never had heard the word; or as if he thought that it belonged, like those other two words, poverty and work, to beings of another order from himself. Now is there any hope for such a man? O, if he were only a fancy sketch! O, if he were not real and actual all through the city! O, if there were not whole hosts of boys, with the capacity in them to be something better, who are growing up with him as the object of their admiration, and becoming year by year more and more like him! Is there any hope of such a man coming to understand that it is not for such a life as he is living that God has made him? I own the only chance I see is in his coming to understand, in some real sense and meaning of those words, that God did make him. I think that is the real knowledge that is needed in our parlors and our clubs; needed there, lacking there, often quite as much as in our drinking saloons and dens of thieves. That a man's life is not an accident, that we are here because God put us here as the master mechanic puts each bolt and shaft of the engine into the place where it is wanted; is not that the quickening, the transforming knowledge? That physical strength, those strong arms and nimble hands, are not accidents; not an accident, that quick perception and that power of endurance; not an accident, that easy temper and careless acceptance of the things of life which might be elevated into faith. Let a man know this, and his sense of fitness must be outraged every day as he hears the life, which he was made for, claiming him, and yet goes on in uselessness. But there is only one way to really know this deeply. The only way to really know that God made us is to let God remake, regenerate us. The only way to be sure that God gave us our physical life is to let Him give us the spiritual life which shall declare for the physical life an adequate and worthy purpose. The only way to realize that we are God's children is to let Christ lead us to our Father. That is the only permanent escape from indolence, from self-indulgence; the grateful and obedient dedication to God through Christ which makes all good work, all self-sacrifice, a privilege and joy instead of a hardship, since it is done for Him.

The curse of Meroz is the curse of uselessness; and these are the sources out of which it comes—cowardice and false humility and indolence. They are the stones piled upon the sepulchres of vigor and energy and work for God, whose crushing weight cannot be computed. Who shall roll us away those stones? Nothing can do it but the power of Christ. The manhood that is touched by Him rises into life. I have tried to show you what that means. O my friends, it means this, that when a man has understood the life and cross of Jesus, and really knows that he is redeemed and saved, his soul leaps up in love and wants to serve its Saviour; and then he is afraid of nobody; and however little his own strength is, he wants to give it all; and the cords of his self-indulgence snap like cobwebs. Then he enters the new life of usefulness. And what a change it is! To be working with God, however humbly; to have part of that service which suns and stars, which angels and archangels, which strong and patient and holy men and women in all times have done; to be, in some small corner of the field, stout and brave and at last triumphant in our fight with lust and cruelty and falsehood, with want or woe or ignorance, with unbelief and scorn, with any of the enemies of God; to be distinctly on God's side, though the weight of the work we do may be utterly inappreciable,—what a change it is when a poor, selfish, cowardly, fastidious, idle human creature comes to this! Blessed is he that cometh to the help of the Lord, to the help of the Lord against the mighty. There is no curse for him. No wounds that he can receive while he is fighting on that side can harm him. To fight there is itself to conquer, even though the victory comes through pain and death, as it came to Him under whom we fight, the Captain of our Salvation, Jesus Christ.

VISIONS AND TASKS

"While Peter thought on the vision, the Spirit said unto him, Behold, three men seek thee."—ACTS x. 19.

THESE words recall to many of you a most familiar picture, for the story of St. Peter's vision is one of those passages of the New Testament which have almost become the proverbs of mankind. Peter had been sitting on the top of Simon's house at Jaffa, and there had been shown to him the sight of the great sheet full of all living beasts, of which he had been bidden to take and eat. And when he hesitated, you remember how a voice had spoken to him, and rebuked the narrow punctiliousness with which he drew distinctions, and thought some of God's creatures clean and others unclean. He was sitting there, pondering this vision, "doubting in himself what the vision which he had seen should mean." A new idea had come to him. He saw it very vaguely; and its developments, what it would lead to if he followed it out, he could not see at all. It was all abstract and impalpable. It just bewildered and eluded him. But as he sat there, steps were heard below, and to his mind the Spirit spoke, saying, "Three men are asking for thee." They were the servants of Cornelius, the Gentile, coming to ask him to visit their master. Their visit gave him immediately the chance to put in action the idea which had possessed him. Our verse shows him then standing between the vision and its application. On the one side of him was the mysterious sheet full of the multitude of beasts; on the other side were the three men who needed just the principle which the sheet-full of beasts involved. It was a critical moment. The question was whether the vision could pass through Peter to the three men and Cornelius. When on the morrow he "went away with them," the question was decided, and the idea and its appropriate duty had joined hands.

Man standing between his visions and his tasks—that is the subject of our verse then. That is our subject for this morning. It is the place where certain men are often called upon peculiarly to stand; and in some degree it is the place in which all men are standing always. For every man has visions, glimpses clearer or duller, now bright and beautiful, now clouded and obscure, of what is absolutely and abstractly true; and every man also has pressing on him the warm, clear lives of fellow-men. There is the world of truths on one side, and there is the world of men upon the other. Between the two stands man; and these two worlds, if man is what he ought to be, meet through his nature.

Think of an instance, and you will see what I mean. Here are you, a thoughtful, meditative man. You have been pondering and studying. Somehow it has become clear to you, let us say, that there is a God. The supernatural behind the natural, the will behind all forces, has revealed itself to you. For the moment, it is enough for you just to know that mighty truth. Turning it this way and that, you think in one view and another how mighty it is. But very soon, if you are a true man, your nature begins to hear and feel a stir upon the other side of it. Under the windows which look towards the world, the tumult of the needy life of your fellow-men comes rising up to you. Perhaps it is more definite than that, and certain special fellow-men come, with footsteps which you can hear, up to your hearts' doors and knock. At first their coming seems to be only an intrusion. Why can they not leave you alone with your great idea? What right have they to claim a share of the sunshine in which you are sitting? But by-and-by you see more wisely. You begin to wonder whether their coming on this side of you is not the true correlative and correspondent of the coming of the vision on the other side of you. You begin to feel that the practical life may be needed to complete the meditative life. If you open the door to your intrusive fellow-men you find that it indeed is so. Your idea of God falling upon the many mirrors of their various needs and natures, gains new interpretations and illuminations. Their human hearts get hold of the reality of God, which they never could have found out for themselves, through your belief in it. And your own life, open on both sides, on this side to the vision, and on that side to the men, grows rich and sacred as being the room in which that most deep and interesting transaction which the world can witness, the meeting of truth with the human mind, takes place.

Truth is vague and helpless until men believe it. Men are weak and frivolous till they believe in truth. To furnish truth to the believing heart, and to furnish believing hearts to truth, certainly there is no nobler office for a human life than that; and the doctrine which I want to preach to you to-day is that the human life or human nature is so made as to fulfil just that office. How can we better tell the story of you who first believe in God yourself and then are drawn out to make your fellow-men believe in Him, and in making them believe in Him find your own belief grow steadier and clearer—how shall we better depict this human life which never learns anything without hearing other human lives clamoring to share the blessings of its knowledge than by recurring to the story of Peter, to whom, "as he thought on the vision, the Spirit said, Behold three men seek thee."

It is illustrated, this central and critical position in which a man may stand, by the way in which the artist stands between the whole world of beautiful ideas and the hard world of matter, in which these ideas at last find their expression through him. The artist dreams his dream, and as he thinks upon the vision, the Spirit says, Behold the marble seeks thee"; and instantly the chisel is in his hand and the work of carving has begun. Ideas would hover like a great vague cloud over a world all hard and gross and meaningless, if it were not for man who brings the fire down and makes the whole of nature significant and vocal. If civilization has changed the face of nature, and out of rocks and trees built monuments and cities, the whole long history is but the record of the meeting within the transmitting intelligence of man of the abstract idea with the adaptable material.

But to return from our illustration to our truth. There are some moments in life when this position of man, as standing between the visions which he has seen and his fellow-men on whom he is to bring them into power, is peculiarly manifest. There are perhaps some young men here to-day who stand just at one of those moments now. When any process of education has been finished, when the college doors have just dismissed their graduate, when the professional student stands upon the brink of the troubled waters of his profession with the calm scholar-days behind him, when the young minister is just feeling the hands of ordination on his bowed head, in all these days how real this sense of the two worlds between which he stands is to any truly thoughtful man. Between the silence and the stir, between the calm accumulation and the active employment of his truth, the young man stands with a strange consciousness which is never so vividly repeated at any other moment of his life. The two worlds, one on each side of him, receive illumination from each other, and this illumination is sent back and forth through him. Truth never seemed so sacred as when he comes in sight of its true uses; and the world never seemed so well worth living for as when he sees how much it needs his truth. Sad is the lot, sad is the nature of any man who can pass through such a moment and not be solemnized and exalted by it. Sad is the man who can graduate from college and go out into the world, and think of his education only as a drudgery from which he has at last escaped, or as an equipment with which he is to earn his daily bread.

Sad is the lot and nature of any man who sees his youth fading back behind him, finds himself growing out of the specially vision-seeing period of life, and counts his visions as they fade, mere pleasant recollections, or, it may be, things to laugh at and to be ashamed of. Sometimes you see a happy man, of whom, as he grows older, nothing of that kind is true. A man we see sometimes who, as he comes to middle-life, finds his immediate enthusiastic sight of ideal things grown dull; that is the almost necessary condition of his ripening life. He does not spring as quickly as he once did to seize each newly offered hope for man. A thousand disenchantments have made him serious and sober. He looks back, and the glow and sparkle which he once saw in life he sees no longer. He wonders at his recollection of himself, and asks how it is possible that life ever should have seemed to him as he remembers that it did seem. But the fact that it really did once seem so to him is his most valued certainty. He would not part with that assurance for anything. All the hard work that he does now is done in the strength and light of that remembered enthusiasm. To have been born into the world as he is now; never to have had any years in which the sky seemed brighter and the fields greener, and man more noble, and the world more hopeful than they seem to-day, would make all life for him another and a drearier thing. Every day the dreams of his boyhood, which seem dead, are really the live inspirations of his life. To such a man there surely came, some day or other in the past, a Peter-hour, a time at which the visions of his youth and the hard work of his manhood met and knew each other. From that time on the power of his vision passed into his work; and now, as, with his calm, dry face, seeming so unemotional, so unmoved, he goes about his labor, doing his duty and serving his generation, it is really the fire of his youth which no longer blazes, but still burns within him that makes the active power of that dry, prudent, conscientious, useful man. Peter plodding over the dusty hills to reach Cornelius, may seem to have lost the glory which was on his face while he sat and thought upon the vision, and caught glimpses of the essential nobleness of man—but the vision was at the soul of his journey all the time, and was what made his journey different from that of any peddler whom he met upon the road.

One longs to speak to men whom the hard work and dry details of life are just claiming, as they are leaving their youth behind and passing into middle life. You may expect to grow less enthusiastic and excited. Do not be surprised at that. But in the meeting of the facts of life with those accumulated convictions which must be the real heart of any true enthusiast, you ought to be growing more and more earnest the longer that you live. There are trees whose fruit does not ripen till their leaves have fallen; but we are sure that the ripe fruit does not laugh at the fallen leaves whose strength it has drawn out into its own perfected shape and color. If you do not see the visions which you saw when you were a boy, that does not prove that the vision was not true. That boy's belief that man is essentially noble, and the world is full of hope, is as genuinely a part of your total life as this man's experience that men will cheat, and that the world's great wheels move very slowly. The emotions grow less eager and excited, but the convictions ought to be growing always stronger—as the kernel ripens in the withering shell. Believe in man with all your childhood's confidence, while you work for man with all a man's prudence and circumspection. Such union of energy and wisdom makes the completest character, and the most powerful life.

I have been wandering a little from my subject. The power of man to stand between abstract truth upon the one side and the concrete facts of life upon the other, comes from the co-existence in his human nature of two different powers, without the possession of both of which no man possesses a complete humanity. One of these powers is the power of knowing, and the other is the power of loving. I ask you to give to both of the words their fullest meaning, and then how rich the nature grows which has them both—this human nature, which is not truly human if either of them be left out.

The power of knowing, however the knowledge may be sought or won, whether by patient study or quick-leaping intuition, including imagination and all the poetic power, faith, trust in authority, the faculty of getting wisdom by experience, everything by which the human nature comes into direct relationship to truth, and tries to learn, and in any degree, succeeds in knowing—that is one necessary element of manhood. And the other is Love, the power of sympathetic intercourse with things and people, the power to be touched by the personal nature with which we have to do—love therefore, including hate, for hate is only the reverse utterance of love, the negative expression of the soul's affection; to hate anything is vehemently to love its opposite. Love thus, as the whole element of personal affection and relationship of every sort, this too is necessary, in order that a man may really be a man. These two together must be in all men. Not merely in the greatest men. It is not a question of greatness, but of genuineness and completeness. Just as the same chemical elements must be in a raindrop that are in Niagara, and, if they are, then the raindrop is as truly water as the cataract; so the power of learning truth and the power of loving man must be in you or me, as well as in Shakspeare or Socrates; and if they are, then we are as genuinely and completely men as Socrates and Shakspeare.

From this it will immediately follow, that the more perfectly these two constituents of human nature meet, the more absolutely they are proportioned to each other, and the more completely they are blended, so much the more ready will the human nature be for the fulfillment of every function of humanity. And if, as we have seen, one of the loftiest functions of humanity is to stand between the absolute truth and the world's needs, and to transmit the one in such way that it can really reach and help the other, then it will also follow that the more perfectly the knowing faculty and the loving faculty meet in any man, the more that man's life will become a transmitter and interpreter of truth to other men.

That sounds like a dry inference; but it is one of which our own dearest experiences have borne to all of us most precious testimony. If you look back to the men who have taught you most, and in the fuller light where you now stand, study their character, you will surely find that the real secret of their power lay here, in the harmonious blending of the knowing and the loving powers in their nature; in the opening of their nature on both sides, so that truth entered in freely here and you entered in freely there, and you and truth met, as it were, familiarly in the hospitality of their great characters. The man who has only the knowing power active, lets truth in, but it finds no man to feed. The man who has only the loving power active, lets man in, but he finds no truth to feed on. The real teacher welcomes both.

You know this in all who are really teachers. It is most clear of all in that highest of all the teacherships which the world has to show, which comes with its blessing to the beginning of every human life which is not by special misfortune poorer than it ought to be. Ask where a mother's power lies, and surely the answer must be that no being like the true mother stands between visions of the highest truths on one side, and a human soul on the other, and offers a nature in which the knowing power and the loving power are kneaded and moulded together into a perfect oneness, into a sacred and pure transparency for the transmission of the first facts of the universe, and God and Life to the intelligence of her child, who lives in her knowledge by her love. The purest mingling of all elements into one character and nature which we can ever see, is in the Christian mother, in whom the knowledge of all that she knows and the love which she feels for her child, make not two natures, as they often do in men, in fathers, but perfectly and absolutely one. She values knowledge not for its own sake, but for her child. She loves him not with the mere animal fondness with which the brute mother loves her child, but as the utterance and revelation of every truth to her. Thus her love and her intelligence are blended perfectly; and the result is that which we know, the wonderful power of the mother's life to bring the deepest, highest, farthest truths, and win for them their first entrance into the nature of her child.

The New Testament tells us of Jesus that He was full of Grace and Truth. Grace and Truth! These are exactly the two elements of which we have been speaking, and it must have been in the perfect meeting of those two elements in him that His mediatorship, His power to transmute the everlasting truths of God into the immediate help of needy men consisted. He was no rapt self-centered student of the abstract truth; nor was he the merely ready sentimental pitier of the woes of men. But in His whole nature there was finely wrought and combined the union of the abstract and eternal with the special and the personal, which made it possible for him, without an effort, to come down from the mountain where he had been glorified with the light of God, and take up instantly the cure of the poor lunatic in the valley; or to descend from the hill where he had been praying, to save his disciples half-shipwrecked on the lake; or to turn his back on the comforting angels of Gethsemane, that he might give himself into the hands of the soldiers who were to lead him to the cross. "While he thought upon the vision, the Spirit said unto him, Behold three men seek thee." Can any words more typically tell the life of Christ than those!

It is a truth which we have all learned from some experience through which we have been led, that any great experience, seriously and greatly met and passed through, makes the man who has passed through it always afterwards a purer medium through which the highest truth may shine on other men. Have you not seen it? Here is some man whom you have known long. You have seemed to have reached the end of all that it is possible for you to get from him, all that it is possible for him to do for you. Nothing has come through him from behind to you. You have seen him. You have seen a sort of glint glimmer of reflection of God's light upon the surface of His life, as the sun might be reflected on a plate of steel. But nothing of God or God's truth has come through him to you as the sun shines through a lens of glass, pouring its increased intensity upon the wood it sets in flame.

But some day you meet that man, and he is altered. Tenderer, warmer, richer, he seems to be full of truths and revelations which he easily pours out to you. Now you not merely see him; you see through him to things behind. As you talk with him, as you look into his face, you see with new surprising clearness what God is, what man is, what a great thing it is to live, what a great thing it is to die, how mysterious and pathetic are sorrow and happiness, and fear and hope. You cannot begin to tell the change by merely thinking that the man has learned some new facts and is telling them to you, as a book might tell them from its printed page. The very substance of the man is altered, so that he stands between the eternal truths and you no longer as a screen, which shuts them from your sight, but as an atmosphere through which they come to you all radiant. You ask what has come to him, and you hear (if you are near enough for him to tell you his most sacred history), of some profound experience. He has passed through an overwhelming sorrow. He has stood upon the brink of some tremendous danger. He has spent a day and a night in the deep of some bewildering doubt. He has been overmastered by some sudden joy. It may have been one of these or another. The result has been in such a change of the very substance of the nature, that, whereas before it was all thick and muddy, so that whatever light fell upon it was either cast aside or else absorbed into it and lost, now it makes truth first visible, and then clear and convincing to the fellow-men who see truth through it.

And when you try to analyze this change, do you not find that it consists in an impregnation of the nature which has had this new experience with two forces—one a love for truth, the other a love for man? and it is in the perfect combination of these two in any life that the clarifying of that life into a power of transmission and irradiation truly lies. What man goes worthily through sorrow and does not come out hating shams and pretences, hungering for truth; and also full of sympathy for his fellow-man whose capacity for suffering has been revealed to him by his own. It is the perfect blending of those two constituents in the new nature of your tried and patient friend which have given him this wondrous power of showing God and truth to you.

What man goes bravely and faithfully through doubt and does not bring out a soul to which truth seems to be infinitely precious, and the human soul the most mysterious, sacred thing in all the world. Out of the union of those two persuasions has come the prophetship of this life which now you cannot look at without seeing the infinite behind it made clear by it.

Surely, if we can believe this, then the way in which God lets his children encounter great, and sometimes terrible, experiences is not entirely inexplicable. Surely if these souls which now are deep in sorrow, or are being cast up and down and back and forth in doubt, are being thus annealed and purified that they may come to be revealers, mediators between God and their fellow-men, then into our wonder at the existence of doubt and sorrow in God's world there comes a little ray of light. Who would not bear anything that could refine his life into fitness for such a privilege as that?

I had meant to speak of several of the special visions which, through the soul that is prepared for such an office, become transformed into influence and blessing to mankind. I can only indicate them in the slightest way. Suppose that God has let you see His goodness. A strong, unalterable persuasion that God is merciful and kind has been poured onto your life, into your mind. That fact itself, once known, absorbs your contemplation. If you and God were all the universe, the knowledge of His goodness would be everything to you. You would sit lonely in the empty world and fill your soul with gazing on the brightness of that truth. So you do sit to-day, as if you and God were indeed alone, and no one in the universe except you two. And then, as you sit so, there comes some sort of appeal from fellow-men. The three men are down at the door while you are dreaming on the housetop. Your child comes to you with some childish joy and wants its explanation; some puzzled neighbor cries across to you, from his life to yours, and wants to know if you have any clue to all this snarl of living. Somehow the cry awakens you, and you go down and put your truth into your brother's hands. At first it seems almost a profanation. The truth is so sacred and seems so thoroughly your own. But as you give it to your brother, new lights come out in it. For God to be good means something more when the goodness turns to new forms of blessing in the new need of this new life. O you who think you know that God is merciful because of the mercy which He has shewed to you, be sure there is a richness in your truth which you have not reached yet, which you will never reach until you let Him make your life the interpreter of His goodness to some other soul!

Or again perhaps the truth which you have learned, the vision which you have seen, is the sinfulness of sin—what a terrible thing it is for any child of God to disobey his Father. Overwhelmed with that knowledge you sit and brood upon your sad estate. I think that all religious history bears witness that that conviction, if it remains purely a personal truth of our own life, certainly grows tyrannical and morbid and brings despair. As soon as it becomes a stimulus, inspiring us to go and help our brethren escape out of their sin, it becomes salutary and blessed. If I knew any soul to-day, haggard and weary with its consciousness of sin and danger, I think that what I would try to do to help it would be this—make it see in its own sinfulness the revelation of the sinfulness of all the world; then let it forget its own sinfulness and keep only the impulse that must come out of its sight of how horrible the world's sin is; then let it go, full of that impulse, and try to save the world. So it must find its own salvation.

So of the truth of immortality. Not as a personal privilege of mine, but as a token of the greatness and worth of the human soul, making every service which I can render to it more imperious and delightful—so do I come to understand with the fullest faith the fact that man never dies.

So of such a truth as the Trinity. Not as a puzzle or a satisfaction of the intellect, but as an expression of the manifold helpfulness with which the divine nature offers itself to the human, so it will be to me the richest and the holiest creed.

There are no limits to our doctrine. Every truth which it is possible for man to know it is good for him to know with reference to his brother men. Only in that way is the truth which he knows kept at its loftiest and purest. This is the daily meaning which I want to find in the picture of Peter sitting before his vision, on the house-top and the three men knocking in the street below.

There is a danger, which we all recognize, of selfishness in our religion. It comes in various forms. It makes one man say: "I am content, for I have seen the Lord." To that man the great host of his fellow-men who need his Lord as much as he, are nothing. He will leave them unheard in the street and sit within, wrapped in the complacency of his assured salvation. Another man says, "What business is it of any one except myself if I close my eyes and do not see the Lord? Does it hurt any one but me? Who has a right to interfere or urge me?" To both of these men is there not a message in the story of Peter which we have been studying this morning? To the first man it says: The seeing of your own vision is but half, and half without the other half grows weak and perishes. Your religion, kept solely for yourself, will certainly decay. Up, up, and go abroad and find the men who need your Christ, to whom you can bring Him, in giving Him to whom alone you can make your own faith in Him complete and strong.

To the other man it says, Indeed it is the business of other men than you, it is the whole world's business whether or not you are a Christian! Indeed it does rob other souls than yours, if you will not live spiritually and see the truth which God is showing to your soul. If there are men whom, being yourself a Christian, you might bring to Christ, then you rob not only yourself but them, if you refuse to come to Christ. The window which makes itself dark, darkens not merely itself, but also all the room into which the light might have shone through it.

I dare to hope that some generous nature may feel this appeal. Be spiritual, be religious, come to Christ. Cast off your sins, not for yourself, but for some soul which possibly may learn from you, what it could not learn in any other way, how good and strong and forgiving is the sinner's God.

It is a terrible thing to have seen the vision, and to be so wrapped up in its contemplation as not to hear the knock of needy hands upon our doors.

It is a terrible thing to hear the knock and have no vision to declare to the one who knocks.

But there is no greater happiness in all the world than for a man to love Christ for the mercy Christ has shown his soul, and then to open his whole heart outward and help to save his brethren's souls with the same salvation in which he rejoices for himself. May none of us go through life so poor as never to have known that happiness.

IS IT I?

"And as they did eat, Jesus said, Verily I say unto you, that one of you shall betray me. And they were exceeding sorrowful, and began every one of them to say unto Him, Lord, is it I?"—MATT. xxvi. 21, 22.

IT WAS a moment of dismay among the disciples of Jesus. Their Master, sitting with them at the supper, had just declared that one of them should commit an act of the basest treachery and betray Him to His enemies. There could be no deed more contemptible. Every obligation of duty and affection was violated by it. One who stood by, in the rude upper chamber where they ate the supper, might well have watched with curiosity to see how these plain men would take the words of Jesus. Will they break out in indignant remonstrance? Will they fall to accusing one another? Will each draw back from his brother apostle in horror at the thought that possibly that brother apostle is the man who is to do this dreadful thing? Instead of these, there is a different result from either, and one that certainly surprises us. Each man's anxiety seems to be turned, not towards his brother, but towards himself, and you hear them asking, one after another, "Lord, is it I?" "Lord, is it I?" Peter, Bartholomew, John, James, Thomas, each speaks for himself, and the quick questions come pouring in out of their simple hearts, "Lord, is it I?" "Lord, is it I?"

Certainly there is something that is strange in this. These men were genuine. There could not be any affectation in their question. A real live fear came over them at Jesus's prophecy. And it was a good sign, no doubt, that the first thought of each of them was about the possibility of his own sin. When a man foresees a great temptation that is coming, it is always better that, instead of turning to his neighbors and saying, as he searches their faces, "I wonder who will do this wicked thing," he should turn to himself and say, "Is it possible that I am the man who will do it?" When the wind is rising it is good for each ship at sea to look to its own ropes and sails, and not stand gazing to see how ready the other ships are to meet it. We all feel that we would rather hear a man asking about himself anxiously than to see him so sure of himself that the question never occurred to him. We should be surer of his standing firm if we saw that he knew he was in danger of a fall. Now, all this is illustrated in Christ's disciples. It must have been that their life with Him had deepened the sense of the mystery of their lives. They had seen themselves, in their intercourse with Him, as capable of much more profound and various spiritual experience than they had thought possible before. And this possible life, this possible experience, had run in both directions, up and down. They had recognized a before unknown capacity for holiness, and they had seen also a before unknown power of wickedness. Their sluggishness had been broken up, and they had seen that they were capable of divine things. Their self-satisfied pride had been broken up, and they had seen that they were capable of brutal things. Heaven and hell had opened above their heads and under their feet. They had not thought it incredible when Christ said, "I go to prepare a place for you, and I will come again and receive you to myself," and now they did not think it incredible when He said, "One of you shall betray me." The life with Christ had melted the ice in which they had been frozen, and they felt it in them either to rise to the sky or to sink into the depths. That was and that always is Christ's revelation of the possibilities of life. To one who really lives with Him the heights above and the depths below both grow more profound. A new goodness and a new badness become possible. He makes men know that they are the children of God, and that as God's children they have a chance to be far better or far worse than they could be when they thought themselves only His slaves. All this Christ did for those first disciples and the same change of life, the same deepening of its possibilities, has come to all who have really lived with Him since then.

There are times in the lives of all of us, I think, when that comes to us which came here to Christ's disciples. Of such times and their position in our lives and their effect upon our lives let us speak this morning. Beneath us as beneath them the worse possibilities of our nature sometimes reveal themselves. There are times when it seems to us not impossible that we should commit very great sins. Just as there are some times when we catch sight of the possibility of holiness which lies above us, and comprehend with rapturous hope how good it is in our power to become; so there are these other times when the mysteriousness of our nature opens its other side, and the crimes and vices, at which we and all men tremble, seem to be not wholly impossible to us. Such times are not our worst times certainly. Often they are times which, by their very sense of danger, are the safest and strongest of our lives. But they are often moments that dismay us. They come in upon our self-complacency and shock it with their ominous presence, these moments when we suspect ourselves and see that inevitably to the power of being very good if we will, is linked the other power of being very bad if we will, too. Let us consider what some of the times are which waken this darker self-consciousness, this sense of our own possibilities of sin.

One of them is the time when we see deep and flagrant sin in some other man. When some great crime is done, when through the community there runs the story of some frightful cruelty, or dreadful fraud, I think that almost all of us are conscious of a strange mixture of two emotions, one of horror and the other of a terrible familiarity. The act is repugnant to all our conscientiousness, but the powers that did the act, and the motives that persuaded the doing of it, are powers which we possess and motives which we have felt. They are human powers and human motives. It is a human act. If we could watch the sinning of another race with a wholly different nature, I think that it would stir no such self-consciousness. If we could stand by and see the wickedness of fiends or fallen angels, it might excite our hatred, our disgust, but it would make no such deep questionings as come when we recognize our own humanity in the sinning man, and find our nature bearing witness that it has in it the same powers by which he has been so wicked. A being of a higher race might see our sin and sorrow with pity, with pain, with wonder; but the pain would be all free from self-reproach, and the wonder would all exhaust itself outside of him. It would be the innocent bewilderment with which I remember, in a picture by Domenichino at Bologna, an angel stands at the foot of the empty cross, and tries with his finger one of the sharp points in the crown of thorns which the Saviour had worn during His passion. It is all a sad inexplicable wonder to him. It appeals to no experience of wickedness and woe in his pure and angelic nature. But when you or I take the crown of thorns into our hands we know in our own hearts the meanness, the jealousy, the hatred which it represents. The possible enemy of righteousness and crucifier of the Saviour stirs to self-consciousness in us. When you read the story of yesterday's defaulter fleeing to-day, an exile and an outcast, or sitting gloomily behind his prison bars, it is not with an angel's innocent wonder what a sin like his can mean; it is with the understanding of a man who has felt the same temptation to which this poor wretch has yielded, that you deplore his fate. It is always the difference between an angel's pity and a man's pity. With simple wonder an angel might walk through our State Prison halls; but a man must walk there full of humbleness and charity; for, as the best man that ever lived finds something of common humanity in us which makes his goodness seem not impossible to us, so the worst of men stirs by the sight of his human sin some sense of what human power of sinfulness we too possess.

2. Another of the occasions which lets us see our own possibility of sin, which opens to us a glimpse of how wicked we might be, is when we do some small sin and recognize the deep power of sinfulness by which we do it. The Bible is full of this idea. Look at Adam with the forbidden apple. Is it only that one sin which terrifies him, and makes him dread the coming of God which had been once the joy of the garden day? Is it not that pressing up behind that sin he sees the long procession of sins which he and his descendants will commit? A boy paints his first stumbling, ill-drawn picture, and, as he gazes at it, he sees, already, the glowing canvas which he is some day to cover. It grows possible to him. A boy makes his first boyish bargain, and the trade-impulse rises in him, and, already, he sees himself a merchant. It is the same thing. A pure, honest boy cheats with his first little timid fraud, and on the other side, the bad side of him, the door flies open and he sees the possibility that he, too, should be the swindler whose enormous frauds make the whole city tremble. The slightest crumbling of the earth under your feet makes you aware of the precipice. The least impurity makes you ready to cry out, as some image of hideous lust rises before you, "Oh, is it I? Can I come to that?"

3. And yet another occasion when we become aware of our own bad possibility is the expression of any suspicion about us by another person. Perfectly unwarrantable and false we may know the charge to be which is brought against us, but the mere fastening of the sin and our name together, the fact that any man could mention the two in the same breath, must turn our eyes in upon ourselves

and set us to asking, "Is it impossible?" "I did not do this thing indeed. My conscience is all clear. I did not commit this cruelty. I did not prove so ungrateful and treacherous as this charge would make me. Perhaps I could not, perhaps I know I could not do this special villainy. But can I blaze up into fiery indignation at men's daring to suspect me without remembering what badness I am capable of. Can I resent suspicion as an angel might, who, standing in the light of God, dreaded and felt no sin?" I think that for you or me to find our names linked to-morrow in this community with some great crime, of which we knew that we were totally innocent, must stir the mystery of our inner life, and make us see what capacity of sin is lying there. I think our disavowal of the sin that we were charged with would be not boisterously angry, but quiet and solemn and humble, with a sense of danger and a gratitude for preservation. I think that ought to be the influence. And even the boisterousness with which some men deny a charge against their characters is still a sign in a worse way of how their conscience has been touched. Would you want the clerk in your store to be charged with dishonesty, and not go back to his work, when the charge had been disproved, with a deepened perception of temptation, and a quickened watchfulness and care?

4. Or yet again. By a strange but very natural process, the same result often comes from just the opposite cause. Not merely when men suspect us and charge us with wrong doing, but when men praise us and say that we are good, this same recognition of how bad we have the power to be often arises. Suppose that you are going on in a dull and lifeless way, not conscious of anything about yourself except just the practical powers by which you do your work from day to day. You have forgotten the mystery of your spiritual life. You have grown wholly unaware of the moral extremes whose folded capacities are in you. You never think how wicked you may be, or how good you may be. "Take thine ease, eat, drink, and be merry." You have come to that. And then suppose that some fellow-being, under the influence of some delusion, begins to praise you. He takes some little thing which you have done; he conceives for it lofty motives which you never dreamed of; he purifies it of all selfishness; he holds it up and says, "See what a true deep spiritual man it must have been that did this thing." What is in your heart as you see your poor little deed held up above the world, shining with

the light that this friend's imagination has thrown into it, and with
the eyes of all men fastened upon it? Is there no shame? You must
be a very poor sort of man if there is not. Is there no breaking up of
the dead equilibrium of self-content? Is it not as if the net in which
a bird had been held, with its wings helpless and useless, were torn
to pieces, and the bird had either to fall to the ground or to fly to the
sky. Its danger and its chance were revealed to it together. A man
comes up to our life and looking round upon the crowd of our fellow-men, he says, "See, I will strike the life of this brother of ours
and you shall hear how true it rings." He does strike it, and it does
seem to them to ring true, and they shout their applause; but we
whose life is struck feel running all through us at the stroke the sense
of hollowness. Our soul sinks as we hear the praises. They start desire but they reveal weakness. No true man is ever so humble and so
afraid of himself as when other men are praising him most loudly.

5. I must name one time more. It is not true that every temptation
which comes to us, however bravely and successfully it may be resisted, opens to us the sight of some of our human capacity of sin.
To resist temptation is never, I think, an exhilarating experience. We
remember too vividly how near we came to yielding. We come out
of battle thankful that we are safe and sound, but the night after the
battle is not a light-hearted or jovial time. There are too many vacant
places in the tent which only yesterday were full. The shriek of the
bullet and the sight of the bursting shell are still too fresh and vivid.
We are too much surprised to find that we are safe. Our escape has
been too narrow. Job, as his wealth rolls back to him, takes it with
thankful hands, but he cannot laugh over it when he remembers
how from the heights of his misery he looked over into the possibility of cursing God. Simeon, when the child Christ is brought to him,
thanks God that he has lived to see the fulfilment of his hopes; but
he may well have remembered how often he had been almost ready
to despair and give up his long watch. Nay, even Jesus Himself, what
shall we think was the kind of step with which He came down the
mountain? He had seen Satan. He had seen with what greedy and
confident eyes Satan looked at that humanity of His, as if it were
something that belonged to Him. Nay, in His own humanity He
had felt a treacherous something, that was ready to respond to
Satan and to own his mastery. Strong and victorious He came away.
But was there no new solemn insight into this humanity which He

had taken? Was not the Incarnation more than ever awful to the Incarnate One? He, the sinless, had gone up and looked over the edge into the deepest depths of sin. He needed the ministry of angels, and He surely came down the mountain serious and sad. And so it is with you, when you follow your Lord into that experience. It may be that you come out by His grace pure and thankful, but you come out like Him, serious and sad, for you have looked down as He looked into the possibility of sin. The man who dares to laugh at a temptation which he has felt and resisted is not yet wholly safe out of its power.

I name these times then in which the possibility of our own great wickedness appears to us. No doubt the list might be made longer, but these are enough. When other men sin flagrantly; when we sin in any degree; when men suspect us although we are innocent; when men praise us; when we are tempted and resist,—at all those times the ground opens under our feet, and, though we stand safe and firm, we see whither we might have fallen. What is this but saying that in every serious moment of life the possibility of sin stands up before us? None but the man who has no serious moments, none but he who makes all life a play, escapes the sight. To every other man, nay, may we not say to every man, since no man is literally always a trifler, to every man at some time the clouds roll back, the spell is broken, and he sees what a power of being wicked as of being good belongs to him just as man. And now is it good for him to see this? Will it help him or harm him? Perhaps it is a question that is needless. He cannot help himself. He must see it. When it has once opened on him, he cannot shut his eyes and forget it if he would. He will see it still behind his folded lids. But still we may ask the question: Will it help or harm him? And that will depend upon the way it works in him. It may become in him either paralysis or inspiration. One man sees his danger and stands powerless. Another man sees his danger and every faculty is strung to its intensest strength. It is like the way in which the knowledge of the shortness of life may affect a man. One man it fills with dismay; another man it turns into a hero. What you want in both cases is to realize the conviction as a motive, and not as a mere emotion. I remember reading of how some one once asked a veteran surgeon what was the effect of the constant sight of human pain which filled his life,—how he could bear it. And his answer was wise and philosophical. He said that, as near as he could state it, the sight of pain ceased with the surgeon to act as a source of emotion, but continued to be effective as a motive for action. The misery at seeing it passed away, but the desire to relieve it grew stronger and stronger. So I think it is with the best sense of our danger of sin. Not as an emotion, not as something that we sit down and weep over, but as a motive, as something that makes us watch and work and pray, does it do its best work for us. The knees need not tremble, nor the heart grow sick. If the feet are set more resolutely toward goodness, and the hands lay hold more firmly upon help, it is good for us to know how wicked we may be, how great our danger is.

And what is it that makes that difference? How is the consciousness of our danger prevented from becoming a depressing emotion and turned into an inspiring motive? It must be by opening the life upon the other side. It must be by realizing the possibilities of our human life for good as well as for evil, by seeing and never forgetting how good we have a chance to be, as well as how bad we may become. This is the power of hope; and hope is the true master of fear. Hope uses fear. It demands its service by a natural right. It is fear's essential superior. Under hope fear works well. But in a life that has no hope fear is a surly tyrant. Now our human nature cannot bear being shut up in its present condition. No man's nature can. Your nature feels its own mysterious capacities too much to believe for a moment that it can be nothing different from what it is. It crowds and presses for an outlet. If it can find an outlet only on the lower side, toward its possibility of sinfulness, it will go forth there and contemplate the evil that lies within its power until it grows into stony hopelessness. But if it finds an opening on the upper side of its present condition, it prefers that, and going out there, aspiring instead of despairing, it is simply driven on toward that which it is already seeking, by the knowledge of what lies behind it if by any chance it should fall back. This is always the relation between hope and fear in healthy life. A merchant hopes to be rich, and the fear of being poor, instead of being a vexing anxiety, becomes the humble servant of his expectation, and helps him on toward wealth. The fear of death is terrible to a sick man until the hope of life and strength and activity opens before him; and then in his convalescence the fear of death has ceased to depress him as a feeling, and only remains with him as a motive to caution and watchfulness. Thus fear is always good when it has hope to rule it. And now if you saw a young man overwhelmed with the sight on which our eyes have been fixed to-day; if you saw him so full of the consciousness of the power of sin in his life, the possibility of the badness that he might do and be, that he was wretched and paralyzed, what would you do for him? Would you try to make him forget what he had seen? Would you try to shut out the mystery of his life from him, and make him live again the life of narrow satisfaction in the present which he lived before he looked down into the deep gulf? You could not do it; but if you could would it be well? Surely not. What you need to do for him is to make him lift up his eyes and see the heights above him. You want to make him like the climber on a ladder, who looks up and not down, who climbs not to escape the gulf below him, but to reach the top above him, and who feels the gulf below him only as a power that makes the hold of foot and hand on every round of the ladder which they strike more firm. Now it is the glory of the Christian Gospel that in the treatment of man's spiritual nature it preserves this true relation between hope and fear perfectly. Christ is the very embodiment of what I have just now been saying. Read your New Testament. As the man who feels its influence leaves his sin and strives towards holiness, what is the power of his progress? Is it the fear of what he leaves behind? Is it not always primarily the desire for the holiness he seeks? And yet the saved of the Saviour as He is borne onward into His salvation never can lose the sense of the great deep below him, into which he must fall if he lets the Saviour go. But that sense only tightens more closely the grasp of the hands which have first seized the hope that was set before them out of ardent desire. This, I am sure, is always the proportion of the Gospel. "Flee from the wrath to come" is always an ally and humble servant of the great "Come unto me." "Come unto me" might stand alone, even if there were no "Flee from the wrath to come." But what would "Flee from the wrath to come" be without "Come unto me"? One is almost ready to say: Better lose sight of the mysterious capacity of life altogether, than to see only one side of it. Hide your eyes. Forget that you are a sinner; never dare look down and see what a sinner you may be, if there is no Saviour from your sin. But if there is, and if you see Him, then feel the depth below you and let it make you cling to Him more closely; realize the power of sinfulness, which has in it the cruelty and falseness and impurity of the worst men that have lived, that you may realize also the power of holiness which has in it the truth and bravery and gentleness of all the saints; let the gulf under your feet measure for you the sky overhead. Know what a sinner you might have been only that you may know more deeply and gratefully the salvation which has saved you.

I suggested just now the analogy between our physical and moral consciousness, between our consciousness of the power to be sick and the consciousness of the power to sin. It is an analogy which illustrates what I have just been saying. There is a nervousness about health which is all morbid. It is full of imaginations. There are people who can never hear a disease described without thinking that they have it. They never hear a sick man talk without feeling all his symptoms repeated in themselves. You think of such a person and realize his wretchedness. Then you look away from him to a perfectly healthy man who seldom thinks about being sick at all. But yet he is something different from what he would be if there were no power of sickness in him. Unconscious for the most part, but now and then coming forth into consciousness, there is always present with him a sense of his humanity with all the liabilities which that involves. He does not do what a man would do who had literally a frame of iron. And that is just the condition of the man with the healthy soul. He does not nervously believe, when he hears of any flagrant crime, that he is just upon the brink of that crime himself. He lives in doing righteousness, but all the time he keeps the consciousness that sin, even out to its worst possibilities, sin even to the cruelty of Cain, the lust of David, the treachery of Judas, is open to him. This consciousness surrounds all his duty. His righteousness is not an angel's righteousness. It is always a man's righteousness, always pervaded, solemnized, strengthened, ay, sweetened to him by the knowledge that there is a bad corresponding to every good, and that he might do one instead of the other just because he is a man.

I do not care to go one step into the theological mysteries of compelling grace and final perseverance. I do not care to ask whether it is possible for man, still being man, to come to such a point that this of which I have spoken to-day, this possibility of flagrant and terrible sin, should utterly and absolutely be left behind and pass away. I think that what I have been saying lately shows us that a man, as the power of the hope of holiness takes stronger and stronger hold upon him, does pass more and more out of the fear of sin. And since his hope of holiness always comes to him as the gift of God, and depends on his dependence on God, we can see that as man by experience grows sure of God, and morally certain that he never can be separated from Him, he passes to a profound belief that he will not fall into the flagrant sin, which yet, because he is a man, remains possible for him. This moral certainty of his comes from his confidence in God. It is not confidence in himself. Here it seems to me is the true escape from whatever has seemed harsh or hopeless in the truth which I have preached to you to-day. The disciples heard Jesus tell of the coming treason, and each of them thought with horror that he might be the traitor. "Lord, is it I?" and "Is it I?" they cried. They knew that they loved their Lord, but they dared not be sure that they would not desert Him. Sufficient spiritual light had come to them to make them see the mystery of their own hearts. Once, before they had this spiritual light, they would have cast aside such a suspicion as an insult. "Am I not an honorable man?" "Is not such a mean act impossible for me?" Now Christ in showing them their higher chance has shown them their lower chance, their danger too, and each wonders whether it can be he who is to do this dreadful thing. Now open a later page of the apostolic history and hear St. Paul writing to his Romans: "Who shall separate us from the love of Christ? Shall tribulation, or distress, or persecution, or famine, or nakedness, or peril, or the sword? Nay, in all these things we are more than conquerors through Him who loved us." See what a change. Here is confidence! Here is a moral certainty! Whoever else may turn traitor, Paul is sure that it will not be he. But it is confidence—not in himself nor in his manliness or honor—only in Christ and in the power of His grace and love. "More than conqueror," but "more than conqueror through Him who loved us." Is there not here the beautiful progress of a moral nature as regards the whole matter of confidence? At the first a pure blank self-reliance, the solid and unbroken self-content of a man who thinks himself able to meet and conquer all temptations. Then an insight into the mysterious capacity of sinning, which breaks and scatters the confidence in self, and leaves the poor soul full of fears and doubts. Then an entrance into Christ and His love and power, where the soul, given to Him, finds a new confidence in His strength, and is sure with a sureness which has no warrant but its trust in Him.

Have you ever watched one of the waterfalls that come over the perpendicular side of a steep mountain? Do you remember how it changes from the top to the bottom of its fall. At first where it comes over the brink it is one solid mass of dark-green water, compact and all sure of itself. Then half-way down the perpendicular face over which it descends, see what a change has come. Its solidness has gone. It is all mist and vapor. You can hardly find it. Only like a thin haze it hangs in front of the dark rock behind it. But once more, as it gets farther down, see how it gathers again. The mist collects, and is once more a stream; a new solidity appears; and at the mountain's foot the brook, restored out of its distraction, starts singing on its way down the bright valley, white still with the memory of the confusion into which it has been thrown. So is it with the confidence of man. It begins full of self-trust. It scatters and seems lost as his experience deepens and he learns his own possibility of sin. It is gathered anew and goes out in happiness and helpfulness when he finds Christ and gives his poor bewildered and endangered soul into His love for keeping.

This is the Bible picture of human life. Where shall we look for any other that is as reasonable or as complete? The fearless truster of himself; the distressed doubter of himself; the faithful truster of Christ! They are all here. We lay the Bible picture down beside our human life and it explains everything. In life, too, there is the stout believer in himself, the frightened disbeliever in himself, and the sure believer in God. As a man comes into Christ, that experience deepens itself around him till he has fulfilled it all. First, a stripping away of his own righteousness, and then a clothing with the righteousness which is in Jesus. First, a light thrown upon himself, till it seems as if there were no wickedness he might not do, and then a drawing of his self into Christ's self till he sees there is no holiness which he may not attain. First, the weakness which comes of self-knowledge, and then the strength which is "strong in the Lord and in the power of His might." First, the fear which cries, "Is it I?" as it hears the announcement of some dreadful sin; and then the wondering faith which cries, "Is it I?" as the doors are opened and they who are Christ's are called to enter in to His everlasting life.

THE SEA OF GLASS
MINGLED WITH FIRE

"And I saw as it were a sea of glass mingled with fire, and them that had gotten the victory over the beast" . . . *stand on the sea of glass, having the "harps of God."*—Revelation xv. 2.

WITH all the mysteriousness of the Book of the Revelation, one thing we are sure of; that in it we have the summing up of the moral processes of all time. There may or may not be a more special meaning discoverable in its pictures, but this there certainly is. Many people find great pleasure in tracing out elaborate analogies between its phophecies and certain particular events in the world's career. "Here," they cry, pointing to some particular event of contemporary history, "do you not see that this is what these chapters mean?" —"Yes," we may generally answer, "they very possibly do mean that, but they mean so much besides that. They mean that, and all other events in which the same universal and eternal causes were at work. These special examples fall in under them, but do not certainly exhaust their application. They are much larger and include much more. They take in the whole circle of great spiritual and moral principles."

In this way I look at, and shall ask you this afternoon to study with me, the verse which is our text. I take it to represent, in a highly figurative way, the result of all moral contest. We may call that our subject.

It surely is no unimportant one. It is a subject that ought to touch all of us very closely, to waken our interest and deep anxiety. I am not to speak to you of imaginary or unreal conditions, not of unheard of depths of sin, or unimagined heights of holy rapture, but only of moral contest, of this struggle with suffering and wickedness, of trial, of that state which every earnest man who is conscious of his own inner life at all knows full well. What is to be the end of it all? How is it all coming out? These are the questions for which I find some suggestion of an answer in the pictorial prophecy of St. John.

They who had gotten the victory over the Beast stood on a sea of glass, mingled with fire. What is the meaning of this imagery? I confess that I do not pretend to know in full what is intended in the Revelation by this term "the Beast." But on the principle which I just stated, I think it certainly means in its largest sense the whole power of evil in all its earthly manifestations; everything that tempts the soul of man to sin or tries his constancy with suffering. Others assert more personal meanings for the name. One very large school says that it means the Church of Rome; another set of commentators used to make "the Beast" to be Napoleon the Third. Perhaps the name may well include them both, in so far as both stand for badness and mischief in the world; but for our present purpose at least, it will be well not to meddle with any of that sort of partial, precarious interpretation, but to hold what certainly is true, that "the Beast," in its largest sense, means all that is beastly, all that is low and base and tries to drag down what is high and noble; all sin and temptation; and so that "they who have gotten the victory over the Beast," are they who have come out of sin holy, and out of trial pure, and out of much tribulation have entered into the kingdom of heaven.

These are to walk upon "a sea of glass, mingled with fire." What does that imagery mean? The sea of glass, the glassy sea, with its smooth transparency settled into solid stillness without a ripple or the possibility of a storm, calm, clear, placid—evidently that is the type of repose, of rest, of peace. And fire, with its quick, eager, searching nature, testing all things, consuming what is evil, purifying what is good, never resting a moment, never sparing pain; fire, all through the Bible, is the type of active trial of every sort, of struggle. "The fire shall try every man's work of what sort it is." "The sea of glass," then, "mingled with fire," is repose mingled with struggle. It is peace and rest and achievement, with the power of trial and suffering yet alive and working within it. It is calmness still pervaded by the discipline through which it has been reached.

This is our doctrine—the permanent value of trial—that when a man conquers his adversaries and his difficulties, it is not as if he never had encountered them. Their power, still kept, is in all his future life. They are not only events in his past history, they are elements in all his present character. His victory is colored with the hard struggle that won it. His sea of glass is always mingled with fire, just as this peaceful crust of the earth on which we live, with its wheat fields, and vineyards, and orchards, and flower-beds, is full still of the power of the convulsion that wrought it into its present shape, of the floods and volcanoes and glaciers which have rent it, or drowned it, or tortured it. Just as the whole fruitful earth, deep in its heart, is still mingled with the ever-burning fire that is working out its chemical fitness for its work, just so the life that has been overturned and overturned by the strong hand of God, filled with the deep revolutionary forces of suffering, purified by the strong fires of temptation, keeps its long discipline forever, roots in that discipline the deepest growths of the most sunny and luxuriant spiritual life that it is ever able to attain.

How wide this doctrine is. The health of the grown man is something different from the health of the little child, because it has been reached through so many strains and tests and dangers. His strong body carries within it not only the record, but the power of all that it has passed through. His bones are strong by every tug and wrench and burden they have borne. His pulse beats even and true with the steady purposeful power which it has learned from many a period of feverish excitement. His blood flows cool, his eye is clear with the simple and healthy action which they have gathered out of many a time of danger that has come since the rosy untried health of babyhood. He is stronger by the accumulated strength of trial. His sea of glass is mingled with fire.

So take the strong man who has won a large property through many disappointments and reverses, and compare him with the baby of fortune who has just dropped by inheritance into money which he never earned. Compare the rich fathers who have made the fortunes with the rich sons who spend them. Is there no keener and more intelligent sense of the value of money in one than in the other? Sometimes indeed the sense is only keener and not more intelligent. Sometimes the father is a miser, while the son is a pattern of judicious liberality. These differences are personal; but always, either for good or bad, the old contest, the long, hard days of patience, the courage, the perseverance which earned the fortune color its whole possession and use. The repose of old age is full of the character that came from the early struggle. The sea of glass is mingled with fire.

Or shall we take the man whose life has known bereavement, who has passed sometime through those days and nights which I may not try to describe to you, but which come up to so many of you as I say the old word, death? Days and nights when he watched the slow untwisting of some silver cord on which his very life was hung, or suddenly felt the golden bowl dash down and broken of which his very life had drank. The first shock became dulled. The first agony grew calm. The lips subsided into serenity. But was there not something in him that made him greater and purer and richer than of old; something that let any one see who watched the change, that it was "better to have loved and lost than never to have loved at all." A whole new quality, that rich quality which the Bible calls by its large word "patience," the power of his trial, was in his new serenity, until he died. His sea of glass was always mingled with fire.

So it is with the world; so it is with nations. A people that has fought for its life, that has had its institutions and ideas subjected to the fiery ordeal, can never be again what it has been. It is not simply older by so many years, but deeper and truer by so much suffering. Besides the mere value which men learn to put into what they have had to fight for, however worthless it may be in itself, the nation that has been saved by struggle, if it has faith enough to believe that it was really saved by struggle and not by accident, by the strength of its ideas and not by the chance turning of the weathercock of battle, must always, in whatever times of peace may follow, deal with its ideas with greater reverence for the strength that has come out of them in war. Under its safest security it will always want to feel still the capacity for the same vigorous self-defence if it should ever again be needed. Thus its sea of glass will always be mingled with fire.

These are all illustrations of our doctrine. But the trouble will be that, however much we recognize the general rule, the exceptions to it, the variations in the effect of trial upon character, will be so numerous as to perplex us. We meet with so many people whose character seems not to be elevated or fired, but depressed and smothered by suffering. They come out of adversity apparently with a great loss of what was noblest and most attractive in them before. Men who were smooth and gracious in health, become rough and peevish in sickness. Men who were cordial and liberal in wealth, turn proud and reserved and close as poverty overtakes them. If trial kindles and stirs up some sluggish natures, on the other hand it quenches and subdues many vigorous and ardent hearts and sends

them crushed and self-distrustful to their graves. It seems sometimes as if trouble, trial, suffering were in the world like the old
fabulous river in Epirus of which the legend ran that its wonderful
waters kindled every unlighted torch that was dipped into them,
and quenched every torch that was lighted.

But however much difficulty this may give us in single cases, it
falls in well with our general doctrine. For it makes trial an absolutely necessary element in all perfected character. If so much
character does really go to pieces at its first contact with suffering
and struggle, then all the more, no matter how terrible the waste
may be, we see the need of keeping struggle and suffering as tests
of character. We see that to sweep them away would be both an insult and a cruel harm to the nature which was meant to meet them,
to crush and conquer and analyze them, to assimilate their strength
out of them as a plant assimilates the nutriment out of the hindering ground through which it has to fight its way up into the sunshine, and to grow strong by struggle. You may just fling your
seed upon the surface, and it will easily come to a sort of sickly ger-
mination. It has no earth to fight its way through, but then it has no
earth to feed on, either; and the first of it is almost the last of it too.

We cannot exaggerate the importance of the change which
comes to pass in a man's life when he once thoroughly has learnt
this simple truth. Disappointments of every sort, sorrows, sufferings, trials, struggles, restlessness and dissatisfaction, false friends,
poor health, low tastes and standards all about us—who shall enu-
merate the million forms, new to each man's new appreciation, in
which life is to each man dark and not bright, bitter and not
sweet? Who shall catalogue the troubles of human life? But who
shall tell the difference between two men who live in different
aspects of all these things? Are they intrusions, accidents, thwartings
and disappointments of the will of God? Or are they (this is what
our doctrine says they are) Messiahs, things sent, having like the
ships that sail to our ports from far-off lands of barbarian richness,
rare spices and fragrant oils and choice foods that we cannot find at
home, whose foreign luxuriance forces its odorous way through
the coarse and uncouth coverings in which their wealth was packed
away in the savage lands from which they came? Are they prolific
sources of spiritual culture, contributing what our best happiness
could not have except from them, the energy and vitality which

there is no way of stirring up in human nature but by some sense of danger, the fire to mingle with the glass.

In sick-rooms, in prisons, in dreary, unsympathetic homes, in stores where failure brooded like the first haze of a coming eastern storm, everywhere where men have suffered, to some among the sufferers this truth has come. They lifted their heads up and were strong. Life was a new thing to them. They were no longer the victims of a mistaking chance or of a malignant devil, but the subjects of an educating God. They no longer just waited doggedly for the trouble to pass away. They did not know that it ever would pass away. If it ever did it must go despoiled of its power. Whether it passed or stayed, that was not the point, but that the strength that was in it should pass into the sufferer who wrestled with it; that the fire should not only make the glass and then go out, leaving it cold and hard and brittle. The fire must abide in the glass that it has made, giving it forever its own warmth and life and elastic toughness. This is the great revelation of the permanent value of suffering and struggle.

But some lives still grow old, some men live strongly and purely in this world, you say, and then go safely and serenely up to heaven, who have no struggle anywhere, who never know what struggle is. What shall we say of them? How are they ripened and saved? How does the fire get into their sea of glass? Ah, my dear friend, first you must find your man. And you may search all the ages for him. You may go through the crowded streets of heaven, asking each saint how he came there, and you will look in vain everywhere for a man morally and spiritually strong, whose strength did not come to him in struggle. Will you take the man who never had a disappointment, who never knew a want, whose friends all love him, whose health never knew a suspicion of its perfectness, on whom every sun shines and against whose sails all winds, as if by special commission, are sent to blow, and who still is great and good and true and unselfish and holy, as happy in his inner as in his outer life? Was there no struggle there? Do you suppose that man has never wrestled with his own success and happiness, that he has never prayed, and emphasized his prayer with labor, "In all time of my prosperity, Good Lord, deliver me!—"Deliver me!"—that is the cry of a man in danger, of a man with an antagonist. For years that man and his prosperity have been looking each other in the face and grappling one another. Whether he should rule it or it should rule him, that was the question. He saw plenty of men whose prosperity ruled them, had them for its slaves, bound them, and drove them, and beat them, and taunted them, mocked them with the splendid livery it made them wear, which was only the symbol of their servitude to it; that dreadful prosperity of theirs which they must obey, no matter what it asked of them, to which they must give up soul and body. He was determined it should not be so with him. He wrestled with his prosperity and mastered it. His soul is not the slave of his rich store or of his comfortable house. They are the slaves of his soul. They must minister to its support and culture. *He* rules *His*, and that is a supremacy that was not won without a struggle, than which there in no harder on the earth.

So that even here there is no exception. There is no exception anywhere. Every true strength is gained in struggle. Every poor soul that the Lord heals and frees goes up the street like the man at Capernaum, carrying its bed upon its back, the trophy of its conquered palsy. There are no glassy seas which will really bear the weight of strong men but those that have the fiery mingling. All others are counterfeits, and crack or break.

There are several special applications of our doctrine to the Christian life, which it is interesting to observe.

I. It touches all the variations of Christian feeling. In almost every Christian's experience comes times of despondency and gloom, when there seems to be a depletion of the spiritual life, when the fountains that used to burst and sing with water are grown dry; when love is loveless, and hope hopeless, and enthusiasm so utterly dead and buried that it is hard for us to believe that it ever lived. At such times there is nothing for us to do but hold with eager hands to the bare rocky truths of our religion as a shipwrecked man hangs to a strong ragged cliff when the great retiring wave and all the little eddies all together are trying to sweep him back into the deep. The rough rock tears his hands, but still he clings to it. And so the bold bare truths of God and Christ, of responsibility and eternity, unclothed for the time of all the dearness that they used to have, however sometimes we have just to clutch and hold fast by them in our darkness to keep from being swept off into recklessness and despair. Then when the tide returns, and we can hold ourselves lightly where we once had to hang heavily, when faith grows easy and God and Christ and responsibility and eternity are once more the glory and delight of happy days and peaceful nights, then certainly there is something new in them, a new color, a new warmth. The soul has caught a new idea of God's love when it has not only been fed but rescued by Him. The sheep has a new conception of his shepherd's care when he has not merely been made "to lie down in green pastures," but also has heard the voice of him who had left the ninety and nine in the wilderness and gone after that which had wandered astray until he found it. The weakness of our own nature and the strength of that on which we rely: danger and its correlative, duty; watchfulness, and its great privilege, trust, come in together, and are the new life of the soul, the active power in its restored peace, the fire in its glassy sea.

The same applies to doubt and belief. "Why do things seem so hard to me?" you say; "why does every conceivable objection and difficulty start up in a moment, just as soon as I attempt to lay hold upon the Christian's faith? Why is it so easy for these others to believe, so hard for me?" One cannot answer certainly until he knows you better. There is a willful and an unwilling unbelief. If it is willful unbelief, the fault is yours. Man must not certainly complain that the sun does not shine on him, because he shuts his eyes. But if it is unwilling unbelief; if you really want the truth; if you are not afraid to submit to it as soon as you shall see it, and it is something in your constitution, or in your circumstances, or in the side of Christian truth that has been held out to you that makes it more difficult for you to grasp it than your neighbor; then you are not to be pitied. You have a higher chance than he. To climb the mountain on its hardest side, where its rough granite ribs press out most ruggedly to make your climbing difficult, where you must skirt round chasms and clamber down and up ravines, all this has its compensations. You know the mountain better when you reach its top. It is a realler, a nobler, and so a dearer thing.

If there be such here, let me speak to them. The world has slowly learnt that Christianity is true. If you learn slowly, it is only the old way over again. The man who learns slowly learns completely, if he learns at last at all. If you can only keep on bravely, perseveringly, seeking the truth, saying I must have it or I die; saying that till you do die; dying at last, if needs be, in the search; then I declare not only that somewhere, here or in some better world, the truth shall come to you; but that when it comes the peace and the serenity of it shall be made vital with the energy of your long search. Yours shall be that faith with which a pure, truth-loving soul may stand unashamed before the throne of God, and hear his work called "Well-done," and blessed and consecrated to perpetual value. You will believe better even in heaven for these earthly difficulties bravely met. For perfect truthfulness must find the truth at last, or where is God?

As we look out, the applications of our doctrine widen everywhere. What is the whole history of the world under the Gospel of forgiveness, from its first to its last, but one vast application of it. Here are men whose condition as perverted, mistaken, sinful beings makes it absolutely necessary that the dispensation that shall save them must be one not of mere culture and development but of rescue and repentance. Let the great future of those men be what it will; let the sublimest regions of calm unbroken holiness be reached in some celestial sphere; let truth and godliness become the atmosphere and the unconscious life-blood of the perfected man, still the perfected man must carry somewhere in the nature which holds high converse with the angels and worships with affectionate awe close to the throne of God, the story of its sin and its escape. Redeemed, its great redemption must forever be the shaping and the coloring element of all its glorious life. "Worthy is He who hath redeemed us"—that song the purest lips and the most exalted heart never will outgrow.

Simon Peter is forgiven, re-adopted, becomes the preacher of the first sermon, the converter of the first Gentiles, the founder of churches, the writer of epistles, the champion of faith; but he is always, to the last, the same Simon Peter who denied his Master and struggled with himself in all the bitterness of tears, upon the crucifixion night. Paul mounts up to the third heaven, hears wonderful voices, sees unutterable things, can give in bold humility the autobiography of the eleventh chapter to the Corinthians, but he never ceases to be the Paul who stood by at the stoning of Stephen, and had his great darkness rent asunder by the bright light that he saw upon the road from Jerusalem to Damascus. You and I, brethren, come by Christ's grace into sweet communion with God, but the power of our conversion—does it ever leave us? Are not we prodigals still, with the best robe and the ring and the shoes upon us, and the fatted calf before us in our father's house, conscious always that our filial love is full of the strength of hard repentance which first made us turn our faces homeward from among the swine? And so the saved world never can forget that it was once the lost world. All of a history such as its has been accumulates, and none of it is lost. It will forever shine with a peculiar light, sing a psalm among its fellows that shall be all its own. The redeemed world—all the strong vitality which that name records, will be the fire that will mingle with the glassy serenity of its obedient and rescued life.

Here then we have the picture of the everlasting life. What will heaven be? What will be the substance on which they shall stand who worship God and praise him in the ages of eternity? I find manifold fitness in the answer that tells us that it shall be a "sea of glass mingled with fire." Is it not a most graphic picture of that experience of rest always pervaded with activity; of calm, transparent contemplation, always pervaded and kept alive by eager work and service, which is our highest and most Christian hope of heaven? Let us be sure that our expectations regarding heaven are scriptural and true. Heaven will not be pure stagnation, not idleness, not any mere luxurious dreaming over the spiritual repose that has been safely and forever won; but active, tireless, earnest work; fresh, live enthusiasm for the high labors which eternity will offer. These vivid inspirations will play through our deep repose and make it more mighty in the service of God than any feverish and unsatisfied toil of earth has ever been. The sea of glass will be mingled with fire.

Here too we have the type and standard of that heavenliness of character which ought to be ripening in all of us now, as we are getting ready for that spiritual life. As men by the grace of God gradually win the "victory over the beast," they begin already to walk upon the sea of glass mingled with fire. Let this be the lesson with which we close our thoughts upon our text. Surely, dear friends, there is a very high and happy life conceivable, which very few of us attain, and yet which our religion most evidently intends for all of us. Calm and yet active, peaceful and yet thoroughly alive, resting always completely upon truth, but never sleeping on it for a moment, working always intensely, but serene and certain of results, never driven crazy by our work, grounded and settled, yet always moving forward in still but sure progress, always secure, yet always alert—glass mingled with fire.

That life which we dream of in ourselves we see in Jesus. Where was there ever gentleness so full of energy? What life as still as his was ever so pervaded with untiring and restless power? Who ever knew the purposes for which he worked to be so sure, and yet so labored for them as if they were uncertain? Who ever believed his truths so entirely, and yet believed them so vividly as Jesus? Such perfect peace that never grew listless for a moment; such perfect activity that never grew restless or excited; these are the wonders of the life of Him who going up and down the rugged ways of Palestine, was spiritually walking on "the sea of glass mingled with fire."

As more and more we get the victory over the beast, we too are lifted up to walk where he walked. For this all trial, all suffering, and all struggle are sent. May God grant us all much of that grace through which we can be "more than conquerors through him who loved us," and so begin now to "walk with him in white," upon "the sea of glass mingled with fire."

INDIVIDUAL AND COLLECTIVE HUMANITY

"Jesus then lifted up his eyes and saw a great company."—JOHN vi. 5.

THE sight of a crowd of human beings always is impressive. The crowd may be of any sort and gathered on any occasion. It may be a great, rapt multitude listening together to exalted and exalting music. It may be a mob, wild and tumultuous with passion. It may be an army marching like one great, marvellous machine, to meet the enemy. It may be the chance gathering of passengers whom some accidental obstruction has stopped upon the street. Whatever be its cause, it is a crowd; and it is interesting to any truly human soul that stands and watches it. It is not simply for the special thoughts which it suggests. It is not Xerxes weeping at the sight of the army of which in a few years no man will be left alive. It is not so definite as that. It is the general sense of human life, the very essence of this mysterious and mighty thing, apart from particular conditions, apart from curious speculations upon it. It is the fact of life laid on the heart of the living man that makes the interest of a great crowd. A sensitive child will feel it. It is in some sense the personal impression broadened and deepened and richened; but there is also something in it which no contact with the individual produces,—a pure impression of humanity, as if you were able to extricate from all its entanglements the one essential, universal quality which makes a man a man; and, making it concrete and visible, yet preserving all the broadness of abstraction, to hold it before your eyes and let it impress itself upon your heart.

This is the general impressiveness of a crowd. But, no doubt, the impression cannot be uniform. It must vary with the character of the observer, of the human being upon whom the impression falls. In the words of my text, Christ is the Observer. He has crossed the sea of Tiberias with His disciples. He is sitting on a hillside of the Eastern country. He has been pondering, and perhaps praying. By and by He lifts up His eyes and sees a great company. The multitude whom He left beyond the lake has followed Him across, and He is face to face with them again. He cannot escape from men. Then He accepts them into His life and deals with them. And we can feel, I think, that as they impress themselves on Him we are getting, as it were, the largest and truest impression which humanity has ever made on man. That which I tried to say just now of the essential life making itself known, must have been more real with Jesus Christ than with any other watcher of his fellow-men that ever lived; for here was Man in His completeness receiving men in their completeness. More and more we come to see that this was what the Incarnation meant. It was the Son of man, in whom the whole of all the life of man was gathered up, who sat and watched the multitude and first realized Himself in them, and then knew them in Himself as they had never been known before.

Let us think for a while about Christ looking upon a crowd of men. And first, let us try to see the picture which is in the words with which the scene is introduced to us. It is an old Bible phrase, one that recurs very often in the Bible story, in which the Saviour is described as "lifting up his eyes" to see the people. The picture is of a man sitting with his eyes bent down. He is in thought and contemplation. He is seeing with the inward sight. He is seeing the invisible. He is looking at truth. He is questioning Himself. So sitting, Jesus is the type of all introspection and meditation and study, of all that occupation of mankind which is turned away from active human life and is dwelling on the unseen things. We recognize at once the quiet, absorbed Figure on the hillside.

Do we not also recognize at once the quick response with which, in answer to the bustling feet of the approaching crowd, Christ turns and looks up, and listens and is ready for them, and gives Himself in answer to their claim. He is theirs. No self-indulgence, even in the deepest thought or highest vision, even in prayer to His Father, must make Him deaf or blind to human life appealing to Him and requiring His help. Therefore He lifts up His eyes.

Could the conditions and obligations of our human life be more vividly set forth than here? There is no study or dream, no meditation or prayer, which must not hold itself subject to the demand of men. It is not simply that the dream or study is less important, and must sacrifice itself when the human need requires; it is more than that. It is that the study and the dream need for their rectification and fulfilment this readiness to report themselves to man and his nature. They must justify and know themselves before the face of human life looking to them out of its anxieties and hopes.

The illustrations of this are everywhere. Philosophers study and ponder to adjust their system of the universe to man. They cannot, they must not, be satisfied with their systems till they have lifted up their eyes and seen the "great company." Will their philosophy watch the world and explain it? they ask themselves. Can they tell man what his life is, and how to live it? The abstract student of political science must sooner or later see before him men waiting to be governed. The military theorists must tell how this especial battle is to be fought and won. The medical inquirer must know that there is sickness crying out to be cured. The theologians must be aware of eager souls appealing to them with the pathetic question, "What must I do to be saved?" The safety of man, the rescue of the thinker from the perils of his thought, the assurance that the farthest and deepest shall always be at the service of the immediate and pressing, lies in this readiness of all true men to lift up their eyes and see the "great company."

There are students and dreamers and theorists enough who are not ready. Sometimes their absorption and irresponsiveness makes other men rudely and crudely denounce all meditation and speculation, and say that the far-off heavens shine only for their own luxury, and have no light to give to the darkened earth. But such vexation is slight and temporary. The crowd looks to the scholar and the dreamer and the saint, and does not look in vain. It is a history full of instruction and encouragement that He who saw the deepest vision and prayed the holiest prayer was the very first to turn away from both, to lift up His eyes and see the multitude, and love them, and come down to break for them the bread of life.

But let us, before we come directly to the thought of how Christ looked upon the crowd, consider somewhat more fully what the sight of a host of his fellow-beings may be to any man who looks them in the face. May it not be summed up by saying that a crowd may be to any man a mirror into which he looks and sees what he is, and what he ought to be.

There is, first, the revelation of what a man is which comes to him in the presence of a crowd. I mean of what he is essentially, intrinsically, behind and separate from the countless accidents of his existence and the peculiar characteristics of his lot. This belongs with what we saw of the power which a great crowd has to present essential and absolute humanity to our minds. Facing that great presentation, many things which are not essential drop off and fall away. You go out from your individual life, from your self-absorbed existence, and stand face to face with a great host of your fellow-men, and as you stand there (have you not felt it?) all that is really human in you throbs with vitality. It is alive with sympathy, while that which is not human manifests its weak vitality and begins to die. Your artificialnesses are exposed. You feel what shams your shams are, how selfish are your selfishnesses. Thus you see yourself in the mirror.

In the same mirror, in the face of the same crowd, you see also what you ought to be. For, along with the sense of how thoroughly your humanity is one with that of the crowd on which you look— not interfering with it, but increased and deepened by it,—there is the other sense of how distinct your life is from the lives of all these men. You are a separate being. There are some things which specialize in you the universal human life. The gifts and endowments which you possess become real to you; all the privileges of your life grow clear. You are entirely unable to be proud of them. They are yours for the sake of this multitude. They become the personal expression of the universal life, bound to restore themselves in service to those human necessities which look into your face with their appeal out of this one great face of the crowd.

I think that no man of true sensitiveness has come forth from his studies and contemplations into the storm and host of human living, without this becoming his revelation. He was himself for all of these. They claimed all that he was and had. If he was rich when they were poor, it was their riches that he held. If he was wise when they were ignorant, it was their wisdom. Who was it that had made him to differ? Even the Father who had first made him one with them. And so humility and responsibility, which are so often in contention and stand apart from one another, meet in the heart of the true man who stands face to face with the crowd of his fellow-men.

It is these things, then, which all true men find, and which Jesus Christ, we cannot doubt, found in the presence of a multitude,— self-revelation and noble impulse—these two together. When He saw the gathering in the Temple at the time of the journey which He made there in His boyhood, when He looked upon the host who were waiting for their baptism at Jordan, when He came down from the mountain and found the crowd waiting in the plain, when He preached in the thronged synagogue at Capernaum, when He walked the streets of Jerusalem or stood in the courts of the great Temple,—everywhere these two things were taking place: He was knowing how truly He was one with man, and He was feeling that that in Him which was more than man was being claimed by the human need. The woods and mountains could not do these things for Him; therefore He turned from mountains and woods to the places where men were.

We cannot picture Christ to ourselves as a mere dreamer. The Oriental standard of the holy man—the mystic sitting in rapt, useless meditation year after year—wholly fails in Him. The nature-worshipper, listening to what the trees and streamlets have to say, drinking in, after our modern notion of him, the unarticulated wisdom of the clouds and the flowers,—that is not the Jesus of the Gospels, the Jesus of the Christian faith. He is a man of men. Any day the murmur of a crowd will draw Him from the silence of the hillside. For the deep knowledge of Himself and the impulse of service pour into Him out of the eager faces and the pictures of suffering and joy which throng upon Him.

These are the elements out of which character is made. And so it is in presence of the world, in contact with the world, that character has birth. This was the truth which Goethe taught, the truth of a talent shaping itself in stillness, but a character in the activity of life. It is character, not talent, for the lack of which the world suffers. It is because of too little character, not because of too little talent, that the careers of human beings come to wreck. Therefore that which makes character must always be the true salvation of mankind. Therefore man, and not nature, is the true school of Human Life.

With this general truth concerning Christ's relation to the multitude of men clear in our mind, we are prepared to go on and speak of two or three of the special effects which it produced in Him. And the first which I ask you to observe is this: the perfect mingling of respect and pity in the way in which He felt about mankind. It would be useless to deny that pity, as we ordinarily know it, has in it almost always a mixture of contempt. It is not respectful to the nature of the man whom it pities. That is the reason why it is resented almost as if it were insulting. "Do not pity me," the proud man cries. "Neglect me if you will; abuse me, but do not pity me." It is not simply that pity declares of necessity the misfortune of him on whom the pity is bestowed. That is inevitable. It is that pity, as we give it, seems to interpret and comment on misfortune. It seems to say that the man must be not worth much who could come to this. It seems to set the pitier over against the pitied in an assertion of superior desert.

Your friend has passed into some one of the great clouds of sorrow which darken the houses and the hearts of men. You, from outside the cloud, radiant with the sunshine of prosperity, speak in to him and tell him how you pity him. Do you not know the feeling of suspense with which you listen to hear how he will receive your words? Do you not know how hard it is, first to keep, and then to make him know that you keep, a true respect for him through all his suffering; and that there is no slightest latent spark of the consciousness of superiority in the commiseration which you offer him? The Book of Job, with the supercilious comfort of the prosperous friends, repeats itself in countless homes of sorrow.

It is the absolute absence of all this in Jesus Christ which makes the wonder of His life. There is never a touch of contempt in His dealing with distress. When He touches the blind man's eyes and gives him sight; when He steps across the threshold of the dead girl's chamber; when, by the Pool of Bethesda, He probes the intention and desire of the sick man's soul; when He calls to the buried Lazarus at Bethany;—everywhere, do you not feel the infinite and exquisite reverence which is in His touch and His voice for the human nature to which His word is spoken, or on which His hand is laid?

It is not merely that Christ is a sufferer Himself. It is not merely that He is poor, and so is in special sympathy with poverty and distress. That would make Him the friend of a class, almost the partisan of a party among men—the party of the wretched and distressed. It is something larger and deeper than that. It is the reverence of the Lord of human nature for the human nature which He rules,—nay, of the Creator of man for the man whom He created. Who knows the wonder and mystery of the organ like the man who built it, who piled pipe on pipe, each with its capacity of various sound? And so, who is it that shall touch the jarred and untuned organ, and call it back to harmony, like him in whose soul the organ's primitive and ideal harmony forever dwells, and to whom all its discord and disorder is a sadness and a shame?

Therefore it is that Jesus Christ pities not merely the sorrow and the poverty which He knows by fellow-feeling, by being sorrowful and poor himself. He pities far more the sin and meanness and moral misery which He knows by its contrast with His own soul, and its departure from that purpose of human nature which lies always in the depths of His divine and human soul. He pities sorrow, but He pities sin far more. Pilate and Herod and Judas and the Pharisees,—these are the truly pitiable creatures of the earth for Him. And yet, even for them the reverence is not lost in the pitifulness. The mystery and richness of their human nature still abides behind their cowardice and selfishness. Can you not feel it in the marvellous loftiness and courtesy of that conversation at the judgment seat? Does it not tremble even in the simple words with which, at the Last Supper, the Lord dismisses the traitor to his dreadful work?

The work of the Gospel on the soul which it saves, bears the conclusive witness of the respect which mingles with the pity which is the power of salvation. Where is the soul, rejoicing in the work which Christ has done for it, that has not wondered when it saw how the very visitation of Divinity which made its sin manifest, and bowed it down with penitence, also made manifest its preciousness, and opened visions of its possible attainment! You knew how you needed salvation when you met Christ. You knew how worth saving you were when you met Christ. The awe which a soul feels before itself as its spiritual capacity is being revealed in its conversion,—what is it but the reflection and echo of the reverence which is in the heart of Christ for the soul which He is saving by His grace?

What the soul feels the world feels. There is a certain insolence in most reformers. It hinders the triumphs of reform. It sullies the splendor of much of the noblest progress which the world has made. The leader stands before the host, and bids them to the battle almost with a taunt and a jeer. There is nothing of that in Christ. There is a profound reverence for the army which He leads. Therefore the army has followed Him as it has followed no other captain. And when He leads it into its final victory, the victory will be sure.

Let me pass on to another impressive point in the way in which Christ looks at the crowd of men. It is something which we feel rather than see; but I do not think that we can be mistaken regarding it. It is the way in which the individual and the combined life do not hinder, but help each other, to His mind. To us the individual loses himself in the crowd, and we cannot find him. A new being—the multitude—takes his place. We cannot think that it was so with Jesus. We are sure that, to Him, each person in the crowd remained distinct, in spite of the host by whom He was surrounded.

Nay, more than that, are we not sure that the person was more distinct because of the host in whose midst his life was set? There was one token of this being so in one event of Christ's life. Do you remember where the poor Syrian woman crept up and laid a timid finger on His robes, and, when Christ recognized and owned it, His disciples almost rebuked Him with their surprise? "Master, the multitude throng Thee and press Thee; and sayest Thou, who touched me?" The blurring of the single face in the great sea of faces, the loss of the one in the many, the sacrifice of personality to society,—all this, with which we are familiar, we think of as wholly absent from the life of Jesus Christ. When the great company came pouring up the hill upon the other side of Gennesaret, it was as a whole, making each part of which it was composed more vividly distinct, that Jesus saw the advancing multitude when He "lifted up His eyes."

We wrestle with the problem of socialism and individualism, the problem of the many and the one; and we wonder which of the two must be sacrificed to the other, which of the two shall ultimately overcome the other and remain the triumphant principle of human life. Let us be sure that to Christ, to God, there is no problem. Let us be sure, therefore, that in the end it shall not be by the victory of either over the other, but by the perfect harmonizing of the two, that the perfect condition of human life shall be attained. When society shall be complete, it shall perfectly develop the freedom of the individual. When the individual shall be perfect, he will make in his free and original life his appointed contribution to society.

Therefore—and here is what it is good for us to remember—it is not by elaborate plans for the building of the social structure; nor, on the other hand, by frantic assertions of personal independence; but by patiently and unselfishly being his own best self for the great good of all, that every man best helps the dawning of the Golden

Age. Many a patient and unselfish worker is making valuable contribution to the great end who never dreams of what he is doing. Every man makes such a contribution who looks upon the crowded swarm of human life as Christ looked upon it; neither losing the man in the multitude, nor the multitude in the man; neither letting the forest drown the trees, nor letting the trees dissipate and destroy the forest.

Sometimes, when for a moment we catch the view of Christ and share His vision, there comes great clearness into our spiritual experience, and that which has sometimes been the source of confusion and obscurity becomes the fountain of enlightenment and strength. Do you not know how, sometimes, it is because of the countless multitude of souls that the experience of each soul grows vague and unreal? In such a host does the great Captain know and care for every soldier? Does God feed and guard and educate me, individually, when all these millions are His children? Does the Holy Spirit bring His special gift to this one nature among all the innumerable natures which must have His grace? And at the last, shall this one little life, which goes trembling out of this familiar existence through the vast door of death, be surely kept sacred, and separate, and precious, and imperishable in the great world of life beyond? These are the haunting questions which beset our souls. Where are the answers to them, except in this which we believe to have been true of Jesus Christ,—that the more men there were, the more clearly did each man stand out distinct to Him who knew and loved them all. The crowd intensified and not obscured the individual.

Let that truth of the Incarnation be true in all the care of God for man, and does not our anxiety—what is sometimes almost our terror—pass away? Because I am one among millions of needy souls, the Holy Spirit shall the more surely find me with my own peculiar food. Because no man can number the immortal, therefore my immortality is the more certain, and He who keeps all spirits will keep mine. With such assurance I look up and face the overwhelming multitude of life, and am not overwhelmed, but filled with buoyant faith and carried onward as on a flood of strength.

One other impression of the "great company" upon the mind of Jesus, I may allude to in a few words. He must have been filled, as He looked at them, with a sense of danger, and a sense of hope together. Danger and hope, so it would seem, belong together in this world where we are now living. Sometime a world may come where hope may be conceived entirely apart from danger; but now and here, when man looks far ahead and dares to anticipate great things, the certainty that great evil as well as great good may come starts up at once and will not be forgotten. It started up to Christ, and He never tried to forget it. No eyes ever saw more distinctly than His eyes saw the peril of human life. He read it in every human face. He had learned it in the temptation in the wilderness. Only, because He was God and knew the evil to be weaker than the good, He always kept the hope behind and within the danger. Because man had in him the power to be this dreadful thing, therefore he also had in him the power to be this splendid thing. I know that, if we had been in Jerusalem, and had met the blessed Saviour in the street, we should have read all this in His features: the fear and hope together, the hope intensified by the fear, but always conquering it and making Him eager to call every human creature with the invitation of the divine Love, whose might He knew.

Shall we not see all that in His face as He looks at us? We have not begun to know our danger as He knows it. He is anxious for your soul as you never began to be. But He hopes for you as you never hoped for yourself. Let His hope take possession of you! Lift up your heart and know, as He knows, how perfectly you can be saved!

Thus, then, it is that Jesus Christ looks upon the crowded world: with reverence and pity; with the sight of the whole and also the recognition of the single life; with the sense of danger and the sense of hope. The result of it all, in Him, is that glorious consecration of his whole Being to the world, by which He is its Saviour. Let us see mankind as nobly as He does, and we shall be consecrated like Him; and in some true, deep, blessed way, we shall share His Saviourship, —perhaps by the sharing of His Cross, but we *shall* share His Saviourship. What more could man ask than that?

THE FIRE AND THE CALF*

"So they gave it me: then I cast it into the fire and there came out this calf."
—Exodus xxxii. 24.

IN THE story from which these words are taken we see Moses go up
into the mountain to hold communion with God. While he is gone
the Israelites begin to murmur and complain. They want other gods,
gods of their own. Aaron, the brother of Moses, was their priest.
He yielded to the people, and when they brought him their golden
earrings he made out of them a golden calf for them to worship.
When Moses came down from the mountain he found the people
deep in their idolatry. He was indignant. First he destroyed the idol,
"He burnt it in the fire, and ground it to powder, and strawed it
upon the water, and made the children of Israel drink of it." Then
he turned to Aaron. "What did this people unto thee," he said,
"that thou hast brought so great a sin upon them?" And Aaron
meanly answered, "Let not the anger of my lord wax hot: thou
knowest the people, that they are set on mischief. For they said unto
me, Make us gods, which shall go before us. . . . And I said unto
them, Whosoever hath any gold, let them break it off. So they gave
it me: then I cast it into the fire, and there came out this calf." That
was his mean reply. The real story of what actually happened had
been written earlier in the chapter. When the people brought Aaron
their golden earrings "he received them at their hand, and fashioned it with a graving tool, after he had made it a molten calf: and
they said, These by thy gods, O Israel, which brought thee up out
of the land of Egypt." That was what really happened, and this is
the description which Aaron gave of it to Moses: "So they gave it
me: then I cast it into the fire, and there came out this calf."

Aaron was frightened at what he had done. He was afraid of the
act itself, and he was afraid of what Moses would say about it. Like
all timid men, he trembled before the storm which he had raised.

* Preached at Christ Church, Lancaster Gate, London, Sunday morning, 27th
May 1883.

183

And so he tried to persuade Moses, and perhaps in some degree even to persuade himself, that it was not he that had done this thing. He lays the blame upon the furnace. "The fire did it," he declares. He will not blankly face his sin, and yet he will not tell a lie in words. He tells what is literally true. He had cast the earrings into the fire, and this calf had come out. But he leaves out the one important point, his own personal agency in it all; the fact that he had moulded the earrings into the calf's shape, and that he had taken it out and set it on its pedestal for the people to adore. He tells it so that it shall all look automatic. It is a curious, ingenious, but transparent lie.

Let us look at Aaron's speech a little while this morning, and see what it represents. For it does represent something. There never was a speech more true to one disposition of our human nature. We are all ready to lay the blame upon the furnaces. "The fire did it," we are all of us ready enough to say. Here is a man all gross and sensual, a man still young who has already lost the freshness and the glory and the purity of youth. He is profane; he is cruel; he is licentious; all his brightness has grown lurid; all his wit is ribaldry. You know the man. As far as a man can be, he is a brute. Suppose you question that man about his life. You expect him to be ashamed, to be repentant. There is not a sign of anything like that! He says, "I am the victim of circumstances. What a corrupt, licentious, profane age this is in which we live! When I was in college I got into a bad set. When I went into business I was surrounded by bad influences. When I grew rich, men flattered me. When I grew poor, men bullied me. The world has made me what I am, this fiery, passionate, wicked world. I had in my hands the gold of my boyhood which God gave me. Then I cast it into the fire, and there came out this calf." And so the poor wronged miserable creature looks into your face with his bleared eyes and asks your pity. Another man is not a profligate, but is a miser, or a mere business machine. "What can you ask of me," he says, "this is a mercantile community. The business man who does not attend to his business goes to the wall. I am what this intense commercial life has made me. I put my life in there, and it came out this." And then he gazes fondly at his golden calf, and his knees bend under him with the old long habit of worshipping it, and he loves it still, even while he abuses and disowns it. And so with the woman of society. "The fire made me this," she says of her frivolity and pride. And so of the politician and his selfishness and partisan-ship. "I put my principles into the furnace, and this came out." And so of the bigot and his bigotry, the one-sided conservative with his stubborn resistance to all progress, the one-sided radical with his ruthless iconoclasm. So of all partial and fanatical men. "The furnace made us," they are ready to declare. "These times compel us to be this. In better times we might have been better, broader men; but now, behold. God put us into the fire, and we came out this." It is what one is perpetually hearing about disbelief. "The times have made me sceptical. How is it possible for a man to live in days like these and yet believe in God and Jesus and the Resurrection. You ask me how I, who was brought up in the faith and in the Church, became a disbeliever. Oh, you remember that I lived five years here," or "three years there." "You know I have been very much thrown with this set or with that. You know the temper of our town. I cast myself into the fire, and I came out this." One is all ready to understand, my friends, how the true soul, struggling for truth, seems often to be worsted in the struggle. One is ready to have tolerance, respect, and hope for any man who, reaching after God, is awed by God's immensity and his own littleness, and falls back crushed and doubtful. His is a doubt which is born in the secret chambers of his own personal conscientiousness. It is independent of his circumstances and surroundings. The soul which has truly come to a personal doubt finds it hard to conceive of any ages of most implicit faith in which it could have lived in which that doubt would not have been in it. It faces its doubt in a solitude where there is none but it and God. All that one understands, and the more he understands it the more unintelligible does it seem to him, that any earnest soul can really lay its doubt upon the age, the set, or the society it lives in. No; our age, our society is what, with this figure taken out of the old story of Exodus, we have been calling it. It is the furnace. Its fire can set and fix and fasten what the man puts into it. But, properly speaking, it can create no character. It can make no truly faithful soul a doubter. It never did. It never can.

Remember that the subtlety and attractiveness of this excuse, this plausible attributing of power to inanimate things and exterior con-ditions to create what only man can make, extends not only to the results which we see coming forth in ourselves; it covers also the fortunes of those for whom we are responsible. The father says of his profligate son whom he has never done one wise or vigorous thing to make a noble and pure-minded man: "I cannot tell how it has come. It has not been my fault. I put him into the world and this came out." The father whose faith has been mean and selfish says the same of his boy who is a sceptic. Everywhere there is this cowardly casting off of responsibilities upon the dead circumstances around us. It is a very hard treatment of the poor, dumb, helpless world which cannot answer to defend itself. It takes us as we give ourselves to it. It is our minister fulfilling our commissions for us upon our own souls. If we say to it, "Make us noble," it does make us noble. If we say to it, "Make us mean," it does make us mean. And then we take the nobility and say, "Behold, how noble I have made myself." And we take the meanness and say, "See how mean the world has made me."

You see, I am sure, how perpetual a thing the temper of Aaron is, how his excuse is heard everywhere and always. I need not multiply illustrations. But now, if all the world is full of it, the next question is, What does it mean? Is it mere pure deception, or is there also delusion, self-deception in it? Take Aaron's case. Was he simply telling a lie to Moses and trying to hide the truth from his brother whom he dreaded, when he said, "I cast the earrings into the fire, and this calf came out"? Or was he in some dim degree, in some half-conscious way, deceiving himself? Was he allowing himself to attribute some power to the furnace in the making of the calf? Perhaps as we read the verse above in which it is so distinctly said that Aaron fashioned the idol with a graving tool, any such supposition seems incredible. But yet I cannot but think that some degree, however dim, of such self-deception was in Aaron's heart. The fire was mysterious. He was a priest. Who could say that some strange creative power had not been at work there in the heart of the furnace which had done for him what he seemed to do for himself. There was a human heart under that ancient ephod, and it is hard to think that Aaron did not succeed in bringing himself to be somewhat imposed upon by his own words, and hiding his responsibility in the heart of the hot furnace. But however it may have been with Aaron, there can be no doubt that in almost all cases this is so. Very rarely indeed does a man excuse himself to other men and yet remain absolutely unexcused in his own eyes. When Pilate stands washing the responsibility of Christ's murder from his hands before the

people, was he not feeling himself as if his hands grew cleaner while
he washed? When Shakespeare paints Macbeth with the guilty
ambition which was to be his ruin first rising in his heart, you remember how he makes him hide his newborn purpose to be king
even from himself, and pretend that he believes that he is willing to
accept the kingdom only if it shall come to him out of the working
of things, for which he is not responsible, without an effort of his
own.

"If chance will have me King, why, chance may crown me, Without my stir."

That was the first stage of the growing crime which finally was
murder. Often it takes this form. Often the very way to help ourselves most to a result which we have set before ourselves is just to
put ourselves into a current which is sweeping on that way, and
then lie still and let the current do the rest; and in all such cases it is
so easy to ignore or to forget the first step, which was that we chose
that current for our resting-place, and so to say that it is only the
drift of the current which is to blame for the dreary shore on which
at last our lives are cast up by the stream. Suppose you are to-day
a scornful man, a man case-hardened in conceit and full of disbelief
in anything generous or supernatural, destitute of all enthusiasm,
contemptuous, supercilious. You say the time you live in has made
you so. You point to one large tendency in the community which
always sets that way. You parade the specimens of enthusiastic people whom you have known who have been fanatical and silly. You
tell me what your favourite journal has been saying in your ears
every week for years. You bid me catch the tone of the brightest
people whom you live among, and then you turn to me and say,
"How could one live in such an atmosphere and not grow cynical?
Behold, my times have made me what I am." What does that mean?
Are you merely trying to hide from me, or are you also hiding from
yourself, the certain fact that you have chosen that special current
to launch your boat upon, that you have given your whole attention
to certain kinds of facts and shut your eyes to certain others, that
you have constantly valued the brightness which went to the depreciation of humanity and despised the urgency with which a
healthier spirit has argued for the good in man and for his everlasting hope? Is it not evident that you yourself have been able to half
forget all this, and so when the stream on which you launched your

boat at last drives it upon the beach to which it has been flowing all the time, there is a certain lurking genuineness in the innocent surprise with which you look around upon the desolate shore on which you land, and say to yourself, "How unhappy I am that I should have fallen upon these evil days, in which it is impossible that a man should genuinely respect or love his fellowmen"?

For there are currents flowing always in all bad directions. There is a perpetual river flowing towards sensuality and vice. There is a river flowing perpetually towards hypocrisy and religious pretence. There is a river always running towards scepticism and infidelity. And when you once have given yourself up to either of these rivers, then there is quite enough in the continual pressure, in that great movement like a fate beneath your keel, to make you lose the sense and remembrance that it is by your own will that you are there, and only think of the resistless flow of the river which is always in your eyes and ears. This is the mysterious, bewildering mixture of the consciousness of guilt and the consciousness of misery in all our sin. We live in a perpetual confusion of self-pity and self-blame. We go up to the scaffolds where we are to suffer, half like culprits crawling to the gallows and half like martyrs proudly striding to their stakes. When we think of what sort of reception is to meet us in the other world as the sum and judgment of the life we have been living here, we find ourselves ready, according to the moment's mood, either for the bitterest denunciation, as of souls who have lived in deliberate sin; or for tender petting and refreshment, as of souls who have been buffeted and knocked about by all the storms of time, and for whom now there ought to be soft beds in eternity. The confusion of men's minds about the judgments of the eternal world is only the echo of their confusion about the responsibilities of the life which they are living now.

Suppose there is a man here this morning who committed a fraud in business yesterday. He did it in a hurry. He did not stop to think about it then. But now, here, in this quiet church, with everything calm and peaceful round him, with the words of prayer which have taken God for granted sinking into his ears, he has been thinking it over. How does it look to him? Is he not certainly sitting in the mixture of self-pity and self-reproach of which I spoke? He did the sin, and he is sorry as a sinner. The sin did itself, and he is sorry as a victim. Nay, perhaps in the next pew to him, or perhaps in the same pew, or perhaps in the same body, there is sitting a man who means to do a fraud to-morrow. In him too is there not the same confusion? One moment he looks it right in the face and says, "To-morrow night I shall despise myself." The next moment he is quietly thinking that the sin will do itself and give him all its advantage, and he need not interfere.

"If chance will make me cheat, why, chance may crown me, Without my stir."

Both thoughts are in his mind, and if he has listened to our service, it is likely enough that he has found something in it—something even in the words of the Bible—for each thought to feed upon.

I own this freely, and yet I do believe, and I call you to bear me witness, that such self-deception almost never is absolutely complete. We feel its incompleteness the moment that any one else attempts to excuse us with the same excuse with which we have excused ourselves. Suppose that some one of the Israelites who stood by had spoken up in Aaron's behalf and said to Moses, "Oh, he did not do it. It was not his act. He only cast the gold into the fire, and there came out this calf." Must not Aaron as he listened have felt the wretchedness of such a telling of the story, and been ashamed, and even cried out and claimed his responsibility and his sin? Very often it is good for us to imagine some one saying aloud in our be-half what we are silently saying to ourselves in self-apology. We see its thinness when another hand holds it up against the sun, and we stand off and look at it. If I might turn again to Shakespeare and his wonderful treasury of human character, there is a scene in Hamlet which exactly illustrates what I mean. The king has determined that Hamlet must die, and is just sending him off upon the voyage from which he means that he is never to return. And the king has fully explained the act to his own conscience, and accepted the crime as a necessity. And then he meets the courtiers, Rosencrantz and Guildenstern, who are to have the execution of the base com-mission. And they, like courtiers, try to repeat to the king the argu-ments with which he has convinced himself. One says—

"Most holy and religious fear it is
To keep those many many bodies safe
That live and feed upon your majesty."

And the other takes up the strain and says—

> "The single and peculiar life is bound,
> With all the strength and armour of the mind,
> To keep itself from 'noyance; but much more
> That spirit upon whose weal depend and rest
> The lives of many."

They are the king's own arguments. With them he has persuaded his own soul to tolerate the murder. But when they come to him from these other lips, he will none of them. He cuts them short. He cannot hear from others what he has said over and over to himself.

> "Arm you, I pray you, to this speedy voyage."

So he cries out and interrupts them. Let the deed be done, but let not these echoes of his self-excuse parade before him the way in which he is trifling with his own soul.

So it is always. I think of the mysterious judgment-day, and sometimes it appears to me as if our souls would need no more than merely that voices outside ourselves should utter in our ears the very self-same pleas and apologies with which we, here upon the earth, have extenuated our own wickedness. They of themselves, heard in the open air of eternity, would let us see how weak they were, and so we should be judged. Is not that partly the reason why we hate the scene of some old sin? The room in which we did it seems to ring for ever with the sophistries by which we persuaded ourselves that it was right, and will not let us live in comfortable delusion. Our life there is an anticipated judgment-day.

I doubt not that this tendency to self-deception and apology with reference to the sins which they commit differs exceedingly with different men. Men differ, perhaps, nowhere else more than in their disposition to face the acts of their lives and to recognise their own personal part in and responsibility for the things they do. Look, for instance, at this Aaron and his brother Moses. The two men are characterised and illustrated by their two sins. The sin of Aaron was a denial or concealment of his own personal agency. "I cast it into the fire, and there came out this calf." The sin of Moses, you remember, was just the opposite. As he stood with his thirsty people in front of the rock in Horeb, he intruded his personal agency where it had no right. "Hear now, ye rebels; must we fetch you water out of this rock?" To be sure, in the case of Moses it was a good act of mercy to which he put in his claim, while in Aaron's case it was a wicked act whose responsibility he desired to avoid. And men are always ready to claim the good deeds in which they have the smallest share, even when they try to disown the sins which are entirely their own. But still the actions seem to mark the men. Moses is the franker, manlier, braver man. In Aaron the priest there is something in that oversubtle, artificial, complicated character, that power of becoming morally confused even in the midst of pious feeling, that lack of simplicity, and of the disposition to look things frankly in the eye; in a word, that vague and defective sense of personality and its responsibilities which has often in the history of religion made the very name of priestcraft a reproach. Moses is the prophet. His distinct mission is the utterance of truth. He is always simple; never more simple than when he is most profound; never more sure of the fundamental principles of right and wrong, of honesty and truth, than when he is deepest in the mystery of God; never more conscious of himself and his responsibilities than when he is most conscious of God and His power.

And this brings me to my last point, which I must not longer delay to reach. If the world is thus full of the Aaron spirit, of the disposition to throw the blame of wrong-doing upon other things and other people, to represent to others, and to our own souls, that our sins do themselves, what is the real spiritual source of such a tendency, and where are we to look to find its cure? I have just intimated what seems to me to be its source. It is a vague and defective sense of personality. Anything which makes less clear to a man the fact that he, standing here on his few inches of the earth, is a distinct separate being, in whom is lodged a unit of life, with his own soul, his own character, his own chances, his own responsibilities, distinct and separate from any other man's in all the world; anything that makes all that less clear demoralises a man, and opens the door to endless self-excuses. And you know, surely, how many tendencies there are to-day which are doing just that for men. Every man's personality, his clear sense of himself, seems to be standing to-day where almost all the live forces of the time are making their attacks upon it. It is like a tree in the open field from which every bird carries away some fruit. The enlargement of our knowledge of the world, the growing tendency of men to work in large companies, the increased despotism of social life, the interesting studies of hereditation, the externality of a large part of our action, the rush and competition for the prizes which represent the most material sort of success, the spread of knowledge by which at once all men are seen to know much, and, at the same time, no man is seen to know everything; all these causes enfeeble the sense of personality. The very prominence of the truth of a universal humanity, in which our philanthropy justly glories, obscures the clearness of the individual human life. Once it was hard to conceive of man, because the personalities of men were so distinct. Once people found it hard, as the old saying was, to see the forest for the trees. Now it is just the opposite. To hundreds of people it is almost impossible to see the trees for the forest. Man is so clear that men become obscure. As the Laureate of the century sings of the time which he so well knows: "The individual withers and the race is more and more." These are the special causes, working in our time, of that which has its general causes in our human nature working everywhere and always.

And if this is the trouble, where, then, is the help? If this is the disease, where is the cure? I cannot look for it anywhere short of that great assertion of the human personality which is made when a man personally enters into the power of Jesus Christ. Think of it! Here is some Aaron of our modern life trying to cover up some sin which he has done. The fact of the sin is clear enough. There is no possibility of concealing that. It stands out wholly undisputed. It is not by denying that the thing was done but by beclouding the fact that he did it with his own hands, with his own will; thus it is that the man would cover up his sin. He has been nothing but an agent, nothing but a victim; so he assures his fellowmen, so he assures himself. And now suppose that while he is doing that, the great change comes to that man by which he is made a disciple and servant of Jesus Christ. It becomes known to him as a certain fact that God loves him individually, and is educating him with a separate personal education which is all his own. The clear individuality of Jesus stands distinctly out and says to him, "Follow me!" Jesus stops in front of where he is working just as evidently, with just as manifest intention of calling him as that with which He stopped in front of the booth where Matthew was sitting collecting taxes, and says, "Follow me." He is called separately, and separately he does give himself to Christ. Remember all that is essential to a Christian faith. You cannot blur it all into indistinctness and generality. In the true light of the redeeming Incarnation, every man in the multitude stands out as every blade of grass on the hillside stands distinct from every other when the sun has risen. In this sense, as in many another, this is the true light which lighteneth every man that cometh into the world.

The Bible calls it a new birth, and in that name too there are many meanings. And among other meanings in it must there not be this—the separateness and personality of every soul in Christ? Birth is the moment of distinctness. The meanest child in the poorest hovel in the city, who by and by is to be lost in the great whirlpool of human life, here at the outset where his being comes, a new fact, into the crowded world, is felt in his distinctness, has his own personal tending, excites his own personal emotion. When he is born and when he dies, but perhaps most of all when he is born, the commonest, most commonplace and undistinguished of mankind asserts the fact of privilege of his separateness. And so when the possession of the soul by Christ is called the "New Birth," one of the meanings of that name is this, that then there is a reassertion of personality, and the soul which had lost itself in the slavery of the multitude finds itself again in the obedience of Christ.

And now what will be the attitude of this man, with his newly-awakened selfhood, towards that sin which he has been telling himself that his hands did, but that he did not do? May we not almost say that he will need that sin for his self-identification? Who is he? A being whom Christ has forgiven, and then in virtue of that forgiveness made His servant. All his new life dates from and begins with his sin. He cannot afford to find his consciousness of himself only in the noble parts of his life, which it makes him proud and happy to remember. There is not enough of that to make for him a complete and continuous personality. It will have great gaps if he disowns the wicked demonstrations of his self-hood and says, "It was not I," wherever he has done wrong. No! Out of his sin, out of the bad, base, cowardly acts which are truly his, out of the weak and wretched passages of his life which it makes him ashamed to remember, but which he forces himself to recollect and own, out of these he gathers the consciousness of a self all astray with self-will which he then brings to Christ and offers in submission and obedience to His perfect will.

You try to tell some soul rejoicing in the Lord's salvation that the sins over whose forgiveness by its Lord it is gratefully rejoicing, were not truly its; and see what strange thing comes. The soul seems to draw back from your assurance as if, if it were true, it would be robbed of all its surest confidence and brightest hope. You meant to comfort the poor penitent, and he looks into your face as if you were striking him a blow. And you can see what such a strange sight means. It is not that the poor creature loves those sins or is glad that he did them, or dreams for an instant of ever doing them again. It is only that through those sins, which are all the real experience he has had, he has found himself, and finding himself has found his Saviour and the new life.

So the only hope for any of us is in a perfectly honest manliness to claim our sins. "I did it, I did it," let me say of all my wickedness. Let me refuse to listen for one moment to any voice which would make my sins less mine. It is the only honest and the only hopeful way, the only way to know and be ourselves. When we have done that, then we are ready for the Gospel, ready for all that Christ wants to show us that we may become, and for all the powerful grace by which He wants to make us be it perfectly.

THE SYMMETRY OF LIFE

"The Length and the Breadth and the Height of it are equal."—Rev. xxi. 16.

St. John in his great vision sees the mystic city, "the holy Jerusalem," descending out of heaven from God. It is the picture of glorified humanity, of humanity as it shall be when it is brought to its completeness by being thoroughly filled with God. And one of the glories of the city which he saw was its symmetry. Our cities, our developments and presentations of human life, are partial and one-sided. This city out of heaven was symmetrical. In all its three dimensions it was complete. Neither was sacrificed to the other. "The length and the breadth and the height of it are equal."

No man can say what mysteries of the yet unopened future are hidden in the picture of the mystic city; but if that city represents, as I have said, the glorified humanity, then there is much of it that we can understand already. It declares that the perfect life of man will be perfect on every side. One token of its perfectness will be its symmetry. In each of its three dimensions it will be complete.

So much of the noblest life which the world has seen dissatisfies us with its partialness; so many of the greatest men we see are great only upon certain sides, and have their other sides all shrunken, flat, and small, that it may be well for us to dwell upon the picture, which these words suggest, of a humanity rich and full and strong all round, complete on every side, the perfect cube of human life which comes down out of heaven from God.

As I speak I should like to keep before my mind and before yours, that picture which I think is the most interesting that the world has to show, the picture of a young man, brave and strong and generous, just starting out into life, and meaning with all his might to be the very best and most perfect man he can; meaning to make life the fullest and most genuine success. Let us see him before us as I speak. We shall see how natural his dangers and temptations are; we shall see how his very strength tends to partialness; we shall see how every power that is in him will grow doubly strong if he can but-

tress and steady it with strength upon the other sides, if in his growing character he can attain the symmetry and completeness of the
new Jerusalem.

There are, then, three directions or dimensions of human life to
which we may fitly give these three names, Length and Breadth and
Height. The Length of a life, in this meaning of it, is, of course, not
its duration. It is rather the reaching on and out of a man, in the
line of activity and thought and self-development, which is indicated
and prophesied by the character which is natural within him, by
the special ambitions which spring up out of his special powers. It
is the push of a life forward to its own personal ends and ambitions.
The Breadth of a life, on the other hand, is its outreach laterally, if
we may say so. It is the constantly diffusive tendency which is always drawing a man outward into sympathy with other men. And
the Height of a life is its reach upward towards God; its sense of
childhood; its consciousness of the Divine Life over it with which it
tries to live in love, communion, and obedience. These are the three
dimensions of a life,—its length and breadth and height,—without
the due development of all of which no life becomes complete.

Think first about the Length of life in this understanding of the
word. Here is a man who, as he comes to self-consciousness, recognizes in himself a certain nature. He cannot be mistaken. Other men
have their special powers and dispositions. As this young man studies
himself he finds that he has his. That nature which he has discovered
in himself decides for him his career. He says to himself "Whatever
I am to do in the world must be done in this direction." It is a fascinating discovery. It is an ever-memorable time for a man when he
first makes it. It is almost as if a star woke to some subtle knowledge
of itself, and felt within its shining frame the forces which decided
what its orbit was to be. Because it is the star it is, that track through
space must be its track. Out on that track it looks; along that line
which sweeps through the great host of stars it sends out all its hopes;
and all the rest of space is merely the field through which that track
is flung; all the great host of stars is but the audience which wait to
hear it as it goes singing on its way. So starts the young life which
has come to self-discovery and found out what it is to do by finding
out what it is. It starts to do that destined thing; to run out that appointed course. Nay, the man when he arrives at this self-discovery
finds that his nature has not waited for him to recognize himself.

What he is, even before he knows it, has decided what he does. It may be late in life before he learns to say of himself "This is what I am." But then he looks back and discerns that, even without his knowing himself enough to have found it out, his life has run out in a line which had the promise and potency of its direction in the nature which his birth and education gave him. But if he does know it, the course is yet more definite and clear. Every act that he does is a new section of that line which runs between his nature and his appointed work. Just in proportion to the definiteness with which he has measured and understood himself, is the sharpness of that line which every thought and act and word is projecting a little farther, through the host of human lives, towards the purpose of his living, towards the thing which he believes that he is set into the world to do.

Your own experience will tell you what I mean. Have you known any young man who early found out what his nature was; found out, for instance, that he had a legal mind and character? He said to himself "I am made to be a lawyer." Instantly with that discovery it was as if two points stood out clearly to him; he with his legal nature here; the full, completed lawyer's work and fame afar off there. Two unconnected points they seemed at first, which simply beckoned to each other across the great distance, and knew that, however unconnected they might be, they had to do with one another and must ultimately meet. Then that man's life became one long extension of his nature and his powers and his will along a line which should at last attain that distant goal. All his self-culture strove that way. He read no book, he sought no friend, he gave himself no recreation, which was not somehow going to help him to his end and make him a better lawyer. Through the confusion and whirl of human lives, his life ran in one sharp, narrow line, almost as straight and clear as the railroad track across a continent, from what he knew he was, to what he meant to be and do. As the railroad track sweeps through the towns which string themselves along it, climbs mountains and plunges into valleys, hides itself in forests and flashes out again into broad plains and along the sunny sides of happy lakes, and evidently cares nothing for them all except as they just give it ground on which to roll out its length towards its end by the shore of the Pacific,—so this man's life pierces right on through all the tempting and perplexing complications of our human living, and will not rest until it has attained the mastery of legal power. That clear, straight line of its unswerving intention, that struggle and push right onward to the end,—that is the length of this man's life.

And if you recognize this, as of course you do, then you know also how necessary an element or dimension of any useful and successful life this is. To have an end and seek it eagerly, no man does anything in the world without that. If we let our thoughts leap at once to the summit of human living, and think of Jesus, we see it in perfection. The onward reach, the struggle to an apprehended purpose, the straight clear line right from His own self-knowledge to His work, was perfect in the Lord. "For this cause was I born," He cried. His life pierced like an arrow through the cloud of aimless lives, never for a moment losing its direction, hurrying on with a haste and assurance which were divine. And this which He illustrates perfectly is, in our own fashion, one of the favorite thoughts of our own time. No man finds less tolerance to-day than the aimless man, the man whose life lies and swings like a pool, instead of flowing straight onward like a river. We revel in the making of specialists. Often it seems as if the more narrow and straight we could make the line which runs between the nature and its work, the more beautiful we thought it. We make our boys choose their electives when they go to college, decide at once on what they mean to do, and pour all the stream of knowledge down the sluiceway which leads to that one wheel. Perhaps we overdo it, but no thinking man dreams of saying that the thing itself is wrong. This movement of a man's whole life along some clearly apprehended line of self-development and self-accomplishment, this reaching of a life out forward to its own best attainment, no man can live as a man ought to live without it. The men who have no purpose, the men in whose life this first dimension of length is wanting or is very weak, are good for nothing. They lie in the world like mere pulpy masses, giving it no strength or interest or character.

Set yourself earnestly to see what you were made to do, and then set yourself earnestly to do it. That is the first thing that we want to say to our young man in the building of whose life we feel an interest. As we say it we feel almost a hesitation, it may be, because the exhortation sounds so selfish. Self-study and self-culture, surely that makes a very selfish life. Indeed it does. But he has thought very little who has not discovered two things concerning selfishness.

First, that there is a lofty selfishness, a high care for our own culture, which is a duty, and not a fault. And secondly, that he who in this highest way cares for himself and seeks for himself his own best good, must, whether he thinks of doing it or not, help other men's development as well as his own. It is only the line which is seeking something that is low, that can pierce through the live mass of men's lives and interests and be as wholly independent of them all as I pictured just now. Even the railroad track, hurrying to the Pacific, must leave something of civilizing influence on the prairies which it crosses. In the highest and purest sense of the word there certainly was selfishness in Jesus. No man might tempt or force Him from the resolute determination to unfold His appointed life and be His perfect self. The world is right when it follows its blind instinct and stands, with some kind of gratitude though not a gratitude of the most loving sort, beside the grave of some man who in life has been loftily possessed with the passion for self-culture, and has never thought of benefiting the world; for if his passion for self-culture has really been of the most lofty kind, the world must be the better for it.

Therefore we may freely say to any young man, Find your purpose and fling your life out to it; and the loftier your purpose is, the more sure you will be to make the world richer with every enrichment of yourself. And this, you see, comes to the same thing as saying that this first dimension of life, which we call Length, the more loftily it is sought, has always a tendency to produce the second dimension of life, which we called Breadth. Of that second dimension let us go on now to speak. I have ventured to call this quality of breadth in a man's life its outreach laterally. When that tendency of which I have just been talking, the tendency of a man's career, the more loftily it is pursued, to bring him into sympathy and relationship with other men,—when that tendency, I say, is consciously and deliberately acknowledged, and a man comes to value his own personal career because of the way in which it relates him to his brethren and the help which it permits him to offer them, then his life has distinctly begun to open in this new direction, and to its length it has added breadth. There are men enough with whom no such opening seems to take place. You know them well; men eager, earnest, and intense, reaching forward toward their prize, living straight onward in their clearly apprehended line of life; but to all appearance, so far as you and I can see, living exactly as they would live if they were the only living beings on the surface of the earth, or as if all the other beings with whom they came in contact were only like the wooden rounds upon the ladder by which they climbed to their own personal ambition. Such men you have all known; men who could not conceive of any other life as valuable, happy, or respectable, except their own; men "wrapped up in themselves," as we say,—an envelope as thick as leather, through which no pressure of any other life or character could reach them. And the one feeling that you have about such perfect specialists is the wonder that so great intelligence can be compressed into such narrowness. They are as bright and sharp as needles, and as hard and narrow.

But when a man has length and breadth of life together, we feel at once how the two help each other. Length without breadth is hard and narrow. Breadth without length,—sympathy with others in a man who has no intense and clear direction for himself,—is soft and weak. You see this in the instinctive and strong dislike which all men have for the professional reformer and philanthropist. The world dislikes a man who, with no definite occupation of his own, not trying to be anything particular himself, devotes himself to telling other people what they ought to be. It may allow his good intentions, but it will not feel his influence. The man whom the world delights to feel is the man who has evidently conceived some strong and distinct purpose for himself, from which he will allow nothing to turn his feet aside, who means to be something with all his soul; and yet who finds, in his own earnest effort to fill out his own career, the interpretation of the careers of other men; and also finds, in sympathy with other men, the transfiguration and sustainment of his own appointed struggle.

Indeed these are the two ways in which the relation between the length and breadth of a man's life, between his energy in his own career and his sympathy with the careers of other men, comes out and shows itself. First, the man's own career becomes to him the interpretation of the careers of other men; and secondly, by his sympathy with other men, his own life displays to him its best capacity. The first of these is very beautiful to watch. Imagine the reformer, whom I spoke of, suddenly called to forget the work of helping other men, and to plunge into some work of his own. With what surprise at his own increase of wisdom he would come back, by and by, to the help of his brethren! What far wiser and more reverent hands he would lay upon their lives; with what tones of deepened understanding he would speak to their needs and sins and temptations, after he had himself tried to live a true life of his own! This is the reason, I suppose, why, in the Bible, the ministry of angels to mankind, while it is clearly intimated, is made so little of. It is because, however real it is, it could not be brought very close to the intelligence and gratitude of men, so long as the personal lives of the angels are hidden in mystery. Only he who lives a life of his own can help the lives of other men. Surely there is here one of the simplest and strongest views which a man possibly can take of his own life. "Let me live," he may say, "as fully as I can, in order that in this life of mine I may learn what life really is, and so be fit to understand and help the lives of men about me. Let me make my own career as vivid and successful as possible, that in it I may get at the secret of life, which, when I have once found it, will surely be the key to other lives besides my own." He who should talk and think so of his own career would evidently have gone far towards solving the problem of the apparent incompatibility between intense devotion to one's own pursuit and cordial sympathy with other men. He would find, in the very heart of his own work, the clew to the works of other men. He would be no mere specialist, and yet he would toil hardest of all men in the special task in which he was engaged. But his task would be always glorified and kept from narrowness by his perpetual demand upon it, that it should give him such a broad understanding of human life in general as should make him fit to read and touch and help all other kinds of life.

And if thus the special life does much to make the sympathy with other lives intelligent and strong, the debt is yet not wholly on one side. There is a wonderful power in sympathy to open and display the hidden richness of a man's own seemingly narrow life. You think that God has been training you in one sort of discipline, but when you let yourself go out in sympathy with other men whose disciplines have been completely different from your own, you find that in your discipline the power of theirs was hidden. This is the power which sympathy has to multiply life and make out of one experience the substance and value of a hundred. The well man sympathizes with the sick man, and thereby exchanges, as it were, some of the superfluous riches of his health into the other coin of sickness, gets something of the culture which would have come to him if he had himself been sick. The sick man, in return, gets something, even in all his pain and weakness, of the discipline of health and strength. The same is true about the sympathy of the rich with the poor, of the believer with the doubter, of the hopeful with the despondent, of the liberal with the bigoted; aye, even of the saint with the sinner. The holiest soul, pitying the brother-soul which has fallen into vilest vice, gains, while it keeps its own purity unsoiled, something of the sight of that other side of God, the side where justice and forgiveness blend in the opal mystery of grace, which it would seem as if only the soul that looked up out of the depths of guilt could see. All this is perfect in the vicariousness of Christ; and what was perfect there, is echoed imperfectly in the way in which every man's special life becomes enlarged and multiplied as he looks abroad from it in sympathy with other men.

So much I say about the length and breadth of life. One other dimension still remains. The length and breadth and height of it are equal. The Height of life is its reach upward toward something distinctly greater than humanity. Evidently all that I have yet described, all the length and breadth of life, might exist, and yet man be a creature wholly of the earth. He might move on straight forward in his own career. He might even enter into living sympathy with his brother-men; and yet never look up, never seem to have anything to do with anything above this flat and level plain of human life. A world without a sky! How near any one man's life here and there may come to that, I dare not undertake to say. Some men will earnestly insist that that is just their life; that there is no divine appetite, no reaching Godward in them anywhere. But to a man who thoroughly believes in God, I think that it will always seem that such a life, however any man may think that he is living it, must always be impossible for every man. There cannot be a God and yet any one of His creatures live exactly and entirely as if there was no God.

The reaching of mankind towards God! Evidently, in order that that may become a true dimension of a man's life, it must not be a special action. It must be something which pervades all that he is and does. It must not be a solitary column set on one holy spot of the nature. It must be a movement of the whole nature upward. Here has been one of the great hinderances of the power of religion in the world. Religion has been treated as if it were a special exercise of a special power, not as if it were the possible loftiness of everything that a man could think or be or do. The result has been that certain men and certain parts of men have stood forth as distinctively religious, and that the possible religiousness of all life has been but very imperfectly felt and acknowledged. This has made religion weak. Man's strongest powers, man's intensest passions, have been involved in the working out of his career, and in the development of his relations with his fellow-men. What has been left over for religion has been the weakest part of him, his sentiments and fears; and so religion, very often, has come to seem a thing of mystic moods and frightened superstitions. This picture from the city of the Revelation seems to me to make the matter very clear. The height of life, its reach toward God, must be coextensive with, must be part of the one same symmetrical whole with, the length of life or its reach towards its personal ambition, and the breadth of life or its reach towards the sympathy of brother-lives. It is when a man begins to know the ambition of his life not simply as the choice of his own will but as the wise assignment of God's love; and to know his relations to his brethren not simply as the result of his own impulsive affections but as the seeking of his soul for these souls because they all belong to the great Father-soul; it is then that life for that man begins to lift itself all over and to grow towards completion upward through all its length and breadth. That is a noble time, a bewildering and exalting time in any of our lives, when into everything that we are doing enters the spirit of God, and thenceforth moving ever up toward the God to whom it belongs, that Spirit, dwelling in our life, carries our life up with it; not separating our life from the earth, but making every part of it while it still keeps its hold on earth, soar up and have to do with heaven; so completing life in its height, by making it divine.

To any man in whom that uplifting of life has genuinely begun, all life without it must seem very flat and poor. My dear friends, this is Advent Sunday. Once more wrought into all our service, pressed into all our hearts, has come to-day the rich, wonderful truth that God once came into our world. And that one coming of God we know gets its great value from being the type and promise of the truth that God is always coming. And for God to come into the world means for Him to come into our lives. On Advent Sunday, then, let us get close hold of this truth. These lives of ours, hurrying on in their ambitions, spreading out in their loves, they are capable of being filled with God, possessed by His love, eager after His communion; and, if they can be, if they are, then, without losing their eager pursuit of their appointed task, without losing their cordial reaching after the lives around them, they shall be quietly, steadily, nobly lifted into something of the peace and dignity of the God whom they aspire to. The fret and restlessness shall fade out of their ambitions; the jealousy shall disappear out of their loves. Love for themselves and love for their brethren, robed and enfolded into the love for God, shall be purified and cleared of all meanness, shall be filled with a strength as calm as it is strong. O, my dear friends, there is room for that new dimension over the lives that all of you are living. Above the head of the most earthly of you heaven is open. You may aspire into it and complete yourself upward if you will. All that you are now imperfectly, as an energetic, sympathetic man, you may be perfectly as the child of God, knowing your Father and living in consecrated obedience to Him.

These are the three dimensions then of a full human life, its length, its breadth, its height. The life which has only length, only intensity of ambition, is narrow. The life that has length and breadth, intense ambition and broad humanity, is thin. It is like a great, flat plain, of which one wearies, and which sooner or later wearies of itself. The life which to its length and breadth adds height, which to its personal ambition and sympathy with man, adds the love and obedience of God, completes itself into the cube of the eternal city and is the life complete.

Think for a moment of the life of the great apostle, the manly, many-sided Paul. "I press toward the mark for the prize of my high calling," he writes to the Philippians. That is the length of life for him. "I will gladly spend and be spent for you;" he writes to the Corinthians. There is the breadth of life for him. "God hath raised us up and made us sit together in heavenly places in Christ Jesus;" he writes to the Ephesians. There is the height of life for him. You can add nothing to these three dimensions when you try to account to yourself for the impression of completeness which comes to you out of his simple, lofty story.

We need not stop with him. Look at the Lord of Paul. See how in Christ the same symmetrical manhood shines yet more complete.

See what intense ambition to complete His work, what tender sympathy with every struggling brother by His side, and at the same time what a perpetual dependence on His Father is in Him. "For this cause came I into the world." "For their sakes I sanctify myself." "Now, O Father, glorify Thou me." Leave either of those out and you have not the perfect Christ, not the entire symmetry of manhood.

If we try to gather into shape some picture of what the perfect man of heaven is to be, still we must keep the symmetry of these his three dimensions. It must be that forever before each glorified spirit in the other life there shall be set one goal of peculiar ambition, his goal, after which he is peculiarly to strive, the struggle after which is to make his eternal life to be forever different from every other among all the hosts of heaven. And yet it must be that as each soul strives towards his own attainment he shall be knit forever into closer and closer union with all the other countless souls which are striving after theirs. And the inspiring power of it all, the source of all the energy and all the love, must then be clear beyond all doubt; the ceaseless flood of light forever pouring forth from the self-living God to fill and feed the open lives of his redeemed who live by Him. There is the symmetry of manhood perfect. There, in redeemed and glorified human nature, is the true heavenly Jerusalem.

I hope that we are all striving and praying now that we may come to some such symmetrical completeness. This is the glory of a young man's life. Do not dare to live without some clear intention toward which your living shall be bent. Mean to be something with all your might. Do not add act to act and day to day in perfect thoughtlessness, never asking yourself whither the growing line is leading. But at the same time do not dare to be so absorbed in your own life, so wrapped up in listening to the sound of your own hurrying wheels, that all this vast pathetic music, made up of the mingled joy and sorrow of your fellow-men, shall not find out your heart and claim it and make you rejoice to give yourself for them. And yet, all the while, keep the upward windows open. Do not dare to think that a child of God can worthily work out his career or worthily serve God's other children unless he does both in the love and fear of God their Father. Be sure that ambition and charity will both grow mean unless they are both inspired and exalted by religion. Energy, love, and faith, those make the perfect man. And

Christ, who is the perfectness of all of them, gives them all three to any young man who, at the very outset of his life, gives up himself to Him. If this morning there is any young man here who generously wants to live a whole life, wants to complete himself on every side, to him Christ, the Lord, stands ready to give these three, energy, love, and faith, and to train them in him all together, till they make in him the perfect man.

THE NEARNESS OF GOD

"That they should seek the Lord, if haply they might feel after him, and find him, though he be not far from every one of us."—Acts xvii. 27.

THE surprise of life always comes in finding how we have missed the things which have lain nearest to us; how we have gone far away to seek that which was close by our side all the time. Men who live best and longest are apt to come, as the result of all their living, to the conviction that life is not only richer but simpler than it seemed to them at first. Men go to vast labor seeking after peace and happiness. It seems to them as if it were far away from them, as if they must go through vast and strange regions to get to it. They must pile up wealth, they must see every possible danger of mishap guarded against, before they can have peace. Upon how many old men has it come with a strange surprise, that peace could come to rich or poor only with contentment; and that they might as well have been content at the very beginning as at the very end of life. They have made a long journey for their treasure, and when at last they stoop to pick it up, lo! it is shining close beside the footprint which they left when they set out to travel in a circle.

So we seek to know our fellow-men, and think that the knowledge can be gained only by long and suspicious experience and watchfulness of their behavior; but all the while the real power of knowledge is sympathy, and many a child has that, and knows men better than we do with all our cautiousness. And so we plot, and lay our schemes, and go long ways about to make men like us, it may be to be famous, when their liking lies right at our feet; to be ours certainly any moment when we will just be simple and true, and forget ourselves, and genuinely care for other men, and let them see that we care for them in frank and unaffected ways. We try to grow powerful by parading what we think that we can do, by displaying the tools of our power before men, by showing them why they ought to feel our influence. Only gradually we learn that power lies as close to us as work lies, that no man can really do real work and not be powerful.

It is a vague sense of all this, I think, that makes a certain confusion and perplexity and mystery in life. The idea that there is much more near us than we understand or know, that we are every hour on the brink of doing things and being things which yet we never do or are,—this is what gives to life a large part of its restlessness, and also a large part of its inspiration. We seem to ourselves, sometimes, like men who are walking in the dark up and down a great, richly furnished house, where tools for every kind of work and supplies for every want are lying on every hand. We find rich things, we taste delicious meats, we recognize the fitness and the care that have provided most ingenious comforts; but all the while we are not sure but there is something even richer, more delicious, more ingenious, which we have almost touched but passed by in the dark.

There comes in life to almost all men, I suppose, a certain sense of fumbling, a consciousness of this vague living in the dark. And out of it there come the everlasting and universal characteristics of humanity, which are in all men of every age and every time, which belong to man as man,—the ever reappearing and unquenched hope, the sense that nothing is quite impossible, the discontent with any settled conditions, the self-pity and pathos with which men always regard their own lives when they are thoughtful, and the self-reproach which is always lying in wait just under the surface of our most complacent vanity. All of these—and all of them belong so to human life that the man who has not any of them is an exception— all of them come from that condition in which men vaguely know that they are always missing the things that they need most, that close beside them are most precious things which they are brushing with their robes, which they are touching with their fingers, but which, lying in the dark, they cannot see.

And now suppose that it were possible for any being, standing where he could look at man, apart from him and yet in fullest sympathy with him, to watch his fumbling with a sight that could see through the darkness. What would his feeling be about this humanity that he saw forever missing the helps and chances that it needed, missing them often only by a finger's breadth? How solemn his sight of man would be! Right by the side of our thinking race to-day lie the inventions and discoveries of the years to come. This seer, to whom the darkness is no darkness, would discern them all. He has always seen how man has missed the nearest things. He saw how for ages the inventions which the world has already reached— the quick-hearted steam, the eager, trembling, vocal electricity, the merciful ether that almost divinely says, "Be still!" to pain,—how all these lay unfound just where the hand of man seemed to touch them a hundred times, and then wandered on unwittingly to play with trifles. He saw how a continent lay hid for ages from the eyes of men. He saw how hearts came and went in this world, always just touching on, just missing of, the great comforting truths of a personal immortality, till Christ with His Gospel brought it to light. He has seen how single souls have gone through life burdened, distressed, perplexed, while just beside them, so close that it seemed as if they could not step an inch without seeing it, so close that it seemed as if they could not move without finding their hot and tired souls bathed in its rich waters, flowed the comfortable faith they wanted, the river of the Water of Life which their death was crying out for.

What must be the feeling of such a being about human life? Pity and awe. A blended sense of what a vast endowment man has, what a vast thing it is to be a man, and at the same time of what a terrible thing it is to miss so much,—the feeling with which even the weakest child of Gaza looks at the blind giant Sampson, helplessly feeling for the great columns of the house. "O Jerusalem, Jerusalem, how often I would have gathered thy children, but thou wouldst not"— Jesus, the Saviour, was having just that view of human nature when He cried out so. And who will say that there was not a reverence for Jerusalem mixed with the pity for Jerusalem in the Lord's heart? And when it is not Jerusalem, but you or I, who is not exalted and solemnized when he is able to rise up and believe that there is not merely pity for the sinner who can be so wicked, but reverence for the child of God who might be so good, blended into that perfect unity of Saving Love with which Jesus stoops to lift even the vilest and most insignificant of us out of his sin?

And now, after all this, let us come to our text. St. Paul is preaching on Mars Hill to the Athenians. We hear a great deal about the eloquence, the skill, the tact of that wonderful discourse; of how St. Paul, with exquisite discrimination, said to those men of Athens just the right thing for them. That is putting it too low. The power of his tact was really love. He felt for those men, and so he said to them what they personally needed. And he was, as regarded them, just where the looker-on whom I was picturing is with regard to the men stumbling and fumbling in the darkness of which I spoke. Never were people on the brink of so many of the highest things, and missed them, as these Athenians. They felt all the mystery, the mysterious suggestiveness of life. They built their altar to the unknown God. The air around them was all tremulous with power. They were always on the brink of faith, without believing; always on the brink of divine charity, yet selfish; always touched by the atmosphere of spirituality, yet with their feet set upon the material and carnal. Of such men there were two views to be taken by one who looked in upon their darkness from a higher light. Easy enough it is to be contemptuous; easy enough to cry out "Hypocrite!" to condemn as hopelessly frivolous and insincere this life which always walked on the brink of earnestness, and yet was never earnest; to condemn, as the sweeping critics of all modern doubt are apt to do, every altar to the "Unknown God" as if those who had built it certainly cared more about and worshipped more the "unknown" than the "God," delighted more in His uncertainty than in His Divinity. Easy enough it is to do this, but possible, at least, it is to do something very different from this, possible to be impressed as St. Paul was with reverence and pity that left no room for contempt, reverence for the men who came so near to so much, and pity for the men who missed it so sadly. Oh, be sure, my friends, that whenever you see a poor bewildered thinker, or a puzzled youth feeling about vainly for his work, his place, his career in life, there are those two thoughts for you to have about them both,—the thought of contempt and the thought of reverence and pity; and be sure that the first thought is mean and unworthy of a fellow-man, and that the second thought is the thought of the best and wisest and divinest men, the thought of St. Paul and of Jesus Christ.

And now, what makes the difference between these two kinds of observation, these two men with their different sight of a human life? It is not hard to see. Is it not simply that the man who looks upon his brother's puzzled life with reverence and pity is the man who sees God there behind the life which he is looking at? The man who looks at his brother's restless life with contempt, is the man who sees no God there, to whom the everlasting human restlessness is nothing but the vain and aimless tossing about of a querulous dissatisfaction. If there is no God whose life and presence, dimly felt, is making men toss and complain, then their tossing and complaining is an insignificant and a contemptible thing. It would be better if they could be calm like the beasts. If there is a God to whom they belong, from whom the thinnest veil separates them; whom they feel through the veil, though they cannot see Him; whom they feel through the veil even when they do not know that it is He whom they feel—then their restlessness, their feverish hope, their dreams and doubts, become solemn and significant, something which any thoughtful man may well delight to study, and may well rejoice if he can at all help them to their satisfaction.

And this is just what St. Paul tells the Athenians. He says, "You are restless and discontented. You are always seeming to be near something which yet you do not reach. Your feet are always pressing the brink of a knowledge which you never come to know. You are always half aware of something which you never see. I will tell you what it means. Your restlessness, your impatience, your discontent, however petty be the forms it takes, is solemn and not petty to me, because of what it means. It means that God is not far from every one of you."

Oh, what a revelation that was! What a preaching that was that day on Mars Hill! It was as if one came to a blind child, sitting in a room where he thought himself alone, and wondering at the restlessness which would not let him settle down to quiet thought and work, and said to him, "I can tell you what it means. You are not alone here though you think you are. Your father is here, though you cannot see him. It is his unseen presence that haunts you and disquiets you. All these many disturbances which your mind undergoes are really one disturbance,—the single disturbance of his being here. It is simply impossible for you to sit here as if he were not here. The only peace for you is to know and own his presence, to rise up and go to him, to make your whole thought and life centre and revolve about the fact that he certainly is here, to quiet your disturbance in the bosom of that presence, known, out of which, unknown, your disturbance came."

And that is what Christianity reveals. What St. Paul said to the men of Athens, Christ says to everybody, to you and me and all these multitudes. He comes to you, and says it: "You are restless, always on the brink of something which you never reach, always on the point of grasping something which eludes you, always haunted by something which makes it impossible for you to settle down into absolute rest. Behold, I tell you what it means. It is God with you. It is Emmanuel. His presence it is that will not let you be at peace. You do not see Him, but He is close by you. You never will have peace until you do see Him and come to Him to find the peace which He will not let you find away from Him. Come unto me, and I will give you rest." That was the revelation of the Incarnation. Listen, how across all the centuries you can hear the Saviour giving that revelation, that interpretation of their own troubled lives to multitudes; now to Nicodemus, now to the Samaritan woman, now to Pontius Pilate, and all along, every day, to His disciples by what they saw from hour to hour of His peace in His Father.

Listen again. Hear Christ giving the same revelation to-day; and ask yourself this: "If it were true, if God in His perfectness, with His perfect standards in Himself, with His perfect hopes for me, God in His complete holiness and His complete love,—if He were here close to me, only separated from me by the thin veil of my blindness, would it not explain everything in my life?" There is the everlasting question, my dear friends, to which there is only one answer. What else can explain this mysterious, bewildering, fluttering, hoping, fearing, dreaming, dreading, waiting, human life,—what but this, which is the Incarnation truth, that God from whom this life came is always close to it, that He is always doing what He can do for it, even when men do not see Him, and that He cannot do for them all His love would do only because of the veil that hangs between Him and them? "Not far from every one of us!"—there is the secret of our life—weak and wicked because we will not live with God; restless, unable to be at peace in our weakness and wickedness, because God is not far from us.

But it is time for us to take this idea of God very near us, and giving Himself to all of us just as fully as we will receive Him, and follow it out more in detail. God is to men wisdom and comfort and spiritual salvation. See how our truth applies to each of these.

1. And first about God's wisdom. I can conceive of a humanity which, up to the limits of its human powers, should understand God. No cloud should come in anywhere. It should know everything about Him which it was within the range of its nature to compre-

hend. Then I can conceive of another humanity which should not understand God at all, to which God should not even try to communicate Himself, which He should govern as He governs the unintelligent plants, without an effort to let them know His nature or His plans. Now which of these two is this humanity of ours? Certainly, neither of them. Certainly not the humanity which knows God perfectly, for see how ignorant we are! But certainly, upon the other hand, not the humanity that knows nothing of God; for behold how much we do know, how precious to our hearts is what we know of Him!

What then? I look back over all the history of man's acquaintance with God, all the religions, all the theologies, and it seems to me to be all so plain. Here has been God forever desiring, forever trying, to give the knowledge of Himself to man. There has been never anything like playing with man's mind, like leading men on to ask questions and then wilfully holding back the knowledge which men asked for; always God has been trying to make men understand Him. Never has He turned and gone away in anger, and left man in his ignorance. He has hovered about man's mind with an unbroken presence. Wherever there was any chink, He has thrust in some knowledge of Himself. Thus man in every age, in every condition, even in his own despite, has learned that God is just, that God is merciful, that He governs the world in obedience to His own perfect nature, that He therefore must punish and that He must reward. These are not guesses about God which man has made. They are not beliefs about Him which men have reasoned out from their own natures. They are the truths about Himself which God has been able to press into the human understanding, even through every veil which man drew between himself and God.

I love to think of this; I love to think that there is no man so ignorant, so careless, so indifferent about what God is and what God is doing, that God is not all the time pressing upon that man's life, and crowding into it all the knowledge of Himself that it will take. As the air crowds upon everything, upon the solidest and hardest stone, and on the softest and most porous earth, and into each presses what measure of itself each will receive; so God limits the revelation of Himself by nothing but by the capacity of every man to take and hold His revelation. This is not hard to understand or to believe. Into a roomful of people who differ in natural capacity and education, comes one man whose nature is rich, whom to know is itself a culture. The various people in the room do know him, all of them; but one knows him far more intimately, takes him far more deeply into his understanding, than another. All grades of knowledge about this newcomer are in that room, from almost total ignorance to almost perfect intimacy; but it is not that he has nicely discriminated and determined to whom he shall give himself, to whom he shall deny himself, and just how much he shall give himself to each. He has given the knowledge of himself just as bounteously to each, just as far into each, as he could.

I love to think that that is true of God. The blindest, dullest man is pressed upon by the same knowledge of God, eager to give itself away, that presses on the wisest saint. The man does not wait till our missionary comes to him. You are not kept waiting until all your doubts are settled and your fogs dispersed. At this moment, on every soul in this wide world, God is shedding that degree of the knowledge of Himself which the condition of that soul will allow. Is not that where what we call the false religions come from? They are imperfect religions. If they are religions at all, as indeed they are, it is because of what they know of God. Our missionaries must go to them with our religion as the elder brother goes to the younger brother, speaking of the father, of whom they both know something, out of the fuller knowledge which has come to him, but with sincere respect and reverence for all that his brother has been able to learn already.

Remember, God is teaching you always just as much truth as you can learn. If you are in sorrow at your ignorance then, still you must not despair. Be capable of more knowledge and it shall be given to you. What hinders you from knowing God perfectly is not God's unwillingness but your imperfectness. Grow better and purer, and diviner wisdom shall come to you, not given as wages, as reward, but simply admitted into a nature grown more capable of receiving it. Here is our old text again: "If any man will do his will, he shall know of the doctrine." Here is Christ's old promise again: "Behold, I stand at the door and knock. If any man will open unto me, I will come in and sup with him."

2. But see again how true our truth is when we think of God as the giver not of wisdom, but of comfort. Two men are in deep suffering; the same great woe has fallen upon each of them. They

need, with their poor bruised and mangled souls, they both need some healing, some strength which they cannot make for themselves. What is the reason that one of them seems to get it and the other fails? Why is it that one lifts up his head and goes looking at the stars, while the other bends and stoops, and goes with his eyes upon the ground? Is one God's favorite more than the other? Is God near to one and far off from the other? We dream such unhealthy dreams! We fancy such unreal discriminations and favoritisms! We think that one soul is held in the great warm hands, while the other is cast out on the cold ground! But then comes in our truth: "He is not far from every one of us." *From every one of us!* The difference, then, cannot be in God and in His willingness; it must be in the souls.

What, then, can we say to any soul that seems to be left comfortless when other souls all around it are gathering in comfort plentifully? There are two things that we may say, I think; and oh, that I could say them to any of your souls that need them! The first is this: God is comforting and helping you even when you do not know it. Do not let yourself imagine for a moment that God's help to you is limited by what you can feel and recognize. Here is a man upon whom one of the great blows of life has fallen. He is not embittered by it. He is not proud and sullen. He goes to God and knows that his only help is in Him. He goes away and comes back to the same mercy seat, and goes away and comes again; and always he seems to himself to be carrying his whole burden. He cannot feel it grow any lighter on his shoulders. But all the time he goes about his work. He does his duty. He will not let his sorrow break down his conscience. Do not I know something about that man which he does not know about himself? Do not I know that God is helping him when he thinks himself most unhelped? Do not I know that his burden is a very different thing from what it would be to him if there were no God? Believe and remember that, I beseech you, about your own suffering. If you are really looking to God for help, He is sending you help although you do not know it. Believe it also about your temptation. If you are really asking strength, He is giving you strength, although you do not feel it. Feeling is not the test. Your soul is feeding on it, though your eyes may not see it, any more than they can see the sweet and wholesome air by which you live.

And then, when this is said; and when there still remains the evident difference in the nearness of two men's souls to God which this cannot explain; remember then that the difference must be in the men. In something that you are, not in anything that God is, must be the secret of the darkness of your soul. Do not let yourself for one moment think or feel that God has turned His back upon you, that He has gone away from you and left you to your fate. Don't ask yourself, if He had, who are you that you should call Him back? Who is He that He should turn round at your calling? That way lies despair. No, "He is not far from every one of us." He is not far from you. It is you that must turn to Him; and when you turn His light is already shining full upon you. What a great truth it is, how full of courage, this truth that man may go away from God, but God cannot go away from man! How God loves His own great character of faithfulness! He cannot turn His back upon His child. If His face is not shining upon you, it must be that your back is turned on Him. And if you have turned away from Him, you can turn back to Him again. That is the courage which always comes to one who takes all the blame of life upon himself, and does not cast it upon God. In humility there is always comfort and strength.

3. But we must not stop here. Where is the God who brings the spiritual salvation, who makes a man know his sin, and gives him the blessing of forgiveness and the peace of the new life? Is He, too, near to every man, ready to help, always trying to help all men to be deeply and spiritually good? This, it seems to me, is what a great many men find it harder to believe than they do that the God of wisdom or comfort is near His children. Many men believe that they can understand God and lay claim to His consolations, who seem to hold that His spiritual presence, the softening, elevating, purifying power of His grace, belongs to certain men only. Indeed, is it not the growing heresy of our time that what we call the Christian character, the beauty of self-sacrifice, devotion, spiritual duty, is possible for some men, but for other men, perhaps for most men, is impossible? That Christian character is not denied; its charm is felt. But it seems to belong to certain constitutions, and to be quite out of the power of others.

Ah, how the human mind swings back forever to a few first ideas, and holds them in some new form in each new age, but does not get beyond them! This feeling about the few men who are supposed

to be capable of Christian experience is but the naturalistic statement, in a naturalistic age, of the same idea which in a legal and
governmental age was stated as the doctrine of election. The man
who, two hundred years ago, would have seen his brethren around
him coming to Christ, and have sat down in submissive or sullen
misery, saying, "Well, there is no chance for me. Others are called,
but I am non-elect,"—that same man now, catching the tone of the
age, looks round upon the praying and believing multitude, and
says more or less sadly, but with no more real self-reproach than
the soul which recognized its reprobation: "Religion is a thing of
temperament, and I am non-religious." Against them both, protesting
that both are false and shallow views of this solemn human life of
ours,—against them both, whether souls are hiding in them as excuses, or crushed under them as burdens, there stands the everlasting simple Bible truth of the universal nearness of God: "He is
not far from every one of us."

And just as soon as men really get below the surface, and have
broken through the superficial look and current theories of things,
and really have come to real study of their own spiritual lives, I believe that it is absolutely true that they always find that there is
nothing which so meets the story of their lives, nothing which can
so explain themselves to themselves, as this; which you may call at
first an hypothesis if you will, but which verifies itself to us as all
hypotheses must verify themselves, by the way in which it meets the
facts which have to be explained; the hypothesis of God present
with and always trying to work upon our souls, to make them good,
pure, strong, true, brave; unseen by us, but always close to us; and,
because He is God, always working, always hindered by our ignorance, our obstinacy, our wickedness, but never discouraged, never
turning away, doing all that omnipotent Love can do upon unwilling
human souls to make them live to Him.

If that were true, what would our life be? Think it out; think how
a being would live, how he would feel, that was thus ever touched
and pressed upon by a God he did not see, trying to persuade him to
holiness, trying to convince him of sin; and then run back over the
life you have been living ever since you can remember, and tell me
if they do not perfectly match and coincide. Restless, self-accusing,
dreaming of goodness which you never reached; fitfully trying tasks
which all your old experience told you were impossible; haunted by

wishes which you dared to laugh at, but did not dare to chase away; with two sets of standards about right and wrong, one which you kept for the world, the other which you hid deep in your heart and were more than half ashamed of;—what does all that correspond to but the life that a man must live who is surrounded and pressed upon by an unseen God? God-haunted our lives are, until they give themselves to God, as the brain of a sleeper is haunted by the daylight until he opens his eyes and gives himself a willing servant to the morning.

Or a beast lies tangled in a net. Some kind hands try to unsnarl the cords and let him go. The creature feels them tugging at the strings, and writhes and struggles all the more, and twists himself into a yet more inextricable snarl. But by and by he catches in his dull soul the meaning of the tugs and pulls that he feels, and he enters into sympathy with his deliverers. He lies still while they unbind him, or he moves only so as to help their efforts, and so at last he is free. That is the way in which God sets a soul free from its sins. And therein the soul freed from its sins sees the explanation of all its struggles which have gone before.

This, then, is the story of the present God. What is the meaning of the Incarnation? We picture Christ coming from far, down through the ranks of angels, down from the battlements of heaven; far, far beyond the sun we picture Him leaving His eternal seat and "coming down" to save the world. Then we picture Christ's departure. Back by the way He came, beyond the sun again, once more through the shining hosts, until He takes His everlasting seat at the right hand of God. There is truth in such pictures. But have we not caught more of the spirit of the incarnation if we think of it, not as the bringing to us of a God who had been far away, but as the showing to us of a God who had been hidden? It is as if the cloud parted and the tired and thirsty traveller saw by his side a brook of clear, sweet water, running along close by the road he travelled. Then the cloud closed again, but the traveller who had once seen the brook never could be faint with thirst again. He must always know where to find it and drink of it. Christ was not a God coming out of absence. He was the ever-present God, revealing how near He always was.

And so of the new life of Christ in man. It is not something strange and foreign, brought from far away. It is the deepest possibility of man, revealed and made actual. When you stand at last complete in Christ, it is not some rare adornments which He has lent from His Divinity to clothe your humanity with. Those graces are the signs of your humanity. They are the flower of your human life, drawn out into luxuriance by the sunlight of the divine Love. You take them as your own, and "wear them as the angels wear their wings."

This is what Belief means, then. Not the far-off search for a distant God, but the turning, the looking, the trusting, to a God who has been always present, who is present now. This is what Belief means. "Believe on the Lord Jesus Christ, and thou shalt be saved."

BACKGROUNDS AND FOREGROUNDS

For lo, He that formeth the mountains, and createth the wind, and declareth unto man what is His thought, that maketh the morning darkness, and treadeth upon the high places of the earth,—the Lord, the God of Hosts, is His name. —Amos iv. 13.

THE mountains to the Hebrew were always full of mystery and awe. They stood around the sunlit level of his daily life robed in deep clouds, the home of wandering winds, flowing down with waters, trembling, as it seemed, with the awful footsteps of God.

They made indeed for him the background of all life, as they make the background of every landscape in which they stand. Close to the eye that watches them there are the shrubs and grass; the river murmurs at our feet; the common works of life go on. And then beyond, holding it all in their strong grasp, setting their solid forms against the sky, sending their streams down into the open plain, stand the great hills, which keep the sight from wandering indefinitely into space and throw out in relief all the details of the broad scenery. The foreground of the plain-land rests upon the background of the hills. From them it gains its lights and shadows. The two depend on one another. Take the background away and the foreground which is left is tame and thin, and leads to nothing. Take the foreground away, and the background, with nothing to lead up to it, is misty and unreal. The man who lives and works in the foreground does not think all the time about the background; but it is always there, and he is always unconsciously aware of it. The background and foreground together make the complete landscape in the midst of which a human life is set.

Now all this is true not merely in the world of outer Nature, but also in the world of inner life. There is a foreground and a background to every man's career. There are the things that press themselves immediately upon our attention,—the details of life, the works our hands are doing, the daily thoughts our minds are thinking, the ground and grass on which we tread. Those are the foreground of our living. And then, beyond them, there are the great truths which we believe, the broad and general consecrations of our life which we have made, the large objects of our desire, the great hopes and impulses which keep us at our work. Those are the mountain backgrounds of our life. When we lift our eyes from the immediate task or pleasure, our eyes rest on them. They are our reservoirs of power; out of them come down our streams of strength. Once more the background and the foreground together make the perfect picture. You cannot leave out the foreground of immediate detail. You cannot leave out the background of established principle and truth. Both must be there, and then the picture is complete.

The danger of our life is not ordinarily lest the foreground be forgotten or ignored. Only a dreamer here and there, wrapt in his distant vision, forgets the pressing duties and the tempting pleasures which offer themselves directly to our eyes and hands. They crowd too closely on us. The detail of life at once commands us and attracts us. The danger with most of us is not lest it should be neglected or forgotten. It is the backgrounds of life that we are likely to forget. The mountains sink out of our sight. The highest sources of power do not send us their supply. Shall we discard the figure for a moment and say that to most men the actual immediate circumstances of life are so pressing that they forget the everlasting truths and forces by which those circumstances must be made dignified and strong? Then must come something like the cry of Amos the Prophet, "Lo, He that formeth the mountains, and createth the wind, and declareth unto man what is His Thought, that maketh the morning darkness and treadeth upon the high places of the earth." Is there not in these words, dimly but very grandly and majestically set forth, the great suggestion of the divine background of all life? It is the same which Tennyson has pictured in the Vision of Sin:—

> "At last I heard a voice upon the slope
> Cry to the summit, 'Is there any hope?'
> To which an answer pealed from that high land,
> But in a tongue no man could understand;
> And on the glimmering limit far withdrawn
> God made Himself an awful rose of Dawn."

And now, if I have made my meaning plain, you understand what I intend when I say that I want to make my subject for this morning

The Backgrounds of Life. We are troubled—whoever looks carefully at his fellow-men is troubled—by the superficialness and immediateness of living. There is a need of distance and of depth. And the distance and depth are there if men would only feel them. Let us try to see what and where they are.

I speak especially to those who are young, whose life is just beginning, for it is in youth that the landscape of a life most easily constructs itself in its completeness. Then, in youth, the immediate thoughts and occupations are intensely vivid; and at the same time the great surrounding truths and principles have a reality which they often lose in later life. Sometimes, much later, as the man grows old, the great surrounding truths and principles gather once more into sight. The old man feels again the distance, which the middle life forgot. But with him by that time the immediate interest has grown dull. The present occupations are not pressing and vivid. The beauty, the glory of young life, of the best and healthiest of young life, is that while it is intensely busy with the present it is also aware of and inspired by those larger truths, those everlasting timeless verities out of which all true life must be fed. Youth has the power of realism and idealism most perfectly combined. Its landscape is most harmoniously complete; therefore it is to healthy youth, to life with all its promise opening before it, that one speaks with the surest hope of being understood as he discourses on the backgrounds of life.

I shall be most likely to make myself intelligible if I speak not too generally, but describe to you several of the special ways in which the greater and more lasting stands behind the less and temporary and holds it in its grasp.

Consider first, then, how behind every foreground of action lies the background of character on which the action rests and from which it gets its life and meaning. It matters not whether it be an age, a nation, a church, a man; anything which is capable both of being and of acting must feel its being behind its acting, must make its acting the expression of its being or its existence is very unsatisfactory and thin. What does it mean to me that the French Revolution burst out in fury a hundred years ago, unless in that outburst I see the utterance of the whole character of that crushed, wronged, exasperated time which had gathered into itself the suppressed fury of centuries of selfish despotism? What is it to me that a great reformer arises and sets some old wrong right, unless I see that his coming and the work he does are not mere happy accidents, but the expression of great necessities of human life and of a condition which mankind has reached by slow development and education? What is your brave act without a brave nature behind it? What is your smile unless I know that you are kind? What is your indignant blow unless your heart is on fire? What is all your activity without you? How instantly the impression of a character creates itself, springs into shape behind a deed. A man cannot sell you goods across a counter, or drive you a mile in his carriage on the road, or take your ticket in the cars, or hold the door open to let you pass, without your getting, if you are sensitive, some idea of what sort of man he is, and seeing his deed colored with the complexion of his character.

If this were not so, life would grow very tame and dull. We cannot picture to ourselves how tame and dull it would become. An engine has no background of character. Its deeds are simple deeds. Unless you feel behind it the nature of the man who made it, its actions are complete and final things and suggest and reveal nothing beyond themselves; therefore its monotonous clank and beat grows wearisome. Its very admirable orderliness destroys its interest. You weary of it. Nobody can make an engine the hero of his novel; for man, being character, will care for nothing which has not character behind it, finding expression through its life.

Here is the value of reality, of sincerity. Reality, sincerity, is nothing but the true relation between action and character. Expressed artistically, it is the harmony between the foreground and the background of a life. We have all seen pictures where the background and the foreground were not in harmony with one another; each might be good in itself but the two did not belong together. Nature never would have joined them to each other, and so they did not hold to one another but seemed to spring apart. The hills did not embrace the plain, but flung it away from them; the plain did not rest upon the hills, but recoiled from their embrace. They were a violence to one another. Who does not know human lives of which precisely the same thing is true? The deeds are well enough and the character is well enough, but they do not belong together. The one does not express the other. The man is by nature quiet, earnest, serious, sedate. If he simply expressed his calm and faithful life in calm and faithful deeds, all would be well; but, behold! he tries to be restless, radical, impatient, vehement, and how his meaningless commotion tries us. The man's nature is prosaic and direct, but he makes his actions complicated and romantic. It is the man's nature to believe, and only listen to the scepticism which he chatters! It is the discord of background and foreground, of character and action.

On the other hand, when the two are not in discord but in harmony, every one feels the beauty of the picture which they make. The act which simply utters the thought which is the man, what satisfaction it gives you! The satisfaction is so natural and instinctive that men are ready enough to think, at least, that they prefer a bad man who without reserve, without disguise, expresses his badness in bad deeds, to another bad man who with a futile shame tries to pretend in his activities that he is good. "Let us have sincerity at least," they say. They are not always right. The good deed which the bad man tries to do may be a poor blind clutching at a principle which he does not understand but dimly feels,—the principle of the reaction of the deed upon the character; that principle and its working we must not lose sight of in our study. The heart gives life to the arm. The arm declares the life of the heart; but the heart also gets life from the arm. Its vigorous exertion makes the central furnace of the body to burn more brightly. So the good action may have some sort of power over the character of which at first it expresses not the actual condition but only the shames, the standards, and the hopes.

What will be the rule of life which such a description of life as this must necessarily involve? Will it not include both the watchfulness over character and the watchfulness over action, either of which alone is wofully imperfect? We are familiar enough with a certain lofty talk which seems to make small account of action. "To be rather than to do; not what you do but what you are; be brave and true and generous,"—so some idealists seem to talk. And on the other hand there are hard-headed practical people who have no eyes for anything but action. "Do your duty and do not worry about the condition of your soul; your deed, not you, is what the world desires; get done your stroke of work and die, and the world will take up the issue of your life and use it and never ask what sort of man it was from whom the issue came,—to do and not to be, that you must make your motto."

Oh, the inveterate partialness of man! Oh, his persistent inability to take in the two sides of any truth, the two hemispheres of any globe! "This ought ye to have done and not to leave the other undone"—sometimes it seems as if that were the most continually needed word of Christ. When will men learn that, above all, to feed the fountain of character and yet never to neglect the guiding of the streams of action which flow out of that fountain,—that that in its completeness is the law of life. All the perplexing questions about the contemplative and active life, about faith and practice, about self-discipline and service of our fellow-men have their key and solution hidden somewhere within this truth of the background and the foreground—the background of character and the foreground of action—without both of which together the picture cannot be complete.

Do we ask ourselves what culture there is by which the human life can be at once trained into character and at the same time kept true in active duty? I reply that there is only one culture conceivable by which it may perfectly be done,—that is the culture of personal loyalty, the culture of admiration for a nature and obedience to a will opening together into a resemblance to Him whom we ardently desire and enthusiastically obey.

I recall what Jesus said, "You must be born again,"—that is His inexorable demand for the background of character. "If ye love me, keep my commandments,"—that is His absolute insistence on the foreground of action. And the power of both of them—the power by which they both unite into one life—lies in the personal love and service of Himself.

This is the largest and richest education of a human nature,—not an instruction, not a commandment, but a Friend. It is not God's truth, it is not God's law,—it is God that is the salvation of the world. It is not Christianity, it is not the Christian religion, it is Christ who has done for us, who is doing for us every day, that which our souls require. What has He done for you, my friend? First, He has made you a new creature in Himself. He has given you a new character; and then He has guided you and ruled you, making you do new, good, holy actions in obedience to Him. Not two blessings, not two salvations,—only one! This is His promise to the soul which He invites, "Come, give yourself to me and you shall be new and do new things; you shall have opened within you the fulness of new admirations, new judgments, new standards, new thoughts,—everything which makes new character; and there shall be new power for the daily task, new clearness, new skill in the things which every day brings to be done." The background and the foreground! "This ought ye to have done and not to leave the other undone,"—the full harmonious picture of a life!

Closely related to the background of character, and yet distinguishable from it, is what I may call the background of the greater purpose. It is like travelling on a long journey. You set out with a clear intention of going to some distant place where there is work waiting for you to do. You keep that intention all the way; it governs the direction of your travel; it keeps you moving on and will not let you wander, and will not let you rest; it gives dignity and meaning to every mile. But under and within that intention lie the numberless details, the interesting circumstances of your journey, the people whom you meet, the landscape which you see, the conversations which you hold, the waking and the sleeping, the idleness and occupation of your days. Often and often you forget the greater purpose of your travel in your absorption in its incidents, and yet that greater purpose is always lying behind the incidents and holding them in their place. If it should vanish, they would become instantly insignificant and frivolous. That is exactly the way in which a man's purpose in life lies behind and gives dignity and meaning to everything that the man does or says. He is not always thinking of it. The ambitious lawyer is not always consciously determining to conquer at the bar. The eager scholar is not every moment consciously hungering for knowledge. The avaricious merchant is not always consciously struggling to be rich. The unselfish philanthropist does sometimes cease consciously to labor for his fellow-man. But each of them has always the greater purpose of his life unabandoned, unextinguished, resting behind the lightest and most unprofessional action that he does, and making it different because it is he—this man with this purpose—that does it. No wave that plays most lightly on the beach which does not feel the great solemn ocean with the mysterious heaving of its tide behind.

The greater purpose may be bad or good, horrible or splendid. One man's greater purpose is an undying passion for revenge. Another man's greater purpose is a perpetual desire for the glory of God. Which ever it is, it dominates the life. No word that the man speaks but is reverberated from that background; no act he does that is not shone through by its color. It is what makes two lives which outwardly are just the same, essentially and manifestly different. It is the life. The other, the outward exhibition, is the living.

In the larger experience of men, in what we call history, the same truth is true; the same landscape, the same combination of background and foreground, builds itself. Behind the immediate activity of any people rises what we call the public spirit, by which we mean the general thought or idea or purpose of living which the whole people has conceived. Behind the things which a time is doing there grows up the *Zeitgeist*, or spirit of the time. The countless actions of a State, its laws, its wars, its administrations of justice, its shaping of its institutions,—all go on within the influence of its idea of its own destiny, the thought of why it exists in the world and what its existence means. Poor is the life that is not in sympathy with its time and with its nation. It fastens itself into no complete picture. It is a spot of discord which the harmony of the whole is always trying to cast out and throw away.

In the smaller world, it is a man's profession which makes the most palpable background of his life. If the choice of it has sprung, as it ought to spring, intuitively and almost unconsciously out of the slowly developed dispositions and capacities of a man's nature, it then enfolds itself warmly about all he thinks and does. It is as the merchant, the lawyer, the artist that he does everything. Every most broadly human act—the way in which he walks the streets, the way in which he serves his family, the way in which he reasons about abstract truth—has in it the marks and tokens of the chosen occupation of his life. Thereby they all gather consistency. They are saved from being scattered fragments. The life does not drift, but moves from recognized purpose to assured result, carrying each drop onward in its current.

If this were the only truth it would seem to make life very stiff and rigid; it would hold every act in the slavery of the pre-established purpose. But here again the power of a re-active influence comes in. The foreground tells upon the background, as well as the background on the foreground. The settled purpose, the profession, the dedication of the life is not a fixed and uniform thing. Nothing is fixed and uniform. Everything is played upon and beaten through and through by personal nature. No two buglers blow their bugles, no two prisoners rattle their hoarse chains alike. Therefore the great purpose is ruled by the man, as well as the man by the great purpose, and it is the complicated result of the mutual ruling that makes the life. It is the background and foreground telling on each other, that make the picture.

And let us notice this, that both the great purpose of a life and its immediate activities are provided with their safeguards that they may not be lost. The great purpose has its impressiveness and its solemnity. The immediate activities have their absorbing present interest. So strong is this last that the great purpose often ceases to be conscious; yet let us not think that this makes it cease to be powerful. I forgot to think about the thing I have resolved to be; I am not pondering upon the dignity of the law or the sacredness of the ministry the livelong day; I am busy, I am delighted with the detail of life which my career involves, but none the less I am in the power of the idea with which I undertook it, I am sensible in an instant to any impulse which turns me out of its course, and I am ready to claim the triumph when the gates of success open before me at the end.

Once more we ask ourselves, as we asked before, What kind of life will the presence of this background, the background of great purposes, involve? And our answer is, once more, that it involves a double life,—a life of practical alertness and a life of profound consecration, a life intensely conscious of the present temporary forms of duty and a life also deeply conscious of the unchangeable, eternal, ever-identical substance of duty. Men lose the first, and they become vague dreamers; men lose the second, and they become clattering machines; men keep them both, and they are sons of God, living in their Father's house, filled with its unchanging spirit, and yet faithful and happy in its ever-changing tasks.

We ask ourselves, How shall a life like that be won? And again we must answer as we answered before, By personal allegiance. No other power is large enough and flexible enough at once to make it. Loving obedience, loving obedience is the only atmosphere in which the vision of the general purpose and the faithfulness in special work grow in their true proportion and relation to each other. The distant hills with the glory on their summits, and the close meadow where the grass waits for the scythe,—they meet completely in the broad kingdom of a loved and obeyed Lord. And who is Lord but Christ? And where but in the soul of him who finds in Christ the worthy revealer of the life's purpose and the sufficient master of every deed shall the great ideals of life and the petty details of life come harmoniously together? Obey Him, love Him, and nothing is too great, nothing is too little; for love knows no struggle of great or little. No impulse is too splendid for the simplest task; no task is too simple for the most splendid impulse.

I hasten to say a word or two upon another of the backgrounds of life, which every earnest heart will recognize the moment it is pointed out. I mean the background of prayer. Every true prayer has its background and its foreground. The foreground of prayer is the intense, immediate desire for a certain blessing which seems to be absolutely necessary for the soul to have; the background of prayer is the quiet, earnest desire that the will of God, whatever it may be, should be done. What a picture is the perfect prayer of Jesus in Gethsemane! In front, burns the strong desire to escape death and to live; but, behind, there stands, calm and strong, the craving of the whole life for the doing of the will of God. In front, the man's eagerness for life; behind, "He that formeth the mountains and createth the winds and declareth unto man His thought, that maketh the morning darkness, and treadeth upon the high places of the earth." In front, the teeming plain; behind, the solemn hills. I can see the picture of the prayer with absolute clearness. Leave out the foreground—let there be no expression of the wish of Him who prays—and there is left a pure submission which is almost fatalism. Leave out the background—let there be no acceptance of the will of God—and the prayer is only an expression of self-will, a petulant claiming of the uncorrected choice of Him who prays. Only when the two, foreground and background, are there together, —the special desire resting on the universal submission, the universal submission opening into the special desire,—only then is the picture perfect and the prayer complete!

What Christ's prayer was all prayers may be, all true prayers must be. What is it that you ask for when you kneel and pray? Directly, no doubt, it is some special mercy. It is the coming in of your ship; it is the recovery of your friend; it is the opportunity of usefulness which you desire for yourself. But do you want any of those things if God does not see that it is best that you should have them? Would they not fade out of your desire if you should know that they were not His will? Do you not wish them because it seems to you that they must be best, and therefore must be His will? Is it not, then, His will which is your real, your fundamental, your essential prayer? You must keep that essential prayer very clear or the special prayer becomes wilful and trivial. You must pray with the great prayer in sight. You must feel the mountains above you while you work upon your little garden. Little by little your special wishes and the eternal will of God will grow into harmony with one another,—the background will draw the foreground to itself. Foreground and background at last will blend in perfect harmony. All conflict will die away and the great spiritual landscape from horizon to horizon be but one. That is the prayer of eternity—the prayer of heaven—to which we may come, no one can say how near, on earth.

I must not multiply my series of suggestions. I hope you see that they are mere suggestions and instances of that which pervades all life. All life has this construction of the foreground and the background. Everywhere there must be the background on which the foreground rests; everywhere the foreground grows thin and false if the background is destroyed or ignored. The love for truth behind the belief in the special creed, the sense of duty behind the conviction that this particular thing must be done, the joy in life behind the enjoyment of this single pleasure, all human history behind the present age, the whole man's culture behind the training of one particular power, the good of all behind the good of each,—all these are instances among a hundred others of the backgrounds of life, and bear witness of how the construction of life is everywhere the same.

Wherever the background is lost, the foreground grows false and thin. What is this foolish realism in our literature but the loss of the background of the ideal, without which every real is base and sordid? In how many bright books there is no God treading on the high places of the earth; nay, there are no high places of the earth for God to tread upon. What is the practical man's contempt for theory? What is the modern man's contempt for history? What is the ethical man's contempt for religion? All of them are the denials of the background of life. All of them therefore are thin and weak.

Again I say that it is only in personal love and loyalty that life completes itself. Only when man loves and enthusiastically obeys God, does the background of the universal and the eternal rise around the special and temporary, and the scenery of life become complete.

Therefore it is that Christ, who brings God to us and brings us to God, is the great background-builder. You give yourself to Him, and oh, the wondrous widening, the wondrous deepening of life! Behind the present opens eternity; behind the thing to do opens the thing to be; behind selfishness opens sacrifice; behind duty opens love; behind every bondage and limitation opens the glorious liberty of the child of God. So may we give ourselves to Him, and life become complete for all of us!

HELP FROM THE HILLS

"I will lift up mine eyes unto the hills, from whence cometh my help."—PSALM cxxi. 1.

MANY people seem to think that the escape from trouble is everything, without regard to the door by which escape is made; and that the finding of help in need is everything, no matter who may be the person of whom the help is sought. But really the door by which we escape from trouble is of more importance than the escape itself. There are many troubles from which it is better for a man not to escape than to escape wrongly; and there are many difficulties in which it is better to struggle and to fail than to be helped by a wrong hand. In these first words of one of the greatest psalms of David, the nobleness which we immediately feel seems to lie in this, that David will seek help only from the highest source. "I will lift up mine eyes unto the hills, from whence cometh my help." Nothing less than God's help can really meet his needs. He will not peer into the valleys. He will not turn to fellow-men, to nature, to work, to pleasure, as if they had the relief he needed. "I will lift up mine eyes unto the hills from whence cometh my help. My help cometh from the Lord who hath made heaven and earth."

How instantly we feel the greatness of a man who could write such words as those. He is great in his understanding of his own essential human greatness. Not every man is able to think so loftily of himself as to realize that in every true sorrow of his there is something which only God "who hath made heaven and earth" can comfort; and that in every weakness of his there is something which only God "who hath made heaven and earth" can help. This is what we mean, I think, in large part, when we so often say that trouble tests men and shows what sort of men they are. It is the time of need that lets us see what men think of themselves, how seriously they contemplate their own existence, how they estimate their need, by letting us see where they seek their help. Have you never been struck by it? One mourner in the hour of bereavement rushes into society

232

or to Europe; another turns to self-forgetting charity and spiritual thoughtfulness. One bankrupt begins to abuse the world for prospering while he is failing; another rejoices, and finds the relief of his own misery in rejoicing, that some part of the world, at least, is better off by the action of the same forces which have ruined him. One man turns instinctively to the lowest and another to the highest, in his need; and so it is that, in their own way, our hours of need become our judgment-days.

I want to speak this morning of the duty of every man to seek help from the highest in every department of his life. I will not say only from the highest, for we shall see, I think, how the lower helps come in in their true places; but we need to be reminded that no trouble is fully met and no difficulty thoroughly mastered unless the trouble is filled with the profoundest consolation and the difficulty conquered with the greatest strength of which its nature makes it capable. It is the forgetfulness of this truth, I think, which causes a large part of the superficialness and ineffectiveness of all our lives.

For the truth rests upon another truth which we are also always ready to forget, which is that the final purpose of all consolation and help is revelation. The reason why we are led into trouble and out again is not merely that we may value happiness the more from having lost it once and found it again, but that we may know something which we could not know except by that teaching, that we may bear upon our nature some impress which could not have been stamped except on natures just so softened to receive it. There stands your man who has been through some terrible experience and found relief. Perhaps it was a terrible sickness in which he was drawn back from the very gates of death. Perhaps it was some mighty task which the world seemed to single him out to do, to fail in which would have been ruin, and in which it seemed at one time certain that he must fail. Perhaps it was a midnight darkness that settled down over all truth, so that it seemed hopeless ever again to know anything truly of God or man. Whatever it was, the experience has come and passed. There stands your man, relieved, released, out in the sunlight on the other side of it. What do you ask of him as he stands there? Is your sense of fitness satisfied if he is only relieved, released; if he is only like a man who, after a hard fight with the waves, has got his footing once more just where he was when he was swept away? Certainly not. The human sense of fitness asks more than that. He must have seen something in the dark, or in the transition from the dark back to the light again, which pure, unclouded light could not have shown him. Into this kneaded and tortured life there must have been pressed some knowledge which the life in its best health was too hard and unsensitive to take, some knowledge which the life, restored to health, shall carry as the secret of inexhaustible happiness forth into eternity. Without these revelations the midnight and the torture would be inexplicable and hideous. But these revelations depend upon the way the soul's eyes look for help. A man may stand in the darkness looking at the ground, and when the dawn gathers round him he will only be glad of the light, but will have no perpetual and precious memory of sunrise. This is the real reason why no release from difficulty or trouble is all that it might be to us, unless we have sought it from the highest and thank the highest for it when it comes. The eye comes out of the darkness trained by looking up. Let yourself be helped by the noblest who can help you, that you may know the noblest with that intimate knowledge with which the helped knows the helper, and that the power of knowing nobleness may be awakened and developed in you.

1. But we shall understand this better and feel it more strongly if we pass at once to special applications of our truth and see it in its workings. Take first the everlasting struggle with Temptation. Every man who is more than a brute knows what it is. All men whose consciences are not entirely dead engage in it with some degree of earnestness. But how perfectly clear it is that any man who undertakes that struggle may look either to the valleys or to the hills for help, may call the lower or the higher powers to his aid. Suppose a man is wrestling with his passions. Some miserable dissipation which he never hates and despises so much as just when he is ready to yield to it, is haunting him all the time. His lust is all awake. His appetite is one day smiling and persuasive, the next day arrogant and brutal. "You must, you shall give way to me," it seems to cry to him. But still he fights. And in his weakness he looks round for help. Where shall he find it? It seems to lie close by him, in the very structure of the body in which the lust is raging. There are the laws of health. Shall not they be his safeguard? Let him be convinced that if he gives himself the bad indulgence which he craves, he will feel the quick answer in certain pain and drag a miserable body

through a wretched life to a dishonored grave. Let him know that, and will it not give him the strength for resistance that he needs? No doubt it will help him, though it will not be his highest help. Many a man is held back to-day from iniquity which his whole heart desires by the inevitable prospect of the pain, the sickness, the misery, the death, that an indulgence will incur. Indeed it seems as if some people thought that herein lay the gospel for the coming age; that just as soon as men had learned the laws of health completely, vice would be all abolished, and temperance and purity reign where the passions have so long trodden them under foot. Or take another case, and see a man tempted to dishonesty in some dealings with his fellow-men. Where shall he turn for strength to his integrity? Let him picture to himself the disgrace that must come if he is found out, the loss of reputation and of his fellow-men's esteem. Let him imagine himself walking the streets a despised, avoided man, with scornful fingers pointed at the detected cheat. Such visions, such fears as those, may help him, and he may resist the temptation to fraud, and keep his integrity unsoiled. Or yet again when a man is tempted to cruelty or quarrelsomeness he may resist because he considers that, after all, the discomfort of a quarrel is greater than the satisfaction of a grudge indulged. Or one who feels the weakness of indolence creeping over him may put himself into the midst of the most active and energetic men he knows and get the contagion of their energy and be kept alive and awake by very shame. All these are perfectly legitimate helpers for the man beset by his temptation. The fear of pain, the fear of disgrace, the fear of discomfort, and the shame that comes with the loftiest companionship,—we may have to appeal to them all for support in the hours, which come so often in our lives, when we are very weak. But, after all, the appeal to these helpers is not the final cry of the soul. They are like the bits of wood that the drowning sailor clutches when he must have something at the instant or he perishes. They are not the solid shore on which at last he drops his tired feet and knows that he is safe. Or rather, perhaps, the man who trusts them is like a dweller in some valley down which a freshet pours, who drives the stakes of his imperilled tent deeper into the ground not like one who leaves the valley altogether and escapes to the mountain where the freshet never comes. "I will lift up mine eyes unto the hills," says David. Not until a man has laid hold "behind and above everything else" upon the absolute assurance that the right is right and that the God of righteousness will give His strength to any feeblest will in all His universe which tries to do the right in simple unquestioning consecration; not until he has thus appealed to duty and to the dear God of whose voice she is the "stern daughter;" not till then has he summoned to his aid the final perfect help; only then has he really looked up to the hills.

I have already said that when a tried and tempted soul thus flees to God and to the absolute righteousness, he does not cast the lower hels away. Still as he looks up to the hills his eye is led there along the gradually rising ground of lower motives. The man who keeps his purity and honesty and strength because he is God's child and must do his Father's will, may still care for his health and his reputation and cultivate a healthy shame before his fellow-men. But these are not the king he serves. They are only, as it were, the servants who bring him the king's orders; to be heeded and obeyed, but not for themselves but for their king who sends them.

This will seem clear enough if we remember how there come times in all the deepest lives when the servant has to be disobeyed in order that the obedience to the king may be complete. The preservation of health, the care for reputation, cannot be the final safeguards and citadels of purity and integrity, because there come times in which, just in order that purity may be kept, health and even life have to be cast away. Just in order that a man may still be upright he has to walk directly across his fellow-men's standards and forfeit their regard. But the time never comes when a man to be good has to disobey God. Therefore it is that obedience to God is the only final and infallible help of the soul in its struggle with temptation. The rest are the fortifications around the city. Sometime their destruction may be the only way to save the city which they were meant to guard; but the heart of the city itself, the citadel where the king sits, the city cannot perish so long as that is safe; and when that falls, the city's life is over.

I beg you, my dear friends, old men and young men, all surrounded with temptations which will not give you rest, to know and never to forget that there is no safety that is final and complete until your eye is fixed upon the highest, until it is the fear and love of God that is keeping you from sin. It is good for every man to care for his life and his reputation. Let the doctors show us more and more how every wrong we do our bodies shortens and impairs our life. Let experience teach us more and more that he who is mean and base will surely some day find himself despised. But these are not enough. The rectitude which they alone protect is not the highest rectitude. It is a selfish, calculating thing. And it is wholly possible that they may themselves become the betrayers of the rectitude which they are sent to guard; so that a man, to keep his life, may do his body wrong, and to keep his reputation may go down into the most miserable meanness. You are never wholly safe until your eye is fixed on God, and until it is because He is so awful and so dear that you will not do the sin which tempts you.

2. I pass on to speak about another of the emergencies of life in which it makes vast difference whether the soul looks to the hills for help or to the valleys. Not merely in temptation but in sorrow a man may seek the assistance of the highest, or of some other power which is far lower. What does it mean when, the blow of some great grief having fallen on a man, his friends gather round him and dwell upon the blessed relief that time will bring him? Nay, the man speaks to his own heart and says: "Let me drag on awhile and time will help me. It will not be so bad when the days have made me used to it. Let me live on and the burden will grow lighter." As these words are often said, they are unutterably sad and dreadful. If they mean anything distinct, they mean that by and by the poor man will forget. The face he misses now will grow more dim before his memory. The sweet music of the days that he has lost will grow fainter and fainter in the distance. How terrible that comfort is. How the true soul cries out against it: "I do not want relief which comes by forgetting. I will not seek comfort in the thought that my affection is too feeble and brutish to keep its vividness forever. Let me remember forever, even though everlasting memory only means everlasting pain. You add a new pang to my sorrow when you tell me that some day I shall escape it by forgetfulness." That is the cry of every noble soul. And no less does it break out in remonstrance when the other relief, the relief of distraction, is offered to it. "Come, busy yourself in some absorbing occupation, take some exacting work or some fascinating pleasure, and so your pain shall lose its hold on you." That is only the same thing in another form. That is only offering the man escape by a side door instead of by the far off gate through which the other offer promised him that he should some

day go forth into forgetfulness of his grief. No wonder that the heart, with such relief set before it, grows jealous of the proffered distraction and morbidly shuts itself in upon its sorrow and will have nothing to do with those occupations which it is told are to dissolve and melt away the pain which, with all its painfulness, still has at its heart the preciousness of love. All this is looking to the valleys and the depths for comfort. "I will lift up mine eyes unto the hills," says David. By and by the soul, vexed and distressed by its poor comforters, turns away from them. They have bid it avoid its grief, and the very horror which their advice has brought has shown the soul where its real relief must lie. It must be somewhere in the grief that the help of the grief is hidden. It must be in some discovery of the divine side of the sorrow that the consolation of the sorrow will be found. It is a wondrous change when a man stops asking of his distress, "How can I throw this off?" and asks instead, "What did God mean by sending this?" Then, he may well believe that time and work will help him. Time, with its necessary calming of the first wild surface-tumult, will let him look deeper and ever deeper into the divine purpose of the sorrow, will let its deepest and most precious meanings gradually come forth so that he may see them. Work, done in the sorrow, will bring him into ever new relations to the God in whom alone the full interpretation and relief of the sorrow lies. Time and work, not as means of escape from distress but as the hands in which distress shall be turned hither and thither that the light of God may freely play upon it; time and work so acting as servants of God, not as substitutes for God, are full of unspeakably precious ministries to the suffering soul. But the real relief, the only final comfort, is God; and He relieves the soul always in its suffering, not from its suffering; nay, he relieves the soul by its suffering, by the new knowledge and possession of Himself which could come only through that atmosphere of pain.

There are no times in life when opportunity, the chance to be and do, gathers so richly about the soul as when it has to suffer. Then everything depends on whether the man turns to the lower or the higher helps. If he resorts to mere expedients and tricks, the opportunity is lost. He comes out no richer nor greater; nay, he comes out harder, poorer, smaller for his pain. But if he turns to God, the hour of suffering is the turning hour of his life. Opportunity opens before him as the ocean opens before one who sails out of a river.

Men have done the best and worst, the noblest and the basest things the world has seen, under the pressure of excessive pain. Everything depended on whether they looked to the depths or to the hills for help.

3. Again, our truth is nowhere more true than in the next region where we watch its application, the region of doubt and perplexity of mind. A man is uncertain what is true, what he ought to believe, especially about religion, the most important of all subjects, and, as he thinks sometimes, the most uncertain as it is the most important. He wants help. He wants some power to lead him into certainty. Where shall he turn? At once the lower resource presents itself on every side. He is offered authority. Close by his side starts up some man, some church, which says, "I have the truth. It has been given to me to tell to you. Believe what I declare simply as I declare it and your doubt is gone. The trouble is all over." It seems an easy thing to do. Nothing is stranger than the satisfied way in which men who, on every other subject, use their own minds and seek the truth by its own proper methods, here in religion only seem to ask that some one shall speak with overwhelming positiveness and they will believe him. Indeed here, in religion, men seem to bring forth their most wanton credulity and their most wanton scepticism. Here, in religion, is where you can find men believing without any evidence at all; and, again, disbelieving against all the evidence which the nature of the case admits. A very large part of the power of the Church of Rome to-day comes simply here, that men, bewildered and perplexed, demand an infallible authority upon religious things; and since the Church of Rome stands forth the loudest and most confident and most splendid claimant of infallibility, they give themselves to her. It is not that they have convinced themselves that she is infallible. It is rather that she alone really claims to be; and they have started with the assumption that an infallible authority they must have, and here is the only one that offers. Now of such an escape from doubt as that what shall we say? The deepest, truest thing that we can say about it is that it is not a real escape, because that into which it brings the soul is not really and properly belief. "What should we think," says a wise writer, "of any man who knew Euclid, but only accepted the demonstrations on the authority of the book?" He who holds a truth of religion, not because he himself has found it to be true but because some trusted friend here by his side,

or some great father in the ancient church, or some council which voted on it once, has told him it is true, does not really and properly hold the truth. He has no more escaped from doubt than you have escaped the rain when you have crept under some other man's umbrella who for the moment is going your way, but who may any moment turn aside, and whose umbrella in the mean time is not big enough for two.

And, besides this, even if the condition which is reached by pure submission to authority could properly be called faith, it would still be weak by the lack of all that personal effort after truth, that struggle to be serious and fair, that athletic, patient, self-denying life which is the subjective element of faith; as true and necessary a part of the full act as is the acceptance of any most perfectly proved objective truth. No; he who looks to authority for his religion is not lifting up his eyes unto the hills. That comes only when a seeker after truth dares to believe that God Himself sends to every one of His children the truth which that child needs; that while God uses the Bible, the church, and the experience of other souls as channels for His teaching, He Himself is always behind them all as the great teacher and the final source of truth; that He bids each child in His family use the powers which belong distinctively to him, and apprehend truth in that special form in which the Father chooses to send it into his life. It is this directness of relationship to God, it is this appeal of the life directly to Him, it is this certainty that no authority on earth is so sacred but that every soul may—nay, that every soul must—judge of its teachings by its own God-given faculties enlightened and purified by devout consecration to God; it is this which makes the true experience of faith. What comes to the soul in such an experience is not infallible certainty on all the articles on which man craves enlightenment, but it is something better. It is an hourly communion with the Lord of truth. It is a constant anxiety to turn the truth which He has already shown into obedience, and a constant eagerness to see what new truth He may be making known. It is a thorough truthfulness. I beg you, my dear friends, not to believe, because of the supposed need of infallible certainty in all religious questions, that therefore religion is a matter of authority. There is no authority short of God. Look up to Him. Expect His teaching. And though between you and the hill-tops clouds of uncertainty may come, never let them make you turn your eyes away in discouragement, or think that on the earth you can find that guidance which is not a thing of earth but which must come to us from heaven.

4. I want to speak in very few words of only one more application of our truth. It is with reference to man's escape from sin. There is a need of help which, when any soul has once felt it, seems to surpass all others. "What shall become of the wickedness that I have done? How shall I cast my sin away and be once more as if I had not sinned?" And then there always have stood up, there always will stand up, two answers. One answer says, "God will forgive your sin. He will remit its penalties. He will not punish you. In view of this or that persuasion every penalty of sin is lifted off and you are free." The other answer says, "You cannot be wholly free from sin till you cease to be sinful. No taking away of penalties can free you. You must be another creature. God will give you a new heart if you will be obedient to Him. Every release from punishment has value only as it wins your grateful soul for Him who pardons you and makes you ready to receive the new heart which He has to give." No doubt both answers have their truth. But no doubt also, the second answer promises a more divine and perfect mercy than the first. The help of transformation is a loftier benefit than the help of remission. I can picture to myself the first without the second. I can image a soul with all its penalties removed, but yet not saved. I cannot picture to myself the second without the first. I cannot imagine a soul in any region of God's universe, turned from its wickedness and made holy by His grace and yet bearing still the spiritual penalties of the sins which it committed long ago. Therefore it is that the best spiritual ambition seeks directly holiness. It seeks pardon as a means to holiness. So it lifts its eyes up at once to the very highest hills. I wish that I could make the thoughtful men, especially the young men who are just deep in perplexity about Christianity, see this. You must not think of Christ's redemption as a great scheme to save you from the punishment of sin. That is too negative. That is too low. It is the great opening of the celestial possibilities of man. Expect to escape, know that you can escape,' from the consequences of having been wicked, only by being good. Crave the most perfect mercy. Ask for the new life as the only real release from death. So only can your religion glow with enthusiasm and open into endless hope.

In these four illustrations then I have tried to enforce the message that I wanted to bring. O for that spirit which is content with nothing less or lower than the highest help. To turn in temptation directly to the power of God; to cry out in sorrow for God's company; to be satisfied in doubt with nothing short of the assurance that God gives; to know that there is no real escape from sin except in being made holy by God's holiness,—these are what make the man's complete salvation. I turn to Jesus, and in all His human life there seems to me nothing more divine than the instinctive and unerring way in which He always reached up to the highest, and refused to be satisfied with any lower help. In the desert the Devil offered Him bread, good wholesome bread. Apparently He could have had it if He would; but He replied, "Man shall not live by bread alone but by the word of God." At Jacob's well His disciples brought Him food and said, "Master, eat;" but He answered, "I have meat to eat which ye know not of. My meat is to do the will of Him that sent Me." On the cross they held up to Him the sponge full of vinegar; but the thirst that was in Him demanded a deeper satisfaction, and He gave His soul to His Father and finished His obedient work. So it was everywhere with Him. The souls beside Him found their helps and satisfactions in the superficial things of earth. They laid hold on petty distractions, outside ceremonies, superficial assurances, and so seemed to forget their cares and questionings. He could not rest anywhere till He had found God His Father, and laid the burden which was crushing Him, into the bosom of the eternal strength and the exhaustless love.

It is your privilege and mine, as children of God, to be satisfied with no help but the help of the highest. When we are content to seek strength or comfort or truth or salvation from any hand short of God's, we are disowning our childhood and dishonoring our Father.

It is better to be restless and unsatisfied than to find rest and satisfaction in anything lower than the highest. But we need not be restless or unsatisfied. There is a rest in expectation, a satisfaction in the assurance that the highest belongs to us though we have not reached it yet. That rest in expectation we may all have now if we believe in God and know we are His children. Every taste of Him that we have ever had becomes a prophecy of His perfect giving of Himself to us. It is as when a pool lies far up in the dry rocks, and hears the tide and knows that her refreshment and replenishing is coming.

How patient she is. The other pools nearer the shore catch the sea first, and she hears them leaping and laughing, but she waits patiently. She knows the tide will not turn back till it has reached her. And by and by the blessed moment comes. The last ridge of rock is overwashed. The stream pours in; at first a trickling thread sent only at the supreme effort of the largest wave; but by and by the great sea in its fulness. It gives the waiting pool itself and she is satisfied. So it will certainly be with us if we wait for the Lord, however He delays, and refuse to let ourselves be satisfied with any supply but Him.

DEEP CALLING UNTO DEEP

Deep calleth unto deep.—PSALM xlii. 7.

IN ONE of the most spiritual of David's Psalms there come, almost incidentally as it were, the most striking pictures of external Nature. He begins by singing, "Like as the hart desireth the water-brooks, so longeth my soul after Thee, O God." Then he goes on to that profound remonstrance with his own oppressed and melancholy heart. "Why art thou so full of heaviness, O my soul? Why art thou so disquieted within me?" And then comes his great appeal to God in Nature,—"Therefore will I remember Thee concerning the land of Jordan and the little hill of Hermon. Deep calleth unto deep at the noise of Thy waterspouts." It is partly a recollection of the causes of his gratitude. It is a remembrance of how Jordan and Hermon had witnessed God's goodness to him; but it is also the effort to lose his own spiritual vexations in the vastness and majesty of the scenes and the phenomena of natural life. He would put his own personal woe where the billows and the tides are sweeping and beating across one another, and make it sensible in their movement of the larger world of which it is a part, and in whose whole there is peace.

This is the way in which David's descriptions of Nature come about. He is no word-painter depicting the beautiful majestic world for the mere pleasure of the exercise of his literary skill. It is all a spiritual experience. "The heavens declare the glory of God, and the firmament showeth His handiwork." It is God and peace and holiness which his soul is seeking when he climbs the mountain, or stands under the starry heavens, or is tossed on the tumult of the resistless sea.

We all know something of what was in the great man's heart. We have all taken a sorrow or a perplexity out into the noontide or the midnight and felt its morbid bitterness drawn out of it, and a great peace descend and fill it from the depth of the majesty under whose arch we stood. It was not consolation. That can come only through the intelligence and reason, or through personal sympathy and love. The sweet and solemn influence which comes to you out of the noontide or the midnight sky does not take away your pain, but it takes out of it its bitterness. It lifts it to a higher peace. It says, "Be still and wait." It gives the reason power and leave and time to work. It gathers the partial into the embrace of the universal. It fills the little with the large. Without mockery or scorn it reminds the small that it is small. The atom floating on the surface hears deep calling unto deep below, and forgets its own restlessness and home-lessness in listening.

This was what Nature in our Psalm is seen doing for the spiritual life of David. But that is not what I want to speak about to-day, al-though I could not help alluding to it as it gives so rich a character to our Psalm.

I want to take now these words by themselves,—"Deep calleth unto deep,"—and let them suggest to us some thoughts with regard to man's relation to the world and his true way of living in it, which I hope will not be without their value. "Deep calleth unto deep." It is the profound responsiveness of life which those words utter. If some great natural philosopher were to speak to us, no doubt he could tell us of the way in which even in physical nature what they suggest is true; of how there is no force which does not correspond with other forces, and find the reason of its own existence in its rela-tionship to them. For such a great rich topic as that, I have no fit-ness. But there is another responsiveness,—the responsiveness of the life of man, the responsiveness of the world and the human nature which inhabits it to one another, which is also worthy of our study. And it is of that that I desire to speak.

How clear they are, and how they call and answer to each other, —the world and man! The world,—this aggregate of conditions and phenomena and events, this multitudinous complexity of things which happen as old habits to which the gray old earth has long been used, and other things which come with sharp and strange surprise and unexpectedness, as if they never had occurred before; the world, —this crowd of circumstances, with a certain subtle spirit and iden-tity and law pervading it; this world, living and yet dead, dead and yet living,—at one moment a thing of mere material of wood and rock and water, at the next moment a thing all instinct with quickness and vitality; the world on one side, and on the other man, sensitive and eager, ready to respond, often responding even when no one speaks to him,—man who seems sometimes to be only the chief of animals, sprung as it were out of the very substance of the world itself, and then at other times seeming to carry on his forehead the star of a supremacy and an authority almost divine,—this world and this man, behold them standing and looking each other in the face, and listening for one another's words! The world hears the man. It answers him with its obediences. It responds to his advancing character. It holds its resources ready as he grows fit to call for them. But even more sensitively the man hears the world. The mass and crowd of things abound in influences which pour forth and tell upon the human creature's life. Its slightest whisper fills him with emotion and works upon his sensitive will. Almost we can think of the angelic beings, full of sympathy, bending and listening to this converse between man and his world, between each man and his circumstances, and knowing how it fares with him by the way in which they speak to him and the way in which he answers.

But then, to take another step, when we look somewhat closer at the world and at man, we find this other thing,—that both in the world and in man there are profounder and there are more superficial parts, there are depths and shallows; and that it makes great and most critical difference which part of the world it is that speaks to which part of the man. The world is deep or shallow. How deep it is! What solemn and perplexing questions come up out of its darknesses! How it is always on the point of vast changes, terrible explosions! How character is always being moulded by the powers which it contains! How souls seem to change their whole nature as they pass through its furnaces! And yet change your point of view and what a shallow thing the world is! How its changes chase one another almost like the idle alternation of joy and sorrow on the face of a child! How much happens in the State and in society, and in the schools, which comes to nothing! What a waving of lights and jingling of bells and playing at hide-and-seek of waves upon the sea a large part of this perpetual activity appears.

And not only the world but man as well is deep or shallow. How deep he is! What struggles may tear the very foundations of his life asunder! On the other hand, what peace which passeth understanding may lie like a great ocean underneath the surface turmoil of his days. How profoundly he can suffer; how profoundly he can enjoy! What rich things are his conscience and his will! And then, all of a sudden, when it seems as if all the universe were in him; when it seems as if he were as high as heaven and as low as hell; when the music of his nature seems to be full of the intensest passion which out-goes expression,—how he will begin, all of a sudden, to chatter like a bird! How nothing is too light for him! How he will play with straws and chase shadows across the fields! How he will make life a frolic, and refuse to be serious even when the heaviest shadows fill the solemn sky!

Thus both the two,—the world and man, whose converse with each other makes the history and poetry, the comedy and tragedy of this planet whereon we live,—both of them have their depths and their shallows. Each of them is capable of seeming profound and rich and serious or superficial and meagre and trivial. And all this makes their talk with one another, their influence on one another, endlessly interesting and pathetic. It is the noblest and completest form of their intercourse—the intercourse of the world and man—which has seemed to me to be suggested by the words from David's Psalm. When the strongest powers of man are brought out by the greatest exigencies of life; when what a man can do is tested to the very bottom by the most awful or splendid exhibition of what the world can be; when a man stands amazed himself at the patience and courage and resource which comes welling up in his soul at the demand of some great suffering or some great opportunity of his fellow-men,—could there be words which could describe the great scene better than these, "Deep calleth unto deep?"

It may be in the region of thought or in the region of action; it may be a great problem awakening the profoundest intelligence, and saying, "Come, find my solution," or it may be a great task summoning the active powers, and saying, "Come, do me;" it may be in an excitement and a tumult which shakes the nature through and through, or it may be in a serene and open calmness which means more than any tumult. The form is nothing; the substance of the experience is everything. When the supreme demand of life calls out the supreme capacity of man, then it is that the picture of the waves is fulfilled in spiritual life and "Deep calleth unto deep."

It is a great inspiring spectacle when this is seen taking place in a young man's life. There is a beautiful exhilaration in it. The mysterious world lifts up its voice and asks its old unanswered questions,

—problems which have puzzled all the generations which have come and gone. Lo! they are not dead—they are still alive. They lift up their undiscouraged voice and ask themselves anew of this new-comer, and he with his audacious heart accepts their challenge. All that is most serious and earnest in him tells him that their answers must be somewhere. His clear eyes question them with hope. Per-haps he can find what all who have gone before have failed to find. So the best which the young man is leaps to wrestle with the hardest which the world can show; so deep answereth to deep.

At the other end of life the same thing comes, only in another way. When the great shadow of the earth lies on the old man's soul, and the light of the life beyond is gathering in the western sky; when wonder deepens and great questions swarm and the supreme prob-lem, "What does it all mean?" stares out at him from all familiar things,—how often then a patience and a faith, a love and trust and spiritual certainty come forth which all the life has been preparing unconsciously; and in the silent days which wait the end, the soul hears the eternity, and "Deep calleth unto deep."

I speak of notable periods which are, as it were, emergencies of life; but I should be sorry to think that this dealing of the deepest part of us with the deepest part of the world was confined to critical occasions and solemn or enthusiastic days. I should be sorry not to think that there are lives in which it is habitual. There are men, not oppressed and gloomy, but serious and happy, whose deepest thought is always busy with the deepest things. Very unhappy is the man who never knows such converse. Happiest of all is he for whom it starts without surprise at any moment, who is always ready to give his deepest thought to deepest questions and his strongest powers to the hardest tasks.

This then is what we mean by deep calling unto deep. You see what kind of life it makes. There is another kind of life by contrast with which this kind may perhaps best be understood. There is a life to which the world seems easy, and so in which the strongest powers of the human nature are not stirred. I call that the life in which shallow calleth unto shallow. Like little pools lying in the rock, none of them more than an inch deep, all of them rippling and twinkling in the sunshine and the breeze,—so lie the small interests of the world and the small powers of man; and they talk with one another, and one perfectly answers the demands which the other

makes. Do you not know all that? The world simply as a place of
enjoyment summons man simply as a being capable of enjoyment.
The whole relationship gets no deeper than that. The material of
pleasure or of pride cries to the power of pleasure or of pride,
"Come, be pleased," or "Come, be proud." It is the invitation of the
surface to the surface,—of the surface of the world to the surface of
the man.

What shall we say of this? It is real. It is legitimate. In its degree
and its proportion it is good; but made the whole of life and cut off
from connection with the deeper converse between the world and
the soul, it is dreadful. The world does say to us, "Enjoy;" and it is
good for us to hear her invitation. But for the world to say, and for
us to hear, nothing better or deeper than "Enjoy" is to turn the relation between the world and man into something hardly better than
that which exists between the corn-field and the crows. It is clothing
oneself with cobwebs. Only when the deeper communion, rich and
full and strong, is going on below, between the depths of life and
the depths of man,—only then is the surface communion healthy
and natural and good. He who is always hearing and answering the
call of life to be thoughtful and brave and self-sacrificing,—he alone
can safely hear the other cry of life, tempting him to be happy and
enjoy.

But look! What multitudes of men have ears only for the summons to enjoyment, who never once seem to hear the call to righteousness and self-sacrifice and truth. Look at the devotees of art to
whom it is never more than a mere vehicle of pleasure. Look at the
slaves of society who never make it their slave by compelling it to
make them generous and good. Look at the business-men who never
make anything out of their business except money. It is shallow
calling unto shallow. It is the tinkling clatter of the lighter instru-
ments with no deep thunder of the organ down below, and oh, how
wearisome it grows!

But there are to other wrong and bad relations between man and
the world he lives in, which result of necessity from what we saw,
—that both the world and man have their shallows and their depths. I
have spoken of deep calling upon deep, which is great and noble;
and of shallow calling upon shallow, which is unsatisfactory and
weak. The words of David suggest to me also that there is such a
thing as deep calling unto shallow,—by which I mean, of course, the

profound and sacred interests of life crying out and finding nothing but the slight and foolish and selfish parts of a man ready to reply. There are a host of men who will not leave great themes and tasks alone and be content to live trivially among trivial things. They are too enterprising, too alive for that. You cannot reduce them to mere dilettantes of the galleries, or exquisites of the parlors, or book-keepers of the exchange; they will meddle with the eternities and the profundities. They have perception enough to hear the great questions and see the great tasks; but they have not earnestness and self-control enough to answer them with serious thought and strong endeavor; so they sing their answer to the thunder, which is not satisfied or answered. This is what I mean by deep calling unto shallow.

If you do not understand what I am thinking of, consider what you see in politics. Is there a greater call than that which comes out of the depths of a nation's needs? "Tell me what this means, and that, in my experience. Tell me how I shall get rid of this corruption and that danger. Tell me how I can best be governed. Help me to self-control." These are the appeals which come out of the nation's heart of hearts. And what is it that they find to cry to? In part, at least, are they not answered back by personal ambitions, by party spirit, by the trickery of selfishness, and by the base love of management? This is the misery of politics,—the disproportion between the interests which are at stake and the men and machineries which deal with them. Those interests need the profoundest thought and the most absolute devotion. In some degree they get it; but how often what they get is only prejudice and passion,—the lightest, least reasonable, most superficial action of our human nature.

If we turn to religion, the same thing is true there as well. What does it mean when out of the profound realities of the soul, of God, of life, of death, of immortality, of duty, there rises to the surface and flaunts itself in the astonished gaze of men—what? The banner of a denominational pride, or the ribbons of a ritualistic decoration, or the rigidities of formal dogma. Listen to what men call a religious discussion. Is this captiousness, this desire to get the advantage of an adversary, this delight in making hits, this passion for machinery, this mixture of the false with the true,—is this the utterance in human speech of the overwhelming dangers, the overwhelming opportunities of the soul of man? The religious newspaper and the religious

convention are often the least religious of all the journals and meetings, the least exalted in their spirit, the most sordid and worldly in
their tone.

I find the same regarding truth of every kind. Truth and the search
for truth are the great food and discipline of human nature. Good is
it when a man, sweeping around some sudden corner of his life, sees
looming up before him a truth which he has not known before. He
has grown used to the old truth; here is another of another kind. How
great the moment is!

> "Then felt I like some watcher of the skies
>   When a new planet swims into his ken,
>   Or like stout Cortez when with eagle eyes
> He stared at the Pacific,—and all his men
> Looked at each other with a wild surmise,—
>   Silent, upon a peak in Darien."

In the heart of the finder of the new truth, as in the heart of the
discoverer of the new ocean, new chambers open for the new-comer
to abide in; new engineries of power leap to life for the new truth
to use. All this sometimes. But sometimes also the new truth stirs
nothing but new jealousies and vanities. A new law opens out of the
complexity of Nature and sometimes—not often, let us be proud to
claim—the naturalists stand quarrelling which it was that saw it first.
A new view of life, a new religion which is very old, is brought by
some disciple of it from his ancient home, and the best use which we
can find to make of it is to use it for the attraction and stimulus of
our flagging social existence, to discuss it in our æsthetic clubs, and
to pretend dilettante conversions to it before we have taken pains to
understand what it really means.

Everywhere the deep calls to the shallow, and the shallow answers
with its competent and flippant tongue. It is earnest questions dealt
with by unearnest men and in unearnest ways which make a large
part of the darkness of the world. "If he would only let it alone," we
feel a thousand times when some flippant trifler takes up some solemn
theme and turns it easily round and round between his thumb and
finger. "Who are these that darken counsel by words without knowledge?" The earnest man to match the earnest question! When he
comes how the light breaks! Oh, my dear friends, I beg you listen to
no other. When deep calls to deep, when the conscience and the

spiritual earnestness of any man—whoever he be—talks with truth, draw near and listen, for you will surely get something; if not great wisdom, from the earnest talker, at least an atmosphere and light in which your own wisdom can work at its best. But when deep calls to shallow, when man deals with great truth in a little spirit and for ends of little selfishness and pride, then turn and go away; for there there is no food or education for your soul.

We have heard the deep calling to the shallow. Now let us turn for a few moments and, with another ear, listen to the shallow calling to the deep. All of our treatment of this imagery will, I am sure, show you what I mean by that. When the mere superficial things of life, which are all legitimate enough in their true places and enlisting their own kind of interest, aspire to lay hold of man's serious anxiety and to enlist his earnest thought, then there is born a sense of disproportion just the opposite of that of which I have been speaking,—a disproportion which seems to be rightly described as the shallow calling to the deep. If we are offended when eternity calls to men, and men chatter about it as if it were a trifle; so we also ought to be offended when some trifle speaks to them and they look solemn and burdened and anxious over it, and discuss it as if it were a thing of everlasting import. Have you never stood in the midst of the world of fashion and marvelled how it was possible that men and women should care, as those around you seemed to care, about the little conventionalities which made the scenery and problems of its life? Natural enough questions many of them were; necessary, perhaps, that they should be settled one way or the other, but certainly questions to be settled in an instant and forgotten,—questions to be settled with the simplest powers and the least anxious thought. You meet your friend some morning and he wears an anxious face. You can seem to see into the depths of his being, and they all are stirred. You picture to yourself some awful woe which has befallen him. You seem to see him wrestling like Jacob in Peniel for his life. You stop him and ask what is the matter, and his answer tells you of some petty disturbance of the household, or some question of a bargain he has made,—whether it will turn out twenty-five or thirty per cent to his advantage. Are you not vexed with a vexation that is almost a sense of personal grievance? The man has no right to conceive things in such disproportion. A man has no right to give to the tint on his parlor walls that anxiety of thought which belongs only to the justification of the ways of God to man. And why? Mainly, I suppose, because the man who has expended his highest powers upon the lightest themes has no new, greater seriousness to give to the great problems when they come, and so either avoids them altogether or else, by a strange perversion, turns back and gives them the light consideration which was what he ought to have given to his headache or the color of his walls. Very often the man in whom the shallow calls to the deep is the same man in whom also the deep calls to the shallow.

There is a noble economy of the deepest life. There is a watchful reserve which keeps guard over the powers of profound anxiety and devoted work, and refuses to give them away to any first applicant who comes and asks. Wealth rolls up to the door and says, "Give me your great anxiety;" and you look up and answer, "No, not for you; here is a little half-indifferent desire which is all that you deserve." Popularity comes and says, "Work with all your might for me;" and you reply, "No; you are not of consequence enough for that. Here is a small fragment of energy which you may have, if you want it; but that is all." Even knowledge comes and says, "Give your whole soul to me;" and you must answer once more, "No; great, good, beautiful as you are, you are not worthy of a man's whole soul. There is something in a man so sacred and so precious that he must keep it in reserve till something even greater than the desire of knowledge demands it." But then at last comes One far more majestic than them all,—God comes with his supreme demand for goodness and for character, and then you open the doors of your whole nature and bid your holiest and profoundest devotion to come trooping forth. Now you rejoice that you kept something which you would not give to any lesser lord. Now here is the deep in life which can call to the deep in you and find its answer.

Oh, my dear friends, at least do this. If you are not ready to give your deepest affections, your most utter loyalty to God and Christ, at least refuse to give them to any other master. None but God is worthy of the total offering of man! Keep your sacredest till the most sacred claims. The very fact that you are keeping it unused will tempt its true use constantly, and by and by the King will take and wear the crown which it has been forbidden any less kingly head than His to wear.

I think that there are men to-day who are living in exactly the condition I describe. Unable to find God and believe in Him in such way that they can give themselves to Him, they yet know themselves to be possessed of powers of love and worship and obedience which it is not possible for them to exercise toward any but a God; therefore they hold these powers sacredly unused and wait. They know their lives imperfect; but they will not try, they will not consent, to complete them by restriction or degradation. If part of the great circle is yet wanting, they will hold the gap open and not draw the line in to fulfil a more limited circumference. To all such waiting souls sooner or later the satisfaction must be given.

Thus I have tried to show how the proportions subsist or fail between the world we live in and the human soul. See what the various conditions are. Sometimes deep calls to deep, and man matches the profoundest exigencies with profound emotions and actions; sometimes shallow calls to shallow, and then there is the surface life of ordinary intercourse and easy carelessness; sometimes deep calls to shallow, and then you see men trifling with eternal things, and playing on the brink of awful truths; sometimes shallow calls to deep, and then the powers which ought to wrestle with the mightiest problems are wasted on the insignificant whims and fancies of the hour.

What is the issue of it all? Does it not sometimes seem as if the struggle of man's history was toward the establishment of the true proportion between man and his world, and as if, when that were reached, every true man and his world would be saved? There is a slow revelation going on by which men are learning that the effort and the purpose must have relation to each other. "Cast not your pearls before swine;" "Render to Caesar that which is Caesar's, and to God that which is God's;" "This ought ye to have done and not to leave the other undone,"—those are the words of Christ which teach the lesson of that proportion. He who hears those words cannot waste his soul's strength on trifles, nor can he think that the great prizes of life are to be had without a struggle, a self-denial, and a patient hope.

There are abundant signs in Jesus of how completely that proportion was maintained in His own life. Men came to Him with selfish little questions about the division of inheritances, and He would not waste His time upon them; but Nicodemus came eager for spiritual light, and Christ would sit all night and teach him. The

one part of our nature which we have been in the habit of think-ing either had nothing to do with our religion or else could only deal with our religion in the coldest and hardest way, but which, indeed, is capable of burning with its own peculiar fire, surely it will be worth our while to study it as carefully as we can. This is why I ask you to think with me this morning, about the Christian loving God with all his mind.

In the first place, then, we want to assure ourselves in general that there is such a power as intellectual affection, and that no man com-pletely and worthily loves any noble thing or person unless he loves it with his mind as well as with his heart and soul. That will not, I think, be very hard to see. Take, for instance, your love for some beautiful scene of nature. There is somewhere upon the earth a lordly landscape which you love. When you are absent from it, you remember it with delight and longing. When you step into the sight of it after long absence, your heart thrills and leaps. While you sit quietly gazing day after day upon it, your whole nature rests in peace and satisfaction. Now, what is it in you that loves that love-liness? Love I take to be the delighted perception of the excellence of things. With what do you delightedly perceive how excellent is all that makes up that landscape's beauty, the bending sky, the roll-ing hill, the sparkling lake, the waving harvest, and the brooding mist? First of all, no doubt, with your senses. It is the seeing eye, the hearing ear, the sense of feeling which in the glowing cheek is soothed or made to tingle, the sense of smell which catches sweet odours from the garden or the hayfield,—it is these that love the landscape first; you love it first with all your senses. But next to that what comes? Suppose that the bright scene is radiant with associa-tions, suppose that by that river you have walked with your most helpful friend; upon that lake you have floated and frolicked when you were a boy; across that field you have guided the staggering plough; over that hill you have climbed in days when life was all sunshine and breeze. That part of you which is capable of delightedly perceiving these associations as they shine up to you from the glow-ing scenery, perceives them with delight and takes the landscape into its affection. You love the scene with all your heart. But yet again, suppose a deeper faculty in you perceives the hand of God in all this wondrous beauty; suppose a glad and earnest gratitude springs up in you and goes to meet the meadow and the sky; suppose that all seems to tell to some deep listening instinct in you that it was all made for you, and made by one who loved you; suppose that it all stands as a rich symbol of yet richer spiritual benefits of which you are aware; what then? Does not another part of you spring up and pour out its affection, your power of reverence and gratefulness; and so you love the landscape then with all your soul. Or yet again, if the whole scene appears to tempt you with invitations to work: the field calling on you to till it, and the river to bridge it, and the hill to set free the preciousness of gold or silver with which its heart is full and heavy; to that too you respond with your power of working; and then you love the scene with all your will, or all your strength.

And now, suppose that, beyond all these, another spirit comes out from the landscape to claim another yet unclaimed part of you; suppose that unsolved problems start out from the earth and from the sky. Glimpses of relationships between things and of qualities in things flit before you, just letting you see enough of them to set your curiosity all astir. The scene which cried before, "Come, admire me," or "Come, work on me," now cries, "Come, study me." What hangs the stars in their places and swings them on their way; how the earth builds the stately tree out of the petty seed; how the river feeds the cornfield; where lie the metals in the mountains—these, and a hundred other questions, leap out from the picture before you and, pressing in, past your senses and your emotions and your practical powers, will not rest till they have found out your intelligence. They appeal to the mind, and the mind responds to them; not coldly, as if it had nothing to do but just to find and register their answers but enthusiastically, perceiving with delight the excellence of the truths at which they point, recognising its appropriate task in their solution, and so loving the nature out of which they spring in its distinctive way.

Is not this clear? Is it not manifestly true that, besides the love of the senses, and the love of the heart, and the love of the soul, and the love of the strength, there is also a love of the mind, without whose entrance into the completeness of the loving man's relation to the object of his love his love is not complete? Think of the patriot's love for his land. Is it complete until the great ideas which lie at the basis of the country's life have appealed to the patriot's intellect, and his mind has enthusiastically recognised their truth and majesty? Is your greatest friend contented with your love before you have come to love him with all your mind? Will any fondness for his person, or association with his habits, or gratitude for his kindness, make up for the absence of intellectual sympathy, for a failure of your understanding to grasp the truths by which he lives? Everywhere we find our assurances that the mind has its affections and enthusiasms, that the intellect is no cold-hearted monster who only thinks and judges, but that it glows with love, not merely perceiving, but delighted to perceive, the beauty of the things with which it has to do.

It would be strange indeed if it were not so; strange indeed if the noblest part of us were incapable of the noblest action; strange indeed if, while our senses could thrill and our hearts leap with affection, the mind must go its way in pure indifference, making its great discoveries with no emotion for the truths which it discovered, and for the men in whom those truths were uttered. But it is not so. The intellect can love. The being who has intellect does not love perfectly unless his intellect takes part in his loving. We know that God loves man. The first article of all our faith in Him, next to His existence, is that He is no cold passive observer or manager of what goes on upon the earth, but that He loves the world and man in whom the deepest interest of the world resides. But can we think about God's love and not feel ever present as an element in it the working of the infinite mind as well as of the perfect heart? There is moral approbation, there is the father's tenderness, there is delight in the beauty of a good character. But the love on which we rest, and from which our most mighty inspirations come, is surely not complete until there also is in it the delight of the perfect intellect in the fitness of things, and joy in the adaptation of part to part, in the perfect sight of all the absolute harmony of laws and forces of which the little stray glimpses which we catch give the world a new sort of dearness in our eyes, and make us glow with enthusiasm as we, with our small judgments, speak God's words after Him and call it Good.

I know that I appear, as I speak thus, to separate into parts that which does really work as one unit. A being who completely loves something which is completely worthy of his love does not analyze himself with any such analysis as this which we have made. His affection is the affection of the one whole man. But when we force ourselves to analyse, I am sure we come to this, that the mind has its true distinctive power of affection, and that there is not a perfectness of love until that giant of the nature is present glowing with delight in truth.

No doubt men's minds differ from one another exceedingly in their capacity of affection. As we enter into the society of the great masters of human thought, it is a difference which we feel at once. Some great thinkers seem to deal with the things of which they think in passionless calmness. It seems as if they flung the truths they find abroad and cared no more for them, as the machine flings out the nails it makes. They seem to be almost like machinery which you can set at work on any material. But always there is another class of students and thinkers whose whole intellectual action is alive and warm. They love the truth they deal with. About such men there always is a charm peculiar to themselves. They evidently have a joy in their own work, and they make other people share their joy. We know such men at once. We are certain that the minds of the great theologians, from Paul to Maurice, loved their truths. We are sure that Shakespeare's intellect had an affection for its wonderful creations. The highest glory of the great students of natural science to-day is in the glowing love of which their minds are full for Nature and her truths. It is the necessity of any really creative genius. It is the soul of any true artistic work. Without it the most massive structures of human thought are as dead and heavy as the pyramids. With it the slightest product of man's mind springs into life, and, however slight it be, compels and fascinates attention.

I am sure that there is no wise and thoughtful teacher of young people whose whole experience has not borne witness often to what I am saying that the mind has a power of directly loving truth which must be awakened before the learner is really able to do his best work. You tell your scholar that he must study because his parents wish it, because he ought to be equal to his fellow-scholars, because he will be poor and dishonoured if he is ignorant. These motives are good, but they are only the kindling under the fire. Not until an enthusiasm of your scholar's own intellect begins and he loves the books you offer him with his mind, because of the way they lay hold of his power of knowing them; not until then has the wood really caught and your fire truly begun to burn. To that end every true teacher must devote himself, and not count his work fairly begun till that is gained. When that is gained the scholar is richer by a new power of loving, the power of loving with his intellect, and he goes on through life, carrying in the midst of all the sufferings and disappointments which he meets a fountain of true joy in his own mind which can fill him with peace and happiness when men about him think that he has only dreariness and poverty and pain.

But now it is quite time to turn to Christ's commandment. I hope that we shall find that what we have been saying will make it clearer and stronger to us. Christ bids His disciples to love God with all their minds. As we hear His words we know that He is speaking for God. Near to God as He is in sympathy, one with God as He is in Nature, we are sure that He is able to tell us what God wants of His children. And the glory of this part of His commandment, which we have chosen for our study, seems to me to be in this assurance which it gives us that God, the Father of men, is not satisfied if His children give Him simply gratitude for His mercies or the most loyal obedience to His will; but that He wants also, as the fulfilment of their love to Him, the enthusiastic use of their intellects, intent to know everything that it is possible for men to know about their Father and His ways. That is what, as I think we have seen, is meant by loving God with the mind. And is there not something sublimely beautiful and touching in this demand of God that the noblest part of His children's nature should come to Him? "Understand me! understand me!" He seems to cry; "I am not wholly loved by you unless your understanding is reaching out after my truth, and with all your powers of thoughtfulness and study you are trying to find out all that you can about my nature and my ways."

If we rightly interpret God when we seem to hear Him saying such words as these, then there must follow a conviction which certainly ought to bring comfort and incitement at once to many souls. It is that it is both man's privilege and duty to reason and think his best about God and the things of God, and that worse than any blunders or mistakes which any man may make in his religious thinking is the abandonment of religious thought altogether, and the consignment of the infinite interests of man to the mere region of feeling and emotion.

If you would know how needful that conviction is, you have only to listen to the strange way in which many people, both believers and unbelievers, talk about God and about religion. Hear what is the tone of many, who call themselves believers. I go to a man who stands holding his Bible clasped with both hands upon his breast. I say to him, "Tell me about that book! What is it? Where did it come from? What is it made up of? How do its parts belong together? What is the ground of its authority? Why do you love it so?" And he turns round to me and says, "I will not ask, I will not hear questions like these! I love this book with all my heart! It has helped me. It has helped my fathers. When its promises speak to me I am calm. When its cry summons me I am brave. I will obey it and I will not question it. I love it with all my heart and soul and strength."

I see another man prostrate at the feet of God. He knows that God. is standing over him. He feels the shadow of the outstretched hand. He hears a voice which takes his will captive. I say to him, "Tell me about God. Try to explain to me what is His nature. Let me understand in some degree how He comes into communication with men's souls." And the grieved worshipper looks up almost in anger, and cries, "Away with such questions! You must not understand. You must not try to understand; you must only listen, and worship, and obey."

I see the soul which Christ has helped, the man for whom all the green earth is different because of the Divine feet that trod it once. I say to Him, "Let us see if we can know anything about the Incarnation. What has this coming of God among men in the wonderful life of His Son to do with that sonship of all men to God, which is an everlasting fact? How did He who came mean to deal with all the remote anticipations of His coming, and cravings after Him, of which the whole religious history of man is full? What were the wonderful works that fell from His hands, which we call miracles?" I ask such questions in the profoundest reverence; and again the lover of Christ turns off from me and says rebukingly, "You must not ask; Christ is above all questions. He bears His own witness to the soul He helps. The less," even so some will speak of Him, "the less I understand of Him the more I love Him."

Yet once again I speak to the saint at His sacrament. I beg of him to let me know what that dear and lofty rite means to him; what are the perpetual faculties and dispositions of our human nature to which it appeals; how it is that he expects to receive his Saviour there. And he cries, "Hush! you must not rationalise. It is a mystery. No man can tell. The reason has no function here."

You will not misunderstand me, I am sure. You will not think that I disparage in the lest degree the noble power of unreasoning love. The Bible, God, Christ, the Sacraments, the Church; these great realities cannot exist without finding out men's hearts, and winning them, and giving precious blessings through the adoration and emotion which they evoke. But what I want to say most earnestly is this, that each of the men I have described, with whatever other parts of himself he loves the object of his affection, does not love it with his mind; that, therefore, his affection is a crippled thing; and that if it be possible for him to bring his intelligence to bear upon his faith, to see the reasonableness which is at the heart of every truth, to discriminate between the true and the false forms of belief, to recognise how Christian truth is bound up with all the truth of which the world is full, and so to understand in some degree what now already he adores; he will, without losing in the least his adoration, gain a new delight in a perception of the beauty of his truth upon another side; his relation to it will be more complete; it will become more truly his; and his whole life will more completely feel its power.

There are Christians all about us who fear to bring their minds to bear upon their religion lest their hearts should lose their hold upon it. Surely there is something terrible in that. Surely it implies a terrible misgiving and distrust about their faith. They fear to think lest they should cease to love. But really it ought to be out of the heart of their thinking power that their deepest love is born. There is a love with most imperfect knowledge. The highest love which man can ever have for God must still live in the company of a knowledge which is so partial that, looked at against the perfect light, it will appear like darkness. But yet it still is true that the deeper is the knowledge the greater becomes the possibility of love. They always have loved God best, they are loving God best to-day, who gaze upon Him with wide-open eyes; who, conscious of their ignorance and weakness, more conscious of it the more they try to know, yet do try with all the powers He has given them, to understand all that they possibly can of Him and of His ways.

I said that the unbeliever as well as the believer needed to recognise, and often failed to recognise, the true place of the mind and thinking powers in religion. Let me tell you what I mean by that. There is a curious way of talking which seems to me to have grown strangely common of late among the men who disbelieve in Christianity. It is patronising, and quietly insulting; it takes for granted that the Christian's faith has no real reason at its heart, nor any trust-worthy grounds for thinking itself true. At the same time it grants that there is a certain weak side of human nature, where the reason does not work, where everything depends on sentiment and feeling, where not what is true, but what is beautiful and comforting and reassuring is the soul's demand; and that side of the nature it gives over to religion. Because that side of the nature is the most promi-nent part, and indeed sometimes seems to be the whole, of weaker kinds of men and women, it accepts the necessity of religion for these weak people, and does not desire its immediate extinction; only it must not pretend to be a reasonable thing. Theology must not call itself a science, and Faith must know it is a dream. "Yes, be religious if you will," this spirit cries, "only do not imagine that your intel-lect has anything to do with it! Be religious; dwell on the beauty of the sacred past; let your lives walk in the twilight of imaginary cloisters; picture to yourselves what the world would be if there were a God; weep over the legendary woes of Jesus; dream of im-mortal life; give yourself up to rapturous emotions, whose source is largely physical; nay, if you will, be stirred by your dreams to noble and self-sacrificing work—do all this and be made happier. Yes, per-haps be made better—if there are such things as good and bad—by doing it; only, do not for a moment think that the mind, the reason, has anything to do with it at all. It is pure sentimentality. Religion is a thing of feelings and of fancies altogether." So pityingly, patron-isingly, and insultingly talks many an unbeliever. Nay, strange as it may seem, there are some men whose minds are wholly sceptical of Christian truth, who yet allow themselves a sort of religion on the weaker side. They let their emotions be religious, while they keep their minds in the hard clear air of disbelief; the heart may worship, while the brain denies. I will not stop to ask the meaning of this last strange condition, interesting as the study might be made. I only want you all to feel how thoroughly Christianity is bound to reject indignantly this whole treatment of itself. Just think how the great masters of religion would receive it! Think of David and his cry— "Thy testimonies are wonderful. I have more understanding than my teachers, for thy testimonies are my study." Think of Paul—"O the depth of the riches both of the wisdom and knowledge of God." Think of Augustine, Luther, Calvin, Milton, Edwards, and a hun-dred more, the men whose minds have found their loftiest inspiration in religion, how would they have received this quiet and contemptuous relegation of the most stupendous subjects of human thought to the region of silly sentiment? They were men who loved the Lord their God with all their minds. The noble relation of their intellects to Him was the supreme satisfaction of their lives. We cannot imagine them for a moment as yielding up that great region of their lives in which their minds delighted in the study and attainment of His truth.

There are ignorant saints who come very near to God, and live in the rich sunlight of His love; but none the less for that is their ignorance a detraction from their sainthood. There are mystics who, seeing how God outgoes human knowledge, choose to assume that God is not a subject of human knowledge at all; that His works are distinct in kind from any of which we know, prompted by other motives, and proceeding upon principles entirely unintelligible to our reason. Such mystics may mount to sublime heights of unreasoning contemplation, but there is an incompleteness in their love; because they rob one part of their nature of all share in their approach to God. Their first assumption is not true; their starting-point is wrong. God's ways are not as our ways. More vast, infinitely more vast in size than ours, they stretch beyond us, as the ocean stretches beyond the little pool of water which it has left, separated from and yet united to itself, behind the extended arm of the outreaching shore. But yet, because we are made in the image of God, His ways are of the same kind as ours, and we may know very much about them as you may know much about the ocean from the study of the waters of the bay, and from the sight of how the tides sweep into it and out again. There is no principle involved in the Atonement of Christ that is not included in its essence in the most sacred relations between man and man. The Bible opens new beauties and depths to any man who studies its history, its geography, its language, with the same intelligence with which men study other books. The Church is an institution built of men, and a knowledge of human nature throws perpetual light upon its character and its hopes. Everywhere, to think that divine truth lies beyond or away from the intelligence of man, is at once to make divine truth unreal and unpractical, and to condemn the human intelligence to dealing not with the highest, but only with the lower themes.

I have pled with you to-day for the use of your intellects in matters of religion. By them you must discriminate between the false and the true. You have no other faculty with which to do that necessary work. You cannot know that one idea is necessarily true because it seems to help you, nor that another idea is false because it wounds and seems to hinder you. Your mind is your faculty for judging what is true; and only by the use of your thoughtful intellect, too, can you preserve your faith in the attacks which come against it on every side. However it may have been in other days, however it may seem to be to-day, in the days which are to come— the days in which the younger people who hear me now will live— there will be ever-increasing demand for thoughtful saints; for men and women, earnest, lofty, spiritual, but also full of intelligence, knowing the meaning and the reasons of the things which they believe, and not content to worship the God to whom they owe everything with less than their whole nature.

I appeal to you, young Christian people, to be ready for that coming time, with all its high demands. I appeal to you upon the highest grounds. Love God with all your mind, because your mind, like all the rest of you, belongs to Him, and it is not right that you should give Him only a part to whom belongs the whole. When the procession of your powers goes up joyfully singing to worship in the temple, do not leave the noblest of them all behind to cook the dinner and to tend the house. Give your intelligence to God. Know all that you can know about Him. In spite of all disappointment and weakness, insist on seeing all that you can see now through the glass darkly, so that hereafter you may be ready when the time for seeing face to face shall come!

May God stir some of us to-day to such ambition, to the consecration of our minds to Him!

THE MITIGATION OF THEOLOGY*

"And Moses said unto him, As soon as I am gone out of the city I will spread abroad my hands unto the Lord; and the thunder shall cease, neither shall there be any more hail, that thou mayest know how that the earth is the Lord's. But as for thee and thy servants I know that ye will not yet fear the Lord God."
—Exodus ix. 29 and 30.

Moses, the deliverer of the Jews, was talking with Pharaoh their oppressor, the King of the Egyptians. Again and again the servant of God had demanded of the monarch that he should let God's people go; again and again as the monarch scornfully refused, God's punishments had come, the terrible quick blows of seven of the plagues. In the midst of all the dreadful discipline, there Pharaoh had stood with the captive people held tight in his relentless fists. The more God's blows beat that closed hand, the more obstinate it seemed to grow. At last the proud king cries for mercy and declares what terms he will make with God. Let God change His whole treatment, let Him spare instead of punishing, let Him lift off His heavy hand, and Pharaoh will yield. "Entreat the Lord (for it is enough) that there be no more mighty thunderings and hail, and I will let you go." And then comes Moses' answer, which I read,—God will change His treatment of you; God will take off His hand; "The thunder shall cease, neither shall there be any more hail." But that change in Him will not bring the change in you that you desire. The milder method will not bring of itself what the severer method failed to bring. The method shall be changed if only to show that God has many methods and will use them all, "that thou mayest know that the earth is the Lord's. But as for thee and thy servants, I know that ye will not yet fear the Lord." No change of treatment of itself can bring a change of heart. Let the heart be right and any treatment of God can interpret Him to His child.

The future proved that Moses spoke the truth. "The heart of Pharaoh was hardened, neither would he let the children of Israel

* This sermon was preached in the year 1878. Ed.

go." That was most natural. Indeed the whole story is full of human nature, so full that it is really a parable of what is happening all the time. It is this value of it which I want to use this morning. I want to make it my text while I try to point out the danger of the newest religious life of our own time. If I am not mistaken, this story of Pharaoh and especially these words which Moses speaks to him, contain the truth which they are much in danger of forgetting, and in much need of remembering, who rejoice most loudly in those changed aspects of the Christian faith which belong to these present days.

The general character of the change which has taken and is taking place in Christian faith is plain. Under many forms as it applies itself to many special doctrines it is one in spirit. It is a desire to escape from the severer, stricter, more formal, more exacting statements of truth and duty, and to lay hold of the gentler, more gracious, more spiritual, more indulgent representations of God and of what He asks of man. I shall have occasion to say before long how deeply I sympathize with this great change in the aspect of faith, how truly I believe that in it there is prophesied a new and richer coming of the kingdom of the Lord of love and life. But now at first I ask you only to note the fact, which no thoughtful and observant man can fail to see, and then to observe how many men among us, how we all perhaps sometimes, are led on to attribute a power to such a change in men's thoughts of God and of His ways which no mere change of thought, however it may be from the less to the more true, ever can possess. We glory in the fuller spirit of the New Testament which pervades our religion. The stern judge of the older dispensation is lost behind the gracious and merciful presence of the Christ. Pity is more than judgment, sympathy more than authority, persuasion more than rebuke, in the God of whom men are thinking, of whom men are preaching now. As we talk thus it sometimes seems to us as if the work of religion for the world and for us would be accomplished when these new and glorious ideas shall have become supreme and universal. Sin will be conquered, man will be saved, when the old, severe theology shall be entirely dethroned and men hear everywhere the truth of truths, that "God is love." At such a time it seems to me that some one ought to speak the very words that Moses spoke to Pharaoh, "The thunder shall cease, neither shall there be any more hail. But as for thee and thy servants

I know that ye will not yet fear the Lord God." The mercy, the pity, the tenderness, the long-suffering, the humanness of God— these shall be shown to man as man has never seen them, but be sure that not these aspects of God nor any others of themselves, not this theology nor any other of itself, can make men good, can turn men from their sins, can do away with the fundamental necessities of personal struggle, personal consecration, personal holiness in human lives. It seems to me that men are very much in danger now of attributing to a liberal and spiritual theology that same impossible virtue which men in other times attributed to a hard and formal theology, —a virtue which really no theology can possess, the virtue of itself to make men good and strong and pure. Against that danger I want to warn you and myself. To many an ardent, many a noisy champion of the love of God as against His sternness and His wrath, it seems as if God must be sadly saying, "Yes, I will show you all my love. But yet I know that you will not fear me."

One striking illustration of what I am saying meets us very often. Constantly in New England, which a generation ago was full of the sternest teachings, I hear the lamentations of men who were brought up under the Puritan theology. I have grown familiar to weariness with the self-excuse of men who say, "Oh, if I had not had the terrors of the Lord so preached to me when I was a boy, if I had not been so confronted with the woes of hell and the awfulness of the judgment day, I should be religious to-day, I should have been religious long ago." My friends, I think I never hear a meaner or a falser speech than that. Men may believe it when they say it—I suppose they do—but it is not true. It is unmanly, I think. It is throwing on their teaching and their teachers, or their fathers and their mothers, the fault which belongs to their own neglect, because they never have taken up the earnest fight with sin and sought through every obstacle for truth and God. It has the essential vice of dogmatism about it, for it claims that a different view of God would have done for them that which no view of God can do, that which must be done, under any system, any teaching, by humility and penitence and struggle and self-sacrifice. Without these no teaching saves the soul. With these, under any teaching, the soul must find its Father.

Again I say that I believe the new is better than the old. The new theology in all its great general characteristics I love with all my heart; I rejoice to preach it as Moses must have felt his heart fill with joy as he went forth to pray for the calm sky and the stilled thunder. But just because I love it and believe in it, I want to say most earnestly that there is no essential power in it to release man from the hard and inexorable necessities and duties by which alone man treads his unbelief and sin under his feet and comes to God.

I hold, then, this, that the change which so delights man's imagination and kindles his ambition, the change from the arbitrary to the essential, from the awful to the gentle, from the narrow to the broad, from the formal to the spiritual, is always a change from the easy to the hard, and not, as men are always choosing to think it, from the hard to the easy. It is so everywhere. In government, the old method of despotism breaks open and the new life of popular freedom comes forth. Men shout as if the race were saved. Now all men will be happy! Now all men will be good! What are we finding? Alas for him whom any dangers that proceed from liberty would drive to think for one base moment of shutting back the tide of freedom behind the hard barriers of personal authority again! His folly is only made harmless by its hopelessness. But alas also for the nation or the citizen which does not learn that to live in freedom is harder than to live as a slave, that liberty of itself makes no people and no man prosperous or good, that self-restraint and honesty and generosity and independence, if they are the crown upon the head of a benignant despotism, are the very life-blood in the veins of a self-governing republic. Or think of education. We used to dictate arbitrary schemes of study to our college students and to what we chose to call our educated men; now we throw open the whole field of learning and say to the studying man, ay, even to the sophomore in our colleges, "Go study what you will, and if you learn it we will call you learned." Is the student's task easier or harder than it used to be? Alas for him who thinks it easier, who thinks that the license to be learned where he will has any way annulled the everlasting law that knowledge only comes by toil! Happy for him who sees at once that the new liberty demands of him severer self-control and a more conscientious just because a freer work! The methods of dictation and despotism attempted less but they were more likely to do what they attempted than the free selection and the personal self-government are to attain their higher ends. Where the boy turns into the man, where the drudge turns into the scholar, where the slave steps forth to liberty, where the Eden of guarded virtue opens into the world of self-deciding moral life, there always the easy changes to the hard, there always the wise soul hears anew the old words of God, "Thorns also and thistles shall it bring forth to thee," and "In the sweat of thy face shalt thou eat bread."

But let us come more directly to our subject. The change of which I spoke in the character of religious faith shows everywhere, and I want to follow it into some of its special manifestations. So we shall best perceive the danger which I said belongs to it. In the first place, then, it involves a change in the whole conception of the religious motive. What is it that religiously makes men good and keeps them from being bad? It used to be, no doubt, the fear of the punishment that God would send them if they sinned. It is becoming more and more the perception of what a high life is set before the soul if it does right, and the sight of God's love which a loving soul dreads to offend. From fear to love! Not that the change is absolute, not that there ever was a Christian faith which was not all pervaded with the power of love, not that there ever can be a true faith in God so loving that it shall not be solemnized by fear, but as the prominent, the conscious, the recognized and trusted power, it is the love of God and not the fear of God that fills the eye of worshipping manhood more and more. This outbreak of protest against the dreadful doctrine of endless punishment is really nothing but an utterance of the profound conviction that not by threats of punishment, however awful and however true, but by the promises of love, are men to be brought into the best obedience to God.

The change which the dethronement of that dogma and all the terrible theology which belonged to it has brought, is so radical that we cannot fully comprehend or state it, but it fills us with joy. It has made religion a new thing for multitudes of souls. It has swept the heavy cloud away and let the sunlight into many a life. It has brought fertility to many a desert. And the thanksgivings of men and women who have found that their religion may be just the love of God because He has loved them, and that in that pure love lies their salvation, make the song and glory of these new years of God. No wonder if amid such joy the danger comes, no wonder if there are men who, thinking they have discovered that there is no hell, seem thereby to have secured their place in heaven, as if to be in heaven were nothing greater and better than to be out of hell. No wonder that one hesitates, even when he believes the truth with all his heart, to go to certain men and declare what he believes, because he knows that it will seem to them as if at once the old need of struggle, the old criticalness of living were gone with the old fear of hell; as if some easy way of holiness had been flung open instead of the straight and narrow way that always has led, that always must lead, to everlasting life. But surely if anywhere our principle is true that the change from the less to the greater is a change not from the hard to the easy, but from the easy to the hard, it is true here. Suppose I am a true believer in the old idea of government by terror. Let it stand to me in its blankest form,—I am trying not to sin because if I do sin I shall go to everlasting torment. Under that fear I study all the law and try to keep it all; I pray, I watch; I give myself no rest; never for a moment is the hand that presses down on me relaxed; never for a moment are those blazing commandments lost from before my eyes. I am afraid to disobey. No doubt the obedience that comes is hard, and narrow, formal, and superficial, but an obedience does come. What such a fear can do it does. But let the liberation dawn. Let the larger faith of love take me into its power. Let me begin to serve God, not for His terror but for His dearness. A larger, nobler, sweeter life at once! The sky is broader and the world is bigger! But oh! the new exactingness of this new service. Oh! the way in which the deep affections, all unstirred before, begin to hear the call of duty. Now they must waken. Not the hands only, now the very heart must obey. As much deeper as this new love lies below that old terror, so much deeper must the new watchfulness and scrupulousness go below the old. Not now to escape from pain, but to be worthy of this divine love the soul aspires. Its dangers become far more subtle and at the same time far more dangerous. A finer spiritual machinery must respond to this finer and more spiritual power; and struggle comes to mean for the soul something so much more intense that it seems as if all that it had before called struggle were the most placid calm.

My dear friend, unless this is its effect in us our milder conception of God's present and future dealing with the souls of men, however true it may be in itself, is a curse to us and not a blessing. Unless it does this for us we are making the truth of God have the power of a lie. We ought to be afraid of any theology which tampers with the sacredness of duty and the awfulness of life. I would far rather be a believer in the most material notions of eternal penalty and get out of that belief the hard and frightened solemnity and scrupulousness which it has to give, than to hold all the sweet broad truth to which God is now leading us and have it make life seem a playtime and the world a game. No! What one wants to plead with every soul whom he sees going, whom perhaps he himself is trying to lead into the new motive of love, away from the old motive of fear, is this: Remember that you are going where duty will grow not less but more imperious. Remember that watchfulness, obedience, righteousness, will mean far more deep and sacred things to you there than they have meant before. Go there expecting life and salvation to become a thousandfold more solemn. Go there expecting sin to be vastly more dreadful. O you who glory in your new faith, see what it asks of you! See what you must be to be worthy of it! See what a deeper vigilance, what a more utter consecration, there must be in this new soul to which it has been shown that he is to be saved not by the fear but by the love of God!

I turn to another somewhat different development of the freer—what some, no doubt, will call the looser—religious thinking which pervades our time, that which concerns the whole matter of belief in doctrine. Orthodoxy used to mean the intelligent and convinced reception of a large number of clearly defined propositions about God and Christ and man. Orthodoxy now, for many men, has come to mean a sympathetic entrance into the spirit and genius of Christianity, and especially a cordial personal loyalty to Jesus. I know that here there is a true and great advance. I know the man who seeks to understand his Saviour is nearer to the New Testament than the man who merely learns his creed? In all those sacred pages the idea of doctrinal orthodoxy is very vague. In the Gospels it hardly shows at all. The idea of personal sympathy and personal loyalty is everything. "Whom say ye that I am?" that is the ceaseless question. And so I know that a man has come nearer to the mind of Christ when he thinks that his work in life is to enter into the genius of Christian truth and to be the friend and disciple of Jesus, rather than to satisfy himself of the truth of many inferential propositions drawn from what Christ and his apostles said. But here, again, the believer in this new and better method is all wrong if he thinks that it opens to him an easier or less exacting spiritual experience than that in which he used to live when he was the champion of doctrines and of creeds. It needs a greater man to be a Christian in the spirit than in the letter of the faith. He who undertakes it must be prepared for deeper mental experiences, for doubts beside which the old doubts shall seem child's play, for a complete obedience of which he never dreamed till he began to seek not only the truth of Christ but Christ the truth. For all experience tells us that a man may pretty easily believe any statement of truth which he wants to believe. Intent, exclusive fixing of the mind upon it will almost certainly make it seem true. But how much more than that is needed when I have to enter into the soul of a great system of salvation like Christianity, or to make myself the disciple, with a discipleship that shall renew me into the likeness of a spiritual Lord like Christ. What repression of myself, what independence of my fellow-men, what opening of the inmost secret places of my life to Him! I know that I could convince a man that a certain theory of the atonement was true, that what Christ did for man upon the Cross was just exactly this or this, with far less strain upon His spiritual power, with far less calling out of his profoundest faith, than I should need in order to make him know the mystery of the Christhood in which our dear Lord not merely wrought but was the perfect atonement for our sins. One would need a persuaded mind; the other needs a quickened soul, alive with all the same purposes that filled the soul of Jesus.

Therefore it is, I say, that the new faith demands a larger man and a profounder belief than that which went before. Oh, do not think that because men no longer dare to ask you whether you believe this or that doctrine and to decide whether or not you are a Christian by your answer, that therefore belief has grown a slight and easy thing. As their poor questions fade and die away, all the more deep and awful in the soul's ear grows the profounder question of the Lord Himself which they used to silence, "What think ye of me?" "Whom say ye that I am?" Be sure that if you are to be a worthy man of the new faith, a worthy Christian of the new time, your heart must be strong to a more heroic capacity of believing what men call impossible. Your thread of unbelief in the new sight you have of its spiritual essence must be far more deep, and your closet must witness far more earnest pleadings with the God of faith than any that the old days of dogmatism ever saw.

3. I take another illustration from the field of man's relation to

his fellow-man in spiritual things. It was a great advance when gradually the idea of spiritual directorship narrowed its range before the progress of the idea of personal responsibility. Once the whole Christian world teemed with confessionals. Certain chosen souls sat by the highways of all life, often with the tenderest solicitude, often too with wondrous skill and experience, all purified and made the more acute by wondrous sympathy, to tell all their puzzled brethren how to unsnarl their skeins of tangled life, what was their duty, in which way they ought to go. It belonged to all kinds of churches of every creed, of every name. That day is past over a very large proportion of the Christian world. Wherever it has passed it never can come back again. Here and there some men who dread the dangers of the new life for their brethren are dragging out the long-overthrown confessional from the rubbish of the ages under which it lies and trying to set its shattered and unsteady framework in its place again; or else they go and borrow one from that part of the Christian world which has not yet disowned its use. Here and there some puzzled soul cries out for it and begs the Church to take a power which her Lord never gave her, and tell it just how it shall sail its most bewildered life. These are anachronisms and exceptions. The world in which we live, the world of progress, the modern world, the modern man wants no confessional and asks the Church to give him not minute rules of duty, but great inspirations and broad principles of life. For the application of those principles, for the special life he ought to live from day to day, from hour to hour, he appeals to his own conscience. Is the modern man right? Indeed he is! The life that he alone must carry up to God at last, he alone must carry through this world of temptation now. He is doing a noble act, an act to which his manhood binds him and in which his manhood is asserted when he goes up to the church, or to the priest, and says, "Give me my life, for I must live it. Help me, advise me, inspire me all you can, but give me my life for I must live it." Only, it is of infinite importance into what sort of hands he takes that life of his, whether into hands trembling with anxiety or into hands greedy and coarse with pride. I think that to the best souls of our time there is, with all the exhilaration that comes of the sense of freedom, a pathos that is almost sad about this new consciousness of personal independence, which no man can disown, with which the light souls play as children might play with battle flags, but in which lies unfolded a possibility of tragedy which no man has begun to fathom. The best souls seem to come to life as the morning comes to the world, all flushed and bright with hope, but pausing, lingering, creeping up the sky as if the day's work it saw before it was too great. Oh, how much easier to find my priest and have him tell me what I ought to do than to seek it and find it for myself in all this maze of doubt, hidden under all this heap of passion, prejudice, and pride! Certainly no man is worthy to live in these new days, and be a modern man in the pure church where no spiritual directorship is tolerated, who dares to be frivolous, who is not constantly and almost overwhelmingly, aware that to guide one's own life is not and cannot be an easy thing, who is not made all the more humbly dependent upon God by the independence of his fellow-men which his soul steadfastly claims.

It would be interesting, if we had time, to trace the clear illustration of our truth in relation to the institutions of religion and the use that men make of them. There, too, a freer method reigns. There, too, the freer method is an advance upon the stricter method just in proportion as it secures more fully the purposes for which the institutions all exist. For instance, there is a less constrained observance of Sunday. There are larger notions of what constitutes the sacredness of the Day of Rest. Is it a gain or a loss, this departure from the severer rules in which we lived some twenty years ago? As Christians we can give but one answer: It is a gain so far as it makes a more reasonable, a more voluntary, a brighter and freer religion possible. If it does that, because it does that, we are glad of the new spirit that fills the Lord's Day. We rejoice that its distinct difference from the Jewish Sabbath has been distinctly shown, because thereby the chance is opened for us to gain perfectly out of our Lord's Day what the Jew could only gain most imperfectly by his most scrupulous Sabbatical propriety. The larger liberty of Sunday is beautiful to us because it means not the throwing away, but the true keeping of the Lord's Day by the man for whom it was made. There is a Sunday conceivable on which no Hebrew shadow rests, a Sunday full of spontaneousness and delight, a Sunday when the soul honors its Lord not merely by turning aside to some fenced and protected regions of its life where alone it seems to it that He abides, but when it touches the familiar things of the other days with new hands and looks on them with new enlightened eyes, and finds them sacred and full of light,—a Sunday whose proper occupations are broadly and freely dictated by the soul's own consciousness of spiritual needs, a Sunday when men shut their shops not by a law of the State but by the law of God in their hearts, His everlasting law that the life is more than meat,—a Sunday when the duty of the human child to know his divine Father, that duty transfigured to a privilege, fills every hour with fresh and eager and ingenious exercise of the best powers that the children of God possess. Every relaxing of the iron laws of Sunday ought to be the opening of the sacred day towards this divine ideal. Oh, let the men who want the Sunday made more free, be sure, as they are Christian men, that they are asking it in the interest of an elevated and not of a degraded spirituality. Let them know that it is not an easier but a harder Sunday that they ask, a Sunday more exacting in the demands it makes upon the peronsal conscience, upon the spiritual ambition, upon the constant, unsleeping vigilance of the soul which on the free day would come freely to the presence of God to its own best life. The man who clearly sees and solemnly accepts that responsibility has a religious right as against every church and teacher to claim the full freedom of his holy day.

All these same things are true about all religious observances, about coming to church, about stated times of prayer, about free intercourse with every kind of worship. In every case the tight, hard rule does to a large extent accomplish what it undertakes, but it cannot undertake the best. He who launches out into a freer life sets sail for higher things, but he ought to know all the dangers of the voyage and be ready for all the patience and watchfulness and sacrifice it will require. If he has faced all that, then let him sail, but not till then. That is the true law of all liberty.

I think that no man carefully reads the words of Christ and does not feel how full his soul is always of this truth which I have tried to preach to-day. He came to lead His people out to freedom. He came to show the love of God. I think that as He stands there in the porch of the Hebrew temple preaching His Christian Gospel we can often seem to see upon His face and to hear trembling in His voice a deep anxiety. He evidently dreads lest to these people freedom and love should seem to be the abrogation and not the consummation of the Law. "Think not that I am come to destroy, I am not come to destroy but to fulfil," these are His earnest warning words. The

broad is more exacting than the narrow; the complete makes larger
demands than the partial; how He is always insisting upon that! It
was said by them of old time "Thou shalt not forswear thyself. But
I say unto you, swear not at all." "Ye have heard that it hath been
said an eye for an eye and a tooth for a tooth, but I say unto you resist not evil." Everywhere He is so anxious that His Gospel should
seem to be not the corruption but the transfiguration of duty. That
the broad is more exacting than the narrow, that the complete makes
larger demands than the partial, that no theology is really an advance
on what has gone before it unless it deepens the sense of personal
duty and the awfulness of living,—these are the convictions which
we want to see firmly set in the minds and consciences of men; and
then there is no need to fear,—nay, we may rejoice in and be thankful or every sign of liberal thought and action, every claim of personal freedom which men make for the belief and worship of their
souls.

There is a picture which one dares to hope is being realized in
many a brave and faithful spirit in these days of ours. A true and
earnest man longs for a larger view of God and for a chance to live
more freely in His service. By and by he finds that he can have such
a chance, that it belongs to him as God's child. He takes it joyfully.
He lives in larger doctrine, in more spiritual relation to all ordi-
nances; and yet as he grows more free he grows more scrupulously,
more eagerly obedient. Every wish of God, discerned by free spiritual sympathy, holds him like a law, and his daily delight lies in finding how strong is love to do the work which once he thought
could not be done except by fear. Every new theological breadth
means a new obligation to be pure and true and holy. It is as if the
world had been hooped with iron and kept shut up in a vacuum till
some day it was flung freely abroad into its atmosphere, and found
its iron hoops no longer needed, only because its new liberty held it
so close into a sphere. That is the picture of the best progress of
earth, and the promise of the best blessedness of heaven.

We have wandered far enough from the old banks of the Nile
where stands King Pharaoh vainly promising that if the thunder
and the hail will only cease he will be good. But I hope in all our
morning's wandering we have been learning that the ceasing of hail
and thunder of itself makes no man good, that no mitigation of theology, no truer presentation of God, no fading out of old threats,

no relaxing of discipline, however they may sweetly tempt men to a higher life, can ever abolish that which is the first law and the highest privilege of human life, the everlasting need of moral struggle, of patient watchfulness over ourselves, of resolute fight with ourselves and of humble prayer to God, and of brotherly devotion to our brethren which alone makes us truly men.

THE LIGHT OF THE WORLD

Then spake Jesus again unto them, saying, I am the Light of the World: he that followeth me shall not walk in Darkness, but shall have the Light of Life.
—JOHN viii. 12.

SOMETIMES Jesus gathers His work and nature up in one descriptive word, and offers it, as it were out of a wide-open hand, complete to His disciples. In such a word all the details of His relation to the soul and to the world are comprehensively included. As the disciple listens and receives it, he feels all his fragmentary and scattered experiences drawing together and rounding into unity. As, having heard it, he carries it forth with him into his life, he finds all future experiences claiming their places within it, and getting their meaning from it. Such words of Jesus are like spheres of crystal into which the world is gathered, and where the past and future, the small and great, may all be read.

It seems to me as if there were days on which we wanted to set one of these comprehensive words of Christ before our eyes and study it. There are days when we must give ourselves to some particular detail of Christian truth or conduct. There are other days when we are faced by the question of the whole meaning of the Christian faith and its relation to the great world of life. Vague and perplexed the soul is to which its faith does not come with distinct and special touches, pressing directly on every movement of its life. But poor and petty is the soul which has no large conception of its faith, always abiding around and enfolding its details and giving them the dignity and unity they need.

One of these comprehensive words of Jesus is our text this morning.

I want to ask you then to think with me what Jesus means when He declares Himself to be the "Light of the World" or the "Light of Life." The words come down to us out of the old Hebrew temple where He spoke them first. They pierce into the centre of our modern life. Nay, they have done much to make our modern life, and to make it different from the old Hebrew temple where they were spoken first. It will be good indeed if we can feel something of the power that is in them, and understand how clear is the conception of Life which they include, how far our present Christianity is an embodiment of that conception, how far it fails of it, how certain it is in being ever truer and truer to that conception that the faith of Christ must come to be the Master of the soul and of the world.

We may begin, then, by considering what would be the idea of Christ and His relation to the world which we should get if this were all we knew of Him,—if He as yet had told us nothing of Himself but what is wrapped up in these rich and simple words, "I am the Light of the World," "I am the Light of Life." They send us instantly abroad into the world of Nature. They set us on the hilltop watching the sunrise as it fills the east with glory. They show us the great plain flooded and beaten and quivering with the noonday sun. They hush and elevate us with the mystery and sweetness and suggestiveness of the evening's glow. There could be no image so abundant in its meaning; no fact plucked from the world of Nature could have such vast variety of truth to tell; and yet one meaning shines out from the depth of the figure and irradiates all its messages. They all are true by its truth. What is that meaning? It is the essential richness and possibility of the world and its essential belonging to the sun. Light may be great and glorious in itself. The sun may be tumultuous with fiery splendor; the atmosphere may roll in billows of glory for its million miles; but light as related to earth has its significance in the earth's possibilities. The sun, as the world's sun, is nothing without the world, on which it shines, and whose essential character and glory it displays.

Do you see what I mean? When the sun rose this morning it found the world here. It did not make the world. It did not fling forth on its earliest ray this solid globe, which was not and would not have been but for the sun's rising. What did it do? It found the world in darkness, torpid and heavy and asleep; with powers all wrapped up in sluggishness; with life that was hardly better or more alive than death. The sun found this great sleeping world and woke it. It bade it be itself. It quickened every slow and sluggish faculty. It called to the dull streams, and said, "Be quick;" to the dull birds and bade them sing; to the dull fields and made them grow; to the dull men and bade them talk and think and work. It flashed electric invitation to the whole mass of sleeping power which really was the world, and summoned it to action. It did not make the world. It did not sweep a dead world off and set a live world in its place. It did not start another set of processes unlike those which had been sluggishly moving in the darkness. It poured strength into the essential processes which belonged to the very nature of the earth which it illuminated. It glorified, intensified, fulfilled the earth; so that with the sun's work incomplete, with part of the earth illuminated and the rest lying in the darkness still, we can most easily conceive of the dark region looking in its half-life drowsily over to the region which was flooded with light, and saying, "There, there is the true earth! That is the real planet. In light and not in darkness the earth truly is itself."

That is the Parable of the Light. And now it seems to me to be of all importance to remember and assert all that to be distinctly a true parable of Christ. He says it is: "I am the Light of the World." A thousand things that means. A thousand subtle, mystic miracles of deep and intricate relationship between Christ and humanity must be enfolded in those words; but over and behind and within all other meanings, it means this,—the essential richness and possibility of humanity and its essential belonging to Divinity. Christ is unspeakably great and glorious in Himself. The glory which He had with His Father "before the world was," of that we can only meditate and wonder; but the glory which He has had since the world was, the glory which He has had in relation to the world, is all bound up with the world's possibilities, has all consisted in the utterance and revelation and fulfilment of capacities which were in the very nature of the world on which His Light has shone.

Do you see what I mean? Christ rises on a soul. Christ rises on the world. I speak in crude and superficial language. For the moment I make no account of the deep and sacred truth,—the truth which alone is finally and absolutely true,—that Christ has always been with every soul and all the world. I talk in crude and superficial words, and say Christ comes to any soul or to the world. What is it that happens? If the figure of the Light is true, Christ when He comes finds the soul or the world really existent, really having within itself its holiest capabilities, really moving, though dimly and darkly, in spite of all its hindrances, in its true directions; and what He does for it is to quicken it through and through, to sound the bugle of its true life in its ears, to make it feel the nobleness of movements which have seemed to it ignoble, the hopefulness of impulses which have seemed hopeless, to bid it be itself. The little lives which do in little ways that which the life of Jesus does completely, the noble characters of which we think we have the right to say that they are the lights of human history, this is true also of them. They reveal and they inspire. The worthless becomes full of worth, the insignificant becomes full of meaning at their touch. They faintly catch the feeble reflection of His life who is the true Light of the World, the real illumination and inspiration of humanity.

But metaphors bewilder and embarrass us when once we have caught their general meaning, and they begin to tempt us to follow them out into details into which they were not meant to lead us. Let us then leave the figure, and try to grasp the truth in its complete simplicity and see what some of its applications are. The truth is that every higher life to which man comes, and especially the highest life in Christ, is in the true line of man's humanity; there is no transportation to a foreign region. There is the quickening and fulfilling of what man by the very essence of his nature is. The more man becomes irradiated with Divinity, the more, not the less, truly he is man. The fullest Christian experience is simply the fullest life. To enter into it therefore is no wise strange. The wonder and the unnaturalness is that any child of God should live outside of it, and so in all his life should never be himself.

When I repeat such truths they seem self-evident. No man, I think, denies them; and yet I feel the absence of their power all through men's struggles for the Christian life. A sense of foreignness and unnaturalness and strangeness lies like a fog across the entrance of the divine country; a certain wonder whether I, a man, have any business there; an unreality about it all; a break and gulf between what the world is and what we know it ought to be,—all these are elements in the obscurity, the feebleness, the vague remoteness, of religion.

And yet how clear the Bible is about it all! How clear Christ is! It is redemption and fulfilment which he comes to bring to man. Those are his words. There is a true humanity which is to be restored, and all whose unattained possibilities are to be filled out. There is no human affection, of fatherhood, brotherhood, childhood, which is not capable of expressing divine relations. Man is a child of God, for whom his Father's house is waiting. The whole creation is groaning and travailing till man shall be complete. Christ comes not to destroy but to fulfil. What is the spirit of such words as those? Is it not all a claiming of man through all his life for God? Is it not an assertion that just so far as he is not God's he is not truly man? Is it not a declaration that whatever he does in his true human nature, undistorted, unperverted, is divinely done, and therefore that the divine perfection of his life will be in the direction which these efforts of his nature indicate and prophesy?

I bid you to think whether to clearly believe this would not make the world more full of courage and of hope. If you could thoroughly believe that the divine life to which you were called was the completion, and not the abrogation and surrender, of your humanity, would you not be more strong and eager in your entrance on it? If below the superficial currents which so tremendously draw us away from righteousness and truth we always felt the tug and majestic pressure of the profoundest currents setting toward righteousness and truth, would not our souls be stronger? Shall we not think that? Shall we leave it to doubting lips to tell about the "tendency which makes for righteousness"? Shall we not tell of it,—we who believe in Christ, who made in His very being the declaration of the nativeness of righteousness to man, who bade all generations see in Him how the Son of Man is the Son of God in the foundation and intention of His life?

Let us see how all this is true in various applications. Apply it first to the standards of character. We talk of Christian character as if it were some separate and special thing unattempted, unsuggested by the human soul until it became aware of Christ. There would come a great flood of light and reality into it all if we knew thoroughly that the Christian character is nothing but the completed human character. The Christian is nothing but the true man. Nothing but the true man, do I say? As if that were a little thing! As if man, with any inflow of divinity, could be, could wish to be anything more or different from man! But we imagine a certain vague array of qualities which are to belong to the Christian life which are not the intrinsic human qualities; and so our Christian type becomes unreal, and our human type loses its dignity and greatness. Human courage, human patience, human trustiness, human humility,—these filled with the fire of God make the graces of the Christian life. We are still haunted by the false old distinction of the natural virtues and the Christian graces. The Christian graces are nothing but the natural virtues held up into the light of Christ. They are made of the same stuff; they are lifted along the same lines; but they have found their pinnacle. They have caught the illumination which their souls desire. Manliness has not been changed into Godliness; it has fulfilled itself in Godliness.

As soon as we understand all this, then what a great, clear thing salvation becomes. Its one idea is health. Not rescue from suffering, not plucking out of fire, not deportation to some strange, beautiful region where the winds blow with other influences and the skies drop with other dews, not the enchaining of the spirit with some unreal celestial spell, but health,—the cool, calm vigor of the normal human life; the making of the man to be himself; the calling up out of the depths of his being and the filling with vitality of that self which is truly he,—this is salvation!

Of course it all assumes that in this mixture of good and evil which we call Man, this motley and medley which we call human character, it is the good and not the evil which is the foundation color of the whole. Man is a son of God on whom the Devil has laid his hand, not a child of the Devil whom God is trying to steal. That is the first truth of all religion. That is what Christ is teaching everywhere and always. "We called the chess-board white, we call it black;" but it is, this chess-board of our human life, white not black, —black spotted on white, not white spotted upon black.

It is easy to make this question of precedence and intrusion seem unimportant. "If man stands here to-day half bad, half good, what matters it how it came about,—whether the good intruded on the bad, or the bad upon the good? Here is the present actual condition. Is not that enough?" No, surely it is not. Everything depends in the great world upon whether Peace or War is the Intruder and the Rebel, upon whether Liberty or Slavery is the ideal possessor of the field. Everything depends in personal life upon whether Cowardice has invaded the rightful realm of Courage, or Courage has pitched its white tent on dusky fields which belong to Cowardice, or whether Truth or Falsehood is the ultimate king to whom the realm belongs. The great truth of Redemption, the great idea of Salvation, is that the realm belongs to Truth, that the Lie is everywhere and always an intruder and a foe. He came in, therefore he may be driven out. When he is driven out, and man is purely man, then man is saved. It is the glory and preciousness of the first mysterious, poetic chapters of Genesis that they are radiant through all their sadness with that truth.

Does this make smaller or less important that great Power of God whereby the human life passes from the old condition to the new,—the power of conversion? Certainly not! What task could be more worthy of the Father's power and love than this assertion and fulfilment of His child? All of our Christian thinking and talking has been and is haunted by a certain idea of failure and recommencement. Man is a failure, so there shall be a new attempt; and in place of the man we will make the Christian! There is nothing of that tone about what Jesus says. The Christian to Jesus is the man. The Christian, to all who think the thought of Jesus after Him, is the perfected and completed man.

Just see what this involves. Hear with what naturalness it clothes the invitations of the Gospel. They are not strange summons to some distant, unknown land; they are God's call to you to be yourself. They appeal to a homesickness in your own heart and make it their confederate. That you should be the thing you have been, and not be that better thing, that new man which is the oldest man, the first type and image of your being, is unnatural and awful. The world in the new light of the Gospel expects it of you, is longing for it. The creation, in Saint Paul's great phrase, is groaning and travailing, waiting for the manifestation of this child of God which is hidden in your life.

And all this vindicates itself by a mysterious and beautiful familiarity in the new life when you have begun to live it. With confidence I know that I could appeal to the experience of many of you who hear me, to recognize what I mean. I take a plant whose home is in the tropics, but which has grown to stunted life amid the granite of Vermont. I carry it and set it where its nature essentially belongs. Does it not know the warm earth, and does not the warm earth know it? Do not the palm-trees, and the sky which it sees through their broad leaves, and the warmer stars which glorify the sky at night speak to the amazed but satisfied heart of the poor plant in tones which it understands? And when a soul is set there where its nature always has belonged, in the obedience of God, in the dear love of Christ, does it not know the new life which embraces it? Ah, it has lived in it always in the idea of its being, in the conception of existence which has been always at its heart. It has walked the great halls of the divine obedience. It has stood by this river of divine refreshment. It has seen these great prospects of the celestial hope. It has climbed to these hill-tops of prophetic vision. They are not wholly strange. Nothing is wholly strange to any man when he becomes it, which it has always been in his nature to become. Because it has always been in man to become the fulfilled man, which is the Christian, therefore for a man to have become a Christian is never wholly strange.

See also here what a true ground there is for the appeal which you desire to make to other souls. It must be from the naturalness of the new life that you call out to your brethren. You must claim your brother for the holiness to which his nature essentially belongs. "Come home!" "Come home!" "I have found the homestead!" "I have found the Father!" "I have found the true manhood!" "I have found what you and I and all men were made to be!" So the soul out of the tropics cries out to its brother souls still lingering among the granite hills, and the voice has all the persuasiveness of Nature. The soft southern winds which bring it tell the souls to which it comes that it is true.

There are two sorts of attraction which draw, two sorts of fascination which hold, human nature everywhere,—the attraction of the natural and the attraction of the unnatural. The attraction of the natural everywhere is healthiest and highest. The attraction of the natural is the true attraction of Religion,—most of all, the attraction of the Christian Gospel.

And yet again this makes the higher life intelligible, and so makes it real. This alone makes such a thing as Christian Manliness conceivable. Christian Unmanliness is what a great many of men's pious, earnest struggles have been seeking. If the saint on to all eternity is to be the ever-ripening man, never changing into any new and unknown thing which he was not before, never to all eternity unfolding one capacity which was not in the substance of his humanity from its creation, then it follows that the most celestial and transcendent goodnesses must still be one in kind with the familiar virtues which sometimes in their crude and earthly shapes seem low and commonplace. Courage in all the worlds is the same courage. Truth before the throne of God is the same thing as when neighbor talks with neighbor on the street. Mercy will grow tenderer and finer, but will be the old blessed balm of life in the fields of eternity that it was in your workshop and your home. Unselfishness will expand and richen till it enfolds the life like sunshine, but it will be the same self-denial, opening into a richer self-indulgence, which it was when it first stole in with one thin sunbeam on the startled soul. There is no new world of virtues in any heaven or in any heavenly experience of life. God is good and man is good; and as man becomes more good, he becomes not merely more like God, but more himself. As he becomes more godly, he becomes more manly too.

It is so hard for us to believe in the Mystery of Man. "Behold man is this," we say, shutting down some near gate which falls only just beyond, quite in sight of, what human nature already has attained. If man would go beyond that he must be something else than man. And just then something breaks the gate away, and lo, far out beyond where we can see stretches the Mystery of Man. The beautiful, the awful mystery of man! To him, to man, all lower lines have climbed, and having come to him, have found a field where evolution may go on forever.

The mystery of man! How Christ believed in that! Oh, my dear friends, he who does not believe in that cannot enter into the full glory of the Incarnation, cannot really believe in Christ. Where the mysterious reach of manhood touches the divine, there Christ appears. No mere development of human nature outgoing any other reach that it has made, yet still not incapable of being matched, perhaps of being overcome; not that, not that,—unique and separate forever,—but possible, because of this same mystery of man in which the least of us has share. To him who knows the hither edges of that mystery in his own life, the story of how in, on, at its depths it should be able to receive and to contain divinity cannot seem incredible; may I not say, cannot seem strange?

Men talk about the Christhood, and say, "How strange it is! Strange that Christ should have been,—strange that Christ should have suffered for mankind." I cannot see that so we most magnify Him or bring Him nearest to us. Once feel the mystery of man and is it strange? Once think it possible that God should fill a humanity with Himself, once see humanity capable of being filled with God, and can you conceive of His not doing it? Must there not be an

Incarnation? Do you not instantly begin to search earth for the holy steps? Once think it possible that Christ can, and are you not sure that Christ must give himself for our Redemption? So only, when it seems inevitable and natural, does the Christhood become our pattern. Then only does it shine on the mountain-top up toward which we can feel the low lines of our low life aspiring. The Son of God is also the Son of Man. Then in us, the sons of men, there is the key to the secret of His being and His work. Know Christ that you may know yourself. But, oh, also know yourself that you may know Christ!

I think to every Christian there come times when all the strangeness disappears from the divine humanity which stands radiant at the centre of his faith. He finds it hard to believe in himself and in his brethren perhaps; but that Christ should be and should be Christ appears the one reasonable, natural, certain thing in all the universe. In Him all broken lines unite; in Him all scattered sounds are gathered into harmony; and out of the consummate certainty of Him, the soul comes back to find the certainty of common things which the lower faith holds, which advancing faith loses, and then finds again in Christ.

How every truth attains to its enlargement and reality in this great truth,—that the soul of man carries the highest possibilities within itself, and that what Christ does for it is to kindle and call forth these possibilities to actual existence. We do not understand the Church until we understand this truth. Seen in its light the Christian Church is nothing in the world except the promise and prophecy and picture of what the world in its idea is and always has been, and in its completion must visibly become. It is the primary crystallization of humanity. It is no favored, elect body caught from the ruin, given a salvation in which the rest can have no part. It is an attempt to realize the universal possibility. All men are its potential members. The strange thing for any man is not that he should be within it, but that he should be without it. Every good movement of any most secular sort is a struggle toward it, a part of its activity. All the world's history is ecclesiastical history, is the story of the success and failure, the advance and hindrance of the ideal humanity, the Church of the living God. Well may the prophet poet greet it,—

"O heart of mine, keep patience; looking forth
    As from the Mount of Vision I behold
  Pure, just, and free the Church of Christ on earth,—
    The martyr's dream, the golden age foretold."

Tell me, my friends, can we not all think that we see a progress
and elevation in men's ideas about their souls' conversion which
would seem to show an entrance into the power of this truth? In
old times more than to-day he who entered into the new life of Christ
thought of himself as rescued, snatched from the wreck of a ruined
and sinking world, given an exceptional privilege of safety. To-day
more than in old times the saved soul looks with a delighted and awe-
struck wonder into his new experience, and sees in it the true and
natural destiny of all mankind. "Lo, because I am this, I know that
all men may be it. God has but shown me in my soul's experience
of what all souls are capable." And so the new life does not separate
the soul from, but brings it more deeply into sympathy with, all humanity.

I believe that here also is the real truth and the final satisfaction of
men's minds as concerns the Bible. As the spiritual life with which
the Bible deals is the flower of human life, so the Book which deals
with it is the flower of human books. But it is not thereby an un-
human book. It is the most human of all books. In it is seen the everlasting struggle of the man-life to fulfil itself in God. All books in
which that universal struggle of humanity is told are younger brothers,—less clear and realized and developed utterances of that which
is so vivid in the history of the sacred people and is perfect in the
picture of the divine Man. I will not be puzzled, but rejoice when
I find in all the sacred books, in all deep, serious books of every sort,
foregleams and adumbrations of the lights and shadows which lie
distinct upon the Bible page. I will seek and find the assurance that
my Bible is inspired of God not in virtue of its distance from, but in
virtue of its nearness to, the human experience and heart. It is in
that experience and heart that the real inspiration of God is given,
and thence it issues into the written book:—

"Out of the heart of Nature rolled
  The Burdens of the Bible old.
  The Litanies of the nations came

Like the volcano's tongue of flame;
Up from the burning core below
The Canticles of love and woe."

That book is most inspired which most worthily and deeply tells the story of the most inspired life.

Is there not here the light of every darkness and the key to every riddle? The missionary goes into a heathen land. What shall he make of what he finds there? Shall he not see in it all the raw material and the suggested potency of that divine life which he knows that it is the rightful condition of the Sons of God to live? Shall he not be eager and ingenious, rather than reluctant, to find and recognize and proclaim the truth that the Father has left Himself without witness in no home where His children live? As in the crudest social ways and habits of the savage islanders he sees the beginnings and first efforts toward the most perfect and elaborate civilizations which the world contains,—the germs of constitutions, the promise of senates and cabinets and treaties,—so in the ignorant and half-brutal faiths shall he not discover the upward movement of the soul to which he shall then delight to offer all the rich light of the teaching which has come to his centuries of Christian faith, saying, "Lo, this is what it means: Whom you are ignorantly worshipping, Him declare I unto you"?

Among all the philosophies of history where is there one that matches with this simple story that man is the child of God, forever drawn to his Father, beaten back from Him by base waves of passion, sure to come to Him in the end. There is no philosophy of history which ever has been written like the Parable of the Prodigal Son. The first idea, the wanton wandering, the discontent, the brave return, the cordial welcome,—all are there. It is the history of man's action and man's thought; it is the story of his institutions and of his ideas; it holds the explanation of the past and the promise of the future; its beginning is where the first conception of what man shall be lies in the heart of the Creative Power; its end is in that endless life which man, having been reconciled to God and come to the completion of his idea, is to live in his Father's house forever.

Do we ask ourselves, as well we may, at what point in that long history the world is standing in this rich and interesting period in which we live? Who shall precisely say? But in the wonderful story of the Prodigal Son must there not have been one moment when at the very height of the revel there came a taste of bitterness into the wine, and when the faces of the harlots, in some gleam of fresh morning sunlight which broke into the hot and glaring chamber, seemed tawdry and false and cruel? Must there not have been a moment somewhere then, perhaps just when the carouse seemed most tempestuous and hopeless, a moment when the heart of the exile turned to his home, and the life with his father seemed so strong and simple and natural and real, so cool and sweet and true and healthy, that the miserable tumult and the gaudy glare about him for a moment became unreal and lost its hold? Much, much had yet to come, —the poverty and swine and husks,—before the boy gathered himself together and arose and said, "I will go to my father;" but the tide was turned, the face was set homeward, after that one moment of true sight of the true light in the hall of unnatural revel and resplendent sin. I sometimes think that there, in many ways just there, is where our age is standing with its startled and bewildered face.

I may be wrong or right about our age, I may be wrong or right about many of the ways in which it has appeared to me as if the truth which I have tried to preach to you to-day touches the great problems of religion and of life. But now I turn to you, young men and women, earnest and brave and hopeful—many of you also sorely perplexed and puzzled. What does this truth mean for you? Does it not mean everything for you if Truth and Courage and Unselfishness and Goodness are indeed natural to man and all Evil is unnatural and foreign?

There is indeed a superficial and a deeper nature. I am talking of the deeper nature. I am talking of the nature which belongs to every one of us as the child of God. I am talking, not of the waves which may be blown this way or that way upon the surface, but of the great tide which is heaving shoreward down below.

The man who lives in that deeper nature, the man who believes himself the Son of God, is not surprised at his best moments and his noblest inspirations. He is not amazed when he does a brave thing or an unselfish thing. He is amazed at himself when he is a coward or a liar. He accepts self-restraint only as a temporary condition, an immediate necessity of life. Not self-restraint but self-indulgence, the free, unhindered utterance of the deepest nature, which is good,—that is the only final picture of man's duty which he tolerates. And all the life is one; the specially and specifically religious being but the point at which the diamond for the moment shines, with all the diamond nature waiting in reserve through the whole substance of the precious stone.

Great is the power of a life which knows that its highest experiences are its truest experiences, that it is most itself when it is at its best. For it each high achievement, each splendid vision, is a sign and token of the whole nature's possibility. What a piece of the man was for that shining instant, it is the duty of the whole man to be always. When the hand has once touched the rock the heart cannot be satisfied until the whole frame has been drawn up out of the waves and stands firm on its two feet on the solid stone.

Are there not very many of us to whom the worst that we have been seems ever possible of repetition; but the best that we have ever been shines a strange and splendid miracle which cannot be repeated? The gutter in which we lay one day is always claiming us. The mountain-top on which we stood one glorious morning seems to have vanished from the earth.

The very opposite of all that is the belief of him who knows himself the child of God. For him, for him alone, sin has its true horror. "What! have I, who once have claimed God, whom once God has claimed, have I been down into the den of Devils? Have I brutalized my brain with drink? Have I let my heart burn with lust? Have I, the child of God, cheated and lied and been cruel and trodden on my brethren to satisfy my base ambition?" Oh, believe me, believe me, my dear friends, you never will know the horror and misery of sin till you know the glory and mystery of man. You never can estimate the disaster of an interruption till you know the worth of what it interrupts. You never will understand wickedness by dwelling on the innate depravity of man. You can understand wickedness only by knowing that the very word man means holiness and strength.

Here, too, lies the sublime and beautiful variety of human life. It is as beings come to their reality that they assert their individuality. In the gutter all the poor wretches lie huddled together, one indistinguishable mass of woe; but on the mountain-top each figure stands out separate and clear against the blueness of the sky. The intense variety of Light! The awful monotony of Darkness! Men are various; Christians ought to be various a thousand-fold. Strive for your best, that there you may find your most distinctive life. We cannot dream of what interest the world will have when every being in its human multitude shall shine with his own light and color, and be the child of God which it is possible for him to be,—which he has ever been in the true home-land of his Father's thought.

Do I talk fancies? Do I paint visions upon unsubstantial clouds? If it seem to you that I do, I beg you to come back now, as I close, to those words which I quoted to you at the beginning. "I am the Light of the World," said Jesus. Do you not see now what I meant when I declared that it was in making the world know itself that Christ was primarily the Power of the World's Redemption? The Revealer and the Redeemer are not two persons, but only one,—one Saviour.

What then? If Christ can make you know yourself; if as you walk with Him day by day, He can reveal to you your sonship to the Father; if, keeping daily company with Him, you can come more and more to know how native is goodness and how unnatural sin is to the soul of man; if, dwelling with Him who is both God and Man, you can come to believe both in God and in Man through Him, then you are saved,—saved from contempt, saved from despair, saved into courage and hope and charity and the power to resist temptation, and the passionate pursuit of perfectness.

It is as simple and as clear as that. Our religion is not a system of ideas about Christ. It is Christ. To believe in Him is what? To say a creed? To join a church? No; but to have a great, strong, divine Master, whom we perfectly love, whom we perfectly trust, whom we will follow anywhere, and who, as we follow Him or walk by His side, is always drawing out in us our true nature and making us determined to be true to it through everything, is always compelling us to see through falsehood and find the deepest truth, which is, in one great utterance of it, that we are the sons of God, who is thus always "leading us to the Father."

The hope of the world is in the ever richer naturalness of the highest life. "The earth shall be full of the knowledge of God as the waters cover the sea."

Your hope and mine is the same. The day of our salvation has not come till every voice brings us one message; till Christ, the Light of the world, everywhere reveals to us the divine secret of our life; till everything without joins with the consciousness all alive within, and "the Spirit Itself beareth witness with our spirits that we are the children of God."

THE PATTERN IN THE MOUNT*

"See that thou make all things according to the pattern shewed to thee in the mount."—HEBREWS viii. 5.

THE elements which make a perfect work are two—a perfect workman, and a perfect pattern. A perfect workman must have perfect faithfulness and perfect skill; and so, to make any accomplishment entirely complete, faithfulness and skill must join in the fulfilment of the perfect plan. It is very much like the casting of some great work in metal. There is skill in the mixing of the elements. Faithfulness is like the pervading heat which keeps the whole mass fluid. But the plan or pattern of the work is like the mould into which the well-mixed and molten metal must be poured, that it may get form and value, and not remain a merely shapeless mass.

There are, then, two great reasons why men's works are failures: one is the lack of the personal qualities of faithfulness and skill in the worker; the other is the absence of a pattern, or the presence of a wrong pattern, in which the faithfulness and skill take shape. The first kind of failure is common enough. Plenty of people there are who, with most perfect plans of life, are so unfaithful or unskilful that their lives come to nothing. But the second kind of failure also is abundant. The world is full of men who, with great faithfulness and skill are doing little, because the plan, the standard, the pattern of their life is weak or wrong. To them, and of them, let me speak to-day, using for my text these words out of the old Epistle to the Hebrews: "See that thou make all things according to the pattern shewed to thee in the mount."

The warning had been given to Moses when he was about to make the Tabernacle. The leader of the Jews was full of faithfulness, and all the skill of all the people was at his command. He could make what he would; but never in all the world before had there been

* Preached at St. Botolph's Church, Boston, Lincolnshire, Sunday morning, 2d July 1882; and at the Chapel Royal, Savoy, London, Sunday morning, 20th May 1883.

such a tabernacle as he was now to build. There was no precedent or accepted rule. And so we read in Exodus that God called him up into a high mountain, and there, in some mysterious way, He gave His servant a description of the Tabernacle which He wanted him to build. He showed it to him in elaborate detail, and when, upon the seventh day, Moses came down from Mount Sinai, the unbuilt Tabernacle was already in existence in his mind, as it had been already before in existence in the mind of God. Not yet had it any material existence; but its idea was there. It was not visible or tangible. The gold, the silver, and the brass, the blue and purple and scarlet, the fine linen and goats' hair, the rams' skins dyed red, the brilliant lamps and carved cherubs shone as yet in no earthly sunshine; the fragrance of the spices floated on no earthly air; the curtains waved in no terrestrial breezes; the stakes which held the structure had been driven in no field of our common ground; it was not yet in being as a material fact, a bright, strange apparition, such as by and by moved with the host of the Israelites and filled the tribes of their enemies with wonder. But yet, in a true sense, it was—it had existence, when God had opened the chamber of His will in which the idea of the unbuilt Tabernacle already stood complete, and showed it to His servant. All that afterwards took place, all the slow building of the Tabernacle by the offerings of the people, was but the transference from the region of ideas to the region of realities of that which existed already in the mind of God.

We have only to enlarge the conception which is in this story and to make it general, and we come at once to one of the loftiest and most inspiring thoughts of human life. As the old Tabernacle, before it was built, existed in the mind of God, so all the unborn things of life, the things which are to make the future, are already living in their perfect ideas in Him, and when the future comes, its task will be to match those divine ideas with their material realities, to translate into the visible and tangible shapes of terrestrial life the facts which already have existence in the perfect mind. Surely in the very statement of such a thought of life there is something which ennobles and dignifies our living. It takes something of this dreadful extemporaneousness and superficialness and incoherence out of our life. The things which come to pass here in the world are not mere volunteer efforts of man's enterprise, not self-contained ventures which are responsible to nothing and to no one but themselves. For each of them there is an idea present already in the thought of God, a pattern of what each in its purest perfection is capable of being. Out of the desire to realise that idea must come the highest inspiration. In the degree to which it has realised that idea must be the standard of judgment of every work of man. To-day begins a baby's life. A child is born into the world this Sunday morning. What shall we say about that child's unlived life? No man can tell what it will be. Its lessons are unlearned, its tasks untried, its discoveries unmade, its loves unloved, its growth entirely ungrown, as the little new-born problem lies unsolved on this the first day of its life. Is that all? Is there nowhere in the universe any picture of what that child's life ought to be, and may be? Surely there is. If God is that child's Father, then in the Father's mind, in God's mind, there must surely be a picture of what that child with his peculiar faculties and nature may become in the completeness of his life. Years hence, when that baby of to-day has grown to be the man of forty, the real question of his life will be, what? Not the questions which his fellow-citizens of that remote day will be asking, What reputation has he won? What money has he earned? Not even, What learning has he gained? But, How far has he been able to translate into the visible and tangible realities of a life that idea which was in God's mind on that day in the old year when he was born? How does the tabernacle which he has built correspond with the pattern which is in the mount? Ah, somewhere in the universe of God, dear friends—if not among our brethren beside us, if not by our own hearts—somewhere in the universe, that question is being asked to-day of every one of us who has grown up and left his youth behind him. Moses may, if he will, go on and build a tabernacle to suit himself, and as its self-willed architecture rises, the people may gather around it and call it wonderful, and praise the builder's genius, but God's eye is judging it all the time simply by one standard, simply by its conformity or non-conformity to the pattern which, long before the hewing of the first beam or the weaving of the first curtain, existed in the mount.

All this is true not merely of a whole life as a whole, but of each single act or enterprise of life. We have not thought richly or deeply enough about any undertaking unless we have thought of it as an attempt to put into the form of action that which already has existence in the idea of God. You start upon your profession, and your professional career in its perfect conception shines already in God's sight. Already before Him there is a picture of the good physician, the broad-minded merchant, the fair-minded lawyer, the heroic minister, which you may be. You set yourself down to some hard struggle with temptation, and already in the fields of God's knowledge you are walking as possible victor, clothed in white and with the crown of victory upon your head. You build your house, and found your home. It is an attempt to realise the picture of purity, domestic peace, mutual inspiration and mutual comfort, which God sees already. Your friendship which begins to shape itself to-day out of your intercourse with your companion has its pattern in the vast treasury of God's conceptions of what man, with perfect truthfulness and perfect devotion, may be to his brother man. It is not vulgar fate and destiny; it is not a mere settlement beforehand by God's foreknowledge of what each man must be and do, so that he cannot escape. The man's will is still free. The man may falsify God's picture of him, he certainly will fall short of it; but it is the essential truth of the Father comprehending all His children's lives within His own, the infinite nature containing the finite natures in itself and holding in itself their standard.

The distinction between ideas and forms is one which all men need to know, which many men so often seem to miss. The idea takes shape in the form, the form expresses the idea. The form, without the idea behind it, is thin and hard. The form, continually conscious of its idea, becomes rich, deep, and elastic. He who once gets the sight into that world of ideas which lies unseen behind the world of forms never can lose sight of it again, never can be content with any act of his until he has carried it into that world and matched it with its idea. To the man who is trying to do just or generous things, but who is perpetually conscious of how imperfect is the justice or the generosity of the things he does, it is a constant incentive and comfort to be sure that somewhere, in God, there is the perfect type and pattern of the thing of which he fails. That certainty at once preserves the loftiness of his standard and saves him from despair. This is the power of ideality, of the unfailing sight of the perfect ideas behind the imperfect form of things.

If all that I have said be true, then it would seem as if there ought to be in the world three kinds of men—the men of forms; the men of limited ideals, or of ideals which are not the highest; and the men of unlimited ideals, or the highest ideals, which are the ideals of God. And three such kinds of men there are, very distinct and easy of discovery. First, there are the men of forms, the men who, in all their self-questionings about what they ought to do, and in all their judgments about what they have done, never get beyond the purely formal standards which proceed either from the necessity of their conditions or from the accepted precedents of other people. They never get into the regions of ideas at all. How many such men there are! To them the question of their business life never comes up so high as to mean, "What is the best and loftiest way in which it is possible for this business of mine to be done?" It never gets higher than to mean, "How can I best support myself by my business?" or else, "What are the rules and ways of business which are most accepted in the business world?" To such men the question of religion never becomes: "What are the intrinsic and eternal relations between the Father God and man the child?" but only, "By what religious observances can a man get into heaven?" or else, "What is the most current religion of my fellow-men?" There is no unseen type of things after the pattern of which the seen deed must be shaped. Every deed is single and arbitrary and special, a thing done and to be judged, not by its conformity to some eternal standard of what such a deed ought to be, but simply by its fitness to produce results. Such a man judges a deed like a hatchet, solely by whether it will split wood. The deed no more than the hatchet has any true character, any conformity to or departure from an essential and eternal type. Of course no visions haunt a man like that. He dreams no dreams of finer purity and loftiness which might have given a more subtle and divine success to acts of his which the world calls successful. He lives in a low self-content, and knows no pain or disappointment at his actions unless his act fails of its visible result, or unless other men condemn the method in which he happens to have acted.

It would be sad, indeed, to think that there is any man here to-day who has not at least sometimes in his life got a glimpse into a richer and fuller and more interesting sort of life than this. There is a second sort of man who does distinctly ask himself whether his deed is what it ought to be. He is not satisfied with asking whether it works its visible result or not, whether other men praise it or not. There is another question still, Does it conform to what he knew before he undertook it that it ought to be? If it does not, however it may seem successful, however men may praise it, the doer of the deed turns off from it in discontent. If it does, no matter how it seems to fail, no matter how men blame it, he thanks God for it and is glad. Here is a true idealism; here is a man with an unseen pattern and standard for his work. He lives a loftier, and likewise a more unquiet life. He goes his way with his vision before his eyes. "I know something of what this piece of work ought to have been," he says, "therefore I cannot be satisfied with it as it is." What is the defect of such an idealism as that? It is, that as yet the idea comes only from the man's own self. Therefore, although it lies farther back than the mere form, it does not lie entirely at the back of everything. It is not final; it shares the incompleteness of the man from whom it springs. It may be born of prejudice and selfishness. It is the source very often of bigotry and uncharitableness and superstition. These are not seldom the fruits of narrow ideality. The man of no ideas is not a bigot. The man of largest ideas has outgrown bigotry. It is the man who asks for principles, the man who seeks to conform his life to some conception of what life ought to be, but who seeks his pattern no higher and no deeper than his own convictions, it is he who stands in danger of, and very often falls into narrowness and pride and the insolent, uncharitable demand that all men shall shape their lives in the same form as his.

Therefore it is that something more is needed, and that only the third man's life is wholly satisfactory. I said that he not merely looked for an idea to which he wanted to conform his life, but he looked for that idea in God. Literally and truly he believes that the life he is to live, the act he is to do, lies now, a true reality, already existent and present, in the mind of God; and his object, his privilege, is not simply to see how he can live his life in the way which will look best or produce the most brilliant visible result, not simply to see how he can best carry out his own personal idea of what is highest and best, but how he can most truly reproduce on earth that image of this special life or action which is in the perfect mind. This is the way in which he is to make all things according to the pattern which is in the mount.

Does it sound at first as if there were something almost slavish in such a thought as that? He who thinks so has not begun to apprehend the essential belonging together of the life of God and the life of every man. For man to accept the pattern of his living absolutely from any other being besides God in all the universe would be for him to sacrifice his self and to lose his originality. But for man to find and simply reproduce the picture of his life which is in God is for him not to sacrifice but to find his self. For the man is in God. The ideal, the possible perfection of everything that he can do or be, is there in God; and to be original for any man is not to start aside with headlong recklessness and do what neither brother-man, nor God dreamed of our doing; but it is to do with filial loyalty the act which, because God is God, a being such as we are ought to do under the circumstances, in the conditions in which we stand. Because no other being ever was or ever will be just the same as you, and because precisely the same conditions never before have been and never will be grouped about any other mortal life as are grouped around yours, therefore for you to do and be what you, with your own nature in your own circumstances, ought in the judgment of the perfect mind to do and be, that is originality for you.

What quiet independence, what healthy humility, what confident hope there must be in this man who thus goes up to God to get the pattern of his living. To-morrow morning to that man there comes a great overwhelming sorrow. Bereavement breaks open his house's guarded door, and the unbroken circle is shattered at what seemed its dearest and safest spot. The man looks about and questions himself— What shall he do, what shall he be in this new terrible life, terrible not least because of its awful newness, which has burst upon him? Where shall he find the pattern for his new necessity? Of course he may look about and copy the forms with which the world at large greets and denotes its sorrow, the decent dreadful conventionalities of grief. He may alter his dress and moderate his walk and tone, and even hide himself from sight, and so give all his pain its proper form. That does not satisfy him. The world acknowledges that he has borne his grief most properly, but he is not satisfied. Then, behind all that, he may reason it over with himself, think out what death means, make his philosophy, decide how a man ought to behave in the terrible shipwreck of his hopes. That is a better thing by all means than the other. But this man does something more. The pattern of his new life is not in the world. It is not in himself. It is in God. He goes up to find it. There is, lying in God's mind, an image of him, this very man, with this very peculiar nature of his, of him bearing this particular sorrow, and trained by it into a peculiar strength, which can belong to no other man in all the world. That image is a reality in God's soul before it becomes a visible thing in the man's soul living on the earth. To get up, then, into God, and find that image of his grieved and sorrowing life, and then come back and shape his life after it patiently and cheerfully, that is the struggle of the Christian idealist in his sorrow, of the man who tries to make all things according to the pattern which is in the mount. Can we not see what quiet independence, what healthy humility, what confident hope there must be in that man's struggle to live out through his sorrow the new life which his sorrow has made possible?

But now it is quite time for us to ask another question. Suppose that all which we have said is true; suppose that there is such a pattern of the truest life, and of each truest act of every man lying in God's mind, how shall the man know what that pattern is? We can see into what a mockery our whole truth might be misread. "Yes," one might say, "God has in Himself the true idea of you, but what of that? How will that help you? You cannot go up into His mind to find it there. You must go on still blundering and guessing, only trembling to know that at the last you will be judged by a standard of which you could never get a sight while you were working at your life. Look up, poor soul, out of the valley and know that on the top of yonder shining mountain lies folded safe the secret of your life, the oracle which would, if you could read it, solve all your mysteries and tell you just exactly how you ought to live. Look up out of the valley and know that it is there; and then turn back again into the valley, for in the valley is the home where you must live, and you can never read the oracle which you know is there upon the mountain-top." What mockery could there be like that? How must the poor man bend his head like a beast and go plodding on, refusing to look at, trying to forget, the mountain where his secret lay, and where he must not climb! Is that the fate of man who knows that in God lies the image and the pattern of his life? It might seem to be, it has very often seemed to be, but it can never really be to any one who really knows and believes in the Incarnation, the life of the God-Man among men. Do you not see? Is not Christ the mountain up into which the believer goes, and in which he finds the divine idea of himself. As a mountain seems to be the meeting-place of earth and heaven, the place where the bending skies meet the aspiring planet, the place where the sunshine and the cloud keep closest company with the granite and the grass: so Christ is the meeting-place of divinity and humanity; He is at once the condescension of divinity and the exaltation of humanity; and man wanting to know God's idea of man, any man wanting to know God's idea of him, must go up into Christ, and he will find it there.

I would not have that sound to you fanciful and vague, for I am sure that there is in that statement the most sure and practical of truths. It was so in the old days of the visible incarnation. See how, when Jesus walked on earth, the men and women who were with Him there were always climbing up into the mountain of His life, and seeing there what God's idea of their lives was. A young man, puzzled with matching commandments, weary of wondering which little corner of duty he should make his own, came up to Christ, came up into Christ, and asked, "Lord, which is the great commandment?" and instantly, as Christ looked at him and answered him, the man saw a new vision of himself, a vision of a life filled with a passionate love of the Holy One, and so he went back determined not to rest until he had attained all holiness. If he came down from Christ a larger man, giving his whole life thenceforth to the attainment of the love of God, and letting all duty do itself out of the abundance of that love, that was the way in which he did all things according to the pattern which had been shewed to him on the mount. Into that mountain of the Lord went up John Boanerges, to see God's idea of him as the man of love; and fickle-hearted Peter, to see God's idea of him as the steadfast rock; and trembling Mary Magdalene, to know herself beloved and forgiven. Nay, up that mountain went even Judas Isacriot, far enough to catch sight of God's Judas, of the man resisting temptation and loyally faithful to his Lord. Up that mountain went Pontius Pilate, and for a moment we can see flash before his eyes the ideal of himself, the true Roman, the true man, God's Pilate, brave and honest, unscared by shouting Jews or frowning Cæsar, standing by his convictions and protecting his helpless prisoner against His brutal enemies. Every man who came to Jesus saw in Him the image of his own true self, the thing that he might be and ought to be. Hundreds of them were not ready for the sight, and turned and went their way, to be not what they might be, nor what they ought to be, but what they basely chose to be. But none the less the pattern had been shewed to them in the mount.

And so it has been ever since. All kinds of men have found their ideals in Jesus. Entering into Him, the timid soul has seen a vision of itself all clothed in bravery, and known in an instant that to be brave and not to be cowardly was its proper life. The missionary toiling in the savage island, and thinking his whole life a failure, has gone apart some night into his hut and climbed up into Christ, and seen with perfect sureness, though with most complete amazement, that God counted his life a great success, and so has gone out once more singing to his glorious work. Martyrs on the night before their agony; reformers hesitating at their tasks; scholars wondering whether the long self-denial would be worth their while; fathers and mothers, teachers and preachers whose work had grown monotonous and wearisome, all of these going to Christ have found themselves in Him, have seen the nobleness and privilege of their hard lives, and have come out from their communion with Him to live their lives as they had seen those lives in Him, glorious with the perpetual sense of the privilege of duty, and worthy of the best and most faithful work which they could give.

Cannot you go to Christ to-day and find the idea of yourself in Him. It is certainly there. In Christ's thought at this moment there is a picture of you which is perfectly distinct and separate and clear. It is not a vague blurred picture of a good man with all the special colours washed away, with nothing to distinguish it from any other good man in the town. It is a picture of you. It is you with your own temptations conquered, and your own type of goodness, different from any other man's in all the world, in all the ages, perfectly attained. If you give up your life to serving and loving Christ, one of the blessings of your consecration of yourself to Him, will be, that in Him there will open to you this pattern of yourself. You will see your possible self as He sees it, and then life will have but one purpose and wish for you, which will be that you may realise that idea of yourself which you have seen in Him.

This, then, is the great truth of Christ. The treasury of life, your life and mine, the life of every man and every woman, however different they are from one another, they are all in Him. In Him there is the perfectness of every occupation: the perfect trading, the perfect housekeeping, the perfect handicraft, the perfect school teaching, they are all in Him. In Him lay the completeness of that incomplete act which you did yesterday. In Him lay the possible holiness of that which you made actual sin. In Him lies the absolute purity and loftiness of that worship which we this morning have stained so with impurity and baseness. To go to Him and get the perfect idea of life, and of every action of life, and then to go forth, and by His strength fulfil it, that is the New Testament conception of a strong successful life. How simple and how glorious it is!

We are like Moses, then,—only our privilege is so much more than his. We are like a Moses who at any moment, whenever the building of the tabernacle flagged and hesitated, was able to turn and go up into the mountain and look once more the pattern in the face, and come down strong, ambitious for the best, and full of hope. So any moment we may turn from the poor reality to the great ideal of our own lives, which is in Christ, with one earnest question. "Lord, what wouldst Thou have me to be?" We may pierce through the clouds and reach the summit, and there, seeing His vision of our possibilities, be freed at once from our brethren's tyranny, and from our own content and sluggishness, and set to work with all our might to fulfil God's image of our lives, to be all that He has shown us that it is possible for us to be, to make all things in these valley lives of ours after the pattern shewed to us in the mount.

THE SHORTNESS OF LIFE

"Brethren, the time is short."—1 Cor. vii. 29.

THE tone in which a man speaks often helps us to understand his meaning quite as much as the actual words he says. And with a great and sincere writer there is a tone in writing as well as in speaking, something which gives an intonation to the words he writes, and lets us understand in which of several possible spirits he has written them. "Brethren, the time is short," writes St. Paul to the Corinthians, and there is no tremor of dismay or sadness in his voice. He was in the midst of work, full of the interest and joy of living, holding the reins of many complicated labors in his hands, and he quietly said, "This is not going to last long. Very soon it will be over." It is what men often say to themselves with terror, clutching the things which they hold all the more closely, as if they would hold on to them forever. There is nothing of that about St. Paul. And on the other hand, there is nothing of morbidness or discontent, no rejoicing that the time is short, and wishing that it was still shorter. There is no hatred of life which makes him want to be away. There is no mad impatience for the things which lie beyond. There is simply a calm and satisfied recognition of a fact. There is a reasonable sense of what is good and dear in life, and yet, at the same time, of what must lie beyond life, of what life cannot give us. It is as when the same pen wrote those sublime and simple words, "This corruptible must put on incorruption. This mortal must put on immortality;" the quiet statement of a great, eternal necessity, at which the wise man must feel the same kind of serious joy as that with which he follows the movements of the stars, and looks to see day and night inevitably give place to one another. Or it is like that calm, majestic weighing of two worlds over against each other, and letting his will lie in even balance between them, cordially waiting the will of God, with which the same Paul wrote again, "I am in a strait betwixt two, having a desire to depart and to be with Christ, which is far better: nevertheless, to abide in the flesh is more needful for you: and having this confidence, I know that I shall abide." Or, again, it is like the healthy satisfaction of the healthy boy in his boyhood, knowing all the time the manhood that awaits him, feeling his boyhood pressed upon by it, hoping for it and expecting it, but living now in the concentrated happiness and work of the years whose activity and pleasure is all the more intense because of the sense that it must end.

It does not matter what St. Paul was thinking of when he said the time was short. He may have had his mind upon the death which they were all approaching. He may have thought of the coming of Christ, which he seems to have expected to take place while he was yet alive. I do not think we can be certain which it was. And perhaps the very vagueness about this helps us to his meaning. For he is not, evidently, dwelling upon the nature of the event which is to limit the "time," only upon the simple fact that there is a limit; that the period of earthly life and work lies like an island in the midst of a greater sea of being, the island of time in the ocean of a timeless eternity; and that it is pressed upon and crowded into littleness by the infinite. Not the shore where the sea sets the island its limits, but only the island in the sea, hearing the sea always on its shores; not the experience by which this life should pass into another, but only the compression and intensifying of this life by the certainty that there is another; not death, but the shortness of life—that is what his thoughts are fixed upon, and it is this of which the best men always think the most.

Our theme is this, then—the shortness of human life. How old that theme is, how trite, and oftentimes how dreary. As we look back and listen we hear all the generations wearisomely wasting their little span of life in doleful lamentations that it is not longer. Trite lessons which nobody loves to learn; dull poems which no man can sing; efforts at resignation which do not succeed,—these are what come flocking up about the truth that life is short. It is the ghost at the banquet of human thought. It is the monotonous, miserable undertone that haunts all the bustle and clatter of men's work and all the gay music of their pleasure-making. I wish that I could read its truth to you in another tone and paint its picture in another color. I wish that I could make you hear it, as it seems as if Paul's Corinthians must have heard it, almost like a trumpet,—a call to work and joy. If we can catch his spirit at all, something of that may certainly be possible.

And first, then, let us ask, What is the shortness of life? What do we mean by life's being short? There is a little insect that crawls upon the trees, and creeps, in one short day of ours, through all the experiences of life from birth to death. In a short twenty-four hours his life begins, matures, and ends,—birth, youth, activity, age, decrepitude, all crowded and compressed into these moments that slip away uncounted in one day of our human life. Is his life long or short? Is our life long or short to him? If he could realize it by any struggle of his insect brain, what an eternity our threescore years and ten must seem to him! And then lift up your eyes, lift up your thoughts, and think of God. What look has any life that has any limits to Him? Nothing short of eternity can seem long to Him. He sees the infant's life flash like a ripple into the sunlight of existence and vanish almost before the eye has caught it. And He sees Methuselah's slow existence creep through its nine hundred and sixty-nine years, and find, at last, the grave which had stood waiting so long. Is there a real difference in the length of these two lives to Him? A little longer ripple is the life of the patriarch than was the life of the baby, that is all. And what do we mean then by the shortness of our human life? To the ephemera it looks like an eternity; to God it looks like an instant. Evidently these attributes of length and shortness must be relative; they are not absolute. How shall human life seem then to man? Must it not depend altogether upon where he stands to look at it? If he stands with the ephemera, his life looks long to him. If he stands with God, his life looks short to him. If a man is able, that is, to conceive of immortality; if he can picture to himself a being who can live forever; if he recognizes in himself any powers which can outlast and laugh at death,—then any limit of life must seem narrow; against the broad background of the whole, any part must seem small. On the blue sky the almost million miles of the sun's breadth seem narrow. It is here that the truth about the matter lies. It is only by the dim sense of his immortality, only by the divine sight of himself as a being capable of long, long life, that man thinks his life on earth is short. Only by losing that divine sight of himself, and looking at himself as the beasts look at themselves, can he come to think his life long. The beast's life never seems short to him. Think of yourself as a beast and your life will never seem short to you. It is the divine consciousness in man, the consciousness that he is a child of God, that makes him know he is short-lived. Human life is not long or short, absolutely. It seems short to us because the consciousness of immortality is in us. What then? It could not seem long unless we threw that consciousness away. That we can count it short, then, is the pledge and witness of our nobility. The man who died among us yesterday, oh, realize, my friends, that the very fact that his life could seem to you, as you stood by his coffin, to have been very short, is a sign that you have been able to conceive of his humanity and yours being immortal. Feel this, and is not the shortness of life the crown and glory of our race?

And again, we all know how the shortness of life is bound up with its fulness. It is to him who is most active, always thinking, feeling, working, caring for people and for things, that life seems short. Strip a life empty and it will seem long enough. The day crawls to the idler, and flies to the busy worker. That is the commonplace of living. The shortness of life is closely associated, not merely with the great hopes of the future, but with the real vitality of the present. What then? If you and I complain how short life is, how quick it flies through the grasp with which we try to hold it, we are complaining of that which is the necessary consequence of our vitality. You can make life long only by making it slow; and if you want to make it slow I should think that there were men enough in town who could tell you how; men with idle hands and brains, who seem to have so much trouble to get through life as it is that we cannot imagine that they really wish that there were more of it.

And tell me, then, does not the shortness of life cease to be our sorrow and lamentation; does it not become our crown and privilege and glory, when we see that life is short to us because we are, that life is short to us just in proportion as we are, conscious of immortality and full of vitality? Who would not dread to have his life begin to seem long? Who would not feel that he was losing the proof-marks of his best humanity, forgetting that he was immortal and ceasing to be thoroughly alive?

But let us leave this and go further on. Suppose a man, with more or less of struggle, with what grace he can, has accepted the shortness of life as a conviction. He knows it. It has been forced upon him by some special shock, or it has been pressed into him by his gradual experience, the certainty that life is short, that he is not to be, cannot be, a long time here on the earth. What effect will that conviction have upon his life? What effect ought it to have? Evidently it ought to go deeper than his spirits. It ought to do something more than make him glad or sorry. It ought to have some effect upon his conduct and his character. I should like to suggest to you in several particulars what it seems to me that that effect will be.

1. And first of all must it not make a man try to sift the things that offer themselves to him, and try to find out what his things are? The indiscriminateness of most men's lives impresses us, I think, more and more. The old Greek Epictetus said that for each of men there is one great classification of the universe, into the things which concern him and the things which do not concern him. To how many men that classification is all vague. Many men's souls are like omnibuses, stopping to take up every interest or task that holds up its finger and beckons them from the sidewalk. So many men are satisfied with asking themselves vague questions about whether this thing or that thing is wrong, as if whatever they could not pronounce to be absolutely wrong for every man to do was right for them to do. So many men seem to think it enough that they should see no good reason for not doing a thing, in order to justify their doing it. As if the absence of any reason why they should do it were not reason enough why they should not do it. Such indiscriminateness would be inevitable, you could not hope to control it, if life were indefinitely long. Such indiscriminateness is almost legitimate and necessary in childhood, in the beginning, the freshman year of life. Then life seems endless. Then the quick experimenting senses are ready for whatever strikes them. But as the course goes on, as its limit comes in sight and we see how short it is, the elective system must come in. Out of the mass of things which we have touched, we must choose these which are ours,—the books which we shall read, the men whom we shall know, the power that we shall wield, the pleasure which we shall enjoy, the special point where we shall drop our bit of usefulness into the world's life before we go. We come to be like a party of travellers left at a great city railway station for a couple of hours. All cannot see everything in town. Each has to choose according to his tastes what he will see. They separate into their individualities instead of going wandering about promiscuously, as they would if there were no limit to their time. So conscientiousness, self-knowledge, independence, and the toleration of other men's freedom which always goes with the most serious and deep assertion of our own freedom are closely connected with the sense that life is very short.

2. But again, besides this discrimination of the things with which we ought to deal, the sense of the shortness of life also brings a power of freedom in dealing with the things which we do take to be our own. This, I think, is what St. Paul is speaking of in the words which are in close connection with this text of ours. "Brethren, the time is short," he says; "it remaineth that both they that have wives be as though they had none; and they that weep as though they wept not; and they that rejoice as though they rejoiced not; and they that buy as though they possessed not; and they that use this world as not abusing it: for the fashion of this world passeth away." Not that they should not marry, or weep, or rejoice, or buy, or use the world. The shortness of life was not to paralyze life like that. But they were to do these things as if they did them not. They were to do them with a soul above their details, and in the principles, reasons, and motives which lay beyond them. To take once more the illustration of the travellers: he who has only an hour to stay in some great foreign city will not puzzle and burden himself with all the intricacies of its streets or all the small particulars of its life. He will try, if he is wise, simply to catch its general spirit, to see what sort of town it is and learn its lessons. He must tread its pavements, ride in its carriages, talk with its people; but he will not do these things as the citizens do them; he will not be fastidious about them; he will hold them very loosely, only trying to make each of them give him what help it can towards the understanding of the city. He will do them as if he did them not. Is not that the idea? Just so he who knows he is in the world for a very little while, who knows it and feels it, is not like a man who is to live here forever. He strikes for the centre of living. He cares for the principles and not for the forms of life. He does the little daily things of life, but he does them for their purposes, not for themselves. He is like a climber on a rocky pathway, who sets his foot upon each projecting point of stone, but who treads on each, not for its own sake, but for the sake of the ones above it. The man who knows he is to die to-morrow does all the acts of to-day, but does them as if he did not do them, does them freely, cannot be a slave to their details, has entered already into something of the large liberty of death. That is the way in which the sense that life is short liberates a man from the slavery of details. You say, perhaps, "That is not good. No man can do his work well unless his heart is in it." But is it not also true that a man's heart can really be

only in the heart of his work, and that the most conscientious faithfulness in details will always belong to the man, not who serves the details, but who serves the idea of the work which he has to do? He who holds that the "fashion of this world passeth away" will live in the fashion still as a present means of working, but will get a great deal more out of it, because he holds it a great deal more loosely than the man who treats it as if it were to last forever. Through the freer use of the fashion which passeth away he will come to the substance which cannot pass away,—the love of God, the life and character of man.

3. Closely connected with this is another idea, which is that in the shortness of life the great emotions and experiences by which the human character is ruled and shaped assume their largest power and act with their most ennobling influence. Every emotion which a man can feel, every experience which a man can undergo, has its little form and its great form. Happiness is either a satisfaction that the cushions are soft and the skies clear, or a sublime content in harmony with the good universe of God. Love is either a whim of the eyes, or a devotion and consecration of the soul. Self-confidence is either a petty pride in our own narrowness, or a realization of our duty and privilege as one of God's children. Hope is either a petty wilfulness, or a deep and thoughtful insight. Trust is either laziness or love. Fear is either a fright of the nerves, or the solemn sense of the continuousness and necessary responsibility of life. And grief is either the wrench of a broken habit, or the agony of a wrung soul. So every emotion has its higher and its lower forms. It means but little to me if I know only that a man is happy or unhappy, if I do not know of what sort his joy or sorrow is. But all the emotions are certainly tempted to larger action if it is realized that the world in which they take their birth is but for a little time, that its fashion passes away, that the circumstances of an experience are very transitory. That must drive me down into the essence of every experience and make me realize it in the profoundest and the largest way. Take, for instance, one experience. Think of deep sorrow coming to a man, something which breaks his home and heart by taking suddenly, or slowly, out of them that which is the centre of them both, some life around which all his life has lived. There are two forms in which the sorrow of that death comes to a man. One is in the change of circumstances, the breaking up of sweet companionships and pleas-

ant habits, the loneliness and weariness of living; the other is in the solemn brooding of mystery over the soul and the tumult of love within the soul, the mystery of death, the distress of love. Now if the man who is bereaved sees nothing in the distance, as he looks forward, but one stretch of living, if he realizes most how long life is, it is the first of these aspects of his sorrow that is the most real to him. He multiplies the circumstances of his bereavement into all these coming years. Year after year, year after year, he is to live alone. But if, as it so often happens when death comes very near to us, life seems a very little thing; if, when we stand to watch the spirit which has gone away from earth to heaven, the years of earth which we have yet to live seem very few and short; if it seems but a very little time before we shall go, too, then our grief is exalted to its largest form. It grows unselfish. It is perfectly consistent with a triumphant thankfulness for the dear soul that has entered into rest and glory. It dwells not on the circumstances of bereavement, but upon that mysterious strain in which love has been stretched from this world to the other, and, amid all the pain that the tension brings, is still aware of joy at the new knowledge of its own capacities which has been given it. Ah, you must all know, you must all have seen, that men's griefs are as different as men's lives are. To the man who is all wrapt up in this world, grief comes as the ghosts come to the poor narrow-minded churl,—to plague and tease him, to disturb the circumstances and habits of his living, to pull down his fences and make strange, frightful noises in his quiet rooms. All is petty. To him to whom life is but an episode, a short stage in the existence of eternity, who is always cognizant of the great surrounding world of mystery, grief comes as angels came to the tent of Abraham. Laughter is hushed before them. The mere frolic of life stands still, but the soul takes the grief in as a guest, meets it at the door, kisses its hand, washes its travel-stained feet, spreads its table with the best food, gives it the seat by the fireside, and listens reverently for what it has to say about the God from whom it came. So different are the sorrows that come to two men which seem just the same. So is every emotion great or little, according to the life in which it finds its play. It must find earth too small for it, and open eternity to itself, or it spreads itself out thin and grows petty. I beg you, if God sends you grief, to take it largely by letting it first of all show you how short life is, and then prophesy eternity. Such is the grief of which the poet sings so nobly,—

"Grief should be
Like joy, majestic, equable, sedate;
Confirming, cleansing, raising, making free;
Strong to consume small troubles; to commend
Great thoughts, grave thoughts, thoughts lasting to the end."

But grief, to be all that, must see the end; must bring and forever keep with its pain such a sense of the shortness of life that the pain shall seem but a temporary accident, and that all that is to stay forever after the pain has ceased, the exaltation, the unselfishness, the mystery, the nearness to God, shall seem to be the substance of the sorrow.

4. But let me hasten on and name another power which seems to be bound up with the perception of the shortness of life. I mean the criticalness of life. All men who have believed at all that there was another life, have held in some way that this life was critical. Some have held absolutely that probation wholly stopped when this life ended, and that as the man was when he died, so he was certainly to be forever and ever. Others have only felt that such a change as death involves must have some mighty power to fasten character, and so to fasten destiny, and that the soul, living in any unknown world, must carry forever, deep in its nature and its fortunes, the marks and consequences of what it has been here. That thought of criticalness belongs to every limited period of being which opens into something greater. A boy feels the probation character of his youth, feels that he is making manhood, just in proportion as he vividly realizes the approach of his majority. And man is made so that some sense of criticalness is necessary to the most vigorous and best life always. Let me feel that nothing but this moment depends upon this moment's action, and I am very apt to let this moment act pretty much as it will. Let me see the spirits of the moments yet unborn standing and watching it anxiously, and I must watch it also for their sakes. And it is in this general sense of probation, or of criticalness, this sense that no moment liveth or dieth to itself; it is in this, not stated as a doctrine, but spread out as a great pervading consciousness all through life, it is in this that the strongest moral power of life is found. Now ask yourself: Could this have been if

life had been so long, if life had seemed so long to men, as never to suggest its limits? It is when the brook begins to hear the great river calling it, and knows that its time is short, that it begins to hurry over the rocks and toss its foam into the air and make straight for the valley. Life that never thinks of its end lives in a present and loses the flow and movement of responsibility. It is not so much that the shortness of life makes us prepare for death, as it is that it spreads the feeling of criticalness all through life, and makes each moment prepare for the next, makes life prepare for life. This is its power. Blessed is he who feels it. Blessed is he in whose experiences each day and each hour has all the happiness and all the solemnity of a parent towards the day and the hour to which it gives birth, stands sponsor for it, holds it for baptism at the font of God. Such days are sacred in each other's eyes. The life in which such days succeed each other is a holy family with its moments "bound each to each by natural piety."

5. I take one moment only to suggest one more consequence which comes from the sense of how short life is I mean the feeling that it gives us towards our fellow-men. Do you not know that when your time of intercourse is short with any man, your relations with that man grow true and deep? Two men who have lived side by side for years, with business and social life between them, with a multitude of suspicions and concealments, let them know that they have only an hour more to live together, and, as they look into each other's eyes, do not the suspicions and concealments clear away? They know each other. They trust each other. They think the best of each other. They are ready to do all that they can do for each other in those few moments that remain. Oh, my dear friends, you who are letting miserable misunderstandings run on from year to year, meaning to clear them up some day; you who are keeping wretched quarrels alive because you cannot quite make up your mind that now is the day to sacrifice your pride and kill them; you who are passing men sullenly upon the street, not speaking to them out of some silly spite, and yet knowing that it would fill you with shame and remorse if you heard that one of those men was dead to-morrow morning; you who are letting your neighbor starve, till you hear that he is dying of starvation; or letting your friend's heart ache for a word of appreciation or sympathy, which you mean to give him some day,—if you only could know and see and feel, all

of a sudden, that "the time is short," how it would break the spell! How you would go instantly and do the things which you might never have another chance to do. What a day of friendliness, of brotherliness, of reconciliations, of help, the last day of the world will be, if men shall know how near the awful end is! But need we wait for that? Cannot the men and women whom we live with now be sacred to us by the knowledge of what wonderful, mysterious ground it is that we are walking together, here in this narrow human life, close on the borders of eternity?

"Brethren, the time is short." There is the fact, then, forever pressing on us, and these are the consequences which it ought to bring to those who feel its pressure. Behold, it is no dreary shadow hanging above our heads and shutting out the sunshine. It is an everlasting inspiration. It makes a man know himself and his career. It makes him put his heart into the heart of the career which he knows to be his. It makes the emotions and experiences of life great and not petty to him. It makes life solemn and interesting with criticalness; and it makes friendship magnanimous, and the desire to help our fellow-men real and energetic. It concentrates and invigorates our lives. In the brightest, freshest, clearest mornings, it comes to us not as a cloud, not as a paralysis, but as a new brightness in the sunshine and a new vigor in the arm. "Brethren, the time is short." Only remember the shortness of life is not a reality to us, except as it shows itself against a true realization of eternity. Life is long to any man, however he mourns over its shortness, to whom life is a whole. Life as a part, life set upon the background of eternity, life recognized as the temporary form of that whose substance is everlasting, that is short; we wait for, we expect its end. And remember that to the Christian the interpretation of all this is in the Incarnation of Jesus Christ. "I am He that liveth, and was dead; and behold, I am alive for evermore." The earthly life set against the eternal life, the incorporate earthly form uttering here for a time the everlasting and essential being, those years shut in out of the eternities between the birth and the ascension, that resurrection opening the prospect of the life that never was to end,—these are the never-failing interpretation to the man who believes in them of the temporal and eternal in his own experience. Christ comes and puts His essential life into our human form. In that form He claims the truest brotherhood with us. He shares our lot. He binds His life

with ours so that they never can be separated. What He is we must
be; what we are He must be forever. Finally, by the cross of love,
He, entering into our death, takes us completely into His life.
And when He had done all this He rose. Out of His tomb, standing there among human tombs, He comes, and lo, before Him there
rolls on the unbroken endlessness of Being. And not before Him
alone,—before those also whom He had taken so completely to Himself. His resurrection makes our resurrection sure. Our earthly life,
like His, becomes an episode, a short, special, temporary thing, when
it is seen like His against an immortality.

So the Incarnation is the perpetual interpretation of our life. Jesus
cries, "It is finished," on His cross, and at once it is evident that that
finishing is but a beginning; that it is a breaking to pieces of the
temporal, that it may be lost in the eternal! That cross is the perpetual glorification of the shortness of life. In its light we, too, can stand
by the departing form of our own life, or of some brother's life, and
say, "It is finished," and know that the finishing is really a beginning. The temporary is melting away like a cloud in the sky, that
the great total sky may all be seen. The form in which the man has
lived is decaying, that the real life of the man may be apparent. The
fashion of this world is passing away; the episode, the accident of
earth is over, that the spiritual reality may be clear. It is in the light
of the cross that the exquisite picture of Shelley, who tried so hard
to be heathen and would still be Christian in his own despite, is
really realized,—

> "The one remains, the many change and pass;
>   Heaven's light forever shines; earth's shadows fly;
> Life, like a dome of many-colored glass,
>   Stains the white radiance of eternity,
> Until death tramples it to fragments."

And so what is there to be done? What could be clearer? Only to
him who realizes eternity does the short human life really seem
short and give out of its shortness its true solemnity and blessing. It
is only by binding myself to eternity that I can know the shortness
of time. But how shall I bind myself to eternity except by giving
myself to Him who is eternal in obedient love? Obedient love! Loving obedience! That is what binds the soul of the less to the soul of
the greater everywhere. I give myself to the eternal Christ, and in

His eternity I find my own. In His service I am bound to Him, and the shortness of that life, whose limitations in any way shut me out from Him, becomes an inspiration, not a burden to me. Oh, my dear friends, you who with Christian faith have seen a Christian die, tell me was not this short life then revealed to you in all its beauty? Did you not see completely that no life was too long which Christ had filled with the gift and knowledge of Himself; no life was too short which departed from the earth only to go and be with Him in Heaven forever?

My dear friends, let us think how solemn, how beautiful, the thought of dedication to Christ becomes, when through His voice which calls us sounds the warning and inspiring cry of His disciple, "Brethren, the time is short." There is no time to waste of what belongs entirely to Him. "The time is short." Take your place now. Bind yourself now in with the fortunes of those who are trying to serve Him. This Christian Church which we see here is only the beginning. This poor stained, feeble church of earth is only the germ and promise of the great Church of Heaven, and we who are trying to serve Him together now have a right to take courage from the promise of the Master, who has overcome, "Him that overcometh I will make a pillar in the temple of my God, and He shall go no more out."

HOMAGE AND DEDICATION

"And the four and twenty elders fall down before Him that sat on the throne, and worship Him that liveth for ever and ever, and cast their crowns before the throne."—Revelation iv. 10.

It is impossible for the mind to conceive of a more majestic picture than is presented in this fourth chapter of the Book of Revelation. The Church of Christ, with all her labors done and all her warfare over, stands at length in heaven, before the throne of Him whose servant she has been, and renders up her trust and gives all the glory back to Him. When we hear such a scene described in the few words of John's poetic vision, I think we are met with a strange sort of difficulty. The great impression of the picture is so glorious that we are afraid to touch it with too curious fingers, to analyze its meaning and get at its truth. At the same time we feel sure that there is in it a precise and definitely shaped truth which is blurred to us by the very splendor of the poetry in which it is enveloped. We see on the one hand how often the whole significance of some of the noblest things in Scripture is lost and ruined by people who take hold of them with hard, prosaic hands. Their poetry is necessary to their truth. On the other hand, we see how many of the most sacred truths of revelation float always before many people's eyes in a mere vague halo of mystical splendor, because they never come boldly up to them as Moses went up to the burning bush, to see what they are, and what are the laws by which they act. Shall we interpret the poetry of Scripture into ordinary language or not? No one reads the commentaries without feeling that often it would be better not to do so; but no one sees how many of the false religious ideas and superstitions have come of an intense and dazzled, but blind, perception of Scripture poetry, without feeling how wisely it needs to be interpreted and studied. There is danger of mysticism and vagueness, if you leave the wonderful Bible images unexplained. There is danger of prosaic dulness and the loss of all their life and fire, if you elucidate them overmuch.

It is seen everywhere. The great New Testament image is the cross of Christ, and any one can see how on the one hand the cross has become a mere object of vague and feeble sentiment to multitudes who have been touched by its beauty without trying to understand its meaning; and how, on the other hand, it has become hard and shallow and commercial, all the mystery and depth and power of appeal passed out of it, as men have torn its sacred agony to pieces, and tried to account on mercantile principles for every pang that Jesus suffered and every mercy that His suffering offers to the world.

In view of all this difficulty, what shall we do? It is not hard to tell what we ought to do, but every Scripture image and poetic description, although it may be very hard to do it. We want to draw out its truth without forgetting that it is poetry; we want to get out of it a broad and clear idea, which shall still keep the glow with which it burned while it lay still in the fire of poetic inspiration. We want to leave it in heaven, and yet bring it down to earth. We want to understand it more, and yet feel it just as much. Something of this kind I want to try to do to-day, with reference to the great apocalyptic image of the four and twenty elders casting their crowns before the throne of God.

What is the broad idea, then, of this great spectacle? The four and twenty elders have been often considered to represent the Church in its two great series, the Jewish and the Christian orders. Twelve patriarchs and twelve apostles may be considered as representatively constituting that company who came, with all the fruits and honors of successful life, to offer them to Him by whose great strength they had been won. Such an interpretation seems very likely to be true; but in a yet broader way we have here crowned beings, those who had won some victory and possessed some kingship, giving the very badges and tokens of their victory and glory to another greater than themselves, casting their kingly crowns before the kingly throne of a royalty mightier than their own. I believe that the picture has that special reference to the relations of the Christian Church to its great Head; but does it not also suggest to us still broader ideas which are illustrated through all of human history, and which find their illustrations constantly in all our daily life? Those ideas seem to me to be two. The first is the necessary homage which the higher natures pay to those that are higher than themselves, and especially to the highest of all. The second is the way in which every great attainment gets its best value from being dedicated to somebody or some purpose that is greater still. These two ideas I see coming up out of this picture, as the soul of a man looks out upon you from his face. I want to dwell upon them with you for a while this morning. I think that they can suggest for us a good deal about the whole nature of reverence and worship.

Take, then, the first of these ideas—the necessary homage that high natures pay to others which are higher than themselves, and especially to the highest of all. Here are crowned beings casting their crowns down at the feet of a dimly seen figure which sits upon a throne so much higher than they are that even their crowns can only reach his feet. Shall we take that idea and lay it down by the experience of ordinary life? Does reverence increase as men grow themselves to be more and more, greater and greater? Think of it first with reference to the homage that men come to pay to what is higher than themselves, but not the highest—not to God. Every strong young man starts in a true self-confidence. He is the master of everything. Everything is to be his servant. Centred in himself, he sees all other things revolving around him as if they were to be the ministers of his necessities. If he is going into politics, the country is an arena that has been spread abroad for the race he is to run. If he is to be an artist, the laws of the materials of art are but expedients to utter the beauty and sublimity that is in his soul. If he is going into business, the great adjustments of the business world are the machinery out of which is to be wrought his fortune. There is no reverence in all that. Wrapped up in himself, the eager young aspirant has not caught sight of the true and regal dignity of these masters whom he assumes to treat as servants. But what comes later? Let our young man grow really great in any one of these departments, and I take it to be a universal truth, a truth which all will recognize, that the greater he grows the more he will come to know that those things, which he thought to make servants of, are really masters, and by and by he will pass into a region where he is able to pay them the homage they deserve. The mere tyro in politics thinks the country is made for his ambition; but the great statesman sees his country a great and venerable being for whom it is his privilege to work and live, and perhaps die. The flippant beginner in art thinks that all the laws of art are merely arrangements to help his genius into expression; but the great artist is sure that the noblest task his genius can attempt is only to utter in visible material some of the everlasting laws of beauty. The confident young trader thinks the whole market made for him; but the great merchant has looked wide over all the earth, and is proud to be a part in that great system of interlacing work and mutual credit that covers all the continents. Thus every man, the greater he grows, becomes capable of understanding the greatness of that with which he has to deal, and so enters into the region of a new homage. Newton could reverence the power of gravitation more than the child who ignorantly tosses his ball into the air and sees it fall. Morse was more able to honor the subtle and mighty force of electricity than is the mere telegraph operator who knows nothing but the mere manipulation of his machine. It is a universal rule that he is a poor workman who does not honor and respect his work. A man has no right to be doing any work which, as he grows greater within it, does not offer him new views of itself to call out an ever-increasing reverence and honor. And in all the good occupations of life (one would like to impress it upon every young merchant, young mechanic, and young student whom he can speak to) a man's best proof of growing greatness in himself is a growing perception of the greatness and beauty of his work.

The same is true of men. The greater a man grows, the more quick and ready he will be to recognize and honor another man who is his better. Here again there is no test so certain of whether a man has any greatness as whether he is able to pay intelligent and sincere respect to other men who have more than he has. There seem to be certain states of condition, as it were, with reference to this. Down at the bottom an unenterprising mortal looks with blank and stupid wonder at the really great men who stand at the top of his race. Up a little higher he is moved with envy and begins to disparage them; but when he comes to be great himself, he knows how to understand them, and yet recognizes how much they are above him. He has become capable of truly venerating them. Only those who are kingly themselves can properly honor the kingliest.

And then think of the worship, not merely of that which is higher than a man's self, but of that which is the highest of all—the worship of God. There it is supremely true that men are capable of it only in virtue of and in proportion to something great, something divine in themselves. Only those who have crowns to cast can do true homage before His throne. This seems to me to be bound up with what I have already said. I claimed—and I think you agreed with me—that it was the man most proficient in any profession who saw the depth and range of that profession best, and so reverenced it most deeply. It is the mere smatterer in any profession who thinks it slight and is contemptuous about it. Now, just exactly this is true of life. The more completely a man lives, the more largely alive he is in every part of him,—in brain, and heart, and hands,—the more completely he will comprehend the magnitude of life, and stand in reverence before the Power that moves and governs it. The mere smatterer in life, the amateur in living, so to speak, with his half-vital movements, never realizes the immensity of existence, the vast variety of its complications, the infiniteness of its privileges and its dangers, the range upward and the range downward, and so he goes on satisfied within himself, and offering no tribute of adoration to the Power which moves in, and through, and under all this world of life, which he has never fathomed deep enough to find adorable. But this moving power of all things is God. His nature is what the soul finds, when tired and bewildered, like a frightened bird which has escaped from its own little cage, it flies through the vast expanse of life and comes to the shadow that encloses it. That follows then which I believe that we continually see. The man most thoroughly alive, he who lives most, will be most reverent to God. I do not mean that he will always hold the correctest ideas. The very fulness of the current of his living may sweep out here and there strange eccentricities and abberations in his way of thinking, but he will be most constantly conscious of a power over him, from which he came, out of which streams of influence are always flowing into him, to which he is responsible, to which he must return. The more a man loves, the more he realizes the limitations in which all earthly affection labors, and the more glorious appears to him the Infinite Love. The more a man thinks, the more he sees how all human thought is but a drop of water out of the illimitable ocean of the thought of God. And when a true man puts his hand to it and bravely does an honest piece of work, he sees at once the beauty and the littleness of the work he does, and comprehends the glory of the perfect work of Him through whom are all things, and by whom are all things. Some such necessary connection there seems to be between the largest living and the completest adoration. I have known many scoffers, men who believed that there was a God, but who did not in any way prostrate themselves before Him, paid Him no homage; some of them were very bright men, some of them conscientious and dutiful, some of them affectionate and brave; but—I do not wholly know why—there was something imperfect in the development of their humanity, as it always seemed. They were the men of unsymmetrical culture; the men in whom some one power was overgrown and the rest were sluggish; the men who did not impress you with largeness of life, but with special, almost mechanical, dexterity of action; the men whom you might call upon for certain tasks which require certain skill, but whom you could not trust with that entire confidence which can only rest on character. In one word, they were not kingly men, not men who in any regal way, according to the old idea of a king, represented their race. Men with sharp, ingenious tools in their hands, but no crowns upon their heads. And almost every one of us knows, too, that in his own life there have been scoffing and scornful times, periods of irreverence, when the sacred was not sacred to us, and the venerable excited in us no veneration; times when if we did not scoff at God, it was not because we adored Him, but because the habits of decent, reverential behavior were strong enough to carry us through times of utter selfishness, when nothing seemed great to us beyond ourselves; times of utter demoralization, when nothing was mysterious, or inspiring, or sublime. And what is our impression of such times? Some of them were the smartest periods of all our life. They were perhaps the times when we worked our hardest—our keenest, wittiest, busiest days perhaps, but not our best, not those which we should choose even out of our poor, stained, sordid lives, if we were required to select some which should give a being of another race some notion of the best life of a man. Surely we have been our best at those times when we have most completely worshipped something far better than ourselves. It is when we have cast our crown most humbly before God that our crown has been most real, that we have known that there was indeed a spark of something kingly in our natures.

And then there is one other way of looking at this matter. Think what company you are in when you are most reverential and full of the spirit of worship. When a man is at his business on mere selfish principles, exercising his business shrewdness, providing for himself and for his family, far be it from me to speak with any slight of such practical good occupation; but yet he is not there about the highest labor, nor associating himself with the highest company in the long lines of history. So long as a man is living for himself and honoring himself, there is an association, however remoted it may be, with all the lowest forms of selfishness in which men have lived; but the moment a man begins to live in genuine adoration of the absolute good, and worship God, he parts company from all these lower orders of human life and enters into the richest and best society that earth possesses or ever has possessed. Think who you are with in adoration. When you say to God, "O God, take me, for the highest thing that I can do with myself is to give myself to Thee," when you say that to God, humbly, but with all your heart, kneeling all apart in your chamber, where no one can see you, it is bewildering to me to think into what company you are taken instantly by that prayer of devotion. You sweep into the current of the best, the holiest, and the most richly human of our 'humanity, which in every age has dedicated itself to God. The worshippers of all the world—the Jew, the Greek, the Hindu, the Christian in all his various cultures, take you for their brother. You have part in the offering of Abel's altar, in the worship of Solomon's temple, in the prison talk of Socrates, in the closet adoration of all the saints. You are never in such company as when you are before God's throne offering Him your brightest and most precious. Yes, men are measured by their reverences. All human life is like the annual procession of the Jews, marching up to Jerusalem, to the Holy City. The nearer we are to that place of supreme adoration, the nearer the purpose of our life is fulfilled. What do you adore, what do you really reverence and respect? is the real test question of your life. In an age which makes too little of reverence, let us not dare to let drop the truth that only that which is high can worship the highest, and so covet as the best crown of our existence the power so to know and feel that we can genuinely worship God.

And now let us take the second idea which seemed to be in our text. That idea was, that our highest attainments always get their best value from being offered to others who are dearer to us and higher than ourselves. Go back to our picture again. The four and twenty elders are casting their crowns before the throne of Christ. Those crowns are the attainments of their lives. All that the work of grace had done in them, all the fruit of their long education,—they valued it only as they might offer it to Him who was the object of their reverence and love. How clearly we are touching here upon one of the universal experiences of men. Is it not true that we do all things best, when out beyond the thing that we are doing there stands some one whom we love and admire for whom the task is done? The scholar who is working hard at his problem in order that some day he may take his triumphant solution of it in his hands and go to his master who gave him his first lessons, and say to him, "Take this, this belongs to you, for I never should have done it if you had not taught me;" the soldier who in the midst of battle is inspired by the thought that if he is brave and conquers he will give back life to the country that gave life to him; the school-boy, who, resisting a school temptation, is strengthened by the thought of father and mother at home, who have taught him to be true and generous, and who comes home afterwards and says, "They wanted me to be mean and to lie, and I did not because I remembered you, and so it was your strength that resisted and not mine,"—all these seem to me to be younger brethren of the elders casting their crowns down at the throne-steps of their Master; full of the same spirit, living the same life.

Such influences are certainly stronger and more frequent than we know. We are often working in this way, with a deep reverence for others, when it seems as if we were doing what we do wholly for ourselves. A ship captain sails out on a long voyage, and as he goes it seems as if he carried all his interests and impulses shut up with him in that little ship. He finds his plenteous enjoyment everywhere. He revels in the problems of navigation that his well-trained skill knows how to solve. He spends long nights on deck, and conquers the elements that seem to have marshalled all their fury to decree that the little ship shall not go through. He rules his crew. He feels the daily joy of difficulties overcome. At last he comes to the haven where he wants to be. There all his business crowds his days. He is full of intercourse with men. He accomplishes the purpose of his voyage. He sells his cargo, and with a new one shipped he sails back, through months of work and interest and danger, till he is at the wharf from which he sailed a year ago. And then—what then? Why, he goes up on shore and finds out a little house where a little child, a mere baby-child, is living in a nurse's care, and gives the treasure of his voyage, all that he has earned, into the little hands of his unknowing child, who really was the single cause and inspiration of his toilsome voyage, and really is the reason why he rejoices in its success. He has not seemed—not even to himself—to think of her, but really she has been there in the bottom of his heart all the long time. The whole success is valuable to him because he may make an offering of it to her. If you doubt it, think how it would be if he came back and found her dead—the house empty, and only a little grave for him to lavish his love on. Where would be the value of his treasures then? Who could wake him out of the bitterness of his sorrow by rustling the paper or rattling the money in his ears? How worthless it would seem when she, the little daughter for whom he earned it all, was gone!

Such consecrations of our life to others are very often not less real and powerful because they are unconscious. Often they are not revealed to us ourselves until some sorrow comes, such as I just described. How many of us have known what all this means! We have gone on with our work in life, thinking that the purpose of our work was centred in ourselves! It was our own work that we were doing. We were working for ourselves. But some day a friend died—one who was very near to us, one in whom our life was bound up in many ways. Who has not known sometimes in life the dreadful going out of all the interest of living at the time of such a death? It seemed as if there were nothing left to live for. You looked upon your money, and wondered how you ever could have cared to earn it. The commonest little duties that recurred after the death was over were weariness to you. You looked forward, and it seemed as if you never could live out the long, flat, dreary days that stretched between you and the grave. The days went by, each with its twenty-four hours, each with its sunset and its sunrise, but the zest of them was all gone for you. The public life, the social life, went on, but it called to your dead interest in vain. What did you care for it all? Then you found that you had indeed been working for that dear dead friend, that wife, child, brother, as you never knew. All that you did had taken its value, not from you, but from them. When you thought you were working for yourself, you really had been working for them. And so their death had taken all the spring and impulse from you. It was terrible. But it was blessed if you did not stop there, but, with persistent love that would not be satisfied until it found the object it had lost, you traced the precious life on as it left you, till you followed it into the very bosom of the God who took it, and poured out there the treasures of devotion which had no longer any one dear enough to tempt them on the earth.

One cannot help feeling as he looks at working men that this more than anything else is what makes the difference between them—the presence or absence in their lives of some distinct superior purpose for their work, to which it is all dedicated. It may be the comfort of a family, it may be a good cause, the support of education, the fostering of the great work of the Church; whatever it is, so it be something greater than the work itself, so that the work is turned from an end into a means, it lightens the pressure of the work most wonderfully, it relieves the continual burden. Take two men working in the field together—they dig across the field side by side, but one is always longing for the end where he can lie down and rest. The other rejoices in every stroke of his spade as if it were one more stone laid in the home that he is trying to build, in the cause which he desires to strengthen. And there is no work so lofty in itself that it does not thus need something higher than itself to be done for, something to lift its heavy pressure from the sore and weary backs of men. Even the work of the Lord Jesus, that work in which His soul delighted, the work of telling men of God and saving the world of sin,—I think no one can read the Gospels and not see that He was always lifting the heavy pressure of that work by reminding Himself that He was doing it for His Father. Is it not very touching? He rests, beyond His own pleasure in His work, upon the consciousness that it is His Father's pleasure too. "I have finished the work that Thou gavest me to do." That was the perfect satisfaction with which the Saviour, as it were, folded His hands from His long task and went to hang upon the cross. That was the casting down, as it were, of His crown before His Father's throne.

We have been speaking of the smaller inspirations that come to men to lighten and redeem their labors, but they are all subordinate to this, the sense that the work that we are doing in the world is done for Christ and God. If a man or woman is able to get and keep that, there is no drudgery so mean and crushing that it cannot be lifted and made buoyant—absolutely none. It is good to think how many men and women that seemed to live in slavery have really lived the freest lives, lifted above their slavery by this continual consciousness of work for God. They realized another meaning of those wonderful words of David,—among the most wonderful in all the Bible, I think,

—"I will walk at liberty, for I keep thy commandments." They would know what those words that we used in this morning's service really mean, "O God, whose service is perfect freedom." This was the case with multitudes of the poor slaves who have toiled anywhere in their slavery upon the suffering earth. Flogged to their work, living in misery, torn from their families, stripped of all the sweetness of life that comes from having something, somebody, to work for, what was there to lift off the load of unthanked and unprofitable labor such as theirs? There could be nothing unless there came, as there did come to many a darkened soul among them, a conviction that their weary work, their weary lives, were tributes and offerings to Jesus—that He loved them so, and had so utterly taken them for His, that He was pleased and glorified when they were patient and submissive in the wretchedness from which they could find no escape. As soon as they saw this, all was completely changed. The cabin walls opened and it was a temple. The dreary cotton-field became already, by anticipation and faith, the field beside the river of life under the towers of the New Jerusalem, where they who have served Him faithfully and glorified His name are to walk forever with the Lamb.

We speak of them because their suffering stood out strong and picturesque. But the release that came to faithful Christian hearts among them was nothing different in kind from that which comes to hundreds of patient sufferers everywhere, always. When it enters like a flood of light into the soul of some wretched invalid or some victim of relentless misfortune, that by a faithful patience under his suffering he can glorify God and show forth the power of Christ, then what a change comes to him! How all is transfigured! How full of beauty the hated sickroom grows! There is something behind the suffering for the suffering to rest and steady itself upon. The light has been kindled behind the dark window, and all its fair lines and bright colors shine out. In the purpose of the suffering the escape from the suffering is found; as when Paul and Silas, in the book of Acts, sang praises to God by night in prison, when they turned their imprisonment into a tribute to their Master, then "the foundations of the prison were shaken, and . . . the doors were opened, and every one's bands were loosed."

I am sure that there are many among us who feel the need to have the labor of our life redeemed,—merchants, clerks, lawyers, laborers, teachers, housekeepers, one thing or another,—the chosen or fated task of our life so often seems to be mere drudgery, crowding us down, pressing the life out of us. It is strange how soon many young men get to feel this about the occupations to which they have given up their lives, and all their first enthusiasm dies away. Then come the dreary years of unrelieved and unenthusiastic work, only enlivened by the unhealthy excitement of mere commercial rivalry or professional spite. How many men we have seen restless all their lives, forever changing their work because they could not stand the heavy pressure of mere heavy, hated toil! Does not what we have been saying seem to show that the trouble lies not in the kind of work, but in this—in whether men have beyond their work a purpose to dedicate it to, which can make it light and buoyant? No doubt some works more easily find such a purpose than others do, but any work that is good and honest is capable of it. And this decides the ranks of works and their effects upon the men who do them. No work is necessarily sacred in its influence upon the man who does it, and no legitimate work is necessarily secular and secularizing. It is possible to sell goods for God's glory, and it is possible (as the Church knows only too well) to swing censers and preach sermons for our own; and then there is no doubt that the man who sells goods gets more blessing out of his work than the man who sways the censer or preaches the discourse.

One would wish to urge this very strongly upon every man, especially upon every young man who is just beginning his work in life, and to whom his work, it may be, has already begun to show that in time it may come to be a weariness and a burden. What you need is some purpose beyond. What shall it be? The possible purposes lie in circles stretching one beyond another. If you can do your work for a friend or for a family as well as for yourself, you have already redeemed much of its sordidness. If you can do it for a cause, for the progress of society and the improvement of business, for your country, for your church, then you have lifted it still more. If you can do it for God, in perfect, childlike, loving desire for His glory, then your work, be it as heavy in its nature as it may, leaps of itself from the low ground, and, instead of crushing you with it to the earth, carries you up every day into the presence of the God for whom you do it. That is the continual beauty of a consecrated life, possible under all sorts of circumstances, possible to every kind of man in every kind of task.

Need I tell you the only thing that remains to be told? Need I tell you that the only influence which can really make us consecrate our lives and works to Christ is the profound and joyous confidence that Christ has done that for us, which makes the utter consecration of ourselves only a feeble token of the gratitude we owe and want to give? It is the soul forgiven—the soul to which the cross is everything —the soul living every day in the richness of the new reconciliation to the Father—this is the soul that values all it has and does, only as a possible tribute to its Redeemer and its Lord. This is the soul that casts its Crown of life down at the feet of the Lord of life, and glories in its Crown's richness not for itself, but for the greater praise of Him. Is there a motive of work conceivable so pure, so strong, so joyous, so humbling, so exalting, as this?—that a man should first take Christ's free love and then try to live as full and bounteous a life as possible, that he might have as worthy a tribute as possible to offer to his Lord and Saviour?

THE CHURCH OF THE LIVING GOD

A DOMESTIC MISSIONARY SERMON.

"The Church of the living God."—1 TIM. iii. 15.

I WANT to preach to you to-day about the Church. Not, that is, directly of the personal Christian experience, but of the great corporate body of Christian life throughout the world, and especially of that particular organization in which we live and worship, and whose work in our own country we are to contribute to extend. If the Church is often thought about, and talked about, in a petty and mechanical and formal way, let us be very careful, if we can, to avoid formality and pettiness in our talk of her to-day. Let us try to make her seem what she really is, the Church of the living God, and the Home of living men.

Let us begin then with one of the most picturesque and striking and perhaps perplexing incidents which occur in the Church's life. A minister is called upon to baptize a little dying child. It is an infant of a day. A ray of light has come from heaven, and just flashed for an instant into the great flood of sunlight, and now is being gathered back again into the darkness out of which it came. The minister goes and baptizes the unconscious child. He does an act which perhaps to those who stand around, seems like the blankest superstition. "What does it mean?" they say. "Have a little sprinkled water and a few whispered words any influence upon this flickering flame of life which in a moment is to go out? If the child is to live elsewhere after its brief life here on earth is over, will this ceremony do it any good? If it revives and lives its life out here on earth, will it live any better for this hurried incantation?"

Meanwhile, to the minister, and to the Church of which he is a minister, that baptism of the dying child has a profound and beautiful significance. It is not thought of for a moment as the saving of the child's soul. The child dying unbaptized goes to the same loving care and education which awaits the child baptized. But the baptism is

333

the solemn, grateful, tender recognition, during the brief moments of that infant's life on earth, of the deep meanings of his humanity. It is the human race in its profoundest self-consciousness welcoming this new member to its multitude. Only for a few moments does he tarry in this condition of humanity; his life touches the earth only to leave it; but in those few moments of his tarrying, humanity lifts up its hand and claims him. She says, "You are part of me, and being part of me, you are part of me forever. Your life may disappear from mortal sight almost before we have seen it, but, wherever it may go, it is a human life forever. It belongs to God, as, and because humanity belongs to Him." Humanity, recognizing itself as belonging to God, recognizes this infant portion of herself as belonging to Him, claims it for Him, takes it into her own most consecrated hopes, appropriates for it that redemption of Christ which revealed man's belonging to God, declares it a member of that Church which is simply humanity as belonging to God, the divine conception of humanity, her own realization of herself as it belongs to God.

Can there be any act more full of significance, more free from superstition? And is there not in this act, just because of the feeble unconsciousness of the child to whom it is administered, the most distinct indication of the nature of the Church into which he is admitted? There is no fact developed yet about the child except his pure humanity. We know nothing whatsoever about his talents, or his character. It makes no difference whether he is rich or poor. He may lie cradled in daintiest lace, or in most squalid rags. Beauty or ugliness, brightness or dullness, friendship or friendlessness, good blood or bad blood, are not taken into account; we baptize him, be he what he may, so that only he is a human creature, the child of human parents, the sharer of our human nature; we baptize him into the fellowship of consecrated humanity, into the Church of the living God.

Have we not then presented to us in this simple ceremony, which to one bystander may seem so insignificant and to another so superstitious, the deepest and broadest meaning of the Christian Church? It is the body of redeemed humanity. It is man in his deepest interests, in his spiritual possibilities. It is the under-life, the sacred, the profounder life of man, his re-generation. Every human being in very virtue of birth into the redeemed world is a potential member of the Christian Church. His baptism claims and asserts his membership.

And now suppose that Baptism were universal, and suppose that instead of being, what it is so often, even among Christian people, a formal ceremony, everywhere it were a living act, instinct with meaning, what a world this would be! Every new-born immortal welcomed by the whole spiritual consciousness of his race! There is some true sense, we may well believe, in which the physical life of humanity grows richer through its whole substance by the added life of each new body. Just in proportion as the spiritual is more sensitive than the physical, may we not hold that the spirituality of the whole race is richer for the access of this new soul? Baptism is the utterance of the rejoicing welcome. The whole world of spiritual capacity thrills with delight and expectation. The Church accepts its new member and undertakes his education. For what time he is to be in her, a part of her, before he goes to his eternal place to be a member of the Church in heaven, whether it be for a few short hours or for a long eighty years, the Church belongs to him and he belongs to the Church. If he does good work it is the Church's gain and glory. If he sins, and is profligate, it is as a member of the Church that he is wicked. The Church is spiritual humanity, and he, a spiritual human being, is, by that very fact, a Churchman.

I cannot tell you, my dear friends, how strongly this view takes possession of me the longer that I live. I cannot think, I will not think about the Christian Church as if it were a selection out of humanity. In its idea it is humanity. The hard, iron-faced man whom I meet upon the street, the degraded, sad-faced man who goes to prison, the weak, silly-faced man who haunts society, the discouraged, sad-faced man who drags the chain of drudgery, they are all members of the Church, members of Christ, children of God, heirs of the kingdom of heaven. Their birth made them so. Their baptism declared the truth which their birth made true. It is impossible to estimate their lives aright, unless we give this truth concerning them the first importance.

Think too, what would be the meaning of the other sacrament, if this thought of the Church of the living God were real and universal. The Lord's Supper, the right and need of every man to feed on God, the bread of divine sustenance, the wine of divine inspiration offered to every man, and turned by every man into what form of spiritual force the duty and the nature of each man required, how grand and glorious its mission might become! No longer the initiation rite of a selected brotherhood, but the great sacrament of man! The seeker after truth, with all the world of truth freely open before him, would come to the Lord's table, to refresh the freedom of his soul, to liberate himself from slavery and prejudice. The soldier going forth to battle, the student leaving college, the legislator setting out for Washington, the inventor just upon the brink of the last combination which would make his invention perfect, the merchant getting ready for a sharp financial crisis, all men full of the passion of their work, would come there to the Lord's Supper to fill their passion with the divine fire of consecration. They would meet and know their unity in beautiful diversity—this Christian Church around the Christian feast. There is no other rallying place for all the good activity and worthy hopes of man. It is in the power of the great Christian Sacrament, the great human sacrament, to become that rallying-place. Think how it would be, if some morning all the men, women and children in this city who mean well, from the reformer meaning to meet some giant evil at the peril of his life to the school boy meaning to learn his day's lesson with all his strength, were to meet in a great host at the table of the Lord, and own themselves His children, and claim the strength of His bread and wine, and then go out with calm, strong, earnest faces to their work. How the communion service would lift up its voice and sing itself in triumph, the great anthem of dedicated human life. Ah, my friends, that, nothing less than that, is the real Holy Communion of the Church of the living God.

And then the ministry, the ministers, what a life theirs must be, whenever the Church thus comes to realize itself! We talk today, as if the ministers of the Church were consecrated for the people. The old sacerdotal idea of substitution has not died away. Sometimes it is distinctly proclaimed and taught. What is the release from that idea? Not to teach that the ministers are not consecrated, but to teach that all the people are; not to deny the priesthood of the Clergy, but to assert the priesthood of all men. We can have no hope, I believe, of the destruction of the spirit of hierarchy by direct attack. It may be smitten down a thousand times. A thousand times it will rise again. Only when all men become full of the sense of the sacredness of their own life, will the assumption of supreme clerical sacredness find itself overwhelmed with the great rising tide. The fault of all onslaughts upon the lofty claims of the ministry has been here. They have vociferously declared that ministers were no better than other men. They have not bravely and devotedly claimed for all men, the right and power to be as good and holy and spiritual as any St. John has ever been in his consecrated ministry. When that great claim is made and justified in life, then, not till then, lordship over God's heritage shall disappear and the true greatness of the minister, as the fellow-worker with and servant of the humblest and most struggling child of God, shall shine out on the world.

Yet once more, here must be seen the true place and dignity of truth and doctrine. It is not knowledge anywhere that is the end and purpose of man's labor or of God's government. It is life. It is the full activity of powers. Knowledge is a means to that. Why is it that the Church has magnified doctrine overmuch and throned it where it does not belong? It is because the Church has not cared enough for life. She has not overvalued doctrine; she has undervalued life. When the Church learns that she is in her idea simply identical with all nobly active humanity, when she thinks of herself as the true inspirer and purifier of all the life of man, then she will—what? Not cast her doctrines away, as many of her impetuous advisers bid her do; she will see their value, their precious value, as she never has seen it yet; but she will hold them always as the means of life, and she will insist that out of their depths they shall send forth manifest strength for life which shall justify her holding them.

The decrying of dogma in the interest of life, of creed in the interest of conduct, is very natural, but very superficial. It is superficial because, if it succeeded, it would make life and conduct blind and weak. But it is natural because it is the crude healthy outburst of human protest against the value of dogma for its own sake, of which the Church has always been too full. Let us not join in it. Let us insist that it is good for man to know everything he can know, and believe everything he can believe of the truth of God. But while we will not pull down dogma, let us do all we can to build up life about dogma, and demand of dogma that service which it is the real joy of her heart to render to life. I will not hear men claim that the doctrine of the Trinity has no help or inspiration to give to the merchant or the statesman. It has great help, great inspiration. I will not hear men claim that it means nothing to the scholar or the bricklayer whether he believes or disbelieves in the Atonement. It means very much to either. Out of the heart of those doctrines I must demand the help and inspiration which they have to give. Then I must do all that I can to make the life which needs that help and inspiration hungry for them. I must do all that I can to make the world's ordinary operations know their sacredness and crave the sacred impulse which the dogmas have to give. I must summon all life to look up to the hills. I must teach the world that it is the Church, and needs and has a right to all the Church's privileges, and so make it cry out to the truths of the Trinity and Atonement to open the depths of their helpfulness, as they never have heard the call to open them when only theologians were calling on them to complete their theologic systems, or only a few special souls were asking them for special comforts or assistance. Here, in the assertion of the great human Church, is the true adjustment of the relations of Doctrine and Life! Doctrine kept active by life. Life kept deep by doctrine.

Ah, but you say, this does not sound like the New Testament. There certainly the Church and the world are not the same. They are not merely different; they are hostile to each other. There is a perpetual conflict between the two. Indeed there is. But what Church and what world are fighting together there? The Church is a little handful of half-believers. The world is a great ocean of sensuality and secularity and sin. Of course between those two there is an everlasting conflict, so long as each is what it is. The world distrusts the Church, in part at least, because it feels coming out from it no spiritual power. The Church dreads the world, which is always dragging it down from its imperfect loyalty and consecration. But he has listened very carelessly to the New Testament who has not heard in it the muffled, buried voices of another Church and another world, crying out for life! A church completely strong in faith, not standing guard over herself, but boldly claiming all the world in all of its activities for Christ, and a world conscious of its belonging to divinity, counting its sin and intrusion an anomaly, a world ashamed and hungry, the world of which St. Paul dreamed, the groaning and travailing creation. How often as we read the New Testament, this deeper Church and this deeper world are dimly seen and faintly heard beneath this present faithlessness and sin. How, whenever they are seen and heard, we recognize, beyond a doubt, that they are the true Church, and the true world, and that every departure from or falling short of them is a loss of the Church's or the world's reality. And how, when the true Church and the true world stand before us, we see and know that they are not in conflict; that they are in perfect harmony; nay, far more than that, that they are identical with one another.

There is no fight so fierce and vehement as that which rages between two beings which ought to be perfectly one, but which, because each falls short of what it was designed to be, are now in conflict with each other. So long as the Church and the world are what they are there must be discord. We who are in the Church must keep watchful guard over her, and must dread and oppose the evil influences of the world. But at the same time we never must let ourselves forget that all this is unnatural. We must never lose out of our sight the vision, never lose out of our ears the music of the real Church and the real world struggling each into perfection for itself, and so both into unity and identity with one another.

Very interesting have been in history the pulsations, the brightening and fading, the coming and going of this great truth of the Church and the world ideally identical. That truth is always present in the words of Jesus. He told his disciples how they were to fight with the actual world, to be persecuted by it, even to be murdered by it. But he was always pointing abroad and saying, "The field is the world." The ideal Church, which was the real Church in his eyes, knew no limit but humanity.

By-and-by came the persecutions of the early Church, and they drove the Church in upon itself, and made the few believers think of themselves as outcasts and exceptions. The intensity of their personal experiences dulled and dimmed the thought of their being simply representatives of all humanity. The Church lived like a sect of souls with special privileges and illuminations.

The mediæval Church in its own way caught sight again of the idea of universality, but it was formal and selfish. It did not think of itself as fulfilling the life of the world, but of the world as existing for it, and to be practically swallowed up in its dominion. Still it had some notion of it and of the Church and the world coming to identity with one another.

With the Protestant Reformation came another intense assertion of the personal nature of religion, and the larger aspects, the world-meaning of the Church, was lost or lay in silence. Calvinism was too busy with the intense problem of the individual soul to think much of the great Redemption of the world, of all humanity.

But now, when in these latter days, there are so many signs that we are passing into a new region, beyond the strong immediate power of the Reformation which has prevailed from the sixteenth century till now, it is the relation of the Church to the active world, the conflict and the possible harmony between them, the message of the Church to the world, the turning of the world into the Church, these are the problems and the visions which are more and more occupying the minds of thoughtful vision-seeing men.

Such alternations and pulsations cannot go on forever. The hostility of the Church to the world, and the conformity of the Church to the world, neither of them is the final condition, nor shall the Church vacillate between them always. Gradually, slowly, but at last surely, this must come forth which we saw testified even in the hurried baptism of the little child who made this earth his home but for a single day, that the earth is the Lord's, and so that to be living in this earth is to belong to God; and that all human life is by the very fact of its humanity a portion of His Church.

I think that we can do the best work in the Christian Church only in the light of that truth cordially acknowledged. Because that truth is coming to more and more cordial acknowledgment, I believe that the Christian Church is becoming a better and a better place to work in every year. If I ask where in the Christian Church one can best live and work, I answer myself that it will be where that truth is most vital, where it makes most strongly the real power of the Church's life.

And this brings me to what little I want to say about our own Church. We value and love our Communion very deeply. To many of us she has been the nurse, almost the mother of our spiritual life. To all of us she is endeared by long companionship, and by familiar sympathy in the profoundest experiences through which our souls have passed. When we deliberately turn our backs for a moment upon all these rich and sweet associations, and ask ourselves in colder and more deliberate consideration, why it is that we believe in our Episcopal Church and rejoice to commend her to our fellow-countrymen and fellow-men, the answer which I find myself giving, is that our Church seems to me to be truly trying to realize this relation to the whole world, this sacredness of all life, this ideal belonging of all men to the Church of Christ, which, as I have been saying, is the great truth of active Christianity. I find the signs of such an effort, in the very things for which some people fear or blame our Church. I find it in the importance which she gives to Baptism and in the breadth of her conception of that rite; for Baptism is the strongest visible assertion of this truth. I find it in her simplicty of doctrine. I find it in the value which she sets on worship; her constant summons to all men not merely to be preached to, but to pray; her firm belief in the ability and right of all men to offer prayer to God. I find it in her strong historic spirit, her sense of union with the ages which have past out of sight and of whose men we know only their absolute humanity.

In all these things I recognize the true, strong tendency which our Church has to draw near to the life of the world, and to draw the world's life near to her. In this tendency all true Churchmen must rejoice. Her breadth of doctrine, her devoutness, and her clear hold upon the long history of human life, all these qualify her for a great work in bringing up humanity, and making it know itself for what it is, the true universal Church of the Living God, toward which all ecclesiastical establishments which have thus far existed in the world, have been attempts, of which they have been preparatory studies.

Can our Church do any such great office as this for the America in which she is set? There are some of her children who love to call her in exclusive phrase The American Church. She is not that; and to call her that would be to give her a name to which she has no right. The American Church is the great total body of Christianity in America, in many divisions, under many names, broken, discordant, disjointed, often quarrelsome and disgracefully jealous, part of part, yet as a whole bearing perpetual testimony to the people of America of the authority and love of God, of the redemption of Christ, and of the sacred possibilities of man. If our Church does especial work in our country, it must be by the especial and peculiar way in which she is able to bear that witness. There is no peculiar privilege of commission belonging to her or any other body. The only right of any body lies in the earnest will and in the manifest power. The right to preach the Gospel to America lies in the earnest faith that the Gospel is the only salvation of the people, first as men, and then as Americans; whoever brings that faith has the right to preach; whoever does not bring it has no right, be the fancied regularity of his commission what it may!

In some sense there has been reason to fear, and there is still reason to fear, that what makes part of the strength of our Church, may also make part of her weakness. Her historic sense binds her, in a very live way, to the sources from which she immediately sprang, and tempts her to treasure, perhaps overmuch, her association with the great Churches of other lands. So long as she does that she can never truly be the Church of America. The Episcopal Church's only real chance of powerful life, is in the more and more complete identification of herself with the genius and national life of America.

To do that, she must become a great moral power. No careful preservation of the purity of doctrine, no strictness of ecclesiastical propriety, can take the place of moral strength. It is by the conscience, that the Church must take hold of this people. It is in the conscience, that the nation is uneasy. In its uneasy conscience, it sees the vision and hears the voices of the life it might be living. To the conscience of the nation then, the Church that is must speak to tell the nation of the Church that it might be.

If the Church at the time of the Civil War had bravely cried out against the sin of slavery, she would be more powerful than we can imagine in America to-day. So the Church which to-day effectively denounces intemperance, and the licentiousness of social life, the cruelty or indifference of the rich to the poor, and the prostitution of public office, will become the real Church of America. Our Church has done some good service here. She ought to do much more. If there are rich men in her membership, she ought to rebuke rich men's vices and to stir rich men's torpidity. She ought to blow her trumpet in the ears of the young men of fortune, summoning them from their clubs and their frivolities to do the chivalrous work, which their nobility obliges them to do for fellowman. She ought to speak to Culture, and teach it its responsibility. She ought to make real contributions to the creation of that atmosphere of brotherhood and hope and reverence for man, in which alone there is any chance that the hard social and economical problems of the present and the future can find solution. If she can do such things as these, she will be following in the steps of all the largest minded, deepest-hearted Fathers of the Church, all the way from St. Paul down. That is the true apostolical succession, of which she must not boast, but which she must struggle more and more earnestly to win.

My friends, it is not possible for the true man to think of his Church without thinking of his country. I cannot be the Churchman that I ought without being a patriot. On this Sunday morning let the image of our country stand before us, with her chances, with her dangers, with her glories, with her sins! We are glad indeed that our Church is not the only church which is laboring for the land's salvation. We rejoice in all that our brother Christians of other names are doing; but we believe in the work which our Church has to do. We pray to God, O keep her simple, brave and earnest, free from fantasticalness and cowardice and selfishness, that she may do it. We look onwards, and far, far away, we see the Nation-church, the land all full of Christ, the Nation-church, a true part of the World-church, issuing into glorious life, and swallowing up our small ecclesiasticisms, as the sun grandly climbing up the heavens swallows up the scattered rays which he sent out at his rising. And full of that vision, we are ready to do what we can to make our Church strong for the work which it must do in preparation for that day!

GOING UP TO JERUSALEM

"Then Jesus took unto him the twelve, and said unto them, Behold, we go up to Jerusalem, and all things that are written concerning the Son of man shall be accomplished."—LUKE xviii. 30.

EVERY true life has its Jerusalem, to which it is always going up. A life cannot be really considered as having begun to live until that far-off city in which its destiny awaits it, where its work is to be done, where its problem is to be solved, begins to draw the life towards itself, and the life begins to know and own the summons. Very strange is this quality of our human nature which decrees that unless we feel a future before us we do not live completely in the present where we stand to-day. We have grown so used to it that we do not realize how strange it is. It seems to us to be necessary. But the lower natures, the beasts, do not seem to have anything like it. And we can easily picture to ourselves a human nature which might have been created so that it never should think about the future, but should get all its inspiration out of present things. But that is not our human nature. It always must look forward. The thing which it hopes to become is already a power and decides the thing it is.

And so every true life has its Jerusalem to which it is always going up. At first far off and dimly seen, laying but light hold upon our purpose and our will, then gradually taking us more and more into its power, compelling our study, directing the current of our thoughts, arranging our friendships for us, deciding for us what powers we shall bring out into use, deciding for us what we shall be: so every live man's Jerusalem, his sacred city, calls to him from the hill-top where it stands. One man's Jerusalem is his profession. Another man's Jerusalem is his fortune. Another man's Jerusalem is his cause. Another man's Jerusalem is his faith. Another man's Jerusalem is his character. Another man's Jerusalem is his image of purified society and a worthy human life. You stop the student at his books, the philanthropist at his committee, the saint at his prayers. You say to each of them, "What does it all mean? What are you doing? What is it all for?" And the answer is everywhere the same: "Behold we go up to Jerusalem." We draw back the veil of history, and everywhere it is the same picture that we see. Companies, great and small, climbing mountains to where sacred cities stand awaiting them with open gates upon the top. The man who is going up to no Jerusalem is but the ghost and relic of a man. He has in him no genuine and healthy human life.

There never was an exhibition of all this so fine and perfect as that which we see in Jesus. His manhood shines out nowhere so clear and strong as here. Think how his life gets its glory and beauty from the way in which it is always, from the very first, tending on to the thing which it was at last to reach. That tendency began at his birth, and it never ceased until he was hanging on the cross outside the city gate. Then he had come to Jerusalem and it was finished. The angels sang about Jerusalem when the shepherds heard them. The boy's thoughts were full of Jerusalem as he worked in the carpenter's shop. Egypt, where they carried the babe to get him out of danger was on the way to Jerusalem, where he was finally to be killed. The visit to the temple when he was twelve years old, was a nearer glimpse of the Jerusalem to which he did not then really come, though his feet trod its streets, but which he then accepted as the only sufficient issue of his life. He was baptized in consecration to the life-long journey to Jerusalem. "For this cause was I born. For this cause came I into the world." "My time is not yet come." Those words, and words like those, dropped here and there, along his path, are like foot-prints in the road he walked, all pointing to Jerusalem. At last he came there, and in the tragedy of Good Friday he laid down his life. He had reached Jerusalem at last. The most intense, persistent purpose that the world had ever seen, had reached its completion.

With Christ as the great image and pattern of it all before us, let us speak this morning of the Jerusalem of every life, the steady tendency of every life to come to some appointed result of which it is growingly conscious as it moves upon its way towards it. Let us speak first of the existence of such a result, and then of the struggle by which it is reached.

First, then, may we not say that the appointed result of any man's life will consist of his character multiplied by his circumstances. Find the product of that multiplication, and you can surely tell what the man will attain. It is because both of these terms are vague; because,

look as deep into him as you will, you cannot read his character perfectly; and because, study his circumstances as carefully as you may,
you cannot tell just what is going to happen; for these two causes,
the final issue of his life is not entirely clear; the Jerusalem to which
he is travelling, is vague and cloudlike. And yet it is good, indeed it
is necessary, for us to know that both of these elements do enter into
the decision of a man's life, and that neither of them must be left out.
You leave out a man's character, and think that his circumstances
only must control his destiny, and at once you are a fatalist. On the
other hand you leave out his circumstances, and think only of his
character, and you have set a premium on wilfulness. At once men
go about complaining that the circumstances, which they did not
take into account, are hindering them from being what they have
found it, they think, in their characters to be!

But see! here is a man who has heard the doctrine which I have
preached thus far in this sermon. He wants to apply that doctrine to
himself. "Where is my Jerusalem?" he says. "What is there to which
my life is moving? What is there which I must hope ultimately to
attain?" That man, I say, must multiply his character by his circumstances and see what the product is. He finds himself by character a
scholar, and by circumstances a citizen of America in the nineteenth
century after Christ. Those two things he must put together. As the
result, a certain image of scholarship, humane, practical, broad, hopeful, distinctly modern, distinctly different from mediæval scholarship, burns before him on the hill. On that his eye must be fastened.
To that his feet must struggle.

Or he might have found himself a man with a soldier's heart in the
third century, or with a saint's heart in the first century, or with a
discoverer's disposition in the fifteenth century. The time and the
man together decree the possible career.

Or, if you talk of it within a narrower range; here in town there is
a man poor and full of enterprise; there is a rich man all alive with
sympathy; there is a quiet, meditative soul, pushed on by the accidents of its existence into perpetual contact with fellowmen; there
is a brilliant flashing genius doomed to solitude. In either case it is
the condition and the man, it is the circumstances and the character
multiplied into each other which make the life. The circumstances
are the brick and mortar; the character is like the architect's design;
out of the two Jerusalem is built.

He then who would know his Jerusalem must know both of these elements. He must know himself and he must know his conditions. See how at once the full activity of man is called for. You cannot simply look at what other men are doing and see in their activity the disposition of your time and fling yourself out into their forms of action, regardless of the fitnesses and the limitations which are in your own nature. On the other hand you cannot just study yourself and then demand that the age and the place in which you find yourself shall take you and find use for you, however you may be out of harmony with its disposition and its needs. From both of those causes there have come great failures. Who are the men who have succeeded in the best way? Who are the men who have done good work while they lived, and have left their lives like monuments for the inspiration of mankind? They are the men who have at once known themselves in reference to their circumstances, and known their circumstances in reference to themselves; true men, sure of their own individuality, sure of their own distinctness and difference from every other human life, sure that there was never another man just like them since the world began, that therefore they had their own duties, their own rights, their own work to do, and way to do it; but men also who questioned the circumstances in which they found themselves, and asked what was the best thing which any man in just those circumstances might set himself to do? These are the men before whom there rises by-and-by a dream, which later gathers itself into a hope, and at last solidifies into an achievement. It is something which only they can do, because of their distinctness and uniqueness. It is something which even they could not do in any other circumstances than just these in which they do it now. Columbus discovers America because he is Columbus, and because the study of geography and the enterprise of man have reached to just this point. Luther kindles the Reformation because he is Luther, and because the dry wood of the papacy has come to just the right inflammability. You and I, who are not Luthers nor Columbuses, but simply, by the grace of God, earnest, true-hearted men, conceive some purpose for our lives and keep it clear before us, praying we may not die before we do it; and at last doing it before we die, because we are we, and because the world in which we live is just the world it is. It is every young man's place to realize, to make real to himself, both himself and his circumstances, what he is and where he

is. Are the young men here doing that? If they are not, their lives
are stagnant or drifting, and who knows which of these two is
worse? But if they are, then there is certainly shaping itself in the
misty future a purpose of their life which slowly will grow clear to
them, which they will pursue with ever deeper joy and ardor, which
they will humbly rejoice in when they come to die, and which men
will thank God for, long after they are dead!

"But how shall I realize myself and my circumstances?" some one
says. I wish that I could make you see it as clearly as it seems to me.
The answer is that you must realize them both in God. Jerusalem,
as we go up to it, shines through its atmosphere to us. We see it
through and because of the vital air which is poured around both it
and us. Now God is the atmosphere in which we "live and move and
have our being." He made our characters, and He made our circumstances, and it is His hand that moulds the two together and bids
arise into existence out of them a definite, appropriate purpose for
our life, a thing for us to be and do.

Here are you, let us say, who have seriously decided that you will
be a lawyer in this city and this time. If you have come to that decision seriously and intelligently, and not by mere whim, you have
reached it by a knowledge of your character and your circumstances, as I tried to describe. You have recognized certain powers
in yourself, and certain needs in the community. Tell me, will it
not make both of those recognitions clearer if behind them both you
put the thought, the certainty, of God? If you are able to think of
One who made you for your time, and made your time for you; if
you are able to see, with the eye of faith, as we say, the eye which
sees the unseen—if you are able to see the divine wisdom and foresight standing with your nature in its hands, and saying, "This nature
will need such and such chances," and so making for it this Boston
and this profession of the law, and also see that same wisdom and
foresight standing with this Boston and this legal profession in its
sight, and saying, "They will need such and such a man," and so
making you. "Ah," you say, in your mock humility, "I cannot really
think that I am of as much consequence as that." "Ah," you say, in
your crude independence, "I will not let any power choose and ap-
point my life for me. I will do it for myself." Let the two outbursts
modify and rectify each other. Let your humility make you rejoice
that God has appointed for you the Jerusalem up to which the whole

journey of your life must climb. Let your instinct of independence, your instinct of personal life, give you assurance that God cannot have chosen your Jerusalem for you so absolutely that it will not rest with you to find the way to it through every bewilderment, and to keep it continually in your sight.

All this is illustrated in the life of him to whom the picture of our text belongs. The life of Jesus Christ is full of this atmosphere of God. He calls Himself, "Him whom the Father hath sanctified and sent into the world." What does that mean but just what I have been saying? God made the world and He sent Jesus. The world needed Jesus the Saviour, and Jesus the Saviour bore in His mysterious nature the power to save the world. The two met and there was Jerusalem, the sacred city, the city where the sacrifices had smoked in prophecy for years; the city where Herod and Pilate tarried for their victim; the city where the judgment-seat, the condemnation, the cross, the resurrection morning were waiting. As Jesus goes up to that Jerusalem, He goes because He is He, and Jerusalem is Jerusalem, and because both are themselves in God; because the Father hath sanctified him and sent him into the world. When he came there and the cross seized and held him, character and circumstances had perfectly met in their complete result. The Saviourhood and the world's need of being saved had come together, and here was salvation.

Would it not be a vast thing for us if we could be far more aware than we are now of some such great Christlike sweep of our lives towards a purpose? The truth which Jesus first manifested in his living, and then taught in his doctrine, the truth that man is the child of God, is pregnant with that consciousness. Whenever any man has learned it he grows strong and eager. He no longer loiters and plays. A friend comes to you and says, "Do this with me!" And you quietly reply to him, "I cannot;" and he answers you, "Why not?" And you say, "I am going up to Jerusalem." There is an end of it. You have not to sit on a stone at the road side, undetermined, until every speculative question has been settled, until you have decided just whether the thing is wrong, and just how wrong it is, and just how bad it is for this other man to do it, and just how near a thing to it you may allow yourself to do. Simply the thing is not on the way to your Jerusalem, and so you press on past it and leave it far behind. Ah, how men spend their time in debating just how wrong things are, which, whether they be more or less wrong, these men know that it is not for them to do. It is as if a traveller in a great highway refused to pass by the opening of any side lane until he knew just how deep was the bog or the wilderness into which the lane would lead him if he followed it, which he has no idea of doing. The power of an apprehended purpose saves us from all that. The hope of our Jerusalem draws us on, and will not let us stop.

And, to come to the second part of what I want to say, this power of our purpose, this attraction of Jerusalem, is not destroyed, nay, is not weakened, nay, is intensified and strengthened, when the veil is lifted, and it is distinctly shown to us that our purpose can be attained only by struggle and self-sacrifice and pain. This surely is one of the most interesting things in all our study of mankind. I see a man who has caught sight of how his character and his circumstances unite to designate for him a certain work and destiny. He is inspired by the vision. He has set out with all his soul to realize it. I can see lions in the way which he cannot see. I dread to tell him of the deserts he must cross, the fires through which he must force his way before He can go into that open gate, and be what he has made up his mind to be. At last I feel myself compelled to tell him, and I do tell him with a trembling heart. I look to see him falter and sink down, or else turn and run. Instead of that I see his eye kindle; his whole face glows; his frame stiffens with intense resolution, and I see him a thousand times more eager than before to do this thing which he has recognized as his. Listen to Jesus as he says the words following our text: "Behold we go up to Jerusalem, and all things which are written concerning the Son of man shall be accomplished. For he shall be delivered unto the Gentiles, and shall be mocked and spitefully entreated and spitted on, and they shall scourge him and put him to death." What a catalogue of miseries! How clear and how certain they evidently are, as we hear through the ages that calm voice rehearsing them, while the Lord and the disciples walk along the road. But tell me, as we hear that voice through the ages, is there any faltering in it because of these miseries which it foretells? Are you not sure that the steadfast feet go pressing on all the more steadfastly as they keep time to the tragical catalogue which the calm lips are telling? O this is a wonderful power in man, this power which shines out supremely in the Man of men, this power to be inspired by danger, and to desire a good and great thing all the more because of the deserts and the fire and the death which must be gone through for its attainment!

We hear it said sometimes that it was wonderful that Jesus, having undertaken the world's salvation, did not draw back at the sight of the cross. Would it not have been wonderful if, being Jesus, he had drawn back and refused to go up to Jerusalem because of what was waiting for him there? Can we imagine that? Would we not have said at once, "No, He is not the Christ I thought He was—or else the cross with all its terrors never could have frightened Him."

I think the same is true of all devoted souls—of all souls who have really seen their Jerusalem and set their faces towards it. I do not expect them—they ought not to expect themselves—to be turned back by the difficulties and terrors which stand in the way. The wonders of life are not in deeds, but in characters. Given the character, the deed does not surprise me. Let me look into the martyr's soul and see the perfect consecration which is burning there, and then there is no wonder in my spirit when I see him walking next day to the stake as to a festival. The wonder would be if I saw him turn and run away. Let me thoroughly understand how the humble missionary loves his Master and thinks that Master's service the one precious thing on earth, and then I can perfectly comprehend why he turns his ship's prow all the more steadfastly shoreward when the savages come howling down to the beach to seek his blood. The wonder is that they should be the men they are. When they once are the men they are, the things that they do are not wonderful.

No deed is wonderful except in relation to the strength which does it. It would be wonderful that a robin should swim, but it is not wonderful that a fish should swim. It would be wonderful if you or I should write a Hamlet. It was not wonderful that Shakespeare should do it. The wonder is that he should be Shakespeare; but, he being Shakespeare, Hamlet is no miracle. It would be unspeakably wonderful if any man should stand upon the mountain-top and bid the morning rise out of the sea. But God does it day by day, and we are not astonished. Granted God, and what deed of God is marvellous? God is so marvellous that He exhausts all marvel in Himself. God is the one only wonder of the universe. With Him in the universe, the most stupendous prodigies are natural.

What does this mean for us? What is its bearing on our lives? Something very direct and definite, I think. If you are going up to

Jerusalem, and as you go you become aware that you can only reach your Jerusalem, your purpose, through suffering, perhaps through death. What then? Where shall you look for your release, and the solution of your fear? Shall you expect it in the change of circumstances, in the muzzling of the lions so that they shall not bite you, in the palsying of death so that it shall not kill you? No! you must seek it in the strengthening of your own life, so that it shall be nothing strange for you, being the man you are, to scorn the lions and to laugh at death.

Men watch you. They say, Is it possible that he will not be frightened, but will go on to his appointed end through everything? You, knowing your own heart, are sure that you will not be frightened, sure that you will indeed go on. Some friend who really knows you, quietly says, "Yes, he will conquer," and evidently thinks it nothing strange. It is no gift of prophecy in him. It is simply that he does know you, and knowing your strength, the trial that awaits it does not seem too great.

O, do not pray for easy lives. Pray to be stronger men! Do not pray for tasks equal to your powers. Pray for powers equal to your tasks! Then the doing of your work shall be no miracle. But you shall be a miracle. Every day you shall wonder at yourself, at the richness of life which has come in you by the grace of God.

There is nothing which comes to seem more foolish to us, I think, as years go by, than the limitations which have been quietly set to the moral possibilities of man. They are placedly and perpetually assumed. "You must not expect too much of him," so it is said. "You must remember that he is only a man, after all." "Only a man!" That sounds to me as if one said, "You may launch your boat and sail a little way, but you must not expect to go very far. It is only the Atlantic Ocean." Why man's moral range and reach is practically infinite, at least no man has yet begun to comprehend where its limits lies. Man's powers of conquering temptation, of despising danger, of being true to principle, have never been even indicated, save in Christ. "Only a man!" that means only a Son of God; and who can begin to say what a Son of God, claiming his Father, may become and be and do?

Therefore the fact that with our purpose clear before us, with something which we believe that it is our place to accomplish in the world, there still are fears and pains and difficulties in the way, that fact may not have any power except a power of inspiration. You tell the mother that her child is in danger, and that she cannot save it except by vast self-sacrifice, and the question never arises for an instant whether the sacrifice shall be undertaken and the child saved. The whole power of the tidings is just to summon a deeper flood of that self-sacrifice which is the very essence of her motherhood, and which laughs at danger with a quiet scorn.

So may it be with you! I look across this congregation and I know that to many of these young eyes some Jerusalem has shown itself, some purpose far away upon its hill. You have multiplied your character into your circumstances and seen what you ought to do with your life. I bid you know it is not easy to attain your hope. I bid you clearly know that if the life which you have chosen to be your life is really worthy of you, it involves self-sacrifice and pain. If your Jerusalem really is your sacred city, there is certainly a cross in it. What then? Shall you flinch and draw back? Shall you ask for yourself another life? O no, not another life, but another self. Ask to be born again. Ask God to fill you with Himself, and then calmly look up and go on. Go up to Jerusalem expecting all things that are written concerning you to be fulfilled. Disappointment, mortification, misconception, enmity, pain, death, these may come to you, but if they come to you in doing your duty it is all right. "It cannot be that a prophet perish out of Jerusalem," said Jesus. "It is dreadful to suffer except in doing duty. To suffer there is glorious." That is our translation of his words into our own life.

May God let us all first see our Jerusalem and then attain it. What is that prayer but the great prayer of our Collect in the Prayer Book —that by his holy inspiration we may think those things that are good, and by his merciful guiding may perform the same, through our Lord Jesus Christ. Amen.

ALL SAINTS' DAY

"After this I beheld, and lo, a great multitude, which no man could number, of all nations, and kindreds, and people, and tongues, stood before the throne, and before the Lamb, clothed with white robes, and palms in their hands; and cried with a loud voice, saying, Salvation to our God which sitteth upon the throne, and unto the Lamb."—Rev. vii. 9, 10.

IN THE calendar of the Church to-day is set apart to be celebrated as All Saints' Day. Besides the special commemorations of particular saints, as St. Peter and St. John, one day is given to the commemoration of the great general idea of Sainthood. It seems to gather in all the multitude of the holy, in every age, and bids us think of their characters and follow in their steps. Its Collect prays that "we may so follow God's blessed Saints in all virtuous and godly living, that we may come to those unspeakable joys which He has prepared for those who unfeignedly love Him." This idea of one life following after and strengthening itself by another life which has gone before it seems to be the great idea of All Saints' Day, and to this I invite your study to-night. It opens wide subjects of religion and of life.

What is there in the world for each of us that would not be here if others had not lived before us, if we were the first generation that ever peopled this populous earth of ours? What are the legacies that the past sends down to us? Let us see. First, there are certain circumstances, such as government and society, social improvements, cities, and railroads, and houses, all art, all the furniture and tools of life. All these things men have gradually, in the course of ages, invented and worked out, and they are permanent, and have come down to us in their accumulation. All that makes earth something else than a primeval wilderness when we step into it,—all this is the great bequest of circumstances. Then, besides these, there are certain truths; all the knowledge that man has ever won, of physics, of metaphysics, of morals, of religion, of beauty,—all this we have not to win over again for ourselves. The truths come down to us all found, and we have only to take them and use them. Certain circumstances then and certain truths. These are great legacies surely. But, besides these, there is another gift—of certain inspirations which we find waiting for us in the world. Men have left behind them not only the systems and structures that they built, and the truths that they discovered, but their examples, their enthusiasms, and their standards. The impulse and contagion of their work is waiting everywhere to breathe itself into ours. A thousand incentives to use the circumstances and to learn the truths, a thousand impulses to action press on the new-born life out of the past. The men who are gone seem to have left behind them in the world much of their power of vitality; and I suppose hardly a day passes in which we do not do some act, small or great, under this kind of inspiration from our predecessors, something that we should not have done, or should have done differently, if, even with all the machinery of living and all the truths that we know now, we had had no predecessors, had been the first tenants of our earth.

The power of this inspiration comes in various ways. In some degree it is the mere force of hereditation. Some tastes and tendencies we get in our very blood, just as we get the shape of our features or the color of our eyes. This of course confines the influence to a very narrow range. Then there is the distinct power of example. We see that other men have done certain things, and that they turned out well, and we say we will do the same. Our forefathers have set the step for the great journey of life; they have found out where the quagmires and where the solid ground is likeliest to lie, and we cannot do better than follow in their steps. But besides and above all these, they have set up certain ideals of character, not reducible to precise rules of action, with which we enter into sympathy, and to whose likeness our lives almost unconsciously attempt to shape themselves.

This power of influence may belong to all the past in general. Out of all the living that men have done what young man has not seen gather one complete and total image of what the human life should be? From all the multitude of failures and successes rises up the picture of a true, successful manhood,—the perfect man. That is our leader. Not in any special man, but generally, this ideal of manhood tempts and inspires and entices us to action.

Or yet again we see that power incorporate itself in some great man. Dead or alive, past or contemporary, some mighty character stands out and says, "Come, follow me;" and who can explain the subtle fascination that reaches everywhere, and lays hold of all kinds of men, and turns their lives out of their course to follow his course; to be with him in some sympathy of purpose, and, if possible, to be like him in some similarity of nature? "As I take it," says Carlyle, "Universal History, the history of what man has accomplished in this world, is at bottom the history of the great men who have worked here." So all absorbing seems in his philosophy the leadership of the leaders.

We may go farther than this, and analyze the power of leadership that great men have. It is of three kinds. It may rest in either of three things: 1st. It may be in mere strength of personality. Mere strong individuality, showing itself in any act of prowess, attracts men and influences them. In this case the leader is what we call a hero,—a Charlemagne or Napoleon or Cæsar. Or, 2d. It may be in some truths that he teaches. The leader may lead men by the power of ideas, of superior knowledge. Then the leader is a teacher. Such leaders were Plato and Shakespeare and Bacon. Or, 3d, and above all, it may be in a certain thing which we call holiness, which we cannot define otherwise than that it is a larger and more manifest presence of God in the life of one man than other men have,—more sympathetic nearness to Divinity, which makes men feel that he, more than they, embodies the Divine Spirit and utters the Divine will; that he shows God to them. This is the leadership of the saint. These are the three: the hero, the teacher, and the saint. These are the leaders, the inspirers of men. To each of these we attach ourselves, and draw out strength from them; strength for action from the hero, strength for thought from the teacher, strength for piety and goodness from the saint.

We have reached then this distinctive definition of the saint. He is the man whose power comes of his holiness,—of his godlikeness. It is a special kind of power; and it is the strongest kind of power where it can be brought to bear at all. It must be so because religion is the profoundest interest of our nature, and religious association and religious admiration lay mightier hold of us than any other. There is an attitude which man assumes toward God different from that which he can take toward any of his fellow-beings. Now in the hero man feels that there is something of God's power, but by no means, of necessity, any of God Himself. All power comes from

God; but, horribly misused and perverted as it often is, no man can fall down in adoration before the violent destructiveness of strong personality as it shows itself in a Cæsar or an Attila. And in the teacher there is God's truth, because all truth is God's, but the teacher is only the glass through which it shines; at best the glass which condenses and applies its rays; and everybody feels that it is the light and not the glass which he must worship. But in the saint, in the embodiment of holiness among men, there is something more than the mere power or the mere truth of God. Here is something of God Himself, a real abiding presence of divinity; and the attitude which the observer takes towards Him has somewhat of the character with which he bows himself even before God. The hero demands astonished admiration; the teacher challenges obedient reverence; but the saint wins a sympathetic, loving awe.

It is not easy to make this plain in definitions, but when you call up your experience, I am sure that you must understand me. A purely good man, a holy man, a man whose life and nature you saw always luminous with the presence of God in every thought and act and word,—have you never been conscious of some power in his presence; or if he were dead, of some power in the image of what he was that grew up in you as you read or heard about him, utterly unlike that which far greater men had over you. He was no hero and no teacher. You felt no wonder at his ability, and found no intellectual delight in what he told you, but he brought God close to you. Why, I know books vivid with such a life into which one steps as into the presence of God. I have seen rooms where such men or such women, weak and ignorant perhaps, were breathing out their long days of suffering, which were very Holies of Holies. They conducted divinity wonderfully. They made God real, and interpreted Him with something of the power of the incarnate deity of Christ.

I am anxious to connect our whole notion of sainthood with this idea of power. Saints, as we often think of them, are feeble, nerveless creatures, silly and effeminate, the mere soft padding of the universe. I would present true sainthood to you as the strong chain of God's presence in humanity running down through all history, and making of it a unity, giving it a large and massive strength able to bear great things and to do great things too. This unity which the line of sainthood gives to history is the great point that shows its strength. You go to your saint and find God working and manifest in him. He got near to God by some saint of his that went before him, or that stood beside him, in whom he saw the Divine presence. That saint again lighted his fire at some flame before him; and so the power of the sainthoods animates and fills the world. So holiness and purity, and truth and patience, daring and tenderness, hope and faith, are kept constant and pervading things in our humanity. Each man has not to begin and work them out from the beginning for himself. So there is a church of God as well as souls of God in the earth. This is the truth of All Saints.

And in this truth we get the great corrective that we need of the continual tendency to solitariness and individuality in our religion. This church of all the saints is a great power in the world. Every true servant of God must belong with this mighty service of God; must get his strength through it, and contribute his strength into it. Ever from out the past, from the old saints who lived in other times, from Enoch, David, Paul, and John, Augustine, Jerome, Luther, Leighton, there comes down the power of God to us. Because they were full of it, we, by association with them, grow fuller of it than we could be by ourselves. Our reverence and love for them becomes akin to, and bears like fruit in us with our reverence and love for God. Our faith mounts up with their exultant prayers. Our weak devotion, tired and drooping, rests against the strong pillars of their certain trust. Their quick sight teaches our half-opened eyes the way to look toward the light that shall unseal them wholly. How large a part of our godward life is travelled not by clear landmarks seen far off in the promised land, but as travellers climb a mountain peak, by putting footstep after footstep slowly and patiently into the prints which some one going before us, with keener sight, with stronger nerves, tied to us by the cord of saintly sympathy, has planted deep into the pathless snow of the bleak distance that stretches up between humanity and God. Take away holy example and the inspiration of holy men (and that I would call destroying the church, not the breaking to pieces of any external system, for that is the true apostolical saintly succession, the tactual succession of heart touching heart with fire); take that away and you would depopulate heaven. Only one bold, supreme soul here and there would still be able to scale the height alone, and stand triumphant in the glorious presence of God. And who can say what dis-

tortion and lack of symmetry there might be in its eternal character
by the solitariness of its struggles. So we ascend by one another. We
live by one another's blessings, as we die by one another's cursings.
No man liveth to himself, and no man dieth to himself. We live and
die not only to God but to each other.

And yet remember what we said about these saints who help us
on our way. They were incorporations, not of the power, nor of the
truth, but of the spirit or the character of God. Not heroes nor
teachers, but distinctly saints. Now in God Himself all three, power
and truth and character, must go together; all must be perfect in
their perfect union in Him. And so they will, to some extent, in the
saint, who is God's copy; but not entirely. The saint is God's child;
and the child has the father's character, but not his truth or his
power. You are interested and inspired very likely when you see
the child of a very great man showing his father's qualities, inter-
preting his father to you, bringing you near to him; but you do not
look to see the child of Cæsar conquering another empire, or the
child of Shakespeare writing another Hamlet. You are surprised
if he has not his father's character. You are surprised if he has his
father's talent or his father's knowledge.

Many earnest Christian people suppose that the saints must have
had some power of miracle. It is not enough that they were good
godlike men and women, manifesting God in daily duty and the
patient devotion of holy lives. Mere holiness is not sufficient. God's
power in their acts, as well as God Himself in their characters,
seems necessary for sainthood. So we are overwhelmed with the torrent of stories of the miracles of the saints, hiding from us with a
misty halo of uncertainty the really certain holiness and nobleness
of the great men and women who adorn the books of sainthood.

Among some schools of Christian belief, especially, perhaps, in
our own church, there is another error of essentially the same character as this, that is always hampering the freedom of Christian life
and the progress of Christian truth. We have seen that godliness of
character ought not necessarily to be supposed to imply the possession of divine miraculous power. But surely it is just as true that it
does not imply any sort of miraculous divine knowledge, or wisdom
either. That poor saintly woman by whose hovel bedside you go and
sit, and rise up edified and strengthened, feeling that you have been
very near to God, it matters nothing to you that she is very ignorant,

that you would not value her opinion on any knotty point of history, or doctrine, or economy. What have you to do with those things, sitting there by her. The head monopolizes life. It has more than its share of treasuries to draw on, and fountains to drink from, in the world. It is the poor heart, so often half-starved and thirsty, that is getting sweet refreshment as you sit and draw it from the rich godliness of the suffering saint. Now make this wider. Back into the history of the Christian Church runs the long pedigree of saintship which I have tried to paint before you. Age after age the qualities of God have been taken up into the holy lives of men; and honoring this truth of the perpetuated grace and holiness of the continual church, we call those great religious men who stand out in the several ages high above all the rest, the Fathers. There are the fathers of Primitive Christianity, the fathers of the Reformation, the fathers of the English Church, the fathers of our own American Episcopacy. We hear much in these days about the Fathers and their authority. There are some men who would equate their authority with that of the New Testament, with Christ's and the Apostles'. But if what we have said be true, is it not evident that however deeply we may reverence, however we may be illuminated by the sweet or splendid piety of those old men of God, there is no true presumption of any infallible wisdom, or any inspired knowledge in them, that should make either their views of truth, or their laws of church regulation, the necessary standards for our own thought and action. Wise men, wonderful men, many of them most certainly were; and on the other hand almost all of them sometimes wrote and talked puerilities and blunders, which are not strange when we consider the times in which they lived, but which compel us to believe that their reliableness as teachers must be tested by the ordinary laws by which we try all our teachers, and that they are to be believed only as they convince our reason, or conform to that higher authority of revelation which both they and we allow. From the substance of a doctrine down to the size of a diocese, or the color of a stole, men quote the Fathers of Nice and Alexandria and Rome. Others will tell us that just in this shape the truth of justification must be always held because Luther or Calvin taught it so. The Prayer-book of the English Reformers, and its adaptation by the first bishops of our own church, is clothed, by some people, with almost superstitious sanctity, as if to alter any jot or tittle in it were a sacrilege. This is not well. These men are patterns for our piety, not tyrants of our thought or action. They made mistakes in ritual and government and doctrine. And the old times in which they lived asked of them shapes of outward Christian life and church organization, which the same live religion that made them create them orders us to change. It is their holy temper that consecrates them to us. It is their godliness that makes them great. In that runs the true chain of sainthood, linking the ages together and making the eternal unity of the church. Oh, there have been great souls behind us, brethren. The stream of truth may widen as the years roll on, and sweep us into harbors of thought and knowledge of which they never dreamed. We may unlearn things that they thought were certainties, and take for sure truths that they would have turned from as the wildest dreams. On the one rock we may build structures of another shape from theirs. But does that make us greater than they were? Does it authorize us to be contemptuous and cast them off as useless? Has your mere schoolboy a right to say that he is greater than Plato, because he lives in a house full of luxuries, and can tell you of opinions in which Plato was mistaken, and knows facts that Plato never dreamed of. Put them in their true place, and the Fathers are mighty. We bow before them as they stand through history and win their blessing. Let them not be made despots over us, and I will praise them with the loudest. A poor extemporized thing the church would be without them. If we learn more than they knew, we still owe it all to them, for we learn it all in the directions which their devout and faithful lives first indicated. We learn of God when we look steadily at them, and thank Him for the blessing of the saints and fathers.

I have been anxious to point this out, this absence of power of miracle, or of authority in truth in the saints of the Christian Church, because we must have some doctrine of the sainthood which shall not for a moment dim or distort the leadership and perfect headship of the Christian, and the church which rests in Christ alone. He must do all our great works for us, and teach us all our great lessons. Better that the whole calendar were swept away and every saint forgotten, than that one of them should take anything from that perfect prerogative of saviorship which is the Saviour's own. But this need not be. Christ, as He leads us on to higher things, may still strengthen us with the company of those who have the same road to travel, and are walking it in the same strength. It surely does not lessen Christ to me as the supporter of my sickness, when on my sick-bed I call up the image of some sufferer of old, and see him patient in the power of a divine sympathy, which then I reach out and cry after with all the more certain assurance for myself. Christ is more utterly my sole resource in strong temptation, the only Being I can flee to, when I see strong men of the saintly histories turned into weakness before the power of evil, and fleeing in desperation to that same Christ, to be restrengthened with a higher power than the old. There is a use of the saints that can make Christ nearer, clearer, dearer to our souls. They may be like a mere atmosphere between our souls and Him, whose every particle, filled with Him, has passed on his life to the next particle, and so at last sent him down to us pure, as He is, uncolored with its own blueness, the "light that lighteth every man," lighting us all the more brightly because it has lighted them.

We have been speaking almost altogether of the saints of old times. But our subject is "All Saints." The question comes then, are there no saints to-day? Has the race run out, or is there such a thing as a modern saint? Yes, surely, I reply. If a sainthood means what we have said, the indwelling, the manifest indwelling of God in man, then there must be many a very saintly saint in these late days of ours. We can well conceive indeed that there may be fewer supreme pre-eminent saints, fewer outreaching pinnacles of grace in the long ranges of spiritual life. There does seem to be something arbitrary in our modern canonizations, some absence of reason why this or that one should be chosen for the aureole or the biography, more than a multidude of others who seemed quite as manifestly full of God as he. This is conceivable. As all civilization and human culture advances, great men become less common and less marked. As the general level rises the mountain-tops are less prominent. And so as the presence of God in humanity becomes more visible everywhere (and in spite of all men say, I believe there never has been a time whose large spiritual level was so high as that in which we thank God that we live), as spirituality grows more common the saint-hoods stand out less marked from their surroundings. It is conceivable that a time of such general elevation may come, in this world or another, that the promontories shall be all lost in the lofty tableland of millennial goodness and nobleness.

Still there are saints enough if we only know how to find them.

The result of what I have just spoken of will be that all saintliness now will have less a miraculous and strange appearance, will far more blend in with and manifest itself through the channels of the most familiar life. The old idea of sainthood made sainthood an exceptional, irregular, unusual thing. We cannot surely think that this idea has anything like the real nobleness of that other which conceives that the highest holiness will not work miracles, but only do its duty; will busy itself, not with unusual, but with familiar things, and make itself manifest, not in prodigies, but in the ordinary duties of a common life.

The true father does not ask his son for prodigies of submission to approve his filial loyalty. He sees it in the hourly look and walk of obedience. The headstrong Pharaoh could not see God until He showed Himself in the ten plagues. The loving David saw God in the quiet guidance of his daily life. "By Thee have I been holden up from the womb," he says. I have been struck by a fine instance of this discernment of God, not in miracles, but in the ordinary course of providence, which occurs in the history of Martin Luther. It was a time when things were going very hard with him, a time when all the human props of the Reformation seemed ready to fall away. It was then that "I saw not long since," cried Luther, "a sign in the heavens." Then you begin to listen for some startling prodigy. A falling star, a pillar of fire, a blazing cross held out against the sky. Certainly some miracle is coming. But hear what does come. "I was looking out of my window at night, and beheld the stars, and the whole majestic vault of God, held up without my being able to see the pillars on which the Master had caused it to rest. Men fear that the sky may fall. Poor fools! Is not God always there?" That is all. That is his "sign in the heavens." It is a miracle; but only that old miracle that has been shown nightly since the heavens and the stars were made, that you and I will see when we go out to-night. The eye that sees God there is more clear and more blessed than the eye that has to be scared into seeing Him by lightnings and by fire-brands. It is not, if we understand it rightly, a sign of decreasing, but of increasing spirituality, that miracles have ceased. And so it is a truer discrimination that recognizes the presence of God in men, the saints that are in the world, not by the miracles they work but by the miracles they are, by the way in which they bring the grace of God to bear on the simple duties of the household and the street.

The sainthoods of the fireside and of the market-place—they wear no glory round their heads; they do their duties in the strength of God; they have their martyrdoms and win their palms, and though they get into no calendars, they leave a benediction and a force behind them on the earth when they go up to heaven.

Every time that we say our Creed, to-night, for instance, we profess that we "believe in the communion of saints." I hope that all which we have said has made it a little clearer to us what is the meaning of that article of faith. All the souls, everywhere, in whom God dwells, dwell together in virtue of that occupation. They may be separated very far. They may not know each other's tongue. The Divine presence in them may take the most utterly various forms of expression. Their works in life may be entirely distinct. All these are things external. They live together as they both abide in God. The symbols of that inner life are many; the multitudinous life itself is one. I have preached of the saint as leader. This article of the Creed brings in a higher thought,—the saint as brother and companion. It is a higher aspect of the same thought, rather, for the two are really one. The highest leadership does not stand above its flock to rule them. It comes down among them, and is one of them. And the completest brotherhood is not mere company; it aids and feeds and ministers to its brethren. It is leadership also. So that the leader is the brother, and the brother is the leader, and saint is both to saint. The communion of saints is a mutual ministry of saints. It is a noble thing to think of. Here, and in the antipodes there, and in regions of thought and culture utterly estranged from ours; here, and in the lordliest cathedral and the lowliest camp-meeting; here, and in sick-rooms, in prisons, in poor-houses, in palaces, the great communion reaches. The Holy Catholic Church, the Communion of Saints! Wherever men are praying, loving, trusting, seeking and finding God, it is a true body with all its ministries of part to part. Nay, shall we stop at that poor line, the grave, which all our Christianity is always trying to wipe out and make nothing of, and which we always insist on widening into a great gulf? Shall we not stretch our thought beyond, and feel the life-blood of this holy church, this living body of Christ, pulsing out into the saints who are living there, and coming back throbbing with tidings of their glorious and sympathetic life. It is the very power of this truth of ours to-day, that it lays hold on immortality. It leaps the gulf of death. David and Peter, part of the same body with us, already prophesy to us, the more sluggish and tardy members, of the great things that are before us, the final bright outcome of the struggle in which we are still so blindly toiling on; as the eager eyes send messages down to the slow laboring feet, of the green, soft fields before, on which they are already feasting, and on which, after a little more plodding toil, the tired feet shall rest. What we know of Christ becomes in some measure the property of all.

> Angels, and living saints, and dead,
>   But one communion make:
> All join in Christ, their vital head,
>   And of His love partake.

The true church, the only church worth living in or fighting for, is this communion of saints. It is the answer to the Saviour's prayer, "I in them and Thou in Me, that they all may be one in us." Oh, when I think of what the church really is meaning all this time,— the fellowship of faith and goodness everywhere,—it does make me indignant to hear how some men talk of it in little narrow mechanical phrases, and think that they alone do it worthy honor.

And now do you ask me how can one enter into this society? 'I would not stand outside of all this organism of holiness and truth. I would be in, as well as believe in, the 'communion of saints.'" I have spoken poorly, indeed, unless you see the answer. The saint is he in whom God dwells. But God comes to dwell in men, by His Holy Spirit, in the great work of the personal regeneration. Do you ask then, "How shall I enter in to the company of saints?" You must yield yourself to that power of God which from your birth up until now has been waiting at your heart-doors, to enter in and fill your nature with itself. You have kept your heart full of selfishness. You must turn it all out, and take God in, and straightway, living by Him and for Him, you are one with the living saints and dead. Oh, wondrous moment of conversion! Out to the farthest limits of the perfect body there runs the tidings of a new member added to the unity. Is it strange that "there is joy in heaven?" This doctrine of the communion of the saints alone lets us realize that text. The saints of old know that the body of their Lord, the universal church, is nearer its completion. The saints who stand around feel their own spiritual life move quicker at the access of this new vitality. The whole body knows of it and rejoices with intenser life. The man himself, knowing Christ for his, knows all Christ's brethren and followers his fellows in the holy unity of faith. Oh, wondrous moment of regeneration! Our church rites, our baptisms and confirmations, what we call "joining the church," feebly tries to typify the great event. If the rites seem to you cold and hollow, and do not attract you, is there nothing in this great spiritual event to stir your heart, and make you say, "I, too, will be a Christian."

And now ought there not to be a power to hold men back from sin in this great truth of all saints? The world seems very wrong and wicked. Vice has the upper hand. All is apparently drifting on from worse to worse. Sin has it all its own way. So it seems sometimes, and the young man says, "What is the use of fighting against the current? I never can do better. What is the use of trying? I must yield at last." And just then, what if the clouds can open round him for one moment and let him see how in the old times, and to-day, there always has been, and still is, through all the wickedness, a compact and steady struggle of goodness in the world. Let him see the church as representing thus the sum of the presence of God in human action, struggling and living always, riding the storms, keeping alive the name of Christ, and the possibility of holiness among men. Let him hear this sainthood of the ages calling to him, "Come, come to us, come with us to God." And is there not something in him to which that call will appeal to spur him to one more attempt to make his escape, to burst his chains, to be a good man, and be saved. And having once heard that cry, can he go on and sin, without feeling, always, that he is doubly obstinate; that he is setting himself not merely against God, but against his fellows too; that they are looking on with sorrow and with pity, as he goes to his self-chosen ruin? This is no illegitimate appeal. It does not dishonor the influence of God, the heavenly Father, when you plead also with a wicked boy, by all the love and high example of his holy earthly father or mother, to turn to nobler things. All is God's influence, however it is brought to bear. And this you must know,—I tell it to you solemnly,—you cannot sin as if you were the first and only man that God ever made and put into the world. If you will sin, you sin against every high precedent of goodness; you tread on those examples of holiness that have made the world lustrous and sacred; you sweep away the inspiration of sainthood that comes down out of the past, and gathers up around you from the present, like the very breath of heaven; you turn away and go out, obstinately and deliberately, not merely from the kingdom of God, but from the communion of saints. May God help you, and bring you back.

And now my work to-night is done if I can bid any of you away with this great presence of the saints of God surrounding you. Sin is disintegrating. It breaks up and scatters fellowships. It makes souls live and die in solitude. I appeal to you by all the holy society of Christianity. There is holiness all around you to help you and inspire you. You will have to suffer in doing right. Here are all the martyrs to be your company. You must find Christ and be forgiven by Him. Here is the multitule who have found Him, each with some story of mercy of his own to tell you, till your hopelessness of success shall turn into hope as you listen to them in spite of yourself. You will need patience. Behold all the waiters for God, each at his watching place in all the ages. You have bad habits to conquer. Here is the old battle-field, and the shouts with which other men who have fought down themselves by God's help are hailing their victory in Him, shall be the prophecy of your triumph as you go into the fight. You must not stand alone. All this strength is for you. Come in among these best souls that believe in and are finding God. I lift the words above all low formality that clings to them, and say, Come, join the Church. Not in mere outward act, but in true inward fellowship. Stand boldly with those who are trying to work for God, and willing to suffer for God here; and then in the perfect communion of saints, you shall stand at last among that great multitude which no man can number, who out of all nations and kindreds and people and tongues shall stand before the throne and before the Lamb, clad with white robes, and with palms in their hands, crying with a loud voice, "Salvation to our God, who sitteth upon the throne, and to the Lamb." May God grant it for us all.

STANDING BEFORE GOD

THE life which we are living now is more aware than we know of the life which is to come. Death, which separates the two, is not, as it has been so often pictured, like a great thick wall. It is rather like a soft and yielding curtain, through which we cannot see, but which is always waving and trembling with the impulses that come out of the life which lies upon the other side of it. We are never wholly unaware that the curtain is not the end of everything. Sounds come to us, muffled and dull, but still indubitably real, through its thick folds. Every time that a new soul passes through that veil from mortality to immortality, it seems as if we heard its light footfalls for a moment after the jealous curtain has concealed it from our sight. As each soul passes, it almost seems as if the opening of the curtain to let it through were going to give us a sight of the unseen things beyond; and, though we are forever disappointed, the shadowy expectation always comes back to us again, when we see the curtain stirred by another friend's departure. After our friend has passed, we can almost see the curtain, which he stirred, moving, tremulously for a while, before it settles once more into stillness.

Behind this curtain of death, St. John, in his great vision, passed, and he has written down for us what he saw there. He has not told us many things; and probably we cannot know how great the disappointment must have been if he had tried to translate into our mortal language all the ineffable wonders of eternity. But he has told us much; and most of what we want to know is wrapped up in this simple and sublime declaration, "I saw the dead, small and great, stand before God."

I think that it grows clearer and clearer to us all that what we need are the great truths, the vast and broad assurances within which are included all the special details of life. Let us have them, and we are more and more content to leave the special details unknown. With regard to eternity, for instance, I am sure that we can most easily, nay, most gladly, forego the detailed knowledge of the circumstances and occupations of the other life, if only we can fully know two things—that the dead are, and that they are with God. All beside these two things we can most willingly leave undiscovered. And those two things, if we can believe St. John, are sure.

"I saw the dead, small and great, stand before God." What is meant by "standing before God"? We are apt to picture to ourselves a great dramatic scene. Host beyond host, rank behind rank, the millions who have lived upon the earth, all standing crowded together in the indescribable presence of One who looks not merely at the mass but at the individual, and sees through the whole life and character of every single soul. The picture is sublime, and it is what the words of St. John are intended to suggest. But we must get behind the picture to its meaning. The picture must describe not one scene only, but the whole nature and condition of the everlasting life. The souls of men in the eternal world are always "standing before God." And what does that mean? We understand at once, if we consider that that before which a man stands is the standard, or test, or source of judgment for his life. Every man stands before something which is his judge. The child stands before the father. Not in a single act, making report of what he has been doing on a special day, but in the whole posture of his life, almost as if the father was a mirror in whom he saw himself reflected, and from whose reflection of himself he got at once a judgment as to what he was, and suggestions as to what he ought to be. The poet stands before nature. She is his judge. A certain felt harmony or discord between his nature and her ideal is the test and directing power of his life. The philosopher stands before the unseen and majestic presence of the abstract truth. The philanthropist stands before humanity. The artist stands before beauty. The legislator stands before justice. The politician stands before that vague but awful embodiment of average character, the people, the demons. The fop, in miserable servility, stands before fashion, the feeblest and ficklest of tyrants. The scholar stands before knowledge, and gets the satisfactions or disappointments of his life from the approvals or disapprovals of her serene and gracious lips.

You see what the words mean. Every soul that counts itself capable of judgment and responsibility, stands in some presence by which the nature of its judgment is decreed. The higher the presence, the loftier and greater, though often the more oppressed and anxious, is the life. A weak man, who wants to shirk the seriousness and anxiety of life, goes down into some lower chamber and stands before some baser judge whose standard will be least exacting. A strong, ambitious man presses up from judgment room to judgment room, and is not satisfied with meeting any standard perfectly so long as there is any higher standard which he has not faced. Greater than anything else in education, vastly greater than any question about how many facts and sciences a teacher may have taught his pupil, there must always be this other question, into what presence he has introduced him; before what standard he has made his pupil stand: for in the answer to that question are involved all the deepest issues of the pupil's character and life.

And now St. John declares that when he passed behind the veil, he saw the dead, small and great, stand before God. Do you not see now what that means? Out of all the lower presences with which they have made themselves contented; out of all the chambers where the little easy judges sit with their compromising codes of conduct, with their ideas worked over and worked down to suit the conditions of this earthly life; out of all these partial and imperfect judgment chambers, when men die they are all carried up into the presence of the perfect righteousness, and are judged by that. All previous judgments go for nothing unless they find their confirmation there. Men who have been the pets and favorites of society, and of the populace, and of their own self-esteem, the change that death has made to them is that they have been compelled to face another standard and to feel its unfamiliar awfulness. Just think of it. A man who, all his life on earth since he was a child, has never once asked himself about any action, about any plan of his, is this right? Suddenly, when he is dead, behold, he finds himself in a new world, where that is the only question about everything. His old questions as to whether a thing was comfortable, or was popular, or was profitable, are all gone. The very atmosphere of this new world kills them. And upon the amazed soul, from every side there pours this new, strange, searching question: "Is it right?" Out of the ground he walks on, out of the walls which shelter and restrain him, out of the canopy of glory overhead, out of strange, unexplored recesses of his own newly-awakened life, from every side comes pressing in upon him that one question, "Is it right?" That is what it is for that dead man to "stand before God."

And then there is another soul which, before it passed through death, while it was in this world, had always been struggling after higher presences. Refusing to ask whether acts were popular or profitable, refusing even to care much whether they were comfortable or beautiful, it had insisted upon asking whether each act was right. It had always struggled to keep its moral vision clear. It had climbed to heights of self-sacrifice that it might get above the miasma of low standards which lay upon the earth. In every darkness about what was right, it had been true to the best light it could see. It had grown into a greater and greater incapacity to live in any other presence, as it had struggled longer and longer for this highest company. Think what it must be for that soul, when for it, too, death sweeps every other chamber back and lifts the nature into the pure light of the unclouded righteousness. Now for it, too, the question, "Is it right?" rings from every side; but in that question this soul hears the echo of its own best-loved standard. Not in mockery, but in invitation; not tauntingly, but temptingly; the everlasting goodness seems to look in upon the soul from all that touches it. That is what it is for that soul to "stand before God." God opens his own heart to that soul and is both Judgment and Love. They are not separate. He is Love because He is Judgment; for to be judged by Him, to meet His judgment is what the soul has been long and ardently desiring. Tell me, when two such souls as these stand together "before God," are they not judged by their very standing there? Are not the deep content of one, and the perplexed distress of the other, already their heaven and their hell? Do you need a pit of fire, and a city of gold, to emphasize their difference? When the dead, small and great, stand before God, is not the book already opened, and are not the dead already judged?

"The dead, small and great," St. John says that he saw standing before God. In that great judgment day, another truth is that the difference of sizes among human lives, of which we make so much, passes away, and all human beings, in simple virtue of their human quality, are called to face the everlasting righteousness. The child and the greybeard, the scholar and the boor, however their lives may have been separated here, they come together there. See how this falls in with what I said before. It is upon the moral ground that the most separated souls must always meet. Upon the child and the philosopher alike rests the common obligation not to lie, but to tell the truth. The scholar and the plow-boy both are bound to be pure and to be merciful. Differently as they may have to fulfil their duties, the duties are the same for both. Intellectual sympathies are limited. The more men study, the more they separate themselves into groups with special interests. But moral sympathies are universal. The more men try to do right, the more they come into communion with all other men who are engaged in the same struggle all through the universe. Therefore it is that before the moral judgment seat of God all souls, the small and great, are met together. All may be good—all may be bad; therefore, before Him, whose nature is the decisive touchstone of goodness and badness in every nature which is laid upon it, all souls of all the generations of mankind may be assembled.

Think what a truth that is. We try to find some meeting ground for all humanity, and what we find is always proving itself too narrow or too weak. The one only place where all can meet, and every soul claim its relationship with every other soul, is before the throne of God. The Father's presence alone furnishes the meeting-place for all the children, regardless of differences of age or wisdom. The grave and learned of this earth shall come up there before God, and find, standing in His presence, that all which they have truly learned has not taken them out of the sympathy of the youngest and simplest of their Father's children. On the other hand, the simple child, who has timidly gazed afar off upon the great minds of his race, when he comes to stand with them before God, will find that he is not shut out from them. He has a key which will unlock their doors and let him enter into their lives. Because they are obeying the same God whom he obeys, therefore He has some part in the eternal life of Abraham, and Moses, and Paul. Not directly, but through the God before whom both of them stand, the small and great come together. The humility of the highest and the self-respect of the lowest are both perfectly attained. The children, who have not been able to understand or hold communion with each other directly, meet perfectly together in the Father's house, and the dead, small and great, stand in complete sympathy and oneness before God.

Another thought which is suggested by St. John's verse, is the easy comprehension of the finite by the infinite. All the dead of all the generations stand before God together. How such a picture sends our imagination back. We think how many men have died upon the earth. We think of all the ages and of all the lands. We think of all the uncounted myriads who died before history began. We see the dusk of the world's earliest memory crowded with graves. We let our minds begin to count the countless dead of Asia, with its teeming kingdoms; of this America of ours, with its suggestions of extinguished races. We remember the earthquakes, the battle fields, the pestilences. We hear the helpless wail of infancy, which, in all the generations, has just crept upon the earth long enough to claim life with one plaintive cry, and die. Where should we stop? We know that "All that tread the globe are but a handful to the tribes that slumber in its bosom;" and yet how crowded is the globe to-day. Not one must be left out! We heap up millions upon millions until we weary of the mere reiteration, and numbers cease to have a meaning. And yet not one must be left out! All must be there. All the dead, small and great, out of all the ages; out of all the lands! All the dead, small and great, are standing before God. Is there an effort more staggering than this, the effort to gather up in our imagination all the hosts of humanity, and believe in the true immortality of every one of them?

Here, I think, is where the faith of many men in their own immortality staggers the most. If only there were not so many of us! A man feels his own soul, and its very existence seems to promise him that he is immortal. And in his brethren, whose life he watches, he sees the same signs that for them too there is another life. But when he looks abroad, the multitude dismays him. There are so many souls. What world can hold them all? What care can recognize, and cover and embrace them all? If there only were not so many of us! The thought of one's own immortality sinks like a tired soldier on a battle-field, overwhelmed and buried under the multitude of the dead. Have not many of you felt this bewilderment? I think that it is one of the most common forms in which perplexity, not clear and definite, but vague and terribly oppressive, lays itself upon a human soul. What can we say to it? How can we grasp and believe in this countless army of immortals who come swarming up out of all the lands and all the ages? There is only one way. Multiply numbers as enormously as you will, and the result is finite still. Then set the finite, however large, into the presence of the infinite, and it is small. Its limitations show. There is no finite, however vast, that can overcrowd the infinite; none that the infinite cannot most easily grasp and hold.

Now, St. John says, that he saw all the hosts of the dead stand "before God." We too must see them stand before God, and they will not oppress us. For God is infinite, and a thousand million draughts come no nearer to exhausting infinity than ten would come. Here must be the real solution of our difficulty, in the infinity of God. You say, "I can have five friends and understand them, and discriminate between them, and love them all; but give me fifty friends and you swamp me in the ocean of their needs. I have not intelligence, nor care, nor sympathy enough to comprehend them all." But make yourself infinite, and then the difficulty disappears. Unnumbered souls may stand before you then, and you can open a vastness of nature which shall take them all in, and be to each one just as much a friend as if there were no others; yet being all the while the comprehending and including presence which embraces all.

Be sure that if you will begin not by counting the multitude of the dead, and asking yourself how any celestial meadow where you can picture them assembled can hold them all, but by lifting yourself up and laying hold on the infinity of God, you will find range enough in Him for all the marvellous conception of the immortality of all men. Every thought of man depends upon what you first think of God. Make your thought of God large enough, and there is no thought of man too large for you to think within it.

Take, then, these three ideas, and I think that we can see something of what it must have been for souls to stand, as John the Evangelist in his great vision saw them standing before God. They had gone up above all the small and temporary standards, and laid their lives close upon the one perfect and eternal standard by which men must be judged. No longer did it matter to them whether they were rich or poor, whether men praised them, or abused them, or pitied them. The one question about themselves, into which all other questions gathered and were lost, was whether they were good, whether they were obedient to God.

And then, along with this, there had come to them a true and cordial meeting with their brethren. No child of their Father was too lofty or too low for them to be truly his brethren, when they stood, small and great, together before God.

And yet, again, in presence of the Infinite, they had comprehended their immortality. They had seen how, within that life to which their lives belonged, there was room for a growth which might go on to all eternity.

No wonder that as St. John looked upon that vision it filled all his soul with joy. No wonder that he hastened back to tell it to the men and women who were yet upon the earthward side of the thick curtain of death. "I have seen the dead," he cried. "Those who have gone from us into the darkness, all our friends who have gone so silently, so sorrowfully, holding fast to this life as long as they could, going into the mystery upon the other side only when they must, sending back no word out of the darkness into which they went—I have seen them all! I actually looked upon them. Among the millions who have gone like them out of all the lands, I saw them. They were standing before God. They are living. They are far more living than you are who are left behind them here." Must not the remembrance of such a sight have filled his soul with joy? Must it not have been present with him afterward, whenever he saw a new soul depart to join the vast company whom he had seen standing before God?

There is the difference between his view of death and ours. He saw what souls go to. We are so apt to see only what souls go from. When our friend dies we think of all the warm delights of life, all the sweet friendships, all the interesting occupations, all the splendor of the sunlight which he leaves behind. If we could only know, somewhat as John must have known after his vision, the presence of God into which our friend enters on the other side, the higher standards, the larger fellowship with all his race, and the new assurance of personal immortality in God; if we could know all this, how our poor comfortless efforts of comfort when our friends depart, our feeble raking-over of the ashes of memory, our desperate struggles to think that the inevitable must be all right; how this would all give way to something almost like a burst of triumph, as the soul which we loved went forth to such vast enlargement, to such glorious consummation of its life! We should be able to forget our own sorrow, or at least to bear it gladly, in our thankfulness for him, as the generous farmer-boy might see his brother taken from his side to be made a king, and toil on himself all the more cheerfully at his humble and solitary labor, thinking of the glory to which his brother's life had come.

It is well, then, with those to whom John's vision is fulfilled.

Blessed are the dead who die in the Lord, and stand immortal before Him.

And now one question still remains! Is the fulfilment of the vision of St. John for any man to wait until that man is dead? Can only the dead stand before God? Think for a moment what we found to be the blessings of that standing before God, and then consider that those privileges, however they may be capable of being given more richly to the soul of man in the eternal world, are privileges upon whose enjoyment any man's soul may enter here. Consider this, and the question at once is answered. Already, now, you and I may live by the standards of the eternal righteousness, and we may claim our brotherhood with the least and the greatest of our fellow-men, and we may so lay hold on God that we shall realize our immortality. The soul that has done all that, is now standing before God. It does not need to push aside the curtain, and to enter into the unknown world which lies behind. While the man is living here, walking these common streets, living in closest intercourse with other men, he is already in the everlasting presence, and his heaven has begun.

But now these are the very things which Jesus Christ promises to give, and which he has given to multitudes of men. All who will come to Him and serve Him are brought thereby to the loftiest standards of righteousness, to the broadest and deepest human fellowship, and to such a true knowledge of God that their own immortality becomes real to them.

Is it not true, then, that Christ does for the soul which follows him, that which the experience of the eternal world shall take up and certify, and complete? Already in Him we begin to live the everlasting life. Already its noble independence, its deep discrimination, its generous charity, its large hopefulness, its great abounding and inspiring peace gathers around and fills the soul which lives in obedience to Him. Already, as He himself said, "He that believeth on the Son hath everlasting life."

And yet, while we need not wait till we are dead for the privilege and power of "standing before God," yet still the knowledge of that loftier and more manifest standing before Him, which is to come in the unseen land, of which St. John has told us, may make more possible the true experience of the divine presence which we may have here. Because I am to stand before Him in some yet unimagined way, seeing Him with some keener sight, hearing His words with some quicker hearing which shall belong to some new condition of eternity, therefore I will be sure that my true life here consists in such a degree of realization of His presence, such a standing before Him in obedience, and faith, and love, as is possible for one in this lower life.

When the change comes to any of us, my friends, how little it will be, if we have really been, through the power of Jesus Christ, standing before God, in our poor, half-blind way upon the earth. If now, in the bright freshness of your youth, you give yourself to Christ, and through him do indeed know God as your dearest friend, years and years hence, when the curtain is drawn back for you, and you are bidden to join the host of the dead who stand before God eternally, how slight the change will be. Only the change from the struggle to the victory, only the opening of the dusk and twilight into the perfect day. "Well done, good and faithful servant, thou hast been faithful over a few things. Enter thou into the joy of thy Lord."